Packy Jim

Packy Jim

Folklore and Worldview
on the Irish Border

Ray Cashman

The University of Wisconsin Press

The University of Wisconsin Press
1930 Monroe Street, 3rd Floor
Madison, Wisconsin 53711-2059
uwpress.wisc.edu

3 Henrietta Street, Covent Garden
London WC2E 8LU, United Kingdom
eurospanbookstore.com

Printed in the United States of America

This book may be available in a digital edition.

Library of Congress Cataloging-in-Publication Data

Names: Cashman, Ray, author.
Title: Packy Jim: folklore and worldview on the Irish border / Ray Cashman.
Description: Madison, Wisconsin: The University of Wisconsin Press, [2016] | ©2016
| Includes bibliographical references and index.
Identifiers: LCCN 2015043078 | ISBN 9780299308902 (cloth: alk. paper)
Subjects: LCSH: McGrath, Patrick James, 1933– | Donegal (Ireland: County)—Biography.
| Donegal (Ireland: County)—Folklore. | Folklore—Ireland—Donegal (County)
Classification: LCC DA990.D6 C37 2016 | DDC 941.69/3—dc23
LC record available at http://lccn.loc.gov/2015043078

ISBN 9780299308940 (pbk.: alk. paper)

For Lorraine

Contents

Illustrations

All photos, maps, and drawings are by the author.

Preface: Packy Jim Is Your Man

"You want *real* folklore? Packy Jim is your man." For three months, reports had been filtering to me from many parts about a man out in the mountains of County Donegal, living alone in an old-time stone house without benefit of electricity, running water, or near neighbors. Surely these were exaggerations; and besides, my primary obligation from August 1998 to August 1999 was documenting life and lore in Aghyaran, County Tyrone, Northern Ireland. I was learning through trial and error all the things not taught or perhaps not teachable in graduate seminars about how to conduct ethnographic fieldwork. The ultimate goal was to write a doctoral dissertation and later a book. I had enough on my plate. But the stories kept coming. At the urging of my friend and neighbor, Danny Gallen, I decided to write down his directions for finding one Patrick James McGrath, take a day out, and go on an adventure across the border.

Monday, November 2, 1998—All Souls' Day—was dark, wet, and blowing cold. No news there. Better weather on another day could not be guaranteed, so a little before noon, I grabbed my coat, notebook, camera gear, and a bag of apples I had purchased at Castlederg's annual Apple Fair, then crumpled into the modest, creaky Peugeot I had use of for the year. The directions were relatively simple, but as I progressed the road turned from tarmac to gravel to muddy intermittent gravel. Once the potholes became indistinguishable I considered abandoning the car, but the shotgun-blasted fox draped over the barbed wire fence to my left gave me pause. I stuck it out, in second gear then first, until the path ended at a gate and shed. The worn tires of my underpowered vehicle were no match for the slurry ahead, so I gathered my things and got out.

As I did I heard the distant rumble of a land rover, and I figured I should stay put to explain myself. I did not know whose land I was parked on or whose land I would have to walk through. When the driver finally pulled up and rolled down his window, he was every bit the country farmer right out of central casting. I was relieved that he was neither a policeman nor a soldier given that in my previous encounters no one in a uniform had ever believed my story that I was in Ireland to collect folklore. Reviving a Texas accent from childhood, I introduced myself and asked if it was okay to leave the car and walk through the land past the gate. I explained that I was off to see Packy Jim McGrath. This prompted a furrow of the farmer's brow relieved by an eye roll, the meaning of which I could not discern. We had not met before, and as was standard until I became better known in Aghyaran, the man never offered me his name. But he was friendly enough and interested in talking about the United States, less so folklore. At this point the rain had subsided and we were standing by the gate.

He asked me, "Do you know where you are?"

"Well, Aghyaran, right?"

"Right here is the border. Look." The man bent to pick up a palm-sized stone. Waving it, he said, "This rock is in the North [Northern Ireland], see."

Then with a flick of his wrist he tossed it over the gate.

"Now it's in the State [the Republic of Ireland]. There's many a man who didn't want attention came this way. Mind you close any gates you open. And careful with Packy Jim. Sometimes he can be a bit crabbit [cranky]."

With those words of caution in my ear—and a vague sense of getting away with something—I climbed over the international sheep and cattle barrier then started my trudge into what officialdom considers a different country. The sodden path wound this way and that, gradually climbing uphill as the perennially grassy slopes to my right elevated steeply. On my left were a series of low meadows full of fading rushes, filthy wet sheep, their leavings and occasionally their bones. Beyond the meadows ran a peaty brown stream, and beyond that a mature conifer forestry covered a string of high hills. I forded three more gates and passed a shed and the foundations of old homesteads. After about twenty minutes I crested the highest hill yet and spied a red metal roof and gleaming white walls tucked in a hollow about two hundred yards downhill. A chimney reek of turf smoke announced that Packy Jim was home. I closed the distance between us with some trepidation, both for boggy patches and for what sort of person I would meet in the house ahead of me. The closer I got, however, the better I could appreciate that the house alone was worth the trek for any vernacular architecture enthusiast. The Ulster American Folk Park and the Ulster Folk and Transport Museum are intriguing and educational, but this was the real deal, not a reconstruction, in continuous use for well over a century.

From about fifteen yards I let out a loud "hello," which prompted movement, a peek through the window, and a surprised "Who the hell?!" I waited a moment, then the door swung open and an unshaven man in his mid-sixties wearing a dark suit, sweater, and knit cap peered over the half door separating us. His clear blue eyes narrowed and his expression turned to that of someone not interested in buying a bag of apples or whatever else might be in my shoulder bag. I quickly let him know that I was a friend of his cousin Susan Gallen, Danny's wife. I dropped the names of several others in Aghyaran he would know—Gallagher and McGrath relations mostly—in the hope of putting him at ease. And the apples, I assured him, were not for sale; I just thought he might like to have them. At this, he welcomed me in out of the weather with thanks and slightly less wariness.

Inside I was intrigued by the handsome open-hearth fireplace and hand-forged metal crane from which hung a cast iron potato pot on the boil, amazed to see so many artifacts and architectural features straight out of the folklife scholarship of Estyn Evans, Alan Gailey, Kevin Danaher, and Henry Glassie. This was not a time capsule exactly. He kept a battery-powered flashlight and radio on a deep windowsill, an I ♥ NY mug lay among the crockery, and the traditional delph dresser had been replaced by a modern mass-produced cupboard or "press." But there was much to take in for my inner time-traveling fantasist—a traditional Sacred Heart picture and holy water font by the half door, a hand-carved and foot-smoothed set of solid stone steps leading up to a half loft, a sturdy antique ladder-back chair he offered me as a seat. Sitting down by the fire, my eye was drawn to the couples, purlins, and rafters of the roof. Through this network of bog fir supports I noted the underside of rolled-out scraw (the top grassy layer of bog) and the ends of scallops (sally rods twisted into a U to pin the thatch into the scraw)—all of this later covered with the corrugated metal. From the height of the half loft to the ridgeline of the roof all surfaces had a discernable patina of turf smoke.

Neither my presence nor my gawking kept Packy Jim from his routine. With a swing of the crane away from the fire, he lowered the potato pot to the floor, where he drained it into another pot, mashed the seven or eight spuds in a bowl with diced onions and a generous pat of butter, then proceeded to eat. I felt awkward interrupting his mealtime but took the opportunity to mentally map my surroundings.

Packy Jim's house mostly conforms to a native type common in the northwest of Ireland and particularly Donegal: chimneys on opposite gables, and "office houses" or utilitarian rooms (for use as byre, barn, dairy, stable, or chicken coop) added to either gable along a lateral axis. The door in the middle of the front façade grants direct entry into the kitchen, which extends toward the right, and a doorway through a partition wall to the left leads to a second

Packy Jim's home from the east (*top*) and south (*bottom*)

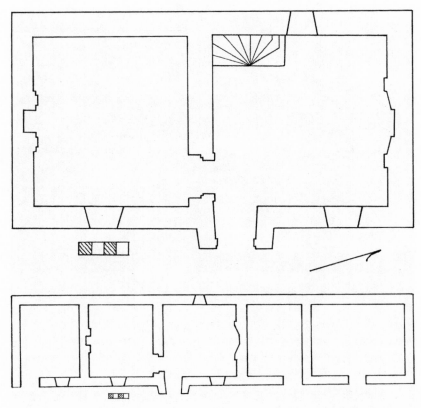

Floor plan of Packy Jim's dwelling house (*above*), and in its larger context with utilitarian rooms off either gable (*below*). Overall, Packy Jim's house conforms to the northwestern Irish type, with noted exceptions. Compare Packy Jim's house with type AC in Gailey (1984:162) and type B in Glassie (1982:590).

room, above which a half loft provides an additional sleeping area and storage space. One thing that makes Packy Jim's house less common is the extended porch-like entryway that affords a greater break from wind and weather for those in the kitchen, where most domestic life takes place. In addition, usually there is a back door opposite the front door where in Packy Jim's house the stone staircase leads to the loft. These opposing doors were necessary in earlier byre-dwellings of the medieval period through the nineteenth century when at night people kept their cattle inside at one end of the house for protection and shared warmth. (It is difficult to maneuver a cow in close quarters, especially backward, hence front and back doors.) With visions of the house under construction—gradually rising three-foot-thick stone walls topped with

Entry to the room off the kitchen

hard-won bog timber, scraw, and thatch — I told Packy Jim how much I admired his house and quizzed him about its history.

In between bites, Packy Jim told me that Edward Roe McGrath — the same man who built the nearby Catholic chapel in Lettercran townland — built the house in the 1850s on the site of an older one. The next owner, John Roe McGrath, hired stonemasons by the name of McGoldrick to cut and install the freestone stairs, which would have replaced a wooden loft ladder (and possibly obscured an original back door). The house changed hands a couple times among different branches of the McGrath family until Packy Jim's grandfather bought it in 1925 and Packy Jim's parents came to live in it in 1932. The hearth crane as well as several pots and a skillet were bought at the Sproules' forge in Killen, County Tyrone, in 1938.

Though I may have gushed about the house, Packy Jim was not overly house-proud. He allowed, however, that although his parents had had many financial worries in days past, the house and land had served them well and they were "never short of grub." Packy Jim remembered his parents quite fondly — unusually, he has no siblings — and remarked that he would be happiest if they were still around "to rule the roost." With domesticity the line of conversation, Packy Jim paused to recall a poem he had memorized from a schoolbook, imagining the thoughts of an itinerant beggar woman who yearns for everything that Packy Jim has.

(*Above*): Stairs to the half loft

(*Left*): Hearth

Oh, to have a little house,
To own the hearth and stool and all,
The heaped up sods against the fire,
The pile of turf against the wall.

To have a clock with weights and chains
And pendulum swinging up and down,
A dresser filled with shining delph,
Speckled and white and blue and brown.

I could be busy all the day
Cleaning and sweeping hearth and floor,
And fixing on the shelf again
My blue and white and speckled store.

Ah, but I'm weary of mist and dark
And roads where there's never a house or bush,
And tired I am of bog and road,
The crying wind and the lonely hush.

And I am praying to God on high,
I am praying Him night and day,
For a little house, a house of my own
Out of the wind and the rain's way.

The poem, transcribed here from a recording made months later, is Padraic
Colum's "An Old Woman of the Roads" (1907), delivered mostly word for
word as published. Back in the moment of his original recitation, I applauded
Packy Jim's spontaneous performance and inwardly hoped more such poems,
songs, or stories might be forthcoming.

   Packy Jim modestly shifted attention to me: "There's probably a thousand
people who've come to visit this house over the years, but you're the first of the
name Cashman to come and to come from so far." Now was my turn to say
more about how I came to be there. Untangling the complicated associations
with the term "folklore" could wait for later, so I explained that I was interested
in collecting and preserving old local stories—comical, historical, mysterious—
and I offered a couple I had heard in Aghyaran as examples. That was all fine,
he said, and he would like to help if he could. But first he wanted to know more
about where I am from. He listened carefully and was interested to review and
expand his knowledge about the world. He knew, for example, that Texas is

roughly the size of France and asked what I could tell him about American Indians.

Eventually I got around to narrating my most recent adventure, which was, in fact, finding his house. I noted that I was amazed a simple livestock gate served as an international boundary in a place where the very existence of that border can be a heated topic and where until recently cross-border roads were blocked or cratered by the British army. Packy Jim explained that, yes, most border roads were severed during the recent Troubles, as well as back in the early 1920s, but the way I had come did not appear on many road maps and had never been obstructed. In fact, that and several other paths over the hills had been active smuggling routes in the 1930s through 1950s. Because of its location, his house had been a prime stopover point for people moving cattle, tea, butter, sugar, tobacco, and any other goods for which there was a sufficient price differential or scarcity to make smuggling, one direction or the other, worth the trouble. Because of his parents' hospitality, most nights they hosted a ceili—a nighttime social gathering for conversation, storytelling, and occasionally singing—that attracted near neighbors and smugglers from further afield. Packy Jim added that there was also a fair amount of poitín—locally pronounced "POTCH-in," the Irish version of untaxed, homemade whiskey—distilled in these remote hills during those decades, including in and around his house.

Forgive an anxious graduate student tasked with collecting folklore, but knowing that Packy Jim would have heard so many visitors conversing in his youth, the pages of Seán Ó Súilleabháin's *A Handbook of Irish Folklore* (1942) flipped through my mind's eye and I could not help launching into questions. I thought it safest and most productive to inquire first about local history, asking if he knew any stories about Famine times (1845–1852). Packy Jim noted that, according to his grandfather, the potato blight was not as bad in this area as in others, but six itinerants fleeing the worst of the Famine in the West died nearby and were buried in an unmarked mass grave at Lettercran Chapel. He also recalled local workhouses filled to capacity and road-building schemes that offered some relief to the destitute but also contributed to the fatigue and spread of disease that killed so many. To this he added two local stories set in the same time period—one about a girl who died trying to save her brother when they got lost in a snowstorm, another about a man framed for crimes by close relatives in order to get him evicted and to take over his land.

With the Famine as the connecting conversational thread, Packy Jim shifted then to another pair of stories about the fairies providing food to a grateful woman in the Castlederg area and to a suspicious, cantankerous man in Aghyaran whom they punished for ingratitude. Telling those opened the door to another story he learned from his mother about the fairies attempting to abduct a bride at her wedding only to be foiled by a man called Nick the Nogginweaver. Hedging, he did not offer these three as true history—they could have happened but he had his doubts. When pressed, he contended that the fairies are real or at least were real in the past. For proof of this he noted that his great grandfather had heard fairy music near Meenabol bush, a fairy thorn tree in the vicinity, and that a man he knew in Aghyaran lost all his hair after cutting down another "gentle bush." With the mysterious side of life on the table, our conversation shifted to cures available at local holy wells and to cures—whether medicinal or involving charms and prayers—that run in families.

I was starting to get almost jittery about the extent of Packy Jim's local lore when we were interrupted by a rumbling in the opposite direction from which I had arrived. For the second time on what was becoming a busy day, Packy Jim jumped up to peer out the window with a "Who the hell?!" Driving a tractor pulling a trailer full of coal was Willie McHugh with his brother, Phillip, both of whom I had met weeks before. "How's Packy Jim?" hollered Willie. "Oh, doing the best," replied Packy Jim.

The McHugh brothers knew that Packy Jim's turf supply had dwindled over the uncommonly wet summer and they decided to save him some trouble by making a delivery. They were surprised to see me but happy for the help unloading the coal bags. After we shooed chickens back into place, we retired to the kitchen, where Packy Jim put the kettle on to boil. He offered Willie (who does not drink alcohol) tea and offered Phillip and me (who do) punch—hot water, whiskey, and sugar, which tasted something like liquid tweed on fire, in a good way.

Willie was chatty and sociable, and after hearing that I had been inquiring about local history, he asked if I had heard of Proinsias Dubh, a local highwayman hanged in 1782. Willie and Phillip are proud of being distant relatives of Proinsias Dubh (also known as Black Francis or Bold Frank McHugh) and proud to live in the same townland where he was born. Priming the pump, Willie launched into an account of how the outlaw began his career of supplying the poor by robbing the Planter class—Protestant incomers who benefited from land confiscations and redistribution, otherwise known as Plantation, following English conquests of the sixteenth and seventeenth centuries. Willie's origin story, of course, prompted Packy Jim, and the two traded their versions of Proinsias Dubh's daring exploits, clever escapes, and inevitable downfall. Perhaps one ulterior motive for the McHughs' visit was for Willie to rehearse his stories about the outlaw in order to hear if Packy Jim had information to help him corroborate or elaborate his store of knowledge. He was probing Packy Jim's repertoire, just as I had been.

After about an hour the McHughs rose to leave, and I figured I should do the same. For someone living on his own, Packy Jim is welcoming—once he knows you—but not desperate for company, and it was clear from the McHughs' visit that he has a strong social and support network despite his living in a remote area. Taking my leave at the half door, I asked Packy Jim if he minded me coming back and whether I could bring a tape recorder. "Oh aye, no bother," was his reply, soon followed by, "Now, I'm not sure what you want to know, so you ask me direct questions and I'll answer them if I can. That's how to get information from me." I told him it was a fine plan, thanked him profusely for his help, and hurried home to Ballymongan townland to write everything down while it was still fresh in my memory.

I was hooked. During the year I lived in County Tyrone, from 1998 to 1999, I returned to Packy Jim in County Donegal with a camera and recording equipment every other week, then returned for one- and two-week stints over summers in 2000, 2002, 2005, 2007, 2008, 2009, 2010, 2011, and most recently 2014. We socialized for countless hours, of which I audio recorded sixty-five and videoed five. We continue to trade letters across the Atlantic.

A Note on Language

I have attempted to represent Packy Jim's oral speech on the page as intuitively as possible through familiar print conventions such as italics for emphasis and capitalization for volume, while indicating pauses and pacing with line breaks and blank space. Even when rendering recorded speech word for word, as I do here, transcription involves a number of stylistic decisions that are already first steps in interpretation. Certain readers will be interested in my decisions, and for them I have made a thorough accounting of the transcription styles used here, in an appendix following the acknowledgments.

Many readers will not be familiar with English as it is spoken on the Donegal-Tyrone-Fermanagh border. For them the following glossary of vernacular terms should be helpful. Ulster Scots and Irish Gaelic are the main sources of influence, and Caroline Macafee's *A Concise Ulster Dictionary* (1996) is a useful resource for further annotation. Similar definitions for those terms also used in Ballymenone, County Fermanagh, can be found in Glassie (1975).

AFEARED   Afraid, as in "I got as afeared of them as if they were ghosts."

AFORE   Before, used as a preposition, as in "A wraith is a ghost of a person that you see afore they die." Can also be used as an adverb or subordinating conjunction.

BEATERS   Feet, human or animal, as in "So they took to their beaters, and they never cried halt 'til they landed at home in Lettercran."

BE'D TO BE   Past habitual tense of the verb "to be," as in "She was very ambitious and the man be'd to be as bad."

BEGOD   By God, an amplifying oath or exclamation.

BRAE   Hill, hillside, or steep slope, pronounced "bray."

BUSH   Tree, not necessarily short or small.

CEILI   Nighttime social visit between neighbors, the site of conversation and storytelling, occasionally singing or music making, inevitably tea and possibly alcohol. Also used as a verb meaning "to visit." Pronounced "KAY-lee."

CHAPEL   A Catholic church, not necessarily small. Compare with Protestant houses of worship known as "churches."

CHILDERS   Children.

CODOLOGY   Also known as codding, the attempt to fool an audience into believing an exaggeration or pure fabrication, either verbally or through the management of expectations as in a practical joke, or cod.

CORN   Oats, typically, but also wheat and rye, not the maize or sweet corn Americans refer to with the same term. Corn is cultivated for the grain—used in bread, cereal, or distillation—but also in the past for the straw stalks that provided thatching materials.

CRABBIT Cranky, ill-tempered, easily angered.

CREEL A wicker basket woven from sally rods harvested from willow tree branches, traditionally used for carrying turf, potatoes, and other agricultural produce.

CUTE Intelligent, clever, and quick-witted, rather than adorable or diminutive as in standard American English.

DELPH From Delftware, meaning crockery, china, or glazed earthenware, but not necessarily from Delft in Holland.

DITCH An earthen and sometimes partly stone wall that subdivides fields, not the low drain that runs parallel and that Americans refer to as a ditch. Hedges often grow out of the top of a ditch.

DOUBT To think or believe, when used as a verb, rather than the opposite. Unlike in standard American English, "I doubt there's something to that" means the speaker believes rather than discredits a given story or piece of information, and "I doubt so" means the same as "I think so." Confusingly, perhaps, when used as a plural noun—as in "I started to have my doubts about Mary Bridget Morris"—the word can convey skepticism rather than belief, as it does in standard American English.

EEJIT Idiot.

GULPIN A rude, slow-witted lout or rustic.

HAET   A thing or bit, as in "I suppose there's nobody could tell you a haet about it in this old world we're living in now, only *me*."

HEDGE   The woody vegetation, often thorn bushes and small trees, that grows out of a ditch, contributing to the subdivision of fields and the corralling of livestock.

LINT   Flax, cultivated for food, oil, and especially fibers used in the production of linen, a textile with a long history of fabrication in the north of Ireland.

LOCK   A small quantity of countable things, such as a lock of nights, yards, or stones. A "brave lock" denotes a considerable quantity.

LOUGH   A lake; compare with the "loch" in Scotland, pronounced roughly the same way.

ONCEST   Once; compare with Manx "wanst" and Scots "ainst."

POITÍN   Homemade, untaxed, illegal moonshine whiskey, traditionally distilled from oats. Sometimes Anglicized unfortunately as poteen. The common Irish Gaelic pronunciation is "poh-CHEEN." The local pronunciation on the Donegal-Tyrone-Fermanagh border is "POTCH-in."

REDD   Verb meaning to clean, clear, or tidy up. Also common in Appalachia and other parts of the United States where Irish and Ulster-Scots immigration was common.

STINT   Verb meaning to put a stop to, or in a case such as "The De'il stint you," meaning "The Devil take you."

STROAN   Also spelled strone in some print sources, a small quantity of milk, such as the stream from one pull of a cow's teat.

THON   An amplifier of quantity, as in "this, that, and thon."

THONDER   An amplifier of distance, as in "here, there, and thonder," not unlike "yonder."

TILL   Preposition meaning "to," as in "I'm going down till the bingo." Also used before an infinitive, as in "These angels that were neutral were condemned till spend their time on this earth." Not to be confused with its homophone, "'til," which is an abbreviation of "until," as in "I'll take you to ceili in Baxter's 'til I come up" or "They never cried halt 'til they landed at home."

TURF   The sods of peat cut from a bog, dried, and burned for fuel.

WELLINGTONS   Waterproof rubber or, more recently, PVC boots that extend above midcalf and typically come in black or green. Also known as wellies, these are essential footwear for rain-saturated Irish fields and bogs.

Packy Jim, 2007

Packy Jim, 2008

Packy Jim, 2009

Packy Jim

Introduction

Using Tradition, Constructing a Self

Growing up on a secluded smuggling route, Packy Jim McGrath regularly heard the news, songs, and stories of the men and women who stopped to pass the time until cover of darkness allowed the Irish border's unofficial economy to resume. Packy Jim says that in his early years he was all ears during these almost nightly ceilis, but now it is his turn to talk.

Indeed, Packy Jim is an imaginative, often animated teller of jokes, tall tales, local character anecdotes, and especially historical and supernatural legends, the largest portion of his storytelling repertoire. He also has several poetic recitations, ballads, and lyric folk songs. Add to this résumé his dressing in the dark suits and wellingtons of a 1940s farmer, living without electricity or running water, and cooking over an open hearth fueled by turf that, until recently, he cut and dried himself. One may be forgiven the initial impression that Packy Jim is the salvage ethnographer's dream informant, a holdover from years past, a keeper of relics.

To some extent, he is all those things but also much more. My intention is neither to celebrate Packy Jim as quintessentially "folk," nor to present him as the typical Irish countryman, Conrad Arensberg's archetype in the flesh (1937). He is, like all of us, both typical and unique, or as he says himself, "I suppose I must be a person that, in some fashion or another, I'm very much like the thousands around me, and in other ways I must be very different."

When I first met Packy Jim, I was a novice fieldworker exhilarated to find someone who embellished everyday conversation with stories of ghosts and fairies, heroic outlaws and hateful landlords—the stuff folklorists traditionally

3

seek. Although a collecting model of fieldwork had brought me to him, my interest in Packy Jim has matured through greater familiarity and friendship to focus less on the stuff, the lore, and more on the uses to which he puts it. That is, I have come to better appreciate that—when conversation is two-way and free-flowing—Packy Jim uses narratives from a range of traditional genres to comprehend and critique his own society, while at the same time seeking to articulate and present a coherent moral self. Packy Jim is as much a storyteller working within a vernacular tradition of Irish narrative we may wish to appreciate in its own right as he is an individual using available narratives to compose a song of the self.

As Mikhail Bakhtin tells us, our mouths are full of the words of others (1981:293, 337), but such a formulation should not challenge our faith in individual agency or indeed genius. Which words and how spoken matter. Packy Jim's talent and dexterity with the inexhaustible potential of narrative guarantees that he is no more contained between his hat and boots than Walt Whitman. Neither is Packy Jim shackled by tradition when he trades in handed-down words, images, and stories to order his complicated world of deep-seated mentalities and provocative change.

Packy Jim mindfully dips into tradition, which Lauri Honko describes as a pool that contains "a multiplicity of traditions, a coexistence of expressive forms and genres, mostly in a latent state, only parts of it becoming activated by the individual user" (2000:18–19). In selecting, applying, and elaborating elements from the pool of tradition, Packy Jim acts as a bricoleur in Claude Lévi-Strauss's memorable term (1966), a crafty recycler who constructs new possibilities out of available handed-down raw materials, meeting present needs. In a very real sense the tale does not exist without the teller and the telling; individuals such as Packy Jim shape tradition, performance by performance.

To claim that Packy Jim is a master of tradition—one assertion of this book—requires that we appreciate two related conceptions of tradition: tradition as process and tradition as resource. Packy Jim in the act of bricolage—creatively recycling inherited ideas, images, and tales—epitomizes tradition as process, which Henry Glassie characterizes as "volitional, temporal action" and "the means for deriving the future from the past" (2003:192). This conception foregrounds the agency of an individual and frees the notion of tradition from any associations with stasis. Here we view tradition as if it were a verb, a doing. But what Packy Jim is doing is working with a collective resource, something noun-like, which comports with Honko's pool image. That is, in addition to tradition as process, we can think about tradition as the accessible raw materials, the handed-down knowledge and ways of knowing, with which someone like Packy Jim may go to work. If tradition as process is not unlike recycling, tradition as resource comprises those things available for recycling.

While decidedly pervasive and influential, tradition is not a superorganic force that pushes us around, and as a resource it is eminently malleable. Some will make more extensive or more competent use of that collective resource than others. Packy Jim is one such person, a master of tradition in both senses. He deserves our attention, both to his personal expressive prowess and to the power and implications of the narratives that he tells.

Motivations and Propositions

For generations of folklorists the study of vernacular expressive culture—particularly oral narrative—has been a means to various ends.[1] One thing I seek through folklore, following in the footsteps of others, is a better understanding of the relationship between the individual and tradition.[2] Attending to a specific individual and his or her range of expression, I seek a window into attitudes, orientations, aesthetics, values, morality, beliefs, ideologies, epistemologies, cosmologies—in other words, into worldview, a sometimes vexing and difficult-to-define concept that nonetheless remains useful.

Folklore scholarship, theory and practice—what Edwin Sidney Hartland called, in his late Victorian terms, "the science of tradition" ([1899] 1968:231)—necessarily begins with close attention to the words, actions, and creations of specific individuals, for traditions do not exist but for the individuals who enact and elaborate them. This is the conceptual basis of and motivation for a performer-centered ethnography such as this one.[3] While most performer-centered ethnographies focus—for good reason—on how certain people play central roles in the instantiation or cultivation of particular traditions, I want to consider the reverse as well: how traditional communicative resources, texts and genres, play a role in the construction and development of a person's sense of self.[4]

An individual self is a persona best understood, like tradition, not as a bounded, natural, or static entity but as an ongoing work in progress—enacted, maintained, and revised through performance, recursive and changeable over time. If we begin with a conception of the individual self as a proposed subjectivity—performed and reperformed through various genres of expression—it follows that there is no such thing as a self except in relation to others, past precedent, and ambient discourse (cf. Goffman 1959:xi). In other words, an individual's understanding and presentation of self is in a very real sense a discursive construction subject to influence and variation over time depending on context, needs, and available handed-down materials and models for expression—texts and ways of creating texts, both verbal and nonverbal (cf. Sawin 2004:4–9). An individual, then, may depend on tradition as much as traditions depend on individuals.[5]

With that in mind, I am interested in the role that tradition as resource plays in the individual as process. Better coming to know a given individual sets tradition in relief as much as tradition sets in relief this individual. Recent models of folklorists approaching single individuals and their creations—particularly Patricia Sawin's treatment of Bessie Eldreth (2004), Glassie's treatments of Haripada Pal (1997) and Prince Twins Seven-Seven (2010), and Levi Gibbs's treatment of Wang Xiangrong (2013)—have been helpful as I confront a very basic question: given an exemplary storyteller and an interestingly complex individual, such as Packy Jim, where and how should a folklorist begin?

Dialogic, discursive, recursive, constructed, performed, revised—an individual's persona may be subject to continual negotiation, but this is not to say that there is no such thing as consistency or at least the drive toward a sense of stable individuality, for both external consumption by others and internal personal contentment. Charlotte Linde observes that in the face of constant negotiation and revision there is typically both a personal and collective desire for coherence in any representation or self-representation of an individual (1993). The self as a construction, then, is analogous to Robert Frost's idea of the poem as "a momentary stay against confusion" (2002:440).

Of course we are not all poets, but many of us—particularly those living in contemporary individualistic Western societies—are inveterate tellers of personal experience narratives—anecdotes of the self with lasting reportability.[6] Working with contemporary American data, Linde focuses her attention on this kind of storytelling as a crucial arena for expressing a sense of self while negotiating that self in relation to others, both present and not. Likewise, Amy Shuman (2005)—also working with American data—has demonstrated how personal narratives are a vehicle for shaping an integrated self out of the fragments and inconsistencies of real thoughts and behaviors. When taken as a whole, an individual's repertoire of personal narratives—rarely told chronologically or all in one sitting—comprise a life story, as discussed by Jeff Todd Titon (1980), Barbara Kirshenblatt-Gimblett (1989), and Ken Plummer (2001). Life stories invent rather than reflect the coherence we seek in our own self-image and in our presentation of self to others (Shuman 2005:58–59).

Sawin, Linde, and Shuman are engaged to greater or lesser extent in what Sawin terms "the ethnography of subject formation" (2004:1) something I, too, am interested in pursuing here. But while investigation may start with personal narratives, it should not end there. Attention to an individual's broader narrative repertoire is necessary for appreciating the full range of consistencies, tensions, preoccupations, and convictions that comprise an individual's sense of self and sense of the world.

My proposition is that polished and repeated personal narratives—first-person autobiographical stories that express one or more aspects of a sense of self—can offer an ideal source for conceptualizing and organizing a study of one person and his or her wider repertoire. There are, of course, many past precedents by folklorists to consider. Roger Abrahams (1970), Michael Owen Jones (1989), and James Porter and Herschel Gower (1995), for example, use autobiographical narratives in their introductions of specific tradition-bearers. In the Irish context, Séamus Ó Duilearga's *Seán Ó Conaill's Book* (1981) provides the clearest example of an established model in which the study begins with a biographical statement about the tradition-bearer followed by documentation and annotation of that person's repertoire, organized by genre. This established model is based on the reasonable assumption that beginning with biography orients the reader and helps illuminate the texts that follow, whether the texts are ballads, customs, or costumes. Ó Duilearga's book, and others of similar conception, serve as extremely valuable historical records, collections that are indispensable for comparative research. This model, however, potentially subordinates personal narratives and aggregated life stories to the contextualization of a tradition-bearer's other forms of lore—typically folktales, myths, and legends, genres that have been more highly valued in the longer history of folklore studies. But there are alternatives.

Recognition of the dialogic and recursive nature of personal narratives has led some folklorists, notably Sawin, to reverse the earlier emphasis on how a life illuminates folklore by focusing on how folklore, including personal narrative, illuminates a life. Whether a life is used to illuminate folklore or the reverse, there is room and need for both approaches, but the latter is not yet fully explored and may offer new room for maneuver.

Starting with personal narratives to privilege an individual's self-construction as an organizing principle in a one-person study is one unambiguous way to pursue the role of tradition as resource in the individual as process. Characterizing personal narratives as traditional may seem at first odd, but these stories are folklore subject to the dynamics of continuity and variation, genre and performance, no less than Mexican corridos, Catalan festivals, or Indian saris. Sandra Dolby (publishing as Sandra Stahl) has argued that personal narratives may not be traditional in content (where we view tradition as a limited number of handed-down ideas and texts), but despite idiosyncratic content they are traditional in construction when viewed as examples of a conventional discourse genre and shared resource for social interaction (1989).[7]

The value of attending first to an individual's most repeated and polished personal narratives is that it alerts us to patterns in that individual's typical moves in proposing coherence. The preoccupations and themes that emerge and re-emerge should guide the representation of an individual on that individual's own terms. For the folklorist, study cannot end here, but building on this foundation, the folklorist's review of that individual's entire repertoire can then proceed along those thematic lines, those typical moves, while identifying others. Personal narratives may suggest a thematic organization for a study that proceeds from an individual's self-conception rather than one that repeats the older biography-plus-repertoire study, arranged in chapters treating one genre then the next.

In some respects the sense of self is not just an opening chapter but rather the whole project. To be clear though, only some of the relevant self-revealing, self-constructing texts will be personal narratives; all the stories an individual shares are inevitably involved in that individual's construction of self. From personal narratives to jokes to myths, these texts are not just an amalgam we lump together conceptually as repertoire then split apart practically to satisfy the organizational needs of a book divided into chapters. Regardless of differences in genre and provenance—and even when some come with identifiable tale type and motif numbers—all stories in a person's repertoire are on some level instrumental in that person's self-conception. Or to put it another way, every story one internalizes or generates plays some greater or lesser role in the intertextual bundle that fills the person-shaped hole. On some level all expression is autobiography.

Personal Narrative and Traditional Idiosyncrasy

Consider how these propositions about the discursive construction of the self apply to Packy Jim and his repertoire. In over seventy hours of recorded sessions since 1998 he has told and retold several personal narratives that emerged naturally in our conversations. They are the sort of stories typically exchanged during the getting-to-know-you phase of any relationship, and they revolve around, in Linde's words, "'what events have made me what I am' or, more precisely, 'what you must know about me to know me'" (1993:20). Even after we came to know each other well, however, Packy Jim continued to tell personal narratives in order to offer glosses on particular threads of conversation, or indeed to pinpoint or amplify the relevance of particular legends or ballads, for example.

The first thing to note is that—perhaps surprising at first—there are not that many personal narratives that Packy Jim tells, whether in response to the everyday flow of conversation or when prompted for a life story. I identify only thirteen first-person narratives that he has repeated to me or to others in my presence with some frequency, to be discussed in detail in the next chapter. Of course, these are not the only personal narratives Packy Jim is capable of generating. On any given day he may narrate his being surprised at rising costs in a local shop or being caught in an unexpected rainstorm. Such anecdotes contribute to conversational give and take, but they may never again require recall, reconstruction, and performance. The told and retold stories I am focusing on here are those that seem to be polished set pieces—what Linda Shopes has termed "iconic stories" (2002)—that are part of Packy Jim's core repertoire and sense of self.

Note, however, that the number of Packy Jim's iconic personal narratives may seem small only when compared to their ubiquity in the face-to-face interactions of mainstream American culture, for example, not to mention their pervasiveness in the self-revelations of social and mass media. Glassie points out that throughout his time in Ballymenone of the 1970s and 1980s, he could elicit fragments of autobiography from individuals, but he recorded only one fully fledged, polished personal experience narrative of the sort I have from Packy Jim (1982:59–62). In my experience on the Donegal-Tyrone-Fermanagh border of the 1990s and 2000s, autobiographical reminiscences can be elicited, but people still place a premium on modesty and want to avoid any associations with self-promotion (Cashman 2008b:138). So having thirteen repeated personal narratives, in fact, sets Packy Jim apart from his neighbors, at least until such time as conversational conventions change, something they may already be in the process of doing.

That said, Packy Jim typically limits his self-presentation to these thirteen stories in part because most of them are appropriately modest. In fact, some do not portray him in the best light. Moreover, they are not entirely about him. These personal narratives often feature and evaluate the behavior of others, and they frequently prompt lectures in which Packy Jim does not hesitate to mount passionate, well-considered critiques of local culture, Irish society, and human nature. For example, one of Packy Jim's most frequently told personal narratives details his confrontation with a smart aleck in a pub who treated him as foolish country rube and made fun of him for being a bachelor. This version from August 2007 succinctly covers the main points that recur in previous and subsequent versions:

> I don't want to have it to be said that I acted ignorantly to anybody. It would be again' my code of conduct to act ignorantly. Unless that I was met with an ignorant cunt.
>
> I seen me going to Jimmy Monaghan's to ceili, and there was a bingo in Castlederg. I didn't know about Jimmy Monaghan and the bingo— I'm not interested in no bingo—but he says, "I'm going down," he says, "till the bingo," and Willie Baxter's was there, an open house, "I'll take you to ceili in Baxter's 'til I come up."
>
> "That's alright."

When we landed at Baxter's, passing Baxter's, there was no *light* there. Willie Baxter was away.

"Go on ahead."

And uh, landed in Castlederg, and there's a bar at the foot of the town there, well down the town, called McHale's. And I was at it a couple of times with Paddy O'Neill. I knowed the bar.

"I'll go in there and I'll have a beer or two while he's up at the bingo. Then he'll come in and go home again."

So uh, I went into that bar, and this boy was there, and—number one, first and foremost—he bought me a drink, that way—a beer—and then, after a time then, he started then . . .

It wasn't that he knowed me too well. He only knowed me by sight, but he seen me with Paddy O'Neill maybe twice before, but he was speaking to Paddy O'Neill more nor me. I was the black stranger.

But that boy looked at me and I suppose I didn't impress him thoroughly, do you understand. That's why I sometimes think that my face is my *enemy*, do you understand. He'd be to see in my face or something, he'd be to say, "This is an innocent ass," or something.

So he started handling me like a kid, old kid stuff, inquiring about my cutting turf, looking for a man to cut turf for him in the bog, and on like that. I said I could cut two days cutting of turf with a spade, or about that. He wanted me to go, like, that he would collect me and take me, and it wasn't two days cutting of turf or anything like that, but a fortnight or three weeks or something like that.

In other words, he was acting the goat, do you understand.

And chatted about—it was just shortly after I got this shoulder here hurted, and it was a kind of working back to normal again. I happened through, you know, old idle chat of one kind or another, to chat about breaking my collar*bone*, and a lump of old chat, and then he went on to say then, that it would be rather difficult to have sex and your collarbone broke. And old stuff of that kind.

I didn't *like* it.

I was sitting at the fire, and I put on my wellingtons middling quick, and I was going to try to get square with him. I signed to the barman to buy the man a drink, do you see, whatever he was taking to get square with him. But I suppose the old sly cunt, he would have give him the wink to not.

But I couldn't get the barman to, as the saying goes, to work. That's neither here nor there, but I wanted to be, as the saying goes, on the level and buy him a drink and then walk out.

That—I'm a long time living—and that's not that many years ago—I never insulted anybody, but I told him, for the first time in my life, "you are an ignorant bastard," and I walked out. And that was that.

I did not want to interrupt such an arresting line as "Unless that I was met with an ignorant cunt," but an aside on semantics is necessary and should not be buried in endnotes. In Packy Jim's world, the term "cunt"—while still considered rude and rarely used in mixed company—is nonetheless not nearly as taboo an expletive as it is in the United States. Moreover, it is not gender-specific. The term is applied by Packy Jim and others throughout Ireland to both men and women, as well as to disagreeable animals and indeed to objectionable inanimate objects. Although you will read the term again in the following pages, Packy Jim is no vulgarian. He uses profanity on occasion—as I do, as many do—to grab his audience's attention, to shift into a more impassioned critical register, to telegraph, in this case, "take me seriously now, for here comes an outrage to evaluate and condemn."

Back in that moment of conversation, with the topic of smart alecks and the theme of condescension raised, Packy Jim then added the following coda:

I'd be a shy person by nature, and like, that old remarks or drawing attention at people, you can be made shyer, you understand. And if you're foolish you can be made foolisher.

It's like what the man said—about the road down there, that had a son that used to work for this other man, periodically, on the land—and they were discussing the son going to this neighbor's house and back again.

"Well," he says—he had been about the house, too, and half reared about the house when he was a young lad, eighty years ago or more.

He says, "If you went to that house with little wit, you *left it with a bit less*," do you understand.

The Irish personality is, if you're a wee bit simple, they'll try and make you worse. Or a bit foolish, they'll try to make you foolisher. They play on what they think would be your weak point. That's the Irish, do you understand. And the Irish, even though you're *not* a fool, in every locality there's somebody and they're a *scapegoat*, do you understand.

That's, as far as I know, one of the tricks of the Irish. It's not nice, but it's something that's ingrained in our personality.

Every Irishman's not like that, now. But there's a quantity of them that's mostly like that. (August 12, 2007)

Several things are going on here. Packy Jim's personal narratives offer a presentation of self—often illuminated through comparison with the behavior of
others—but one that is typically, appropriately modest. Through these stories
he makes a series of direct and indirect statements about being one sort of a
person and not another sort, bothered by some things and not others. Looking
at his repertoire of iconic personal narratives as a whole, we see that he does
not propose too neat an image of a person who is, for example, consistently
virtuous or intelligent. Consistencies add to his coherence, but in many cases
he presents himself as a person caught between certain extremes, animated by
certain irresolvable tensions. Both consistencies and tensions are telling; they
deserve further investigation because they also inform the stories he tells in
other genres of narrative.

In this account of the smart aleck confrontation, we also see a clear example
of how Packy Jim's bid for coherence may simultaneously vault him from
specific personal experience (looking inward) to generalizable observations
about his wider cultural and historical surround (looking outward). Academics
are not the only people engaged in ethnography, as Clifford Geertz (1973) and
Keith Basso (1979) observe. Instances of what Jason Jackson calls ethno-ethnology
offer some of the most informed emic (or insider) perspectives on social life
available.[8] Unlettered by conventional standards—or, more accurately, un-
conventionally lettered—Packy Jim is no less an intellectual, and he marshals
his experiences in concert with relevant handed-down narratives to act as
something like a vernacular social critic. As we will see, using different variables
and expressive means, Packy Jim nonetheless comes to conclusions similar to
those of Max Weber about modernity ([1904–1905] 1976), Émile Durkheim
about anomie ([1893] 1984, [1897] 2006), Karl Marx about class and alienation
([1844] 1964, [1867–1883] 2010, 1994), and Sigmund Freud about self-esteem
and intellectual development ([1920] 1967, [1927] 1961).

There are many themes in Packy Jim's personal narratives to consider in
the next chapter, and they suffuse and shape the nonpersonal narratives discussed in the chapters that follow. But for now a larger methodological point is
clearer. Starting with personal narratives provides a productive way to discern
an individual's tendencies in constructing a coherent self. The exercise highlights inconsistencies and foreshadows tensions; this is the nature of constructed
selves and of life story-telling. But the themes that emerge can and should inform
how we approach the rest of the subject's repertoire. In other words, it is perhaps
more faithful to an individual's perspective and conceptual world to organize
his or her repertoire, not strictly by genre—first a chapter on myths, then
legends, then folktales, and so on—but rather by aspects of the self-image that
individual has taken great care to present to us.

In Packy Jim's case, we note in his personal narratives a preoccupation with the tension between autonomy and submission, or between independence and rule-following. That tension suggests something about his worldview and offers itself as a natural theme for its own chapter (see chapter 2). However, while this chapter must certainly review the relevant personal narratives, it should also take into account narratives from other genres that speak to this same theme. This includes, for example, both literary historical fiction and ballads from oral tradition. In fact, the narratives through which Packy Jim offers his most elaborate meditations on the issue of rules are not personal narratives but rather his legends about the local eighteenth-century outlaw Proinsias Dubh—doing the right thing by breaking the law—and his oral historical accounts of the Irish War of Independence and the more recent Troubles discussed in chapter 3.[9]

Likewise, personal narratives tip us off to the fact that Packy Jim thinks deeply about theology, ontology, teleology, eschatology, and cosmology, but he explores these issues most fully in traditional narratives about wraiths, ghosts, and fairies, discussed in chapters 5 and 6. Such stories are widely considered canonical in Irish folklore—Seán Ó Súilleabháin's *A Handbook of Irish Folklore* (1942) anticipates all of Packy Jim's—and indeed Packy Jim is a worthy steward of this tradition. But these handed-down stories are also core to Packy Jim's personal project of coming to terms with the nature of things while simultaneously conceiving and projecting a coherent self. People do different things through different genres (Seitel 1999; Cashman 2007a), but perhaps when approaching one storyteller, all stories revolving around a particular theme or tension need to be explored together, just as they are in conversation.

Myth and Personalized Tradition

If a personal narrative such as the one about the confrontation with the smart aleck can gesture beyond the individual to global issues and social critique, nonpersonal traditional narratives can certainly resonate with, express, and indeed shape the self. For a case study in the role of tradition in the development of an individual self, let us consider Packy Jim's version of the origin of the fairies—seemingly as traditional a story as Packy Jim's personal narratives are idiosyncratic. Of the three versions I have recorded, the following from July 2002 offers a good starting point:

> Well, the story goes that God got lonely, and He decided to make himself some company.
> And He created what they call the Angelic Creation: angels.
> And there was nine lots of them, called "nine choirs" of angels.

And when He made the angels, He made a place to hold them to, a home for them we call Heaven.

But these angels were placed outside of Heaven on a probationary period. There was no two angels exactly the same. From the greatest to the least there were a big, big variation.

But the greatest and the most intelligent of all the angels was an angel called Lucifer. And that was said to be the first sin committed, against God, if you like: the sin of pride, committed by an angel called *Lucifer*.

So Lucifer got the idea in his head—to put it the best way I can—that he was as good as God. And a whole lot of angels sided with him, took his side. And there was what they called the Angelic Rebellion.

And at that point in time, Hell was made. And the bad angels was put into Hell for to suffer there for their sin, and they're known now as the devils. Well then there was a considerable amount of angels, a vast amount of angels, that didn't take God's side in the rebellion, nor they didn't take the Devil's side in the rebellion—they were *neutral*.

And when the thing was over, then, God made this material creation—the world, and the sun, and the earth, and all the rest of it—and these angels that were neutral were condemned till spend their time on this earth here. And they are known as the fallen angels or the fairies—the neutral angels that didn't take God's side in the rebellion, nor didn't take the Devil's side, they took no side. And they didn't get into Heaven.

God then took in the angels—the angels that took God's side were headed by an angel called Blessed Michael the Archangel, who was supposed to be the greatest angel in Heaven—and they were taken into Heaven, then, to their places in Heaven—there was a place in Heaven, as we're told, for every angel. And the angels were that many that they were numberless, they were millions of billions, maybe mightn't be the right way to term it.

So then there was a big space then, left, in Heaven, a vacancy left in Heaven, according to what the Catholic Church tells us, and I suppose the Protestant churches, too.

So God got the idea, then, of making another type of a creation, a material creation, and another type of beings, so that, as time would go on, succeeding generation after generation of them would move towards Heaven, when they would have their time spent here, and gradually that Heaven would be filled. And when Heaven would be filled this creation that we know now would cease, and that would be that.

We are supposed to be here for till take the place, if we're good, to say it that way, to fill those places in Heaven, that them bad angels left vacant.

I think that's the story of all Christian religions, as I was taught, I think Master Cunningham taught me that, and my mother who knowed a lot, taught me that about the same time or maybe earlier, but that's the *story!* (July 12, 2002)

In this version from 2002, Packy Jim covers all the main points, in the same order, as two other versions I recorded in July 2000 and August 2007. In fact, many of the images and phrasings are similarly constructed in the 2000 and 2007 versions, in some cases word for word. Compare the following pairs:

God made Heaven and he made nine batches of angels, and they were termed "nine choirs." (July 4, 2000)

So God got lonely and desired company, so he made this big tribe of angels, and they were divided into nine lots called "nine choirs." (August 12, 2007)

◎⫴⫴~

And there was no two of them the same. There were a difference between them like the stars in the sky. (July 4, 2000)

And there was no two of them exactly the same. (August 12, 2007)

◎⫴⫴~

He was so great, he was so powerful, that he took it in till his head that he was as good as God. (July 4, 2000)

But the Devil seemingly thought he was as good as God. (August 12, 2007)

◎⫴⫴~

And then this universe was made, and human beings were made—Adam and Eve to start off with. The human race was made, and then they were to increase and multiply, and then when your station on this earth was over, you went into Heaven. And that was to go on, and on, and on, and on, and on, and on until Heaven was again full, that there was every place in Heaven occupied. And then, at that point then, everything finished then. This place come till an end. That's the story. (July 4, 2000)

The human race is supposed till last until such a time that all them seats left vacant in heaven is filled. And when heaven is filled completely, the human race is going to be finished off. It's going to be, I'd say, it ends. That's the story. That's the story: it ends then, when Heaven's filled. (August 12, 2007)

In addition to the consistency between Packy Jim's versions of the origin story, there is consistency between his versions and others recorded in Ireland. The idea of fairies as fallen angels is widespread not only in Ireland and areas of Irish immigration but also farther afield in other Celtic and Scandinavian regions. The idea became popular in Ireland during the Middle Ages for resolving tensions between pre-Christian and Christian cosmologies. Casting the fairies as fallen angels preserved some elements of native tradition by reading between the lines of Christian scripture (Isaiah 14:12 and Revelation 12:7–9), giving the fairies a place in Christian cosmology and eschatology. Moreover, the resulting syncretism offers an opportunity, depending on the telling, to explore the nature of humanity through contrast with an antecedent but co-existing other. The only major element in other recorded versions missing from Packy Jim's is an explanation of fairy abductions of or sexual relations with humans. In many recorded sources, the fairies hope to increase the amount of human blood in their veins in order to secure some chance at salvation on Judgment Day. While this is missing from Packy Jim's origin story, he nonetheless recognizes the fairies' occasional harassment of humans as motivated by jealousy that we still enjoy the possibility of redemption.

Whereas recorded versions have this or that element—Ó hEochaidh's collected version (1977) emphasizes the War in Heaven, Ó Duilearga's (1981) highlights the fairies' hope for salvation, Lady Wilde's (1888) emphasizes their residual powers and envy of humans—Packy Jim's version is a masterful synthesis of the many images, ideas, and motifs handed down to him. As a bricoleur of inherited narratives and fragments, Packy Jim does more than account for the existence and nature of the fairies; he employs traditional materials to define the human individual's ontology and teleology, articulate a charter for moral behavior, and explain the origins, workings, and eventual end of the world. Few stories could offer better material for an exploration of collective belief and worldview (see chapter 5).

Still, Packy Jim, an individual working within an established oral tradition, makes the origin of the fairies story his own in many ways. All three versions display the hallmarks of Richard Bauman's conception of performance as an acceptance of responsibility to an audience for a display of communicative competence. In each telling, Packy Jim draws attention to his breakthrough into performance (Hymes 1975), signaling in effect "I'm on" (Bauman 2004:9), though various keying devices identified by Bauman (1977): *figurative language* (e.g., "There were a difference between them like the stars in the sky" [2000] and "But the devil seemingly thought he was as good as God . . . that's the stool that he fell over" [2007]); *parallelism* (e.g., the eighth and ninth sentences of the 2002 version, ending with emphasis on "an angel called Lucifer," and the repetition of "to go on, and on, and on, and on, and on, and on" [2000]); *appeals to tradition* (e.g., "I think even a Protestant theologian—any *Christian* theologian— will tell you the same thing as I'm telling you. But my mother Maggie Gallagher was the first that I heared at that, and I think Master Cunningham was the next that I heared at that, too. Oh, that's going till the root of the faith" [2000] and "Well, that's the story at the root of all Christians: Protestants, Orthodox, Roman Catholics, the whole damned lot, probably the Jews [2007]); *paralinguistic features* (these are quite numerous, including several mimetic hand gestures, and regular rhythms established through speed, volume, pitch, and tone, then broken for dramatic emphasis).

As Packy Jim assumes responsibility through performance for tradition—in terms of both content and communicative convention—he also reveals much about his personal storytelling style and his individual subjectivity. Packy Jim's use of figurative language in the origin story, for example, reflects his broader preference for expression through analogies, similes, and metaphors that cast even spectacular events in ordinary, familiar terms. Note that in his 2007 version he refers to the Devil committing the original sin of pride—setting in motion our very creation—as tripping over a stool. Also in the 2007 version, Packy Jim depicts the gaping absence left in Heaven after the rebellion in everyday terms: "Then there was a big, big vacancy. It would be like maybe nine or ten people in the chapel and the rest of the chapel empty." His matter-of-fact delivery and everyday imagery often serve as understatements for effect, but they also under-score a certain way of thinking about language, reality, and the problem of representation.

In all three versions of his origin story—and throughout his repertoire as I have recorded it—Packy Jim continually punctuates his descriptive prose with habitual phrases such as "to say it that way," "I'll put it that way," and "to put it the best way I can." Perhaps his most frequent habitual phrase, "as the saying goes," very rarely announces a proverbial phrase. Rather, all these habitual phrases typically presage or mark a moment that advances plot as he makes a bid to represent something in a certain way: "as if." In part, these phrases put the communicative act on display as is common in performance. More to the point, such interjections are fundamentally metacommunicative. They acknowledge and illustrate that storytelling is going on here, that this is a process of representing a reality through the indispensable but ultimately limited faculty of language. Especially when discussing ultimate realities and nonmaterial beings that are completely other, Packy Jim is keen to indicate his awareness that language at best affords us analogies and metaphors rather than a transparent, one-to-one replication of actuality.

> Well, you have to chat about it this way, you know. You don't think about spirits in the way like you think about humans—chatting about an angel "thinking" or a devil "thinking"—but that's the way you must express it. We don't know whether angels or devils or things like that can think, but we must put it that way anyway. (August 12, 2007)

> This is the curiosity about religion, what religion has to say. I suppose we need not liken angels to humans, but we must, as the saying goes, for to put the point over, I must say it this way: he took it in till his head that he was as good as God, do ye understand? (July 4, 2000)

> So then, God took it in till his head—I'm putting it the rude way again— that it would be too bad for to have your place . . . the place not half full. "I'll go about it again and I'll make another creation, but it'll be a different creation." (July 4, 2000)

Laying bare the mechanics of storytelling, highlighting the limitations of language, Packy Jim keys performance while making a bid to express his intellect, dispositions, and personality. Likewise, he regularly tacks back and forth between taking responsibility for the traditional materials at hand, and making more direct pronouncements about himself and the world around him. Just as his personal narrative about confronting the smart aleck in the pub led to a short lecture on scapegoating, Packy Jim's story of the fairies' origin stirs him to comment on the state of the world today and how it relates to the sacred framework established in the beginning:

> But then, I suppose, if you're prepared to believe what we're taught, like the human race, I'm afraid that there's more of them going to Hell nor's going to Heaven at the present time. Barring that there's something in

it that I don't understand, Satan—as the saying goes—Satan's still getting his quota. (July 4, 2000)

Ours is a fallen world—"a valley of tears" in his 2000 version, referencing a phrase in the rosary inspired by the Psalms—and widespread wickedness delays Heaven's completion and the end times. Springboard for social commentary and moral proclamation, index of his predispositions and orientations to the world, Packy Jim's versions of this story do more than explain the origin of the fairies or offer us another instantiation of tradition that can be dated, located, and archived. He has mastered the narrative—having arranged the handed-down parts, having thought deeply about its implications—to articulate a coherent eschatology and a comprehensive cosmology that nonetheless leaves room for mystery. As Packy Jim declares in a coda to his 2002 version:

> All we know about it is that there's some kind of another side, some way or another, that you go till and nobody, as they say, has come back to tell it. But it's there, and I suppose you had better be a good boy as a bad boy, you'd fare better and have less to worry about.
> But I suppose if you're made to be a bad boy—that's the mystery of life—if you're made to be a bad boy, a bad boy you must be. That's the whole of that. It has to be that.
> Aye, I think so.

But neither the discussion nor the recording ended there. With his body tense and agitated, his brow knitted, Packy Jim became louder and quickened his pace:

> And there's another thing about it that the bad people—whatever's about it—some instinct sometimes can tell them when there's a good body, as the saying goes, in their presence.
> And many a reasonably good body or near perfect body—there's none of us a hundred percent, I'll say it that way—but many a time you've got insulted and belittled simply because I think the Devil's at the back of it propping them up to try to shame you, to try to hurt you. Simply because the Devil in some shape or fashion lets them know: there's a person that has lived a good life, no mortal sin never in their life. "I'll hurt 'em, I'll belittle 'em, I'll take 'em *down!*"
> That's the Devil's way, it's said, when he has had contact with people, is to try to take you down. Aye. To belittle you, hurt you on your, on your good and religious points. Like your man at McHale's— (July 12, 2002)

At this point Packy Jim began to segue from the origin of the fairies into what, I am sure, would have been another telling of his confrontation with the smart aleck in the pub, but much to my regret I interrupted with another question about fairies, supposing that he was veering off track. Obligingly Packy Jim answered my stuff-oriented, salvage ethnographer's query, then the conversation shifted elsewhere. It is only in retrospect that I understand that he was not off track at all.

This origin story is not just about cosmology and eschatology, belief and theology. Nor is it merely a handy reflection of Packy Jim's personality as an individual or his style as a storyteller. At least in this instance, he was trying to talk about himself: a reasonably good body confronting no less a figure than the Devil, the Angel of Pride, propping up some uppity pub-lounger to belittle him, to make him out the fool and scapegoat once more. The personal narrative is not the only genre through which we hope to invent the coherence we seek in our own self-image and in our presentation of self to others. No less weighty a genre than collective, sacred myth can play a central role as stories create contexts for each other, making meaning through relation.

Stepping back to view a larger picture, we see that Packy Jim's versions of the origin of the fairies offer a clear example of the individual actively engaged in tradition-as-process, taking responsibility for and molding tradition to present needs. We also observe an equally clear example of tradition-as-resource playing a central role in the construction and articulation of self. Packy Jim as bricoleur masters this story because he needs this story. The slings and arrows of this world—from fairy mischief to hateful neighbors—have a primal sacred origin. Tradition provides Packy Jim both an explanation for evil in the world and a charter for his own moral behavior, helping him comprehend injustice and have faith that in the end the deserving will triumph.

Like the early Christian scribes who found a place for the fairies in the master narrative of scripture, Packy Jim finds through this story a place for himself in this life and, he hopes, the next. Though not a first-person story of experienced events, this collective origin myth can be used in such a way that makes it no less personal, immediate, or useful.[10] Inserting himself imaginatively into this story-world of the Angelic Rebellion and its aftermath, Packy Jim is in no way neutral in the sense that here is something to latch on to, something of which to be sure, a side to take. As it was in the beginning, some will not be allowed into the Kingdom, but unlike the fairies or the Devil's cohort, Packy Jim has reason to hope for salvation. Or as he adds demurely, "I guess that's all we can ask right now is a sporting chance."

Engaged in a tradition of performer-centered ethnography—attending to how individual stories are used rhetorically by particular storytellers in certain performance contexts—we cannot but find instances in which there are few meaningful differences between such apparently divergent genres as collective myth and personal narrative. Both genres and certainly others play crucial roles in the imaginative construction of self and society. In a performer-oriented ethnography of subject formation, what matters is how the stories are told, to what ends, and what "meanings open between stories and proliferate when stories are performed together" (Glassie 2006:255). The range of meanings established through storytelling is our window into worldview.

Worldview

As it was for many before me, worldview is the ultimate quarry; understanding the world from the perspective of others is, for me, the point of studying folklore.[11] In addition to appreciating Packy Jim as a master of tradition—and better appreciating the nature of tradition in the process—another goal of this book is to work thematically through Packy Jim's repertoire in order to understand something about his worldview. But what exactly is worldview?

Gregory Schrempp offers a useful general characterization of worldview as "basic postulates that cognitively and affectively orient humans toward themselves, other humans, the physical environment, indeed the cosmos." Furthermore, "such broader orientations directly inform human action," and therefore "human action is unintelligible apart from them" (1996:21). The anthropologists Robert Redfield (1952, 1953), Clifford Geertz (1957), and Michael Kearney (1975, 1984) to greater or lesser extent systematize worldview as comprising postulates about (some combination of) the self, the other, society, time, space, nature, the supernatural, classification, and causality. Linda Dégh resists such systematization and abstraction, preferring to regard worldview as an interpretive vehicle individuals draw upon during the active process of everyday interaction and communication.[12] She defines the concept of worldview, as studied by folklorists, as

> the sum total of subjective interpretations of perceived and experienced reality of individuals. Any human action is motivated by such a perception. It contains beliefs, opinions, philosophies, conducts, behavioral patterns, social relationships and practices of humans, related both to life on this earth and beyond in the supernatural realm. Worldview, then, permeates all cultural performances, including folklore. Narratives, in particular, are loaded with worldview expressions: they reveal inherited communal and personal views of human conduct—this is their generic goal. (1995:247)

Like Alan Dundes (1980a:70), Dégh argues that because worldview is pervasive, analysis could start with almost any aspect of human life, but folklore offers particularly good materials for the study of worldview because it gives explicit concrete form to implicit internalized frames of mind. Furthermore, Dégh argues that despite folklorists' theoretical detours over time—and regardless of whether it was termed as such—worldview has long been and remains the most important object of study when approaching narratives, no matter the genre, that express "how people feel and think about themselves and the world around them" (1994:246).

To some, worldview may seem a dated concept that betrays misguided assumptions. Visions of holistic, systematized, and integrated mentalscapes—indeed any totalizing ethnographic observations—are suspect from the contemporary academic perspective in which "the reality of human experience is, and has always been, fragmentary, ephemeral, context-bound, and contested" (Schrempp 1996:25). I would argue, as does Schrempp, that there is room in our scholarship for totalizing postulates because the people we study—not least Packy Jim—think in terms of and consciously strive for totalizing postulates about the nature of life, sacred and profane; the shape and meaning of the cosmos; the inner workings of culture and society; the relationship between self and others. Part of the ethnographer's job is to identify and contemplate other people's totalizing postulates in context and on their own terms, then to present them in terms understandable to the ethnographer's audience. Packy Jim undertakes the hard work of theorizing life, most often through storytelling; my somewhat less difficult task is to clear the stage for him and to help build a bridge between his world and worldview and yours.

Admittedly, worldview is a somewhat nebulous term and concept, and as Schrempp points out, it can overlap vaguely with related concepts such as mentality, ethos, cognition, cosmology, even culture. He also notes an inherent tension in various conceptions of worldview: does it revolve more around intellect and cognition or emotion and affect (1996:25)? Geertz (1957) and Dundes ([1972] 2000:131), for example, make a distinction between worldview and ethos, where worldview deals with the cognitive and existential, and ethos deals with the normative and evaluative. Juha Pentikäinen makes another cut by limiting worldview to only the cognitive dimension of religion (1987:38).

Schrempp, however, cautions against such attempts at a precise or delimiting definition, and he gives greater attention to examining the assumptions of the term's supporters and critics—opposing assumptions that may in fact speak to the existence of conflicting worldviews. Likewise, Dégh argues that the vagueness of "worldview" is not a problem but rather a benefit, allowing us to appreciate "a broader spectrum of how narrators think about themselves and the universe" (1995:246). So one advantage of the term having permeable borders is that it can and should be molded to best fit the individuals and texts under study. Given the nature of Packy Jim's stories—given his penchant for using folklore to know himself, critique his social world, and comprehend the natural and supernatural worlds—I lean toward affect and evaluation when discussing Packy Jim's worldview rather than toward more formal aspects of cognition, for example. That said, his repertoire suggests that the intellectual and emotional aspects of worldview exist in a dialectical, mutually constituting relationship. Why not conceive of both under the umbrella of worldview? Following Packy Jim's lead, I use this plastic term in a more inclusive and agglutinating way than Dundes, Geertz, or Pentikäinen.

For some, the term "worldview" comes with certain baggage, negative associations with an earlier notion of culture as static, reified, and self-perpetuating. Here again, however, worldview's nebulousness can be an advantage. It obliges me to specify how I use the term, and its intellectual baggage invites me to state unambiguously: Packy Jim exercises agency; there are no superorganic forces at play. Shaping tradition to meet present needs, however, he is both idiosyncratic and conventional. As a bricoleur of ideas, images, and narratives inherited from others, he is necessarily informed by habits of mind that are not his alone. Our mouths are full of the words of others. But he takes an active role in the construction of his own worldview. He selects and expands on certain available postulates that agree with his personal inclinations and experiences while resisting others. Worldview is not a superorganic force that controls passive human subjects (neither is tradition, neither is culture). Worldview is something much more modest, a label—faulty as all labels are—for the frames of mind and interpretive vehicles that we all develop over a lifetime of living as an individual in a group and that we make explicit, concrete, and localized in interaction and communication, not least through folklore.

As broad as my use of "worldview" may seem, it is in fact narrower than it could be. I agree with Dundes and Dégh that oral traditions provide particularly apt materials for the elucidation of worldview, and my primary focus is on Packy Jim's narrative repertoire. I am under no illusion, however, that worldview shapes and is shaped by narrative alone. The anti-authoritarian, libertarian border mentality I describe in the following chapters emerges as much from practices such as smuggling and illicit distillation—reactions to and survival strategies in a historically specific socioeconomic and political environment—as it does from songs and stories that commemorate or reference these practices. Likewise, Packy Jim's religious beliefs (and skepticism) are as much the amalgamation of a lifetime of ritual and custom as they are of verbal indoctrination, discussion, and debate. Embodiment, practices, and habits—for example, personal and domestic adornment, proxemics, or foodways—are both source and articulation of worldview. But no study is ever exhaustive and cuts have to be made. My privileging discursive evidence, primarily narrative, is not, however, arbitrary. Packy Jim is undoubtedly one of the best storytellers I am ever likely to meet, and the worldview that emerges from his range of verbal expression is at turns fascinating, disconcerting, and compelling.

To an extent I am not following the otherwise good advice of colleagues who would push me away from worldview and its negative baggage toward the more recently formulated concept of *habitus*. Pierre Bourdieu defines habitus as the lifestyle, values, and durable, transposable dispositions that individuals acquire through the everyday practices of living in a group. Habitus develops in response to shared, objective conditions, and it contributes to social reproduction (1977:72–94). My concept of worldview includes and benefits from rather than denies Bourdieu's observation that practices shape mentality. Were I to privilege Packy Jim's practices, habits, and embodiments over his rich discursive materials perhaps habitus would be a better organizing concept, though it would not easily include such things as cosmology, which worldview does. I stick with worldview not out of any lack of regard for Bourdieu or habitus, but because worldview has a longer intellectual history in my discipline and is broad enough to include the range of basic affective and cognitive postulates Packy Jim's repertoire communicates. Worldview is in fact broad and malleable enough to include everything Bourdieu claims for habitus.

Because my privileged materials are discursive, we might entertain a final complementary definition of worldview. David Naugle is a neo-Calvinist theologian who has reviewed the intellectual history of "worldview" from its origin in Immanuel Kant's *Critique of Judgment* ([1790] 1987) to the beginning of the twenty-first century (2002). His main interest is in the concept's utility in Christian apologetics and evangelism. This is not an agenda we share, but because we are both invested in narratives and textual evidence—different ones for different reasons—his definition of worldview offers another close parallel to my use of the term: "I suggest that a worldview is best understood as a semiotic phenomenon, especially as a system of narrative signs that establishes a powerful framework within which people think (reason), interpret (hermeneutics), and know (epistemology)" (2002:xix).

One may consider "worldview" vexingly imprecise or productively malleable, but I agree with Schrempp's conclusion that, although worldview can be a problematic concept, "its salvation lies in the fact that the problems it generates are intriguing and perennial" (1996:23). At any rate, invested in proverbs and the wisdom of others, most folklorists are loath to throw the baby out with the bathwater, and using "worldview"—or any term—is inevitably an act of creative recycling.

Why Packy Jim?

I am partisan. I want you to know about Packy Jim McGrath, his stories, his ways of thinking and being, his worldview. Granted, of all the people on whom to focus attention, Packy Jim might not be the first choice of historians preoccupied with world leaders or of biographers preoccupied with the already famous. But he is my first choice, and the reasons for that invite further explanation.

I will not try to conceal my intrinsic Romantic leanings, passing myself off as an entirely impartial academic only in search of empirical data, nor will I try to win friends in certain circles of the academy by pretending to be a world-weary cosmopolitan unmoved by the old and rustic. There is a good case to be made for mindful and perhaps strategic Romanticism recast as critical nostalgia (Cashman 2006a), but a more complicated argument can wait for now. Tales of the past, whiskey and turf smoke, that house—I had hoped to encounter such things in Ireland and, more than any one person, Packy Jim had such things to offer. That is only one answer—personal but honest—to the question of why I chose initially to study with Packy Jim. Many before me would have done the same. William Butler Yeats, John Millington Synge, Douglas Hyde, and Lady Gregory, later joined by professional folklorists such as Seamus Ó Duilearga, Seán Ó Súilleabháin, Seán Ó hEochaidh, and Michael J. Murphy, would have delighted in conversation with Packy Jim for many of the same reasons I do.

There are, however, compelling countertraditions that critique a naïve beatification of country people as oracles of a lost golden age. In Ireland no one has lampooned the folklorist's Celtic sentimentality more thoroughly than Flann O'Brien in *The Poor Mouth* ([1941] 1974), and both Patrick Kavanagh and Mairtín Ó Cadhain deplored the folklorist's preoccupation with collecting bits of lore to be filed away while doing little to cultivate living traditions (Ó Giolláin 2000:149–153). For some critics of the folklorist's enterprise, the preferred choice of rural informants is no less suspect. Brendan Behan (1957) writes with derision and some trepidation in characterizing the ignorance of "bogmen," a vision of stultifying culchee-ness that edges toward the sinister with the bogmen who populate Pat McCabe's *Butcher Boy* (1992) and later works.

No less than James Joyce may serve as a conflicted but forceful spokesman for this opposition when he wrestles with the tradition of elevating rural dwellers as exemplars of national identity or links to a more authentic past. In *A Portrait of the Artist as a Young Man*, Stephen Dedalus contemplates John Alphonsus

Mulrennan's account of a trip to the West of Ireland, the wellspring of untainted and enduring Irishness for the luminaries of the Irish Literary Revival and fellow travelers.

> He told us he met an old man there in a mountain cabin. Old man had red eyes and short pipe. Old man spoke Irish. Mulrennan spoke Irish. Then old man and Mulrennan spoke English. Mulrennan spoke to him about universe and stars. Old man sat, listened, smoked, spat. Then said:
> —Ah, there must be terrible queer creatures at the latter end of the world.
> I fear him. I fear his redrimmed horny eyes. It is with him I must struggle all through this night till day come, till he or I lie dead, gripping him by the sinewy throat till. . . . Till what? Till he yield to me? No. I mean him no harm. ([1916] 1993:243)

In this passage, Joyce through Dedalus expresses anxiety over being stifled by the orthodoxies of the Irish Ireland agendas of his time, shackled to a narrow equation of authenticity with the ancient and native. The old man Joyce conjures could be a version of the same men Yeats immortalized in *The Celtic Twilight* (1902) and poems such as "The Fisherman" and "To Some I have Talked with by the Fire." The difference of course is how Yeats and Joyce react to this exemplar of the traditional, simple, and pure. Perhaps toward the end of the passage, Joyce softens on the mythologizing of the West, or at least he softens his stance toward the old man who is in fact a reality regardless of the agendas of the many who would represent him. Instead Joyce/Dedalus lets the old man be, leaving Ireland behind to answer the call of international, multicultural, polyglot, cosmopolitan, modern Europe.

Though I may lean more toward Yeats than toward Joyce when it comes to representing old men in mountain cabins, I do understand Joyce's inner conflict, and I do appreciate criticisms of the Revival's conservatism. But to be clear, though I may be soft on cultural nationalism and antimodernism, I returned to Packy Jim over many years, and I commit a version of him to print now, neither to antagonize those who would follow the path of Joyce nor to add a belated postscript to Yeats's *Celtic Twilight*.

The reason, as clearly as I can put it, is that Packy Jim is an incisive, talented, and interestingly complicated individual living at a time and in a part of the world many want to know more about. Regardless of your impression of Packy Jim—whether you are in Joyce's camp or Yeats's or neither—getting to know Packy Jim is simultaneously an examination of his world, an entry into ethnography. If we look to collaborative autobiographies in Ireland, books such as *The Islandman* (Ó Crohan 1935) or *Twenty Years A-Growing* (O'Sullivan 1933), and if we look more broadly to classics in ethnography, books such as *Sun Chief: The Autobiography of a Hopi Indian* (Simmons 1942) or *Tuhami: Portrait of a Moroccan* (Crapanzano 1985), we appreciate that focusing on an individual productively sets his or her cultural surround in relief and vice versa.

Perhaps the most interesting thing about Packy Jim is not that he has stories we might characterize as traditional or uniquely Irish but that he uses them to contemplate and theorize the nature of life, history and society, the sacred and the profane. Moreover, Packy Jim regularly tacks back and forth between traditional and personal narratives in order to contemplate various ideological positions. This serves as a process of reflection leading him to articulate critical insights and aspects of worldview that are inevitably both idiosyncratic and informed by collective dispositions and expressive resources. Let it not be said that privileging one individual as a focus for study is too small a scale, the details too microcosmic, the stakes too low. The individual and tradition: in a very real sense, one does not exist without the other, and we cannot fully appreciate either without grasping their interdependence.

It is my hope that Packy Jim's name may join the list of exemplary thinkers and storytellers who each bear witness to a particular variety of vernacular Irish culture at a specific time and place—Tomás Ó Cathasaigh, Seán Ó Conaill, Timothy and Anastasia Buckley, Tomás Ó Criomhthain, Muiris Ó Súilleabháin, Peig Sayers, Hugh Nolan, Ellen Cutler, among many others.[13] It is my hope that Packy Jim's example will challenge any conception of folklore as strictly a past-tense phenomenon, safely preserved in a filing cabinet or database but fundamentally an artifact with little contemporary relevance. We should and will consider at greater length what "real folklore" might mean, but altogether my time with Packy Jim convinces me it is, simply but profoundly, that which makes life meaningful.

The Structure of the Book

From here I delve into the life and times of Packy Jim McGrath. The next chapter—necessarily the longest one—offers biographical, cultural, and historical context, then shifts to Packy Jim's presentation of self on his own terms through personal narratives. Chapter 1 also considers the nature of representations of him by others, myself included. The patterns and preoccupations that emerge from Packy Jim's own song of the self suggest themes for the following chapters.

Chapter 2 revolves around Packy Jim's ambivalence toward authority and rules, an ambivalence shared by many on the Irish border. Although investigation starts with his personal reminiscences about being torn between obedience and insubordination at the intimate level of family and neighbors, Packy Jim also points me to the broader issue of the competition between interests, otherwise known as politics, found at all levels of society from the micro to the macro. Given the legacy of colonialism, contemplation of power and politics on a broader scale has considerable resonance in the north of Ireland. In chapter 3, Packy Jim's local legends, poetic recitations, and favorite historical fiction speak directly to the shared dilemma of submission versus resistance in the context of violence and injustice. Curator of his community's historical traditions and witness to the Troubles, Packy Jim reveals through storytelling a personal politics founded on convictions about morality, neighborliness, and community that trump all other considerations.

With history and morality conjoined, the choices made and examples set by past individuals provide a range of positive and negative models for behavior in the present. A reliable catalyst to such memories and evaluations—and prominent throughout Packy Jim's repertoire—is place, both near and far. According to Yi-Fu Tuan, place is undifferentiated space transformed and made meaningful through "the steady accretion of sentiment over the years" (1977:32). Tim Cresswell would add "in the context of power" (2004); I might add "quite often through folklore." In Tuan's formulation and its elaborations, place is not a preexisting fact in the world but an achievement. More process than essence, place is a way of knowing, an arena for meaning-making. Indeed, any close consideration of Packy Jim's repertoire reveals the deep resonances of certain places that remind him of narratives about the past, stories freighted with moral lessons, existential conundrums, and confirmations of or challenges to belief. Place is so central to understanding Packy Jim's stories that it organizes the two chapters that follow.

The first of these, chapter 4, focuses attention on how landscape—physically traversed or mentally summoned—provides Packy Jim a vast mnemonic device for stories that throw into further relief the contours of his own morality. Anchoring narratives of human drama, certain places stand in for the prospects of tragedy, treachery, or redemption in this world; they profile the range of virtues and vices that characterize human nature. Through storytelling, Packy Jim reveals that history, place, and morality are inextricable and that sense of place is simultaneously sense of self and others.

Chapter 5 demonstrates that sense of place extends beyond the here and now in stories of supernatural beings crossing the threshold from the Otherworld to our material creation. Packy Jim's deep interest in "queer things" and the "spirit world" is suggested in personal narratives but explored most fully in his stories of encounters with wraiths, ghosts, and fairies in his immediate vicinity. Such stories bear witness to a grand cosmological system of sacred origin and answer fundamental questions about teleology and eschatology.

Like everyone, Packy Jim believes in some things, not in others, and leaves yet others up for debate. Chapter 6 delves deeper into Packy Jim's range of belief and disbelief in the supernatural, including his positions on and qualifications of official Church teachings. Here, legend is the primary genre for expression, and close attention to how Packy Jim rhetorically frames legends as plausible, true, or untrue reveals a large segment of his worldview and offers a glimpse into how his beliefs have evolved over time. As a rational believer, Packy Jim is keen to evaluate the truth status of stories about fairy abductions and water horses, St. Patrick and the Virgin Mary, and he is not afraid to question the authority of his sources, whether neighbors, clergy, or scripture. His findings shape an idiosyncratic yet locally and collectively informed vision of the sacred and profane.

Chapter 7 features a case study in local stories about witchcraft and the evil eye, stories that link Packy Jim's preoccupations with the difficulties of living in community, ambition and competition, morality, power, and the spirit world. The case study demonstrates how aspects of the sacred and profane are completely intertwined in Packy Jim's worldview, anticipating the final chapter.

Chapter 8 reviews, distills, and makes connections between the various aspects of Packy Jim's worldview that have emerged throughout the review of his repertoire. I offer a final consideration of the concept of worldview, noting how one individual's worldview, once grasped and made explicit, inevitably articulates both the personal and collective at the one time. Comparative evidence from my previous work in Aghyaran, County Tyrone, and Henry Glassie's work in Ballymenone, County Fermanagh, helps delineate idiosyncratic and cultural aspects of Packy Jim's worldview, and underscores the ethnographic payoff of attending to Packy Jim, his stories and experiences.

The afterword recalls that, in the beginning, friends in Aghyaran recommended Packy Jim to me as a source for "real folklore." Here I consider what real folklore means to Packy Jim, to scholars, and to me. In folklore studies there has been much talk about the evils of Romanticism and the "invention" of folklore, and some find the term "folklore" too weighted with ideological baggage to continue using it. I take a moment to own, again, my role and agendas in the representation of Packy Jim and his words, while questioning some of the excesses of reflexive critique in folklore studies. There is such a thing as traditional, vernacular, expressive culture that provides people such as Packy Jim an invaluable resource for conceptualizing their world, resisting some aspects, embracing others. I would caution against throwing the baby out with the bathwater, while reiterating that—faulted though it may be—"folklore" is a valuable label for real world phenomena. And folklore—like tradition, culture, and worldview—is best understood, I reiterate, through close attention to how specific individuals use and adapt it to changing present needs.

Finally, let me draw attention to additional resources in the back starting with the appendix, which discusses in detail the decisions made in transcription style. Following this, "Notes on the Recitations, Songs, and Traditional Stories" further illuminates Packy Jim's repertoire with historical and comparative information and includes the full transcripts of texts that were only excerpted in the preceding chapters. Separate but complementary are the endnotes arranged by chapter, which offer contextual information, join ongoing scholarly discussions, and point to supplementary sources. In addition to providing a traditional subject index, I have included indexes of international motifs and migratory legend types found in Packy Jim's stories. These allow readers to more readily access specific aspects of his repertoire and to identify relevant materials for comparison through time and across space.

1

Person and Place, Life and Times

One way to tell the story of a man's life and times is chronological. Although the autobiographical storyteller often abandons chronology for thematic connections and illustrative anecdotes, imposing chronology organizes the constituent components of a life into a tellable whole in a way that is familiar to readers. One cannot stop here with potted chronological biography; elaboration and complication necessarily follow. But neither can one delve into detail nor gesture toward pattern without such a contextual foundation. In generic terms, what follows is life history. These are the basic facts fit to print, arranged chronologically, edited or expanded in conversation with Packy Jim, and supplemented with historical background necessary for those less familiar with twentieth- and twenty-first-century Ireland.

Patrick James McGrath was born on May 29, 1933, the only child of Thomas (Tommy) McGrath and Margaret (Maggie) McGrath, née Gallagher.[1] Tommy and Maggie met in 1926 at a country house dance in Ballymongan townland, County Tyrone.[2] They later married on July 15, 1932, at the ages of forty-one and forty-three, respectively—late by local standards, then and now. As Packy Jim notes, "I suppose, perhaps, it's a minor miracle that I'm here at all."

Belonging to the "Bán" (fair-haired) branch of the McGraths who straddle the Donegal–Tyrone border, Tommy was born in Lettercran townland, County Donegal, on September 11, 1892. Lettercran, the location of a Catholic chapel, is also the name generally used for a larger collection of surrounding townlands—Lettercran, Crilly, Cashelinny, Tybane, Grouselodge, Tievemore, Tullylark, and Cullion—stretching from Pettigo and Lough Derg in the west to the point at which Donegal comes to a stop, pinched between Tyrone and Fermanagh in the west. In Tommy's youth and into adulthood, all of Ireland was part of the United Kingdom, but events of the early twentieth century

31

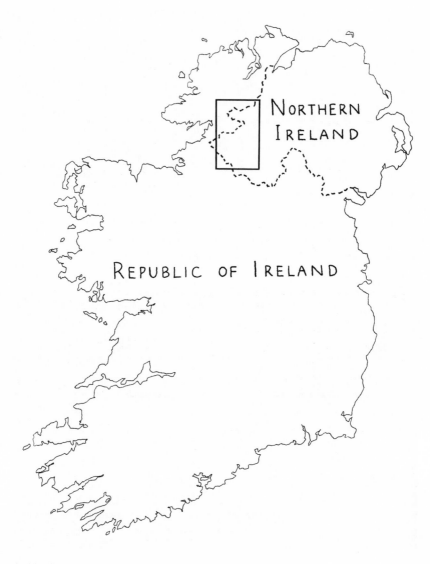

An island-wide perspective

transformed county boundaries into an international border separating the
newly independent Irish Free State and the newly formed British province of
Northern Ireland. In 1922 Donegal became part of the Free State; Tyrone and
Fermanagh remained under British rule. For Tommy and his kin this new official
border would have seemed arbitrary and occasionally inconvenient but did not
weaken their family, social, or economic ties on either side of that invisible line.

Co. DONEGAL

Castlederg

AGHYARAN

Killen

Killeter

Co. TYRONE

Lough
Derg

LETTERCRAN

Drumquin

Pettigo

Ederney

Lower Lough Erne

Co. FERMANAGH

Enniskillen

5 MILES

BALLYMENONE

Packy Jim's broad geographical context

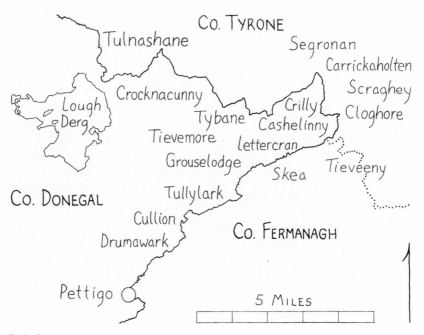

Packy Jim's immediate surroundings with townland names

Of Tommy's siblings, one brother, Jimmy, emigrated to the United States, where he married a Tyrone woman, started a family, and died a troubled veteran of World War II. Another brother, Hugh, stayed in Ireland, married a Tyrone woman, but moved in with relatives after his marriage fell apart. One sister, Mary Ellen, emigrated to the United States, married and had children in New York City, and returned to Ireland for frequent visits in her later years. Another sister, Biddy, never married and stayed in the Lettercran family homeplace. For his part, Tommy seriously considered emigrating to Canada in the 1920s and even gathered maps and began the application paperwork, but he did not follow through. In 1925 Tommy's father, James, bought a house, sixty-four acres, and one rood in Crilly townland, County Donegal, then gave it to Tommy when he married Maggie.

Maggie Gallagher was born on August 27, 1890, and grew up in Tulnashane, County Tyrone, the eldest sibling among four brothers. As she grew older through her thirties and approaching forty, Maggie prepared to be a spinster and keep house for her brother Mick, who, as the eldest son, inherited the farm. Eventually, however, Mick married and sold the homeplace to the next eldest brother, James, and the next eldest, Hugh, moved to his own place in Scraghey, County Tyrone. These shifts put Maggie in the difficult position of either becoming more or less an unpaid servant to James's wife or hiring herself out. Another option was marriage, and she was quite happy to accept Tommy McGrath's proposal.

After decades of cooking, cleaning, hauling water, feeding and milking cattle for her parents and brothers, Maggie was not pleased to receive a five-pound note and a nine-year-old cow for a dowry. While James was away, she packed up as much of the bed clothes, chairs, and other household furnishings as she felt entitled to. This included the family Sacred Heart picture and a large portrait of her brother Patrick. Maggie had been particularly close to Patrick, the youngest, whom she nursed during a terminal disease while he was on remand from imprisonment as a leader of the County Mayo IRA (Irish Republican Army). On the wedding day itself, Tommy and Maggie were married in Aghyaran chapel, County Tyrone, then spent the day in Enniskillen, County Fermanagh, while a hired man carted Maggie's belongings and drove the cow from Tulnashane, County Tyrone, to the new home just across the Donegal border in Crilly townland.

Ten months passed before the minor miracle of Packy Jim's birth, at home with the assistance of a doctor from Pettigo. Like most people, Packy Jim has few memories from his earliest years. As he approached school age, the days for Packy Jim were not overly structured and not much was expected of him beyond basic chores—helping his mother wash eggs, fetch turf, and the like. The nights were filled with the excitement of visitors, many of them smugglers trading news and stories from farther afield. In the mornings, he rose late, as did his parents, as did many other night owls along the border.

From the age of seven, Packy Jim attended Lettercran National School, next to the chapel, where the curriculum was heavily influenced, directly and indirectly, by the Catholic Church, an enthusiastic partner in the nation-building project of the Irish Free State and later Republic. At Lettercran, Packy Jim studied Irish history, Irish Gaelic, reading, math, and geography, with afternoon lessons in Catholic catechism. The focus on Irish history—often delivered in Irish, mostly as a chronicle of great men and momentous events—was part of a government effort to nationalize the historical consciousness of the youngest citizens of the new state. The effort to decenter Britain conceptually was perhaps less successful in that Irish history, as taught to Packy Jim and his generation, cast Britain in a starring role as foil—the age-old tyrant making Ireland the virtuous underdog. The Irish language—two generations dead and irrelevant to economic advancement in Packy Jim's part of Donegal—was nonetheless key to de-Anglicization efforts and legitimating the case for Irish independence founded on cultural and linguistic difference (Hyde 1894). Nevertheless, Packy Jim, like many, did not care for the way that the Irish language was taught:

Tommy and Maggie McGrath (*left*) with nieces Annie McClusky, Bridie Bradley, and Sheila McHugh (all née Gallagher),1955

Packy Jim with a portrait of his uncle Patrick Gallagher

poorly and by rote from a nonnative speaker who treated deficiencies or lack of interest as moral failings of a most unpatriotic variety. Reading in English included the occasional Irish folktale or legend translated from the Irish but emphasized approved British and American writers including Shakespeare, Milton, Longfellow, Wordsworth, and Tennyson. Readers featured none of the Anglo-Irish writers of the Irish Literary Renaissance on the grounds that they were deemed of insufficient quality and too steeped in Protestant values (O'Donoghue 1998:144). Instruction in mathematics was not the only nod to practical realities of making a living; geography was deemed particularly important for Irish school children, many of whom—about half of Packy Jim's classmates—would become emigrants in the not too distant future.

According to Packy Jim and many of his contemporaries, the local school-master, Bernard Cunningham, had a mercurial temperament and frequently meted out corporal punishment. Packy Jim was a frequent victim given that, with his home full of visitors until all hours most nights, he often woke too late to get to school on time. Like the majority of his classmates—bound neither for the clergy nor professions—Packy Jim left school, rather happily, at the age of fourteen. As he remembers,

Oh Lord, when the day come to quit school I thought I'd be happy ever after. It was the greatest relief. Oh Lord God, there was nobody getting out of jail after doing ten years in jail happier nor me when I got rid of that damned place! (August 13, 2007)

In leaving school, however, Packy Jim entered more fully into harsh economic realities that shaped and continue to shape his life and sense of self. From the point of leaving school in 1947, he was expected to take on more responsibility and to contribute financially to his family's livelihood. Packy Jim assisted Tommy with odd jobs including whitewashing, stonework, and thatching. Over time Packy Jim took on a series of his own temporary jobs, mostly agricultural day labor, a few months in the local forestry, and occasional work for the local government council maintaining roads. Unpaid work at home was a continuation, intensification, and expansion of childhood chores. These included splitting wood and cutting and drying turf for fuel; tending the vegetable garden, potatoes, and oats; winning hay, which is to say cutting, drying, and storing grass for winter fodder; helping to milk and look after four cows; and feeding and watering up to sixty hens and an assortment of turkeys, ducks, geese, and guinea hens.

Chores were governed by seasonal animal and crop growing cycles and by when particular goods came into greatest demand. Turkeys, for example, fetched the best price before Christmas, when they would be served at holiday celebrations; maturing goslings were typically sold in mid-August to larger farmers who fattened them on the leftover grain of stubble fields before final sale. Tillage required intensive efforts planting by spade in the spring and harvesting by hand in the fall; summer required weeding and vigilance for pests, while winter required little attention. Milking for Maggie to make and sell butter continued year round but slowed in the winter with the natural dip in dairy production. Proceeds from eggs—under the management of the woman of the house, as was traditional—was the family's most reliable source of income from February to October, again taking into account a natural dip during the winter. Eggs were a particularly valuable commodity during World War II and through the mid-1950s, when rationing in Northern Ireland created a lucrative market for those who were willing—like the McGraths, like most of their neighbors—to smuggle across the border.

All three family members took part in various aspects of the smuggling trade, whether actively smuggling or tending stock and storing goods for smugglers awaiting the most opportune moment to complete their transportation and sale. Smuggling in both directions has always been part of the Irish border experience, but it increased dramatically in the 1930s during the Anglo-Irish Trade War, continued through World War II, and began to taper in the 1950s.[3] Packy Jim, then, simply took smuggling for granted from his youngest days through to adulthood, and indeed smuggling will remain a fact of life for him and others in border counties as long as there are price differentials or subsidies to take advantage of on either side of that otherwise imaginary, ultimately ungovernable line.

Another important source of extralegal income for the McGraths came from poitín-making, the local form of moonshining.[4] Both Tommy and Maggie knew the craft, distilling in a nearby glen with a spring in good weather, at home indoors in bad. They told the preadolescent Packy Jim that the sharp-smelling clear liquid about their house was "lough water," allowing him to maintain his innocence if ever cross-examined by customs men or the Guards.[5] Packy Jim eventually learned the craft as well, though Tommy abruptly stopped distilling in 1951 when the Bishop of Clogher Diocese proscribed poitín-making and poitín-drinking as a special class of sin. (Maggie's response was perhaps less definitive.)

According to Packy Jim, the 1930s, '40s, and '50s were the most financially straitened times. The struggle to piece together jobs and the constant subsistence chores were difficult. Then again, barring sustained bad weather and crop failure, they never went hungry and were more or less self-sufficient, buying only tea and sugar. In 1954 Packy Jim started collecting unemployment benefits. This offered some relief for the family, though this amounted to only eight shillings weekly to start and lasted only from November to March. Starting in 1957, the Irish government provided subsidies for cattle, which offered additional relief. Before that, starting in 1951, Northern Ireland had offered subsidies. Although Tommy had not been a serious smuggler of cattle until that point, like many of his Donegal neighbors he occasionally walked calves across the border to split the subsidy proceeds of £5 a head with a friend or relative willing to "stand for" or claim ownership of the cattle. Tommy or Packy Jim then returned to collect the animals the next day after they had been officially inspected and registered.

As Packy Jim recalls, despite their efforts, his family never prospered beyond basic subsistence until Maggie and Tommy began drawing their weekly government pensions at age seventy, in 1960 and 1962, respectively. This was a watershed moment after which the family was able to pay for certain foods and consumer goods rather than producing it all themselves or making do without. They were also in position for the first time to afford select luxuries, feed their stock better, save money, and make material improvements. Although the McGraths did not elect to pay for bringing electricity to their house, they purchased their first battery powered radio in 1967, enjoying the access to news and music. At Packy Jim's urging, his father covered their thatched roof with corrugated metal, retiring his ladder and thatching tools in June 1977. In 1979 Tommy also retired his debt to the Irish Land Commission, an institution that had inherited the task of subsidizing the redistribution of land from landlords to tenants begun before Irish independence.[6] So when Tommy took over the Crilly farmstead from his father, James, he had taken on a kind of mortgage paid to the Commission guaranteeing his freeholding. Paying off the Commission in 1979 was quite a victory for a family that had struggled for decades. It also meant that when it came time for Packy Jim to inherit, his real property came free and clear of debt, liens, or rent.

The gradual easing of financial strain coincided with the gradual decline of Maggie's and Tommy's ability to perform all the tasks they were accustomed to carrying out, and more responsibility fell to Packy Jim to keep the household going. More troubling, Tommy had a stroke in November 1977, was hospitalized, and recovered to an extent, but other strokes followed. Maggie's health, too, began to fail as she suffered from chronic stomach problems and loss of strength in her legs. With no siblings and little support, Packy Jim dreaded the inevitable, lost sleep, and lost weight. After another stroke took Tommy's ability to speak, he was hospitalized until he died, on May 8, 1980. Maggie did not last much longer, dying in Ballyshannon's Sheil Hospital on March 4, 1982. Packy Jim remembers well the considerable mental and emotional strain of this period, and the grief and relief when it was over.

At the age of fifty, Packy Jim was on his own and relatively well provided for. He had a house and land, his parents' savings from pensions and the sale of livestock, four cows, and fields to graze them on or lease to neighboring farmers. Packy Jim was not suddenly wealthy, but he had sufficient means to continue living in the manner he knew and was most comfortable with. Occasionally in recent years a forestry or wind power firm has approached Packy Jim about buying or leasing his land, but access remains an issue and Packy Jim is in no rush or need to see big changes.

Gradually Packy Jim has shifted from the near total self-sufficiency of raising most of his own provisions, to becoming more of a consumer, albeit a rather frugal one with basic needs and minimal overhead costs. Packy Jim has never missed having electricity. Battery powered and wind-up radios provide his news, and he gets all the television he wants—which is not much—at the houses he visits during the week. Packy Jim has a reliable source for water (and refrigeration) in a cool spring only paces from his southern gable wall. Eventually, in 1989, Packy Jim stopped keeping cattle. With no help to win hay to fodder cattle over the winter, Packy Jim concluded that they were not worth the trouble. He continued to raise chickens for eggs and to provide his own fuel by cutting and drying turf from the bog. Eventually, in 2010, he gave up winning turf as well; it can be bought relatively cheaply or bartered for with grazing rights or other favors. Now Packy Jim shops twice a week (or three times in summer when the milk spoils more quickly) to replenish the same staples: tea, tea biscuits, milk, sugar, bread, butter, potatoes, lard, bacon, mince (hamburger), and Bovril (a granulated beef extract he makes into a gravy).

In a typical week, Packy Jim's chores have shrunk to the basics of cooking, house cleaning, keeping a fire going, taking out the ashes, care and feeding of chickens, and more occasional projects such as splitting wood for kindling or breaking stones to repair the path in and out of his home. This leaves plenty of time for reading—newspapers, true crime magazines, Westerns, and *Ireland's Own*.[7] He also has a significant small library of books, mostly readers leftover from school and gifts.[8] This routine also leaves plenty of time for socializing. His supposed rural isolation is relative, for he maintains one or more bicycles and a motorbike to ceili at night with a network of friends—Francie Duffy, Willie McHugh, Cassie McMenamin, Charlie Hilley, Arthur O'Neill, Charlie Gillespie—and more occasionally with relatives in Tyrone and Donegal. Depending on weather and mood, Packy Jim will ceili between two and five times a week, "enough to keep you going," as he says. More generally he concludes, "Aye, that's my way of going and will be till the day I die."

Life History versus Life Story

Any book focusing on one person requires biographical contextualization up front in a form we may call life history. I gathered the facts reviewed here in roughly two phases. In the earlier years of working with Packy Jim—in nineteen recorded sessions from 1998 through 2009—he was happy to discuss any topic, but he asked that I come with questions to prompt him. So in a typical session I would raise a topic for conversation such as ghosts, smuggling, or holiday customs, not unlike former Irish Folklore Commission collectors did using prompts from Seán Ó Súilleabháin's *A Handbook of Irish Folklore* (1942), which I consulted extensively, particularly in the beginning. This elicited songs, recitations, tall tales, jokes, anecdotes about local characters, historical and supernatural legends, and oral history. This also elicited first-person reminiscences that related thematically to the topic at hand. Although Packy Jim asked me to prompt him with questions, note that recorded interviews rarely proceeded as cross-examinations for very long; prompting led to rather than shut down more free-flowing conversations in which, eventually, I would abandon my agenda and finding lists to follow his lead into the topics that interested him. During this first, longer phase I proceeded as inductively as possible, without a preconceived hypothesis, trusting that a thesis would emerge and knowing that both personal and handed-down narratives would be relevant and would likely speak to each other.

In more recent years, particularly during four recorded sessions in 2011 and another four in 2014, I elicited additional information, sometimes through direct questions, in part with an eye toward fleshing out what I had already recorded. By this point I was sufficiently aware of certain personal narratives that Packy Jim had found occasion to tell me three or more times in the past, and in many cases I steered conversation to invite them again, either directly or more often indirectly. Here the goal was gathering not only facts and connective tissue between stories I was already familiar with but also additional versions of his most frequent narratives.

It can be argued that my first phase of research allowed for these stories to emerge more naturally, as glosses on present conversational threads, whereas in the second phase I prompted personal narratives more consciously while Packy Jim was happy to oblige. In a seminal *Journal of American Folklore* article, Jeff Todd Titon (1980) calls the former—the naturally occurring stuff—"life story" and celebrates it for expressing the storyteller's self-conception. The latter—the elicited and edited stuff—he calls "life history" and criticizes for being coaxed, co-opted, and artificial. At its worst, life history for Titon smacks too much of the editor's agenda, and while claiming the authority of quoted speech, offers a false sense of authenticity and objectivity.

These are issues worth keeping in mind. But consider also that, as Patricia Sawin observes, all stories representing a life, whether emergent or elicited, are collaborative and dialogic and must be understood as such. Autobiographical reminiscence is always a "cooperative achievement between a speaker and an addressee—the Other without whom there would be no point in conceiving of or expressing the self" (2004:20). Certainly it is important to bear in mind Kirshenblatt-Gimblett's (1989) characterization of life history as a construct, a genre of ethnographic writing that comes with certain textual strategies and conventions, such as chronological organization. For my purposes, however, I have not found a rigid dichotomy of the natural versus elicited all that useful.

Life stories, too, are collaborative, complexly situated, fictive constructions, and I am under no illusion that what I gathered and reproduced as life history is complete or entirely accurate biography. Instead, my concern is to try to understand Packy Jim as he understands himself, or at least as he presents himself to me under the typical and specific circumstances of our conversations. Just as we have come to appreciate that identity is neither essential nor fixed but subject to ongoing negotiation through interaction, it follows that the performed self may be the only one there is and certainly the only one any of us will ever get.

So comparing life story versus life history—or as Ken Plummer puts is, naturalistic forms of autobiography versus researched biography (2001:396)—I argue that there is room for both. Life history as a collaboration, knitted into the chronological trajectory audiences expect, efficiently does important contextualizing, orienting work. It may be a constructed, collaborative, and possibly etic genre, but with proper care it can proceed along emic conceptual lines, especially when fleshed out with the personal narratives that are most frequently told and presumably most important to the person in question (cf. Langness and Frank 1981:86).

Personal Narratives and the Presentation of Self

Let us shift here from life history to life story in order to investigate what patterns, preoccupations, and themes emerge and endure through repeated narrations. These can and should guide our understanding of Packy Jim on his own terms. Because Packy Jim's iconic personal narratives are few, briefly summarizing them provides a useful overview. Here and in chapters to come, I will delve into the specifics of certain stories, but taken as a whole, they generally follow the form of developed personal narratives as described by Labov and Waletzky (1967) and Labov (1972; cf. Labov 2013:5–6, 223–224). Typically Packy Jim's personal narratives begin with an orientation to the setting and people involved, then proceed through complicating action to resolution, and include an evaluation that proposes the point of the narrative, including its relevance as a gloss on preceding conversation. Oftentimes Packy Jim provides a coda that returns us, the listeners, to the present moment; connects the previous story with events or behaviors in everyday life, outside the story frame; and/or makes pronouncements or generalizations. Codas often serve also as the jumping-off point for additional narratives that support or complicate the generalizations reached through the preceding narrative.

The following are summaries of Packy Jim's most frequent iconic personal narratives arranged in chronological order of the narrated events:

1. Early in Packy Jim's school years, the schoolmaster cruelly beat him until he had successfully memorized and recited a poem commemorating Christ's sacrifice, written by one of the executed leaders of the 1916 Easter Rising.[9] The irony of being beaten to learn this particular poem is not lost on Packy Jim, who sees himself as a victim of capricious authority. He can still recite that poem "learned in tears" seven decades ago ("I See His Blood upon the Rose" by Joseph Mary Plunkett [1916]).

2. One day, fearing a beating from his schoolmaster for being late, Packy Jim played hooky from school, but it was not worth the massive anxiety this caused. Fear of punishment by the schoolmaster and/or by his parents, and fear of authority more generally, animated the young Packy Jim, in a way that it no longer does. This story provides Packy Jim an opportunity to characterize how he has changed over time. It is something of a minor epic, running between six and twelve minutes.

3. As a boy, Packy Jim was terrified of his mother's talk of the family emigrating and his father's talk of moving the family to another house, some of which was not serious but staged to get a reaction from him. Often Packy Jim includes additional ancillary anecdotes that underscore the theme that he is not now, nor has he ever been, terribly fond of change.

4. At a fair in Pettigo (the nearby village divided by the Northern Ireland–Republic of Ireland border), the young Packy Jim bought a pair of wellingtons on the northern side of the border but was stopped by a southern customs agent who took pity on him as a "middling poor boy" and gave him the option of taking the boots back or paying customs duty. Packy Jim took the boots back to the seller but later retrieved them and smuggled them home.

5. When Packy Jim was twenty or twenty-one he noted the number of his contemporaries who had emigrated and on impulse bought a suitcase from shopkeeper Maggie Haughey with the intent of leaving for Scotland with a couple other young men from Lettercran. Haughey, however, mentioned the purchase to Packy Jim's mother, who became upset and confronted him in tears. Packy Jim immediately gave up his plan and sold his hidden suitcase to another aspiring emigrant. Although he notes the irony that "my suitcase got to Scotland but I never did," he is confident in retrospect that he would have regretted the decision and quickly made his way home.

6. A car ride to and from Shannon airport was as far from home as Packy Jim ever went (although he also mentions being on shorter journeys to Dublin airport and Knock, back and forth). Regrettably, there was little or no time for him to explore his destination(s). He was as glad to be out of the car at the finish of the trip(s) as he had been eager for the trip(s) to begin. He still prefers not to roam far from home.

7. As a teenager Packy Jim was spurned and mocked by more than one girl he attempted to court. He remains bitter.

8. Also during his teenage years, certain neighbors and relatives slighted Packy Jim as a laborer and rejected his help. He remains bitter.

9. In his later forties, Packy Jim experienced great stress and dread over his father and then his mother, both dying after prolonged infirmity. During this five-year period he lost weight, lost sleep, and often experienced a dark shadowy figure dragging him out of bed at night. In codas to this experience, he maintains that today he would be happier were his parents still around "to rule the roost," as he puts it, or to be the "complete boss" and for him to continue living the "sheltered life" under their rule.

10. After seeing to his mother's burial, not long after his father's, Packy Jim at age fifty remembers receiving visitors. This was the first time he could not sit silently to one side. He had to act as the man of the house, and eventually he "came into his own." This story is often extended with an account of his refusing to move in with cousins and relinquish his autonomy once it had been firmly established, as it remains today.

11. In his fifties Packy Jim visited a cousin in the Sperrin Mountains of County Tyrone, Northern Ireland. His hosts convinced an old man in the house that Packy Jim was an IRA man on the run, and Packy Jim did not like being used as a pawn in this bout of "codology," which belittled the old man in the same way Packy Jim believes some people now try to belittle him. More generally, Packy Jim felt uneasy about the number of soldiers and helicopters scouring the countryside, and he was quite happy to return home after his sojourn to Northern Ireland at the height of the Troubles. This story is sometimes amplified by shorter examples of frightening personal encounters with British soldiers closer to home.

12. At sixty Packy Jim encountered and confronted a smart aleck in a pub who made fun of him for remaining a bachelor, questioned his sexuality, and treated him as a foolish country rube. This story is his most frequent illustration of the bad behaviors and unfair stigmas he has to put up with, of a reprehensible streak in the Irish national character, and more generally of the iniquities of human nature. The fact that Packy Jim stood up to the smart aleck is notable and marks for him a change from his more passive younger days. (See the introduction, pp. 9–11, for a transcript of one version of this story.)

13. Packy Jim remembers that he has been "in the jaws of death" three times: in 2011 when a car clipped and destroyed his motorbike at Aghyaran crossroads; another motorbike versus car accident in 1993 that left him with a broken collarbone and a hurt shoulder (often referenced as context in personal narrative 12); and in the 1980s when he sustained a concussion after being knocked off his motorbike in Castlefinn, County Donegal, while not wearing a helmet. Sometimes he adds a fourth near-death incident, mentioning that when he was five years old he nearly fell into a well. In each case, Packy Jim believes that the guardian angel prayer and five Hail Marys he recites twice daily helped save him.

Packy Jim, 1955

Packy Jim, 2014

Again, these iconic personal narratives are polished set pieces, not the only personal experience narratives Packy Jim is capable of performing. These thirteen, however, have been a stable part of his repertoire during the years of our acquaintance. Judging from the frequency with which he tells these stories, they seem to have repeated utility for conveying the self he wants to present to me and to others.

As performance studies and the ethnography of speaking have demonstrated, who is speaking to whom, when, where, how, and to what ends are not only relevant but central to any informed analysis of narratives told in face-to-face settings. We are fortunate not to be working solely with insufficiently contextualized stories from an archive or library, so of course we should pay attention to how and why these personal narratives are marshaled during specific communicative events (as done in the previous chapter where the mismatched expectations of speaker and listener were key). But given the frequency with which Packy Jim tells these thirteen personal narratives, and given the consistencies between multiple versions of them, an overview of common themes is valuable. From this, the contours of a personality emerge, the one that Packy Jim proposes for himself. If we are in the business of illuminating texts, this personal context is an equally important form of context as situational, cultural, socioeconomic, historical, or comparative contexts that have, thus far, been greater preoccupations for folklorists.

So what kind of self-portrait emerges? In some respects personal narrative 13 is not as tightly related in theme or purpose to the other twelve in that near-death experiences are often less concerned with making a bid about subjectivity or coherence. Rather, such stories are somewhat "meta" in that they focus on events that could have ended the life that one is otherwise in the process of characterizing through personal narratives. That being said, personal narrative 13 does establish something very important about Packy Jim. He believes in God, guardian angels, and the power of prayer. This fact alone is enough to call for elaboration in chapters 5 and particularly 6, which address the supernatural, the sacred, and the issue of belief.

Invested in self-image and portraiture, the other twelve personal narratives are perhaps more fully interrelated. Most clearly, Packy Jim sees himself as a virtuous underdog and occasional victim (personal narratives 1, 4, 7, 8, and 12). He is aware of his undesirability as a marriage prospect in the eyes of women (7), his reputation as lazy and unskilled laborer in the eyes of conventional working men (8), and his lowly social status in the eyes of authority figures (teachers, customs men, and soldiers in 1, 4, and 11) and particularly of those who consider themselves to be of higher status (such as the smart aleck pretending to contract him to cut turf in 12). Personal narrative 11 includes a moment of Packy Jim regretting his passive complicity in a moment of "scapegoating," as he calls it, empathizing with an older man being treated badly by those of purportedly higher status.

Packy Jim identifies consistencies in his position, personality, and preoccupations over time but also acknowledges change and personal evolution. For example, he may see himself as the perpetual underdog, but unlike in his earlier life (1, 2, 4, 7, and 8), now he is willing to stand up for himself and to push back against the stigmas projected upon him (12). Likewise, Packy Jim pinpoints fear of change as a life-long concern (3, 5, 9, and to an extent 6 and 11), and this is tied to his preference for what he calls the "sheltered life," which includes simple living, letting his parents make all the major decisions when they were alive, and sticking close to home with his own class of "modest" people (5, 6, 9, 11, 12). As Packy Jim advised his friend and fellow bachelor, Paddy O'Neill, "stick with your own level of people, for them high flyers and progressive people will take a hand at you." That said, when circumstances forced change, Packy Jim was prepared and capable of coming into his own, taking on the social and economic roles of his parents once they were gone (10). As he remembers this transition, "I had to stand up and be counted. I didn't like it, but it had to be faced."

As mentioned in the previous chapter, much of the coherence Packy Jim proposes for himself emerges from consistencies over time—for example, he worries about and always has worried about change, he is and always has been stigmatized by certain types of people. On the other hand, the coherence he proposes for himself also emerges from certain irresolvable tensions—such as between exercising his individual autonomy or following collective rules.

Bearing down first on consistencies over time, consider a few texts for more in-depth illustration. Packy Jim has made pronouncements such as "No, I wouldn't be a big fan of change," from our first (unrecorded) meeting on November 2, 1998, through to the last time I recorded him, on June 21, 2014. Personal narrative 3 speaks most directly to Packy Jim's consistent resistance to change and is in some ways more of a constellation of brief anecdotes than a single, fixed beginning-middle-end narrative. His early memory of Tommy contemplating a move and Maggie contemplating emigration usually prompts the theme, but the related anecdotes of worrying over neighbors moving away or seeing his favorite calf driven off to market have accompanied this reminiscence, in variable order, to illustrate the central point. Of course, in personal narrative 5, Packy Jim is the one contemplating emigration, but it takes very little resistance to this idea, from the chief authority in his life, to make Packy Jim abandon change and the great unknown for familiarity, familial duty, and the status quo.

Packy Jim's most deep-seated trepidation — complementing but surpassing these others — was the impending deaths of his parents, the most significant change he has faced. This dread takes on a power of its own in personal narrative 9:

Oh, that was an awful period. I was in dread, both of them ailing. What's to be done, what's to become of me?

I always slept up on that old loft up there, always, but then there were nights and nights I had no sleep. Lost heaps and heaps of nights, no sleep.

Several times it happened—over a period of time for maybe four or five months—that I'd fall asleep and I thought something *invisible*, something I couldn't *see*, was catching me in the bed clothes, pulling me to the one side, and I'd drop down on to the floor.

And then you'd waken up, then you'd see you were in the bed. You weren't on the floor.

It was *scary*.

Not every night, but more nor once.

And do you know what I done, at that time? Only I hadn't the option. I'd have given anybody a pound to lay with me, at night, for *company*. There was nobody to pay. I'd have given anybody a pound to lay with me. I was that scared.

It was only, I suppose, well, it be'd to be the worry and the annoyance or whatever the Devil, but I thought, like, well, you would know when you'd be thinking about it the next day, it was no ghostly experience. You'd have to come to the conclusion that it was just an old nervous thing.

But this *thing*, like, you know, you didn't see it, but it caught you and it trailed you. And then you wakened up then, well, then, maybe the first instant you were waking up, see were you on the floor? You quickly realized you weren't, you were in the bed.

But it was SCARY! (November 17, 2011)

Although Packy Jim interprets his perception of an invisible force under his bed as a "nervous" reaction to worry — rather than as an actual supernatural being — his mind had conceived a particularly terrifying metaphor for inescapable change. Burdened by a sense of impending doom, Packy Jim got no rest at night as his thoughts dragged him under, helpless, exposed, paralyzed, alone.

Other torments came during the conscious hours of day. Stigma has followed Packy Jim all his life—for being an only child, for living in rustic conditions, for being "middling poor," for remaining a bachelor, for being shorter in stature than many. As the story of Packy Jim's confrontation in McHale's pub (personal narrative 12) suggested in the previous chapter, smart alecks in particular—those who point out and make fun of his supposed shortcomings—are a bane of his existence. This is an old theme, not just a recent outrage. In a version of personal narrative 7 from August 2007, we see Packy Jim insulted and rejected as a useless worker.

I was down about a house about the road there, as I was in so often. And uh, [a local drover and smuggler] come till it, and he was looking about a man for the *bog*. He was looking for the man of the house, the *young* man of the house, for the bog.

And the young man of the house wasn't *there*.

But *I* was *there*.

And my *cousin* was *there*.

And uh, this was outside my hearing—I might have been out doing something, maybe doing some chore for the people, maybe perhaps that was it.

So.

"What about Packy Jim?" she says.

"HE WOULDN'T BE WORTH A *DAMN*!"

That was what he said.

"That's a cousin of *his* there," she pointed to the cutty. "That's a cousin."

"WHAT DO *I* CARE?"

So then, again, that's what—as is chatted about—story carrying does:

Rosie then told it to Mammy.

And Mammy told it to me.

And it's in my head—as the saying goes—*presently*.

And it's like that: I'd have been as good a man as the man he was looking for. But again, I was the wee dwarf. A wee, I suppose, looked-down-on dwarf. So I was just what you might call, to put it in Irishman's words, "a wee useless fucker."

And the other man, when he couldn't be got, "To Hell with that boy."

Well that's in my head to my dying day. That doesn't do you any good either, and it helps to give you what they call an inferior *complex*. It'll do that. And if your character, or if your, your character—or whatever way you like to put it—or subconscious is destroyed once, you hardly ever get the better of it, you have that damned old inferior feeling till the day you die, if you would live to be five hundred.

And I've heared a lump of that, and Rosie shouldn't have told Mammy about it. And if she told Mammy about it, Mammy shouldn't have told me about it, do you understand.

"He wouldn't be worth a damn."

"That's . . . that's . . . that's the cousin there."

"What do I care?"

So [that man] was ignorant. He was a smart man, too, but he knowed fuck all! I would have been as good a man as the man [he] was looking about, but . . .

Ah, to Hell with him.

Here Packy Jim sees himself through the eyes of his judge—a "looked-down-upon dwarf"—and he protests. Evaluation is swift and sure: Packy Jim is the equal of any man for work, that ignorant smart aleck "knows fuck all," the gossip that circulates insults can be as devastating as the original offense. Exercised, he repeats the provocative dialogue in support of his evaluation. But Packy Jim pushes back without the satisfaction of facing his accuser. He can mimic the man's unmannerly bellow. He can disparage the crude, pejorative terms an "Irishman" would use to characterize him, while echoing his previous critique of "the Irish" and their penchant for "scapegoating." But the damage is done, and it is lasting. The coda—"Ah, to Hell with him"—brings us back to the present moment of our recorded conversation, as if nothing more is to be said, but Packy Jim cannot let the theme go.

To underscore this smart aleck's insult as being typical, he followed it immediately with another jibe from a cousin (not the same one as in the previous story) who judged him lazy without knowing the full extent of Packy Jim's industry:

It's like another man, a cousin of mine, that I heared saying—and I heared him too, I wasn't born deaf either—it was easy for me to be, it was easy for me to be supple of myself [fit and well rested], I never done nothing.

But he wasn't at my arse all the time when I was working on the Council and working for old farmers, here and there and thonder, that was trying to take—as the saying goes—the last shilling out of you. He didn't know that, but he come here with sheep or something like that. He seen the wee place here, about thirty or thirty-five rooks of hay, and

a strong man—my daddy—going good, and we're only working half time,
and lying about to dinner time, like that, and lazing about, doing fuck
all. I suppose that that's what he thought.

Aye, easy for me to be supple. Never done nothing.

We know that fellow too, but we'll not name him. I wouldn't have
much time for him either.

Old *smart alecks*! (August 13, 2007)

"Old smart alecks" is both an evaluation of his tormentors and a coda naming
the burning issue that has prompted his reminiscences—the damnable hateful-
ness of some people, thinking themselves great by underestimating Packy Jim,
the virtuous underdog. If the content of what the smart alecks said is unfair, the
style is appalling—to his face by his own cousin, behind his back in the presence
of another cousin who is left to defend him, or not.

Packy Jim points to these early experiences with smart alecks as both singular
and typical. They are a major source of his present sense of having failed in
realms conventionally associated with success. Here he taps into generally
available tenets issuing from Freud to popular understandings of psychology,
looking to originary moments for the root cause of present neurosis such as an
inferiority complex. Packy Jim further generalizes from his own experience to
articulate a truth about living in society, trapped in a competition for status.
Once your lowly status has become conventional wisdom through gossip or
"story carrying," once your confidence has been destroyed, "you hardly ever
get the better of it, you have that damned old inferior feeling till the day you
die."

Packy Jim's interest in girls and young women during his youth met with
similar obstacles, and these experiences further challenged his sense of self-
worth, compounded his growing apprehension over the risks of sociability and
competition for status, and entrenched his views about the wicked types of people
who populate his world. Some of his earlier love interests are still around, and
certain details are too sensitive to publish. But in broad strokes, Packy Jim un-
successfully courted three girls in succession. One in particular humiliated him
at a ceili where he was asked to sing a song. Packy Jim readily agreed, though
his performance was perhaps not that well received. Her sarcastic observation
to the audience, referring to Packy Jim's eagerness to perform, was terse but
devastating: "Good singers are hard to force."

He still has contact, of a sort, with one of his early crushes, and whether or
not his interpretation of her motives is accurate, his lasting bitterness over real
or perceived condescension is stark and not to be questioned.

She's married for years and living in County Donegal. And she takes me
for what you'd call an innocent eejit, with child's wit, somebody with
the wit of about four or five. And I'm sent a Christmas card every year,
but she took good care that Mammy would be dead a couple of years
before it would come, do you understand. When Mammy was living it
didn't come.

But she sends that to me hoping then I'd open that card, if I was
foolish enough, and maybe might think, "Christ of Almighty, I've missed
you. Jimity God, if I'd made a better effort I would have got you."

Maybe I'd sit down and cry.

Maybe I'd do better than that, maybe I'd take that gun and blow the
head off.

And that could be good news to her, do you understand.

That's downright fucking badness.

But uh, I was telling that to Paddy Dolan—you don't know Paddy
Dolan, but he lived down Killeter, he's dead now for a lock of years.
Well, I don't like mentioning names, and I wouldn't mention names,
but I was telling him about this.

"Christ sir, *I'd burn it, sir!*" he said. "*I'd BURN IT, sir!*"

So uh . . . I look at it, and I hang it up there—it's down there in the
room there, among the other Christmas cards—and later, sooner or
later, along about Hall'eve, I'll pick the whole up and I'll burn them.

But it doesn't cost me a thought . . .

But she doesn't know, she thinks I'm the soft innocent body. Well,
maybe at the best I'll break down and cry—cry bitter tears, do you
understand, about what I'd missed.

But she's, she's not hitting the right nail. She's missing, she's
missing, but she's a bad ape. She's a *bad ape*, do you understand. Aye.

That's one of the bad women I've met.

But she thinks poor old innocent Packy Jim out there, when he
gets that, he'll still think, Lord, look what he's missed.

That's the kind of bad apes you meet.

I'm telling you, it's not much wonder there's broken marriages in it.
(August 13, 2007)

Faced with such "a bad ape" who plays with his affections and misjudges him
as an innocent, Packy Jim may claim, for the sake of dignity and self-esteem,
that this abuse does not "cost him a thought." But of course his sense of the

injustice—and the insult to his intelligence—does concern him enough to shape his experience into an impassioned, repeated narrative that can be understood as a gloss on related topics.

As we might expect, in four of the five recorded versions of the previous story, Packy Jim used it as a spring board to discuss women of disagreeable to villainous sorts, the institution of marriage—which he does not take lightly—and morality more generally. (In the remaining version, from February 1999, he segued into a discussion of the foolishness of people, men or women, who assume that a person—and more to the point, Packy Jim—does not have the capacity to improve or mature over time.) Packy Jim is talking here about a "bad ape" of a woman, and he tells stories of other bad women, both fictional and nonfictional, in a range of genres (see, for example, his account of Cassie McFadden's ambitious scheming in chapter 4). But he has no hatred of women across the board, and for his generation and part of the world, he is rather progressive in his attitudes toward gender equality. Packy Jim is, for example, a full-throated supporter of women who want to become priests in the Roman Catholic Church, adding, "I fear—as the saying goes—that men have taken, taken too much of an upper hand in the Church, and government, too."

What agitates Packy Jim, first and foremost, is cruelty, committed by women or by men. Secondarily, he is scandalized by the fallen state of the world today, as indicated clearly for him in degenerating relationships between men and women and in the decline in people's commitment to the sacred bonds of marriage. While most anecdotes supporting his positions here would be too awkward to quote in full—they involve his neighbors and relatives—in general Packy Jim is scandalized by the amount of promiscuity, adultery, illegitimacy, and failed marriages in his world. And here he refers not just to examples from today but also from his childhood, which to him is no golden age of virtue and unwavering morality seen through a nostalgic lens.

Packy Jim's own decision to remain a bachelor was not entirely his. He was not attracted to those who were receptive to him, and those he was attracted to did not sufficiently return his affection. His rural situation and relative poverty may have turned away some or many prospects, and he himself judges that his resources would have been stretched too thin to raise a family in comfort. Still, Packy Jim probably could have married for the sake of marrying, but here he stands on principle. Marrying for lust or for money is "damnable." Mutual love is the only valid reason for Packy Jim, though he says, "I differ from many on this." In the end, he rationalizes that "the celibate life isn't so bad," and more than that, it has saved him and the family that never was a great deal of worry and heartache.

They chat about marrying and this and that and *thon*. But I say this: I was in no position to marry, I had no place to take a woman till, and that was that.

But if I had been married forty years ago, if I had had seven or eight of a family, what were they? They were on the lowest rung of the ladder!

I'm sure of it, I swear to it, do you know. Whether that would be a good thing or a bad thing, I don't know.

But if I had had six or seven, they were the lowest rung of the ladder.

And worrying about how to provide for them, kids maybe having to emigrate for jobs. And maybe a daughter married on a drunken bastard some road or another, too. What do you know?

That's the life that never come for me, do you know. Aye. That's the way of that. (February 18, 1999)

During a later conversation, Packy Jim characterizes marriage as a high stakes gamble; being stuck with a person for life that you did not and perhaps could not fully know before the wedding strikes him as taking a big chance. Moreover, marriage leaves you vulnerable, not least to the betrayal of infidelity.

You meet people now and again—as the saying goes—and you think they're all right, and then if you were seeing more of them as time goes on, you might find out that it was the reverse. It's happened to me time and again.

There's lots and lots of people in the world and they're just exactly as you meet them. But then there's another quantity of people in the world you think they're all right, you go to them to live or something like that, and you find out, unfortunately, that they're a different class of a person.

That is the big *risk*, we'll say, in marrying. That's the big risk, too big a risk I'd say.

No. Better safe than sorry. I'm not so bad, living on my own, not having to worry about nobody, not having to support nobody. Not having to worry about a woman two-timing me neither.

No, leave it, this is my way of living and will be till the day I die.

There's a motto—did I ever tell you—there's a motto I have, it's been in my head maybe sixty years or more. It's:

Love *many*,

Trust *few*,

And always paddle your own *canoe*.[10]
Aye. Isn't that a good one? (November 17, 2011)

By now, Packy Jim is set in his ways, ways not entirely of his choosing but ways he considers to be for the best. Part of this way of being is avoiding the sort of risks he took more often, and regretted, in his youth—putting himself in the public sphere, out on stage at ceilis, out on a limb professing affection to one young woman then another. Avoiding vulnerability, betrayal, and making the wrong choice, Packy Jim is risk-averse to the point that he neither suffers the heartbreak of a marriage that did not work out nor enjoys the happiness of a marriage that did. There is perhaps a parallel here to the risk-averse neutral angels whose fence-sitting during the War in Heaven spared them the torments of Hell but also the ecstasy of Heaven. Unlike the neutral angels on earth, however, Packy Jim is quite content with his situation on the margins of society. In his rationalization of the celibate life, he occasionally goes so far as to feel sorry for married men for their concerns rather than to envy them for their comforts. Better safe than sorry. Love many, trust few, and always paddle your own canoe. It is difficult to argue with proverbial wisdom.

Consistencies evident in Packy Jim's personal narratives may point to a basic conservatism in his resistance to change, in his shunning romantic entanglements, and in his avoidance of public life to escape suffering at the hands of smart alecks. But these personal narratives also point out that some of Packy Jim's attitudes conflict, though without becoming entirely mutually exclusive. That is, some aspects of his personality convey not so much consistency as tension. For example, given the stories that illustrate Packy Jim's victimization, we might expect that Packy Jim has internalized, to some extent, the perspectives of others that he is "not worth a damn" or come to his own conclusion that he has fallen short of society's expectations. Indeed, in a more depressed mood, Packy Jim says it clearly:

I take the view that I'm a failure in life. That's a view I've had for many, many years past. Of course I know there's people far, far worse failures nor me. But uh, I would look upon myself as a failure in life, surely to God. (August 21, 2007)

At the same time, in a different mood, in a different conversational orbit, Packy Jim can be quite agonistic, recognizing his disadvantages but pushing back against the arbitrariness and injustice of his situation, countering the uncharitable estimations of him by some of his neighbors.

I'm as *good* as the *best*, and if I'd have got half a chance, I was about the best human specimen that you could have got in the north of Ireland, and that's the nine counties of *Ulster*! But the abuse that I got and that old smart chat jokes at my expense—you know you can make a dog cross, well the same can happen with a human. (May 28, 1999)

At no point is Packy Jim going to settle for long on either extreme of the spectrum between self-esteem and self-loathing. Context and mood will have their affects, but his self-image will remain—as it does for many of us—in a perpetual pendulum swing. One result of this swing is, in fact, the self-awareness of this swing and perhaps a greater appreciation that all is relative. That said, another lasting effect, no matter where the pendulum may be in its swing, is an inclination toward crossness and a wariness of too much sociability, too much risk. As Packy Jim says,

It's not that my life has been all doom and gloom, and say it that way. It's like the Irish weather, changeable surely. There were times in my life when I could have jumped for joy. Then there were others when I might have ended it then and there. Thank God I didn't.

But by God—as the saying goes—I got the rough edge of life. I can tell you I got the rough edge of it, in many different ways.

And it makes you, too—another thing—it makes you tend to keep more to yourself. To *shun* the world.

But I think that here [living where he does], you're very much in the world, and at the same time, you're very much in a backseat. And I could tell you that is a big, big *appeal* to *me*.

You're very much—as the saying goes—a backseater. And at the same time, you're quite enough in it. (August 21, 2007)

In addition to the tension between pride and humility, another core tension that emerges in Packy Jim's personal narratives is that between doing what he pleases and playing by the rules, or between independence and submission. On the one hand, Packy Jim presents himself as a maverick who jealously guards his autonomy. Throughout the nerve-racking period when his parents were dying, Packy Jim believes that certain relatives were pressuring him to move and possibly taking stock of his property for their own gain. One rather pitiless uncle took him aside to say, "Well, sir, when Tommy and Maggie is finished, you're finished there, too." But as Packy Jim observes with a sense of triumph, "He was supposed to be a smart man and all the rest of it, but what did he know? He's long dead now, and I'm still here." Personal narrative 10, in which Packy Jim must rise to the occasion of acting as the man of the house after both parents are gone, usually concludes with his refusal to move in with cousins now that his autonomy had been established.

> I had my independence, the more I didn't ask for it, not in this manner, anyway. But then my worry was, they'll take over the old land and commandeer me. They'll take over the land. They'll take over me for my work. They'll take over my money.
>
> But no one way was I going to hand it over just. By God, I wasn't going to let them—I would say it that way. I was going to steer my own— as the saying goes—pathway through life. (December 1, 1998)

More recently, Packy Jim suspects that a certain couple were grooming him to be the wife's next husband in the expected event that she might soon be a widow. But Packy Jim sensed greed at the back of this suspected scheme.

> I might have gone to live, but no marriage nor no bed sharing. I think they were looking about money and land, but what was I going to get: an old *bred* out, *redd* out old woman, nearly my own age.
>
> Was I going to be such'n a *fool?*
>
> *Not likely.*
>
> No, it's not so bad, my life, better nor it used to be.
>
> I'm doing the best on the edge of a busy world, my own boss, and that counts for a lot. (August 31, 2007)

Guarding his autonomy, Packy Jim claims his right to do as he pleases "so long as it does nobody harm." Furthermore, he says he would not be too "near-be-going." In other words, he does not feel obligated by principle to follow rules for the sake of following rules. Although it may not be the main point of personal narrative 4, consider Packy Jim's taken-for-granted attitude toward the law illustrated here in a version from February 1999:

> In Pettigo on a fair day, there was standings up on High Street, and uh— clothes, selling clothes, you know.
>
> So, I was a stupid young boy at the time, and I wanted a pair of wellingtons. And I went—I think it was Paddy Campbell—I bought a pair of wellingtons off Paddy Campbell. And he rolled them up roughly in a bit of paper. And I was coming down the street with them.
>
> I was stupid, you know, say it that way.

So far Packy Jim's story establishes an appropriately modest, self-deprecating portrait of himself as a boy. Then comes the complicating action as he walks through the town to return home.

> And who was standing, who was standing on the bridge—on the border bridge—only Goggins the custom man.
> "What have you got there?" he says.
> "Pair of wellingtons."
> "I'll give you two options," he says. "Come down with me to the custom hut and pay the duty on them, or lay them back where you got them."
> "I'll lay them back where I got them." I did.
> It wasn't bad, because, like, I would have been like, well, an unmannerly gulpin in his eyes. Well, he was having—as the saying goes—I suppose, a bit of compassion on me as a stupid young boy, and probably to look at me, maybe a middling poor boy.
> I says, "I'll lay them back," and I left them on the standing.
> So, that wasn't so bad.

Stigma is again a central theme as Packy Jim views his younger self—a foolish country rube—from the perspective of the customs man. But Goggins, the customs man, is not overtly condescending, and he takes pity.

> Well then, when I was going to go out the road home, then, I picked up my bicycle, and then there was *another* road that went around, do you see, a *circular* road that went around, that took you way out—as the saying goes—at a safer distance.
> So I collected my wellingtons from Campbell and still had them home with me.
> Well, I suppose, what the duty would have been on the wellingtons, it could have been maybe three or four or five shillings. It wouldn't have been a great robbery. But I couldn't afford it. When I bought the wellingtons, I wouldn't mind what they were, maybe two pound or whatever. But three or four or five shillings more—that would have been big money for me. Of course, today you'd only call it a pittance. Aye.
> Oh, Goggins wasn't so bad. I think he was from Limerick, or down there, south of Ireland man. (February 18, 1999)

So Packy Jim takes advantage of the customs man's compassion to smuggle his boots home by another lesser-known route. Establishing himself once again as the virtuous underdog, Packy Jim also uses this story to illustrate change in his character over time; as an adult he is more mindful, more clued in to the ways of the world. This story also holds out the possibility of there being people in the world with a modicum of humanity. That being said, note that the humane character here is not a local.

For our more immediate purposes, bear in mind that, although Packy Jim does not directly comment on his attitudes toward the law or the legitimacy of the border that splits his island, what he takes for granted here is telling. Like many of his neighbors on both sides of the border—Catholic and Protestant alike—Packy Jim internalized early on an attitude toward government and taxation as arbitrary intrusions to be outflanked at any opportunity, especially by the less fortunate. He applies this attitude equally toward illicit distillation, an early source of his family's income that was crucial to their subsistence. Moonshine and smuggling are not crimes. They are survival skills. "Wasn't it St. Augustine himself who said stealing a loaf of bread is no sin when you're a starving man?" As Packy Jim concludes an anecdote about his mother selling poitín to a publican and former policeman, "No, I tell you, it's a bad thing to be, what you may call, *too* scrupulous."

On the other hand, for Packy Jim some (but not all) rules are sacrosanct. People he believes to be living in sin receiving communion at the altar rails, for example, causes him great consternation. Likewise, as we have seen, Packy Jim is scandalized by the fact of adultery and will have nothing to do with marriage, in part, because of it. The infidelities and broken marriages among his parents' generation and among his neighbors provide exempla underscoring his conviction here. Moreover, his own early foray into rule-breaking—playing hooky—was nothing short of traumatic, and his accounts of this experiment in truancy—personal narrative 2, discussed in the next chapter—are consistently the longest in his repertoire of personal narratives. As he characterizes his overwrought twelve-year-old sense of guilt and paranoia, "The crime that I had committed was damnable, do you understand. Oh *LORD*, if I had a done the wildest deed—if had picked up a gun and shot ten—that couldn't have been worse in my mind nor that simple little deed." So perhaps Packy Jim is not entirely secure as a brash scofflaw either. Despite his talk in praise of autonomy and independence, he is also adamant—in versions of personal narratives 5 and 9 and at other times—that were his parents still alive he would be more than content to "hand them back the reins" to his life, "to be the little boy again."

Through personal narratives, Packy Jim constructs and projects a persona that is deeply concerned with acting justly but not at all concerned with following rules for the sake of following rules. He represents himself as deeply moralistic yet also selectively flexible and relativistic. He is a maverick, but within certain limits, never crossing certain lines. These core tensions rather than his consistencies alone are what make possible another of Packy Jim's aphoristic pronouncements: "I'm my own man, like, but I play by the rules."

Of course this begs the question: which rules? If he does not obey all rules, there must be some common denominator among the rules he does play by. Here we face an age-old contrast between ethics and morality. The accepted distinction is that while ethics and morals both distinguish between right and wrong conduct, ethical rules derive from or are imposed by an external source such as the law, religion, or more generally society. By way of contrast, morals are principles that one has internalized as that part of worldview delineating how one should and should not live, no matter what anyone else says or what anyone else does.

With that distinction in mind, one could act in accordance with ethical laws without actually having an internalized, personal moral compass. For example, Packy Jim notes that many people in his world—including himself in certain circumstances—will comply with laws of the state or with injunctions from organized religion mostly out of a fear of getting caught and possibly embarrassed or punished for breaking these rules, rather than out of a sense of what is right and wrong. Moreover, breaking an ethical law may get one fired, fined, or even imprisoned or executed without leading to any sense of personal remorse. So for Packy Jim it was an irksome inconvenience rather than a regretted moral failing when the police in Northern Ireland confiscated his motorbike after discovering that it was neither taxed nor insured and therefore illegal to operate. Breaking a moral principle, on the other hand, typically leads to personal remorse because this is a violation of one's fundamental convictions about right and wrong.

Of course, this is not to say that ethics and morals never overlap; frequently they do. Packy Jim has internalized as morality much of the ethical codes his religion imposes—thou shalt honor thy mother and father, thou shalt not commit adultery, for example. As we have seen and will see again, he has a particular hostility for the cardinal sins of lust, greed, and pride. But not everything in the Decalogue or in the rest of Church doctrine and catechism maps one-to-one on his personal moral code. Packy Jim can list several exceptions to religious rules he condones. For example, stealing is not a sin if it is an extreme case of self-preservation, and there are instances such as self-defense in which killing is justifiable. Compulsory Mass attendance is not something he takes seriously in any moral register, though he attends regularly, if not religiously, out of habit. He rarely receives communion but follows his own conscience about whether and when to do so. As a self-described "lukewarm Catholic," Packy Jim has a perhaps healthy disregard for some of the more authoritarian

impulses of the clergy, themselves fallible humans. He recalls dismissing one
parish priest who had lectured him as a youth about mending his ways: "Some
priests would make it a sin to shit, only they had to do it themselves." Moreover, bitter experience has led him to tilt with one of Christ's more memorable
injunctions and a central teaching of the Church.

> Another thing, like, what I can't agree with in the Catholic Church is
> you're supposed to turn the other cheek. Here's what I'll tell you: I'm
> not a believer in that.
>
> In this world, if you're—sometimes you could live your life and live a
> long life and you never would have to hold your own—but another time
> in life, for a lot of people—once nor twice—if you don't hold your own,
> you'd be better off cutting your own throat.
>
> No, I can't get behind "turn the other cheek."
>
> That's not the—as the saying goes—that's not proper Christianity,
> and say it that way. But then, I suppose, I'm not professing to be one of
> the greatest Christians going. (August 23, 2007)

In a similar dynamic, Packy Jim defers to the state, agreeing that murder
(nonjustifiable killing) and theft (except in extreme circumstances) should be
illegal and punished if committed. Slavery is certainly an area where ethics and
morals align for Packy Jim. More pointedly, it is illegal because it is wrong
(*malum in se*) rather than the reverse (*malum prohibitum*). On the other hand, there
are no laws against ambition—indeed, neoliberalism puts a premium on it—
but as I will show in chapter 4, Packy Jim is deeply suspicious of the moral pitfalls
of unchecked ambition. Not everything—and perhaps not much—in the ethical
code established by law carries the weight of moral principle for Packy Jim.
Smuggling, illicit distillation, tax evasion, or collecting subsidies on both sides
of the border ("doing the double") may be crimes technically, but they are
more or less victimless crimes, which is to say, hardly crimes at all. The state—
the legitimacy of which is already suspect in a place such as the Irish border—
loses a small amount of revenue, but it can afford the loss and in any case it
was unlikely to spread the wealth equitably in the form of services and security
(or so a typical attitude along the border maintains). On the border, removed
from the centers of power, such technically illegal activities are viable survival
strategies, neither crimes nor sins.

One may seek parallels in history or literature for the sort of character
Packy Jim seeks to present and in fact to be. But as is perhaps typical of Packy
Jim, and despite his limited access to books and other media, he identified his

own exemplar for me one sunny afternoon in his bee-loud glade when he asked me if I had ever heard of Henry David Thoreau.

Aye, he's some kind of—he wrote books and things of that kind. A Dutchman. Well, he was descended from the Dutch. I got two articles that he, that was wrote or copied from a *Reader's Digest*.

But uh, he would be today, like, totally against the kind of uh—what will you call it—complicated world like you have today and so much—as the saying goes—*red tape* and all the rest of it in it.

His idea was simplify, *simplify*.

If your affairs are twelve or fourteen, make them three or *four*.

If you could count, if you could count in hundreds, count—as the saying goes—three or four or *five* on your *fingers*.

That was his, uh—he chatted about that everybody lived—as the saying goes—in the *nick of time*. Always, he said, always try to improve "*the nick of time*." That's the *here and now*. Never look to *yesterday*, never look to *the DAY*.

Aye.

Oh aye, he had *great ideas*, like.

He died at the age of forty from TB. He was a schoolmaster in his time, and he didn't believe in, at that time, in chastising kids or anything like that, do you understand.

And uh, they—there was some complaint made about that he was too easy on his pupils, or something like that, and somebody that was over him come in and says, "Now, you have got to keep disciplining your kids, *or* it will not be so good for you."

So Henry David Thoreau took one kid and give it a mock battering, and he says, "Right. Good luck to you. I'm away."

And he finished with it. He would have no more of it. "I'm away."

And he was very strong, too, for the, for the—against *slavery*. He was very bigly against that. Slavery was going on in America, enslaving the *black people*.

Aye.

Oh, I heared about that there—like, there's so many *Reader's Digests*, but it was very *interesting* like, you know, articles about him.

But he was all for the simple life and rooting out all the complications that you *can*. He'd have been a God-fearing man, too, and all that type of thing, but he would have been, like, belonged to some branch of Protestantism.

He mapped out land and things like that, and he would have done jobs of handiwork. And then, if he decided then to go fishing or something like that, just you work the day, and the morrow—if it's a good day, if you want to go fishing or something like that—forget about the work. Enjoy the moment. That was what he emphasized a lot—enjoy the moment. You only live in the here and now. Good enough lookout I suppose.

Henry David Thoreau. If you can ever come up across any of his works, he might be interesting reading. If you went to them libraries or places, that's his name, Henry D. Thoreau.

His ideas did appeal to *me*, quite a *bit*.

And I just seen these two small articles in *Reader's Digest*. Only for that I suppose I wouldn't know such'n a person existed as Henry David Thoreau. (August 17, 2007)

Of course. Who else could appeal more to Packy Jim? Clearly his next Christmas present would have to be editions of *Walden* and *Civil Disobedience*.

As with Thoreau, Packy Jim's strong streak of iconoclasm is tempered by his equally strong moral compass—the two forces are suspended in cantilevered tension. Bear in mind, however, that Packy Jim's coherent moral self—as Linde (1993) would put it—is the result of a long maturation process. He is under no misconception that the self he presents today is of an essential, unchangeable nature. The Packy Jim who suffered the schoolmaster's wrath, who lived in fear of punishment for playing hooky, who lived the "sheltered life," is no more. The watershed moment is the death of his parents, but as he recalls, "when I had to stand on my own feet—as the saying goes—and pick up the threads of my life, thank God, I had no bother doing it, but that was some big change alright."

Unlike his earlier more passive self, he pushes back, against those who would impinge on his autonomy, against the kind of smart alecks you find in bars and other public venues. Of course, Packy Jim does not live in constant conflict with those around him; much of his pushing back happens in the personal narratives he tells. But here, in the story realm, he posits an evolving self, a persona born of experience both positive and negative. Or as Packy Jim puts it more succinctly, "You don't go through life and learn nothing. As an old boy said to Mammy one time, 'You may get the young fox asleep, but you'll not get the old one.' Aye."

In the end, how does Packy Jim evaluate his life so far? He makes no secret of the fact that he goes through bouts of depression (his term). He remembers times when, "if I had met a man with a machine gun I would have thanked him to riddle me, do you understand." Moreover, he remembers well the striking words of a frequent visitor in his childhood, Frank McCanny, a man who endured many of the same stigmas Packy Jim does today:

> Oh Christ to God, I heared Frank McCanny sitting in that corner there, in the chair *there*, saying to my mother—he put it this way, and I wasn't old—that some people, if at the end of their life they were getting a chance to go it again and go through the same again . . . *they wouldn't do it.*
>
> It's still in my memory, and it's sixty years ago and more since he said it *there*. That was *his* experience of life. It can't have been that pleasant either.
>
> "There are people," he said, "if they were getting the chance of starting off again, like, when you become near dying, you could go back to the start and go up the ladder again—*they wouldn't do it.*"
>
> Frank McCanny wouldn't *do* it.
>
> I don't think I would *either*. (August 21, 2007)

Counterarguments are many. I have repeated to him his own words about the unassailable value of being one's own boss, argued that the only true failure is not him but rather other people's standards for what constitutes success. Dismiss this as Romanticism or Pollyannaish drivel if you must, but to my mind, Packy Jim's life is a victory, his very existence a small but not insignificant bulwark against cruelty, vanity, arrogance, fraudulence, and all manner of human bullshit. His way of being stands in direct opposition to the excesses and depredations of religious orthodoxy, political and institutional authority, bourgeois consumerist values, and—I would go so far as to say—modernity.

In certain moods, Packy Jim is willing to concede, modestly, some of my points. In certain moods, he is the Packy Jim of "I'm doing the best on the edge of a busy world, my own boss." But of course, I also see what he is up against. I identify with his doubts and recognize his demons, even as I appreciate and am grateful that, undeservedly, I have been dealt an easier hand so far. Try though I might, it is hard to argue with Frank McCanny's point of view, or indeed with Packy Jim.

Prime Time

One Thursday afternoon in late December 2013, Susan Gallen, my friend and former neighbor in County Tyrone and a cousin of Packy Jim's, called me to say that Packy Jim—our Packy Jim, Packy Jim way out on the mountain, Packy

Jim who loves many, trusts few, and always paddles his own canoe—was going to be on television that very night. Stranger things have happened, but not that many. I suppose it should not have surprised me so much; this is still the same person who consented to let me write a book about him and his stories. But this was television, RTÉ One's current affairs show *Prime Time*, to be exact. I can guarantee you, dear reader, that you are one of a select handful who will ever read this book, whereas *Prime Time* has some of the highest ratings on Irish national television.

Apparently, through a series of small world connections, a local community activist had made introductions between Packy Jim and the producers who were putting together a report on the issue of rural isolation, focusing on bachelors, titled "No Country for Old Men" (original air date December 19, 2013). I found the program online at the Raidió Teilifís Éireann (RTÉ) website (see http://www.rte.ie/news/player/prime-time/2013/1219/) and watched the journalist Miriam O'Callaghan interview Packy Jim and two other rural bachelors, then open the program to a discussion including a broadcaster/author and a social worker. In the Packy Jim segment, O'Callaghan pitched many forward questions I would not dream of asking during a first meeting, and I watched with pleasure as Packy Jim batted each one back with confidence and articulate insight. I admit also that I was pleased to see that he told her many of the same things he had told me over time, and in a very similar manner. Of course it matters—who's speaking to whom, when, where, how, why, and to what ends—but then again there may be something to say for the consistency of a personality and a repertoire across conversational contexts.

I quote the interview with Packy Jim here to offer another document in the world that represents him in his own words—one that, to an extent, complements what I have gathered, though it does not share the same methods or goals. Places where I use bracketed ellipses are points where audio and/or visual cues indicate probable edits, where two noncontiguous parts of the interview have been spliced together.

> MO: How long have you lived here in this house? Tell me about your life, Packy Jim.
> PM: Since I was born on the twenty . . . thirtieth of May, 1933. Here. And, unless for a fortnight or two I've been here all my life. I've worked a little on the Council, off and on. I've worked for two months on the forestry one time. And the rest of the time I worked for my daddy. [. . .] My mother was called Maggie Gallagher. She was a very jolly woman, and a very generous woman for what she had, and jolly, and uh, Daddy would have

been a wee bit maybe more serious. [. . .] They got along
reasonably well together, but they had financial troubles. The
place was, wasn't great, the place was again ate out with smuggled
cattle, they [Tommy and Maggie] were getting a bit out of it, but
at the same time maybe they were losing as much as, as much as
they were gaining. [. . .]

MO: What was it like here when you were growing up?

PM: Like, this part of the world was more thickly populated then nor it
is now. There was lots of ceiliers at night, smuggling people and
ceiliers. And there was lots and lots of ghost stories told and all,
all that, all that sort of a thing. [. . .]

MO: Why did you never get married?

PM: Poverty, and the want of money, and poverty, and, uh, not being
a great fancier of all the women I seen—I didn't fancy all the
women I seen. I fancied a few girls in my time. I had no money
or nothing like that. They didn't fancy me, oncest or twicest or
three times. And the only option that I had, if I was a strong-
minded person and wanted to leave, was get away to Hell from
here and go till England. [. . .] When my dad seen that his time
was near up in this world that was his last advice to me that
when Maggie would die for me to get away and leave here and
go to wherever, some other place.

MO: And Maggie was your mum?

PM: Maggie was my mum, aye. Maggie was my mum, aye, aye.

MO: But you didn't take his advice, Packy Jim.

PM: Seemingly I hadn't the power to take the advice, no. [. . .] But to
go till England and leave home, I wouldn't, I just didn't like to
do that. [. . .] The sheltered life is a great thing. Maybe nobody
understands it unless them that, as the saying goes, has been in
that position. But I loved the sheltered life, and I got it until I
was near fifty years of age. [. . .]

MO: Were you lonely after your mum died? [. . .]

PM: I *do* be, of late, I do be *lonely*. I spent a fortnight there down with a
cousin of mine, down in Ballybofey, in Drumboe, it's a housing
estate back of the town. I spent a fortnight there, and do you
know what it is: till an extent it was one of the worst things I ever
done, because there was so many people there, and she had so
many relatives, that when I come home again I was as lonely as
lonely could be. But I'm starting, I suppose, hopefully, to get
over it. [. . .] And I'll tell you another thing, while I was with that

cousin, it was the first shower I ever had, barring a shower that I got out of the sky. The lady told me to go and have a shower — I've had two or three showers, there — that was the first shower I ever *had*!

MO: Did you like it?

PM: I *did*, I did, I *enjoyed* it, to tell you the truth, I *enjoyed* it. [. . .]

MO: You have no running water and no electricity in this house.

PM: No, none, no, no. No, no.

MO: Is that very difficult?

PM: No, I don't miss it. No, I don't miss it in the *slight*est. Not what you never *had*, I suppose that's the answer to that. I don't miss it in the slightest.

MO: Do you think you've had a happy life?

PM: It was like the Irish weather: there were some times you could jump for joy, and there were another few occasions when I was studying of finishing my own life down in that lough down there, when it was bad about fifty years ago, and it would have been one of the nicest — as the saying goes — thoughts that would have been in my *head*, and writing a note and putting it in my pocket. And I thought that my poor old mother and father would be heart broken about it. Then you heared about it that if you committed suicide you went away to Hell, and you heared all them stories, too. Thanks be to God I didn't do it. [. . .]

MO: What makes you happiest in your life?

PM: Well . . . I suppose having reasonably good health. And having neighbors to visit here and there and thonder, two or three or four times a week, or maybe five times a week. I go to Willie McHugh's, I go to Cassie McMenamin's, I go to Arthur O'Neill's, or I'm going down there to Francie Duffy's. And that's what sustains me.

I am gratified to recognize the Packy Jim that I have come to know, even through the chopped up edits of what must have been a much longer interview. That said, I think the report as a whole — and the Packy Jim segment in particular — suffers from a starting presupposition that men such as Packy Jim see themselves as unhappy to be forgotten by society, disadvantaged by isolation.

Listening patiently over time, anyone can learn that Packy Jim has many causes for complaint and that he is no stranger to depression, but neither his rural situation nor his lack of electricity and indoor plumbing are his main

concerns. His isolation is in part a choice and a strategy to maintain his autonomy. He does not miss modern amenities in the slightest. As he quite reasonably
observes, one does not miss what one never had. Those taken-for-granted
aspects of his life certainly never caused him to contemplate ending his life, as
one might be confused by the RTÉ interview to believe.

Let us not forget that—while there may be plenty of antagonists in his
life—Packy Jim has an active network of caring friends and family, and his
isolation has to be seen as relative and, by his own reckoning, manageable.
Packy Jim does not always revel in his solitude, as the report makes clear, but
then the tone of the questions asked of him and the selections made in audio
and visual editing—not to mention the somewhat cloying background score—
cast Packy Jim in an almost pitiable light that his own testimony nicely resists
and complicates.

Or to put it another way, *Prime Time* needed a disadvantaged rural bachelor.
Packy Jim obliged to give them some of that—an anachronistic turf-burning
hearth and a recent memory of his first shower—but he also offered glimpses
into his own agendas and perspectives. The Packy Jim of "I'm doing the best
on the edge of a busy world, my own boss" still peers through the offline edits.

What we have in the *Prime Time* report is a collaboration between Packy Jim
and another party, with an agenda, who is in a position to put Packy Jim's self-
presentations on a stage. This book must be described in the same way. The
difference is that *Prime Time* was working deductively on a fixed schedule,
whereas I am taking whatever time is necessary to work as inductively and
reflexively as my faculties allow. Even as I recognize the ultimate impossibility
of doing this completely, my goal is to follow as closely as possible Packy Jim's
agendas.

The Neighbors, Status, and Perspective

Prime Time stopping by, setting Packy Jim on a national stage, is obviously not
an everyday event. And yet Packy Jim is well aware of the stakes in being represented. One of Packy Jim's agendas—as much of his self-presentation makes
clear—is doing what he can to manage his social status, pushing back against
the stigma projected upon him by some in his most immediate, everyday audience: the neighbors.

If you ask his neighbors about Packy Jim, you will meet ambivalence from
some of them, both praise and the occasional eye role. "He's got all that old
history, all those songs and stories," some chuckle, "and he even lives like we
used to—a century ago." For many at this time and in this part of the world,
the past equals backwardness and memories of not just a lack of privilege but

true poverty. If you consider yourself to be even one rung higher on the social ladder than Packy Jim, then the stigma of poverty associated with the past is the last thing you want to be associated with, especially when conversing with an outsider such as myself. For some of his neighbors Packy Jim is a local analogue of Joyce's old man in the mountain cabin with red-rimmed horny eyes, as much as I am an analogue of the admiring, authenticity-seeking outsider Mulrennan. Some would like to distance themselves from both of those character types and sets of ideas, and sometimes to take them down a peg.

People talk, trading in anecdotes about others that assign greater or lesser social status, fairly or not (Cashman 2008b). To be sure, people talk about Packy Jim and he knows it. His neighbors' acknowledgement of him as a master of local lore is rarely sufficient compensation for the disregard he endures as an elderly bachelor—not a successful family man in the conventional sense—living in what some would characterize as rough and antiquated conditions. Like many marginalized people around the world, however, Packy Jim turns to traditional resources for symbolic compensation and fodder for resistance to dominant hierarchies of value. Prompted, he can rattle off any number of stories one might label folklore, but perhaps more surprising and enlightening are the many instances of him summoning handed-down ideas, images, and genres to present a more sympathetic version of himself and of those inhabiting a similar social position, using tradition to push back against stigma and disregard.

When managing his social status, Packy Jim's typical moves are both direct (telling personal narratives about himself that undermine the anecdotes told about him) and indirect (using legends of the deeds of others in the past that may be read as parables about his own actions and values in the present). Both moves (see chapters 3 and 4) reveal a predisposition toward seriousness and earnestness on Packy Jim's part. He does, however, appreciate and occasionally employ another strategy used to great affect by many in marginalized positions: humor. Here again, speaking of others can be simultaneously a presentation of the self, an application of handed-down resources to personal ends.

For example, Packy Jim recalls a cycle of stories about Pat McMenamin, better known as the Buffer. He was a poor man living alone in a one-room cottage during Packy Jim's grandfather's time, and he eked out an income by helping people haul heavy loads over the steep hills of Scraghey in County Tyrone. Poor though he was, the Buffer's strategy for burnishing his reputation was to spin tall tales about himself that were simultaneously self-effacing in content, acknowledging his poverty and difficult circumstances, but self-aggrandizing in style, amassing cultural capital through comic genius. Originally told in first person as if true stories, these tall tales built through exaggeration until the truth status of the narrated events was thoroughly discredited while the narrator's wit and talent as a wordsmith were firmly established. Consider the following from May 1999, Packy Jim's sampling of the Buffer's tall tales smuggled into conversation through the generic frame of second-hand local character anecdotes:

> The Buffer told one, one time, he was for Scotland, and he made his way down till Derry City. And when he got the length of Derry City, unfortunately the boat had sailed. And there was nothing for it only, only—as the saying goes—to wait for the next day, or the next time the boat was going, perhaps the next day.
>
> So the Buffer was very scarce of money and he had no place to go for his lodging.
>
> So he was wandering about in a frantic state of mind, not knowing—as the saying goes—where to go or what to do. And where did he find himself? On Derry's walls, the walls built by the British, 'round.
>
> And he was wandering 'round Derry's walls, and he come to one of these cannons that the boys had, a big cannon, on the walls—they're still there, I think—and he looked at this cannon, and damn but he says to himself, "I found my lodging."
>
> "I'll slip into the mouth of the cannon and I'll sleep until morning and if it happens to rain it won't rain on me. A grand lodging place."
>
> So he got into the mouth of the cannon, and he lay there, and seemingly somebody had some kind of a queer—as the saying goes—trick that they at a certain time, midnight or something like that, this particular cannon was fired, you know.
>
> Ah, an old yarn!
>
> This particular cannon was fired, and begod it was the cannon that the Buffer was lying in. That was the one that was going to be—as the saying goes—fired.
>
> So the Buffer was lying in the, in the cannon. Whether he was asleep or not, I don't know, but suddenly [claps his hands] out the blarge goes. And away, it happened to be pointing toward Scotland, you understand, in that direction, the right direction.
>
> The blarge goes off, out goes the Buffer, and the next thing the Buffer knowed—as the saying goes—he come down with a thud. And, uh, it was on the streets of Glasgow.
>
> I suppose he was over before the boat that he missed, I suppose. He was over before the boat, come down with a thud on the streets of Glasgow, and he was landed for no money at all.
>
> Isn't that a queer yarn? Aye, that was a queer yarn.

Packy Jim's recollection of the Buffer, so far, highlights the Buffer's ability to undermine disparagement of his poverty and supposed haplessness by playing with the stereotype of the happy-go-lucky Irish migrant worker, taking it to an unbelievable extreme. Packy Jim followed with additional yarns about the Buffer foregrounding his poverty and dire circumstances while playing it for comedy.

> Well then, Barney McHugh went into it one night—an old man that lived in Cloghore—and somebody else, to visit the Buffer. And he lived in one end of a house, like, you know, as if the second room was taken away and the kitchen was all that was left but the room gone. And what there was, they say, was in very rough conditions.
>
> Anyway they, maybe, talked till him about how was he feeling or something like that.
>
> "Ah," he says, "I'm not very well at all. Just very, very poorly. I threw off the full of a creel of leopard's blood last night," he says.
>
> Leopard's blood!
>
> "If yous don't believe me, yous can go down to the *room*. Yous'll see it, maybe, if you don't believe me. It's there yet."
>
> But there was no room in it, like, but that was him: "If yous'll go down to the room yous'll see it yet." Aye. "The full of a creel of leopard's blood." You know, a creel [a sally rod basket] is not a very good thing for holding anything, well, barring turf or something like that.
>
> Well, that was a tale he was at. He was always a great character, I think. He'd have been an uneducated person, do you understand, but he was no less cute: "Threw off a full of a creel of leopard's blood last night. If yous don't believe me, yous can go down to the room there. It's there yet."
>
> He had another good one, too. "I never was as ashamed," he says, "in my life. Do you know what happened? A pickpocket had his hand in my pocket. And he had *nothing to get*. I never was as *ashamed*." That was another one. That's a Buffer story. Aye.
>
> Whether he was in Scotland or not, I don't know. He may have been or he may not, but uh, he lived his lone, like, in that little hut of house, doing the best. (May 28, 1999)

Although Packy Jim typically leans toward the serious and does not compose such tall tales about himself, in telling anecdotes about the Buffer, recalling his tall tales, Packy Jim benefits indirectly from the Buffer's comic strategy for establishing a place in the local economy of reputation. Received social hierarchies assign status based on conventional indications of success—wealth, property, family—but the Buffer who has none of these can still outflank these hierarchies by constructing a witty and sympathetic persona. By extension Packy Jim reaps some of that alternative success by being able to reanimate the Buffer's imaginative fantasies, once again using tradition as resource to meet present needs. Comedy, too, can be serious business.

For Packy Jim, or the Buffer, marshaling traditional resources to challenge dominant hierarchies of value is often a first step toward a broader conceptualization and critique of one's social world. In fact, marginalized people are perhaps in the best position to do so. Transforming social distance into a kind of intellectual distance, people like Packy Jim have a stake in theorizing community and society, which may be possible only from such a remove. Éilís Ní Dhuibne tells me that her most insightful informant/storyteller, Joe MacEachmharcaigh of Gortahork, County Donegal, as well as Bo Almqvist's, Mícháel Ó Gaoithín of the Great Blasket Island, County Kerry, closely fit Packy Jim's profile of being unmarried, not wealthy, and undervalued: "In both those instances, the individuals were, like Packy Jim, held in a certain amount of benign contempt by the other people in the parish. They were regarded as eccentrics and were to some extent figures of fun because they were not successful in ordinary ways."[11] The same may be said of Peter Flanagan of Ballymenone, County Fermanagh, and of creative folk artists farther afield.[12] Their standing in the community, it would seem, varied in inverse proportion to their motivation and ability to represent and analyze that community.

By this point I have provided a solid introduction to Packy Jim's own typical presentations of self: direct and indirect, proclaimed in first-person or telegraphed through handed-down tales, mediated and collaborative as all representations inevitably are. Other genres of expression develop or extend beyond the themes raised by personal narratives. Second-hand legends, jokes, tall tales, local character anecdotes, recitations, and songs do not stand in contradistinction to his first-person accounts. They often speak complementarily to each other, with tradition-as-resource playing a central role in subject-formation, in the individual-as-process. From here I proceed thematically through Packy Jim's repertoire—rather than strictly genre by genre—mindful of the speaker, his preoccupations and dispositions.

2

Authority and Rules

At the age of twelve, Packy Jim played hooky from school and it was a traumatic experience, to say the least. Packy Jim's account of the misadventure, illuminated from both his childhood and adult perspectives, is one of the longest stories in his repertoire, running over twelve minutes in one version. The five versions I have recorded are remarkably similar in organization, detail, and quoted speech. Polished and significant, this iconic narrative can be read, in one sense, as a personal origin myth for a tension that still animates Packy Jim: the tension between exercising individual autonomy versus following received directives, strictures, and norms. As orienting details give way to complicating action, resolution, and evaluation, pay attention to the centrality of rules and attitudes toward authority as I give Packy Jim the floor to narrate at length.

> I used to go to school, but these people, here, there were people coming in at night and ceiliing late, and not leaving in any time. They mightn't have been getting to their bed times 'til a half one or two would have been common. Then my mother was the riser in the morning, and my mother maybe might sleep in odd times, or she got up and got on a fire, and got me up, and got me my breakfast, and got me *going*.
>
> So if you didn't leave *here* at a certain time, then you didn't arrive *there* at that certain time. Different times when I'd be going down the road, Cunningham an odd time maybe might hold back the roll. The roll was to be called I think at ten o'clock. Cunningham might hold back the roll five minutes or so if there were ones hadn't arrived. And I can dimly remember in my later times going down the road and some kid would run across the road like that and back in again, "Aye, he's coming!" So, you'd be marked down, you'd be marked down then as being *there*. But many and many a time I arrived at that school there, Lettercran, and the roll call was over and I was marked absent.

So the government had a *law*, that if a kid missed school without a doctor's orders so many days in the year, a *prosecution* could follow. Your parents could be prosecuted for not putting you out to school. You had a quota to pass. I don't know what the quota was. But periodically, at the end of the year, it used to be called out. And, of course, mostly my quota would have been pretty *low*, you know. It wouldn't have been too high. There were stormy days and you weren't *sent*. And then, besides that, there was the unfortunate days that you went and you were marked absent and, as far as the roll book was concerned, you weren't *there*.

Well I mind, one time, going into school, and this big man was there when I went in, and as far as I mind—if I'm not making a mistake—he had a big brown roughly knitted pullover on him. I didn't know the man from Adam, but he called me up till him and talked to me about the bad attendance at *school* and that—as the saying goes—I would have to pull my socks up—something like that—pull my socks up and attend a whole hell of a lot *better*. Perhaps—as the saying goes—I would maybe take in hand to say he was forecasting—as the saying goes—a *doomsday* situation for myself and my daddy and my mammy. You know, a *doomsday* situation if you *didn't*.

Well I didn't know the big man, but then many, many long years later, I sized up who it was—it was Guard Dowd. He was the—as the saying goes—he was the man that was the attendance officer at the school. Guard Dowd. And I would say Tommy and Maggie could have been often prosecuted, but uh, Maggie's brother was up for years in *Ballina*, a shop boy in Ballina. And he was on the Old IRA, he was the *captain* of the IRA, and Guard Dowd was one of his *squad*. That was one thing that would have helped a bit, and another thing that would have helped a bit, Guard Dowd would have drunk poitín—as the saying goes—if he got it, or any other kind of drink. Every—as the saying goes—every shilling that he could spare was *drunk*—say it that way. And he used to be out here and—again, long years later—I come to the conclusion he was getting an odd bottle *here*.

But Tommy never was prosecuted is all I know. I don't know if them old, old roll books are still in existence or not, but uh, I doubt on a lot of years my, my, my attendance figures for the year would have been low, lower nor most.

But.

Nineteen and . . . forty-*six*, and I had been promised by Master Cunningham that I was going to get as good a—as the saying goes—a slapping across the arse with his ash plant [walking stick] as ever I'd got, from beginning to that *time*, "if you don't come *earlier*."

Well one Friday morning, down the roads I go, the bog road I go, and
I stood at Hilley's swing bars, late as ever I'd *been*. And if I'd have seen
one kid going to school, or two, I would run, maybe try to overtake them.
"Well, you're okay, they're going, you're safe enough," that kind of a
thing.

But there weren't a kid going at all.

I stood there a while, and I considered what's to be done.

I had Cunningham's promise what I was going to get.

No hope.

I decided I would *turn BACK*.

So I headed back up the bog road, turned back along the back of
Patrick Hilley's house. And my Uncle Hughie had an old byre [a cattle
shelter], called the mountain byre, and it was situated above a pad road
[dirt road or path]. And across this pad road, at three o'clock—I surmised—
would go James Morris's youngest daughter, Mary Bridget Morris, would
go across that pad road. And when I would see Mary Bridget Morris
going across that pad road, I would know that it was my time to head
for *home*, you understand.

And I got into this *byre*, and sat in this byre, and time started to
drag, drag, *drag, DRAG*.

So, I went out of the byre, and I went up a short laneway, and there
was a stile across from one side of the ditch to the other. And I sat on
the stile, looking towards Lough Veenagreane. And they were doing a
little job of work on the bog road, nine or ten men or so doing a little
job breaking stones and opening outlets and jobs of that kind, and my
daddy was *one* of them, about a quarter of a mile away.

So I was sitting on that stile looking across at these boys in the
distance, and James Morris was working on the bog road, too. I heard
the thistles [rustling] behind me, and I looked 'round, and there was
James Morris's sister going out to the lough with a bite of food to James
for dinnertime—a sup of tea and bread or whatever it was. That was bad
because she could speak it, that she *seen* me.

I don't know what I told her, like. I suppose I was middling good at
lies. I used to tell Cunningham if I was late, always my excuse at school
was, "The clock's slow. The clock's stopped." I think it was "the clock's
stopped," when the clock *wasn't* stopped. Of course, Cunningham didn't
believe that. He knowed that our clock was a good enough clock, but "the
clock was stopped" I used to tell him.

So uh, I don't mind what I told Maggie Anne, but I wouldn't have
told Maggie Anne that I was lying out from *school*. She went on, but as

soon as she went on, I bored back into the byre again. When she come back, I wasn't to be *seen*.

So, I wasn't too smart at the time, but I'd have had a certain amount of *wit*. I started to have my doubts about Mary Bridget Morris. There was *another* road that she could have come home from school, along the main road, which was further away, a route that I wouldn't see her on *at all*. And then there was another question: maybe Mary Bridget Morris wouldn't be *at* school, where would I be *then*? [*Packy Jim laughs nervously, channeling his childhood anxiety.*]

So uh, after a time, I decided that it was probably roughly near enough time to head for home. *I head away back.*

So I kept along the safe side of the ditch—and say it that way—so that the ditch and the whins [thorny yellow-flowered bushes] on it would shield me from the men working on the lough shore, just in case they'd see me, and *surmise*. I wrought back into this old lane, and down the lane to the lough shore, round the lough shore, and up to the *quarry*.

"Maybe I'd be a wee bit too early. I'll stay a wee while in the quarry."

So sat in the quarry, looking across by Scraghey, and was, I suppose, perhaps happy enough.

But then I heard a rattle *again* and I looked down. What was it only James Hilley the postman on a bicycle coming up to James of the Mountain's up there with a *letter*.

So by God then, I had to—as the saying goes—buckle up and head up the, up the lane with him. I don't mind what I told him. He could have asked me a few sly questions probably, I don't mind. He would have known damned well that I was doing the *mooch* [skulking, concealing himself], but I would have told him some old *stuff*.

And I landed in here, in this house here, at three o'clock or five past three, when the school would have been closing in Lettercran! [*Packy Jim laughs nervously again.*]

So my mother chatted about "who was at school the day," do you understand? And I just can mind one person's name that I named that was at *school*. And that person was Josephine McGrath—Pat John's sister. I told her, I mind telling her that Josephine McGrath was at school. I don't mind about whether I named anybody else or not.

But I got my dinner anyway, and things was going pretty well. There was no—as the saying goes—big, big, big hullabaloo, no big thing in making about it. So I'm over *one hurdle*.

But then Daddy'll be coming up, and he'll be landing in here about a quarter past five. Work stopped at five o'clock on the road. He'll be in here about a quarter past five, and maybe he had seen me, maybe Maggie Anne had mentioned about what the son was doing. Perhaps there could be *trouble THEN.*

But uh, anyway, I think it was the early part of the year—March or so, shorter days. Before Daddy got home, smuggling was going on, and there landed in a little man to this house here from Drumquin with two or three stone of tea that he was taking away by the Donegal town direction to *sell.*

He arrived in, and shortly after that I think *Daddy* arrived in. And right on Daddy's heals landed in three or four or so people more. McGraths men was there, and Johnny Simon, and Davey Elliot the blacksmith, a handy man with two or three spraying machines with him. They were coming to strip the copper off—off the spraying machines—to make a head, to make a new head for a still for making poitín.

So, with Paddy McMenamin being there, and these boys coming and all, I was over the *second* hurdle nicely, the best.

But *then* the crime that I'd committed was *DAMNable*, do you understand? You understand if I'd have *KILLED* some one or *two,* or otherwise I done some *wild* thing, it couldn't have been worse!

So the big danger then was that it could be talked about, and that Cunningham, it could come to Cunningham's *ears.*

But, come Monday morning, you had to go back to school no matter what happened. I landed back at school on Monday morning, and . . .

No problem! [*Packy Jim's expression is wide-eyed and incredulous.*]

Cunningham had heard nothing, so that was the end of that. I had got away with a wild, *wild* transaction. But . . .

Oh LORD, if I had a done the wildest deed—if I could have picked up a gun and I *shot TEN*—that couldn't have been worse in my mind nor that—as the saying goes—that *simple* little deed.

So that was my first and my last attempt—as the saying goes—at *that* job. It was a bit of a failure—as the saying goes—quite a bit of a failure.

That's about nineteen and forty-six, it's a brave while ago. It's a brave while ago. (April 8, 1999)

Despite all the building suspense, Master Cunningham "passed no remarks" when Packy Jim returned to school on Monday, so apparently the flipside of the schoolmaster's rage was his inconsistency and forgetfulness. Yet as Packy Jim's account makes clear, the agony and paranoia endured was as bad as any beating. Slipping dramatically into present tense ("down the roads I go," "I head away back," "So I'm over one hurdle") and occasionally quoting his fevered

The bog road to Lettercran School

thoughts as if in real time ("they're going, you're safe enough" or "maybe I'd be a wee bit too early"), Packy Jim brings the past to life. Laughing with decades-old nervousness about one misstep after another, Packy Jim conjures a former self from "a brave while ago." The affect and aesthetic power of the story derives in large part from Packy Jim's masterful re-creation of the mood of childhood with all its vulnerability and fear of authority. I am reminded of the first chapters of *Great Expectations* in which Pip nearly implodes with anxiety, caught in various fixes while being bullied about by the adults in his life. At the same time, the mature Packy Jim—like Dickens's mature Pip—is a capable narrator, poking a little fun at his overwrought twelve-year-old self without deflating any of our vicarious appreciation of real, past emotion. "*Oh LORD*," Packy Jim intones with melodramatic flare and a bit of an eye roll, "if I had a done the wildest deed—if I could have picked up a gun and I *shot TEN*—that couldn't have been worse in my mind." As an adult, he appreciates and has fun with the fact that his sense of guilt was inflated for "that simple little deed." His bid to illustrate and even make light of his previous manner of thinking establishes a past–present contrast that is eloquent of his adult character and attitudes toward authority. "No, I tell you, it's a bad thing to be, what you may call, *too* scrupulous."

In addition to tone and delivery, we should appreciate the glaring irony that our young protagonist ties himself in knots over rule-breaking and punishment, even as he is surrounded by people who take inconsistent or indeed no notice whatsoever of the law and institutional authority. Every other character in the story—every other authority figure, including his parents—is a smuggler or a moonshiner or a beneficiary of those technically illegal activities. Even Guard James Dowd, the policeman/truancy officer, speaks of prosecution while turning a blind eye in deference to old familial connections (through the proscribed IRA, no less) and to a fondness for the illegal drink Packy Jim's parents supply. In other conversations, Packy Jim has told me that Dowd's opposite number, an ex–Royal Ulster Constabulary officer with a pub in Killen, bought his poitín supply from Tommy and Maggie, and that Master Cunningham, himself, was a loyal customer. Coming of age, these ironies were not lost on Packy Jim as he learned to appreciate the complexity and realpolitik of adult life on the Irish border. The examples of others imply again and again that rules are not to be followed for the sake of following rules. Furthermore, not only is there no shame in breaking arbitrary rules, but there is also an affirming pleasure to be taken in outfoxing such restrictions or otherwise gaming the system.

In Packy Jim's younger days, models abounded for the libertarian mood and cunning ethos of this mature border mentality. For example, in 1951 Maggie and Tommy were in the middle of a poitín distillation in anticipation of the demand at Easter when it was announced from all pulpits of the Clogher Diocese that Bishop Eugene O'Callaghan had declared poitín-making and poitín-drinking a "reserved sin." This meant that one could not seek absolution from ordinary parish clergy; rather, one had to go through the considerable extra trouble of making an appointment with the bishop himself in Monaghan. While the laws of the state had done little or nothing to stop illicit distillation, the intervention of the Church did make an impression on many. Upon hearing the announcement, Tommy decided to stop distilling immediately, but Maggie did not want to let their half-finished batch go to waste. So after Tommy left to ceili, not wanting to be a witness, Maggie finished the job with the help of a willing neighbor, but then, as Packy Jim says, "she was saddled with the sin of it." Unwilling to seek out the bishop, Maggie reasoned or heard a rumor that confessing to non-ordinary clergy while making a pilgrimage at St. Patrick's Purgatory on Station Island in nearby Lough Derg should offer sufficient absolution.[1]

This was a trickier set of moves than open resistance. It was a matter of obeying a version of the letter of the law without complying with the intent, having your cake and eating it too. Maggie's maneuvering also puts one in mind of the common legend in which a man comes to know the location of buried fairy gold and marks the spot with a stick. The fairies cannot remove the stick after the man says an Ave Maria (Hail Mary) over it. Instead, a clever

Poitín maker's glen

fairy, still playing by the rules as it were, fills the field with identical sticks, making it impossible for the man to find the treasure when he returns with a shovel.[2] Whether in real life or in story worlds, it would seem that flanking maneuvers are preferable to surrender when facing superior forces.

Packy Jim would have absorbed this tricky border mentality perhaps more frequently from narratives that he heard on an almost nightly basis starting in his earliest days. During the regular late night ceilis at Packy Jim's house, one of the more common types of story told were anecdotes about local smugglers either cleverly evading detection or, when caught, out-witting the prosecution. In one recorded session, after telling a version of his experience playing hooky, Packy Jim elaborated this theme of rule-breaking with a series of smuggler anecdotes, including this one:

> There was another smuggling woman, Cassie Pat. They called her Cassie Pat Suzanne. I think she might have been McHugh from Corgary [County Tyrone].

And she was up on a—she was up giving evidence about smuggling
or something like that in court in Castlederg, maybe cattle that she was
supposed to have sold to some neighbor or something like that. I think
it was black cattle that was mentioned, and uh, this boy—Captain Fyfe I
think they called him—he was the prosecutor for the Crown.

"And how would you know," he says, "one black heifer from
another?"

This was the question he put at her.

"How would I know that there's a hole in your ass and I never seen
it?"

That's what she said. Oh, that's true, too.

"How would I know there's a hole in your ass and I never seen it?"

Aye.

Cassie Pat Suzanne.

Oh, she's dead maybe for forty years. Don't think she was married.
I think she was a spinster woman. Oh, she would have been bigoted
too, I suppose, a bit too, you know. There might have been a wee bit
of *republican* blood in her, you know, from about Corgary. (August 13,
2007)

This story follows the expected conventions for anecdotes, following the interaction of two characters with dialogue culminating in a subversive punch line.
Such anecdotes are usually framed as a contest of wits in which there is a clear
winner and a clear loser.[3] Given that the smuggler is a northern Catholic from
a known republican area giving testimony in a Crown court, there is a clear
political overtone to her words. This is much more open and hostile resistance
compared to Maggie's under-the-radar exploitation of an institutional loophole. So while rendering unto the Church can be sidestepped with some delicacy,
avoidance of rendering unto Caesar comes with a perhaps cleaner conscience
but no less maneuvering.

Taken together, Packy Jim's hooky story, his recollection of Maggie's calcu-
lated transgression, and his anecdote about Cassie Pat Suzanne establish a
certain relativistic orientation toward rules and authority, ranging in levels of
openness and dissidence. We may gather this orientation from the texts themselves, internal clues, and thematic connections. Put side by side these three
stories build contexts for each other, revealing a certain sharable perspective.
But let us return to the hooky story in particular to consider another, larger
context that would motivate Packy Jim to tell such a tale of rule-breaking and
prevarication about himself.

I heard Packy Jim's hooky story more frequently in the years when he and I were becoming better acquainted. So one motivation for telling it may have been inviting intimacy through entertaining self-revelation. As Sandra Stahl (now Dolby) observes, "nothing creates intimacy quite so well as some confession or exposure of the self" (1983:274), and "the expression of personal values is the hidden agenda in any such storytelling" (1989:21). But of course I am not the only person to whom he has told this story; it lies at the ready for any receptive audience when it is thematically relevant. With thematic relevance in mind, it is interesting to note that in one recording session, he told the hooky story directly after a version of his personal narrative 12, the one where he stands up for himself while confronting the smart aleck in the pub. At the time I did not fully appreciate any connection between the stories other than the fact that they were both personal narratives. It is clearer to me now that the hooky story is not only a commentary on rules and rule-following but it may also serve as a form of resistance in and of itself.

Remember what Packy Jim is up against as he understands it. Some of his neighbors pass the time by trading anecdotes about him and others, stories that require winners and losers and that assign greater or lesser social status. In addition to pointing out Packy Jim's eccentricities as a somewhat reclusive bachelor living an arguably premodern life, some of the anecdotes told about him establish an unflattering portrait of him as spoiled, lazy, backward, and ill-tempered. One locally circulated anecdote sums up this side of his reputation: As a young man, Packy Jim was planting potatoes in the spring with his father, who kept correcting him, telling him that he was not planting properly. Eventually Packy Jim snapped, threw down his spade, and retorted, "Daddy, if that's the way you want it done, you'll have to do it yourself," and then stormed off. As one man editorialized, this was Packy Jim's way of getting out of work. As another commented, "Poor Packy, he really has no practical capabilities." True, the same people who circulate this anecdote also compliment Packy Jim's memory, his acuity, and his way with words. But this anecdote gets repeated to establish the widely held conventional wisdom that it is no wonder Packy Jim is knowledgeable and perceptive. "He does very little work," they say, "and he has few obligations, so of course he has all the time in the world to read and to talk and listen, and to turn those stories over and over in his mind."

Packy Jim is well aware of this aspect of his reputation, which circulates seemingly beyond his control, and he is given to sometimes bitter defensiveness when he encounters hints and echoes of it. He is well aware of his neighbors' more general ambivalence toward him as an admirable master of local lore but also as a symbol of that which is old fashioned and perhaps backwards. People will talk, but then so will Packy Jim. He cannot stop the anecdotes told about him, but he can control the stories he tells about himself, stories that illustrate what foot he wants to put forward.

Consider the persona Packy Jim creates for himself in the hooky story. It is both innocuous and telling. He makes no boasts about his cleverness but returns again and again to his miscalculations and trepidation. Packy Jim the child is charming for his excessive sense of guilt and fear, which draws us into sympathy. Packy Jim the adult narrator is charming for his ability to transport us into the overwrought mind of the child. His choice of persona allows sufficient self-deprecation, so charming us cannot be dismissed as immodest. As a counterbalance to the anecdotes that circulate about him, this personal narrative—and others—serves to typify him, modestly and appropriately, as a lovable character. In conversational give and take, the story fosters a sense of intimacy through self-exposure of forgivable mistakes made. Most importantly, in a local economy of status and respect, this story achieves modesty and self-deprecation while undermining less charitable stories told about him by neighbors and relatives, stories that revolve around other mistakes and unconventional behavior.

As we have seen in Packy Jim's critique of scapegoating—one of the tricks of the Irish—there is an inherent inequity in the generic conventions of anecdotes, which call for a winner and a loser in a battle of wits. If you are a wee bit simple or a wee bit foolish—to paraphrase Packy Jim—the demands of a good anecdote will make you out to be even simpler, even more of a fool. But narrative is fundamentally a tool of human agency and—as it was for the Buffer—it is well within Packy Jim's power to push back appropriately and artfully in the circulation of stories that fuel the local economy of reputation. As much as Packy Jim's account of playing hooky offers commentary on rules and authority—pointing out their relative import and specious inviolability, calling into question reflex fear and automatic submission—the narrative also serves as a form of resistance to representations of Packy Jim propagated by others. This story, among others, is itself an instrument of social power.

3

Power and Politics

Power and politics, as conventionally conceived, have not emerged as obvious major themes in Packy Jim's repertoire so far, with the possible exception of the anecdote about the republican Cassie Pat Suzanne's hostile testimony in a British court. Contemplation of power and politics, nevertheless, shapes, motivates, and serves as a bridge between many of Packy Jim's personal and traditional stories.

Power may be understood as the ability to command or persuade others or to act unilaterally regardless of others. Politics, narrowly defined, is the theory and practice of exercising power—of imposing and enforcing laws, for example, or of establishing by other means a hegemony in which subalterns voluntarily act in ways that further the interests of a social elite. Yet note that power is exercised at all levels of society from interpersonal relationships to the nuclear and extended family, from neighborhoods and local communities to the level of state governments and regional spheres of influence and indeed to the transnational global stage. Politics may be understood more broadly as the competition of interests and ideologies in any arena where power is exercised, from the micro to the macro levels of society. I say competition because always at play in human affairs is the debate over whether power is being wielded justly and legitimately. Should we resist, comply, or indeed never give politics a second thought? The question depends on one's subject position—that mutually constituting mesh of vested social and economic interests, convictions, principles, and worldview.

With politics on the table we may think first of the competition between nationalists and unionists in Northern Ireland, between Democrats and Republicans in the United States, or between left and right in a global context. But we can speak also of the politics of gender, race, or identity or of the politics of respectability, consumption, or development. Here the emphasis shifts from the more literal understanding of politics as having to do with governance to a broader understanding of politics as concerned with power dynamics in any realm of human affairs.

Much of what Packy Jim has been addressing all along—though in his own terms, through his preferred genres of expression—is the politics of representation. Like any good folklorist, linguistic anthropologist, or discourse analyst, or indeed like any good playwright or novelist, Packy Jim recognizes that language and narrative play a primary role in constructing rather than merely reflecting reality. Representation inherently involves a competition over meaning, and any given representation that succeeds—that becomes accepted by a majority of people—will necessarily shape social life. One concern for Packy Jim is how he represents himself and how others represent him. At stake are not only reputation and social status but also his ability to be himself without interference or disparagement. If power is exercised at all levels of society, Packy Jim's self-representations and his anecdotes representing others in a similar position are a matter of politics closer to the micro end of the spectrum where the dynamics of interpersonal relationships are of greatest concern. But many of the same tensions and preoccupations that animate his personal stories also inform his stories concerning the actions of others in the removed but relevant realm of history.

Politics as more conventionally understood—and the debate over who justly and legitimately wields power—is naturally of great concern in Irish local, regional, and national history. In the north of Ireland, in the wake of Plantation and Partition, representations of the past necessarily grapple with sectarianism, nationalism, unionism, and the legacy of colonialism. But Packy Jim is not simply interested *also* in politics on the macro end of the spectrum; his interest is in many ways an extension of his interest in politics at the micro end of the spectrum. Examples from both ends of the spectrum invite contemplation of authority and power, as well as when and what kind of resistance is justifiable.

In particular, which historical figures attract Packy Jim's attention is telling, and how he chooses to represent their actions has evolved, generally from simplicity (involving clear dichotomies between good/bad, us/them, Irish/British, Catholic/Protestant) to greater complexity. As with his beliefs in the supernatural, over time Packy Jim has developed greater skepticism and a willingness to question the grand historical narratives that constitute much of the political discourse of his world. If he were a faculty member in a department of Irish history, he might be labeled a revisionist. On the other hand, certain exemplary stories encapsulate principles and political orientations that, for him, stand the test of time. Though he entertains revisionism and relativism, Packy Jim remains a traditionalist in many respects, especially where history and morality intersect. Deriving from available oral and written narrative, much of Packy Jim's historical repertoire both revolves around politics in the conventional sense—with class, sectarian, and national struggle center stage—and serves as an exercise in the politics of representation. As Packy Jim is well aware, which historical figures get represented, by whom, and how have direct implications for ideology and actions in the present.

Historical Resistance, Transgression, and Evaluation

Asked what sort of things interested him as a child and adolescent, Packy Jim recalls that he did not like history as it was taught in school because it was usually taught in Irish, with which he had little facility or affinity. But he was very interested in the glimpses into Irish national history he got from English-language fiction written from a nationalist perspective. Like his beloved Wild West adventure books in which the small rancher stands up to the encroachments of the evil land baron, nationalist historical fiction offered entertaining fantasies of heroic resistance to an unjust system.

A prime example and one of Packy Jim's favorites is *A Swordsman of the Brigade* (1914), written by Michael O'Hanrahan, who was executed for his role in the 1916 Easter Rising. Set in the wake of dispossession by the English Williamites at the end of the seventeenth century, the novel begins with Piaras Grás, a son of the vanquished Catholic gentry, running afoul of the authorities after wounding a surly English baronet who tried to take his mare, being too fine for a Papist. Piaras then flees to join the Wild Geese or Irish Brigade, a force of Irish Jacobites that became part of the French army after the defeats of 1690 and 1691. He later returns to Ireland as a recruiter for the Irish Brigade and, after many adventures, falls in love with a Planter's daughter, marries her, and takes her back to France.

Fascination with the Wild Geese and "the chance to strike the old foe on another front" also led Packy Jim to memorize a poem from his schoolbook, "Fontenoy, 1745," by Emily Lawless (1922). In this, one of the "exiled sons of Clare" lays awake in anticipation of the chance to right old wrongs fighting against the British "for faith and fame and honor, and the ruined hearths of Clare." Indeed, the British were routed at the Battle of Fontenoy, and the poem immortalizes this event as an Irish national victory, even though it was fought on the Continent in the service of France.

Of course, as Packy Jim is quick to note, not every dispossessed Irishman left with the Jacobites for France. Those who stayed and worked to frustrate their supplanters were termed tories or rapparees, celebrated in song and story as heroic outlaws stealing from the rich and giving to the poor in a charged political context. From childhood, Packy Jim has had a keen interest in these latter-day Robin Hoods as well. One of his favorite songs—in fact, the first song he ever sang for me—is "The Mountains of Pomeroy" by George Sigerson, originally published in 1869. In the song, the heroic rapparee Renardine (meaning fox-like) is

> An outlawed man in a land forlorn,
> He scorned to turn and fly
> But kept the cause of freedom safe
> Upon the mountains high.

Here a nationalist writer repurposes earlier outlaw lore—in this case pertaining to Shane Bernagh from the Cappagh area of County Tyrone—to cast the rapparee as proto-nationalist. Interestingly, like Michael O'Hanrahan, Sigerson chooses a Protestant for his protagonist's love interest, perhaps signaling a hope for reconciliation of native and Planter and for a dismantling of both class and sectarian divides. The same motif is found in *Willy Reilly and His Dear Colleen Bawn*, both the novelization by William Carleton (1855) and the earlier nineteenth-century broadside ballad, with which Packy Jim is familiar. In Sigerson's song, Renardine tries to sooth his lover who fears for his safety, then beckons her to live with him in the wilderness:

> "Fear not, fear not, sweetheart," he cried,
> "Fear not the foe for me.
> No chain shall fall, whate'er betide,
> On the arm which will be free.
> But leave your cruel kin and come
> When the lark it is in the sky
> And it's with my gun that I'll guard you
> On the mountains of Pomeroy." (November 16, 1998)

The song ends tragically, however, when his love, coming to meet him during a tempest, drowns while crossing a flooded mountain stream. Apparently some divides cannot be bridged, at least from the tragic perspective that Sigerson voices.

After singing for me "The Mountains of Pomeroy," Packy Jim transitioned to "Brennan on the Moor," a song about another heroic Irish outlaw set generations later. Over time, the dispossessed Jacobite tories and later rapparees were succeeded by the often romanticized highwayman—technically a criminal but one whose targeting of rich Protestants gave both the historical actor and his folkloric and literary representations wide support among poorer Catholics. "Brennan on the Moor" recalls the career of an actual historical highwayman, William Brennan of County Tipperary, and features many motifs that are typical in Irish outlaw lore—robbing the rich to support the poor, escaping the authorities through wit rather than force, avoiding violence except in extreme cases of self-defense, being betrayed by a close associate, and justifying his actions at his execution. As Brennan exclaims from the gallows:

> I own that I did rob the rich
> And did the poor supply.
> In all the deeds that I have done
> I took no life away.
> The Lord have mercy on my soul
> Against the Judgment Day. (November 16, 1998)

Cunning, dissident, and justified, the outlaw is the ideal hero for anyone marginalized by the status quo, whether the colonial subject, the rebellious teen, or indeed anyone seeking resolution for the binary tension between conformity and nonconformity. Doing the right thing while breaking the law, the heroic outlaw gets to be bad (in the romantic sense) and good (in the moral sense) at the one time. Of course, the heroic outlaw's victories are temporary and typically consist of flanking maneuvers that merely delay the inevitable betrayal and execution. This fated martyrdom, too, adds to his appeal. Just as white boys of a certain generation in the American South fantasized about fighting for the lost cause of the Confederacy—just as Castlederg Orangemen, even more vicariously, annually commemorate the Battle of the Alamo in the shadow of Davy Crockett's ancestral home—the martyrs for a righteous cause available to young Packy Jim and generations of Irish Catholics before him were tories, rapparees, and highwaymen.[1] And if there is any better symbolic figure for the marginalized than a heroic outlaw, it is a *local* heroic outlaw. For Packy Jim, young and old, that hero is Proinsias Dubh, highwayman from Cloghore (aka Meencloghore), one townland away, just across the Tyrone border.

Black Francis in English—pronounced "Prinshis Doo" with a slight "v" sound at the end—Proinsias Dubh was not personally dispossessed by the Williamite conquest, though his family, the McHughs, would have been generations before. As a Catholic born in the mid-1700s, he was subject to the Penal Laws of the time that made it illegal for him or any Catholic to own land, own a horse over £5 in value, possess firearms, marry a Protestant, vote, practice law, or hold public office. In these straitened conditions, Proinsias Dubh embarked on a career of highway robbery and raiding the property of Protestant gentry, ranging from his home base on the Tyrone–Donegal border into Fermanagh, Leitrim, Sligo, and Mayo. His career came to an end when he was caught, convicted, and hanged in 1782. Packy Jim knows several stories about Proinsias Dubh's rise and fall, and he occasionally peppers conversation with this or that exploit when thematically relevant. But once a favorite figure or topic is raised for conversation, Packy Jim is just as likely to tell every story he knows in a long, coherent string. Here is one such disquisition, almost everything he knows about Proinsias Dubh:

Proinsias Dubh was born and reared about a mile from where I'm sitting, down there, in Cloghore, about a mile from where I sit, in a little hut of a house there, in a little place on a brook side they call Pollywoods. And he was reared there, and he was, I suppose, a native Irishman, a Catholic. And he took till raiding royalty, landlord people, and other well-to-do, well-to-do people—the Crowellians or incomers, I suppose you may call them. He was supposed to be a highwayman and a raider that stole from the high rich class and give to the poorer class. He give money and valuables and food, dividing oatmeal among the poor and the like. I think he had that good point. It wasn't just for his own enrichment as far as I know.

I suppose he would have been like many and many another McHugh man that I seen. He'd probably be black-haired and probably about medium sized—a lot of them McHugh men wasn't all that big, like myself.

But he could have went here and there and thonder and mixed with some of these royalty at gatherings and passed off as one of them while he was in reality stock-taking and sizing up would this place be worthwhile to come back and raid. Oh, he was very ingenious and could fake his character, do you know. He acted, he was a bit of an actor—as far as we're told—that could have maybe dressed up in a certain guise and maybe fixed up his accent till fit the English accent and passed off as one of these toffs. And then he wasn't suspect, you see.

And it's reported that he went as far away up as County Sligo and up into County Mayo, on occasion, to raid away up there. But then, he used till—as far as it's said—when the hunt was on after him, take cover up in what they call the Tievemore Mountains, out in the Lough Derg direction, and he used to have that as a refuge out there.

Well then, he was, uh, kind of forced by poverty as a young chap into the robbery business. He enlisted with the Achesons, Achesons down there in Grouselodge below Leonard's down there, that long low house with a—you see the door in the middle of it, like that, you know, with an arch. It was reported that these Achesons were highwaymen. And they were the, uh, Planter class of people too, Protestants. So I don't think it was political for them. No, it was for a grab and greed. But being Protestants they were practically—as the saying goes—not too wild interested, I would say, in religion. They wouldn't have been too very righteously mad about religion. And they say that they killed, too. The Achesons would have killed, too. They believe that there could be a few corpses, could be buried in the locality. But Proinsias Dubh didn't kill. He had the reputation of *never* killing.

Aye, like, these Achesons killed one of their own up there—the more Proinsias Dubh got the blame—but it's supposed it was them, that's presumed. He was a person of the Protestant religion, a man by the name of Glendinning, I suppose an ancestor of Alfred Glendinning's I would say. He was believed to be waylaid by the Achesons on the way to Castlederg fair. Well, his pockets wouldn't have been empty anyway going till a fair, so it was believed that he was killed for money—a couple of guineas or sovereigns—on the way to the fair, up there at Cushey's Bridge. Aye, supposed to be a ghost at that place. I never seen it, but I had to pass many times years ago and I was dreading it.

But. Anyway.

Proinsias Dubh was with them for a while, and then he branched out on his own. He left them. Maybe it was jealousy or the want of a reward—well, he would have been a rival in the locality, and say it that way—but whatever was about it, the Achesons set a trap for him. Acheson sent word, sent a message to Proinsias Dubh, "You and your men come till us for a little bit of a celebration, a little bit of a feast."

This is an old story. I think it's a true one, too.

So Proinsias Dubh landed there, him and two or three or four of his followers—there were one of them Corrigan, called Supple Corrigan, I forget what they called the others—but they landed here, anyway, for this bit of a feast or whatever.

And there was a girl there in the house—I suppose a working girl or a domestic servant—and she was frying herring. Herring was going to be part of the menu. So, well, we'll say Proinsias Dubh was in here by the fire, and the lassie was going back and forth, frying the herring. She knowed about the *plan*, that it was to get him arrested, and she looked brave and sharp at him—looked him in the eye—and she says, "*It's a silly fish that would get caught for its belly.*"

And he took that for a good broad hint, a *warning*. So him and his men—as the saying goes—took to their heels and got to their horses and left. And when the redcoats come they were far away and there was no one to *get*.

But the girl that was in the house was in the know, and this is what she says, "It would be a silly fish would be caught for its belly."

Oh aye, that was true, that's true too. I heared that time and time again.

But, uh, then he was caught then up there in Fermanagh up there, uh, not far from Enniskillen. He was caught and tried and convicted and sentenced to death for highway robbery.

But there was some house that they had visited—him and a number of his folk, three or four or five—and there was a *girl* in the house. Lisgoole Abbey, I think it was, and she was a Miss Armstrong, if I'm not making a mistake. And there was some blackguard of a boy on the gang going to use her badly and probably I suppose—say it that way—probably rape her. But Proinsias Dubh *upbraided* his man for it and put *manners* on him. He wouldn't allow that, *no one way*.

Well, she appreciated that quite a lot—as the saying goes—and thought that he was a gentleman, as he *was* in many, many ways. And by God, she spoke up strong in the court for his reprieve, or at least, like, for him to be transported. But it was no good. When her, her request was, was, *wasn't* listened to, she broke down in tears and was sad about it, the same as if it was a near relative. Only for him, she'd have been badly abused and probably raped, you know. There were always blackguards and whores, either three hundred years ago or three *thousand* years ago. And I suppose she was youngish and attractive and all the rest of it, and she would have belonged to the Protestant Ascendancy. They talk about the Ascendancy class, and they were disliked, and if you abused them you, you couldn't be doing better!

But Proinsias Dubh would have *none* of it, and she appreciated that. That's the old story to that affair.

Well, then, he was coming from some road well up in Fermanagh, way up there by Kinawley or some road that far side of Fermanagh up by the Cavan border, and he was tired, dead beat and ready for a sleep and a rest. And he approached some farmer man and he asked the farmer man—a Protestant man—would it be alright if he could have a rest in his barn. And the farmer man said, "Ok, surely to God, go on ahead and have your rest." And the farmer man then went and he reported it to the redcoats, as they called them, and they come and they got him in his sleep. And that was the finish of Proinsias Dubh. He was arrested and taken up till Enniskillen, got some kind of a trial there, and was condemned to be hung quickly, the next day or so.

And there was a big crowd gathered as there used to be in them times if there was a hanging any road, everybody gathered to watch the *spectacle*. And I think there was, uh, one of his men was there that day, disguised as a woman. It could've been Supple Corrigan. It may have been Supple Corrigan I think was there that day, disguised as a woman in the crowd. But anyway, Proinsias Dubh was given time to say some words, and he prolonged it for a long time, making a speech of it. And the hangman or somebody that was there said, "Cut it a bit *shorter*," this, this speech he was making.

"Ah, gentlemen, the day may be long for *yous*, but it's short for *me!*"

Oh aye, he said that, I think that's right enough:

"Gentlemen, the day may be long for yous, but it's short for me."

But that was that. The trap was sprung, and Proinsias Dubh was *hung*.

And then, I suppose, sympathizers, we may say, sympathizers that was about there got his body. And it was put on a boat and was taken down ten or twelve mile, down Lough Erne to the Waterfoot, and disembarked at the Waterfoot that's below Pettigo, there where that McGrath Castle is, or round about there where them two rivers goes into the Lough, close till them. And then it would have been carried across the moorland, then, I suppose on their shoulders or, like, with the two sticks across, you know, underneath the coffin—I suppose he was in some sort of a coffin—and across to Carn Graveyard, which would have been five or six mile. Buried there for whatever reason, like his burial ground probably was the graveyard in Lettercran at the time, probably. His burial ground you would have thought should have been Lettercran Graveyard. But for whatever reason or another, he was buried in Carn Graveyard in an unmarked grave.

He wouldn't have been oldish or anything like that, nor it wasn't an old man's, an old man's caper. And he'd have been starting that job, we'll say, with the Achesons probably about eighteen or nineteen years of age, and probably around ten or twelve years or so with the Achesons and then on his own. He probably wouldn't have been thirty-five I would say when he got strung up, I would think. (November 16, 2011)

Comprehensive as it is, this string of Proinsias Dubh stories leaves out two ancillary legends: one about a heroic escape by Supple Corrigan, another about Proinsias Dubh's undiscovered buried treasure (both stories are transcribed and discussed in "Notes on the Recitations, Songs, and Traditional Stories" at the back of the book). Asked during an earlier conversation what about Proisias Dubh captured his imagination as a boy, Packy Jim replied:

Well, he was a local man—say it that way—I suppose that gave it a, more of a *flavor*. And ancestors or descendants maybe in the locality, away down, like them McHughs of Cloghore, like, would have been far away down descendants of his.

And you heared it preached about like, here at home and on down the road in other houses. Well, if they weren't chatting about ghost stories, they were chatting about Proinsias Dubh or something like that, but he figured a lot with them, all people around here, all people. Daddy knowed a lot about that, too, do you see. Daddy was big into that thing, too. But not alone my daddy, all people around there. Some of them yet, Owney McGoldrick, Packy McGoldrick, or ones like that could still tell you a lot about it.

When I heared about it first, I thought it was a grand idea, stealing from the rich and giving to the poor, stealing from the Planter class, the incomers. Aye. You would have thought there was nothing wrong about that. The common man against, against, against the rich man, the interloper. That would make it something better nor crime. That's true, something better nor crime. But there's still a kind of, uh, a kind of spiciness you get from them stories.

And then there were that old, that old song, on Pomeroy and Renardine, on the mountain, coming down and raiding the people, falling in with a young lassie and taking a notion about her, a Planter's daughter. Proinsias Dubh was more that older model. He would be different from the modern rascal, that modern, uh, criminal type person. He wouldn't have been so much selfish.

Being a robber, taking from the rich and giving to the poor, and he was a Catholic and him taking from the Cromwellians: no, I would say, I would take in hand to say, like, perhaps, that he wasn't damned for it. When he died, he wouldn't have been damned for it. I wouldn't think so. (August 31, 2007)

Righting wrongs, fighting a corrupt system, redistributing wealth from the illegitimate rich, and doing all this without taking human life, the Proinsias Dubh of folklore provides a model for just resistance and selfless sacrifice, an example of moral clarity in an otherwise contentious field of political struggle. Colonialism remains the original sin that divided society and created a situation in which acting morally includes breaking the law.

But note that Packy Jim's legends about Proinsias Dubh do not amount to a simplistic sectarian revenge fantasy. Rather, they serve to complicate, among other things, a facile partisan vision that would cast all Planters as villains and

Acheson's Hall, where Proinsias Dubh escaped betrayal

all natives as virtuous underdogs. What differences do exist between Protestant and Catholic, rich and poor, are not inherent, essential, or inevitable but rather can be a matter of performance.

Proinsias Dubh has no trouble passing with a shift in accent, clothing, and manners. In his own day, Packy Jim notes that many Protestants who convert at marriage become the most exemplary Catholics. Most importantly, Protestants are not the enemy; the system that privileges some (but not all) of them is. As it is today in Packy Jim's Donegal, Protestants, too, are neighbors and part of the social fabric, however tumultuous the creation of that social fabric may have been. Many of them, too, are poor and in need of championing. In the age of Proinsias Dubh, Dissenters or Presbyterians, in particular, would have been subject to the Penal Laws that repressed all non-Anglicans. So while the illegitimate rich are all Protestants in this story world, Proinsias Dubh's motivations for enforced charity are not primarily sectarian but class-conscious. The landlords and the landlord class must pay.

Still, these legends about Proinsias Dubh are complex enough that—even with the theme of class struggle raised—an entitled member of the Protestant gentry, Miss Armstrong, can be both vulnerable and virtuous. Proinsias Dubh defends her honor against fellow Catholic outlaws motivated by lust and a desire for sectarian vengeance. She then crosses the sectarian divide to return the favor, defending the outlaw as a gentleman by virtue of his noble character, a victim of a discriminatory system that elevates interests over justice. The Protestant Achesons, for their part, complicate assumptions that all Protestants are wealthy, privileged, and law-abiding, while setting Proinsias Dubh's moral compass in relief: unlike his former colleagues, Proinsias Dubh obeys the sacred commandment not to kill. There are just forms of resistance and others that cross a line, not just descending into mere criminality and self-interest but also breaking higher laws, committing sin.

Not every entextualization of Irish outlaw lore is similarly ecumenical or sensitive to the complexities of a plural society. There is an established tradition of mustering songs and stories about tories, rapparees, and highwaymen to grant the IRA and other republican paramilitary groups the authority and legitimacy of being part of a longer, heroic tradition of armed resistance to British colonization (Cashman 2000b, 2000d). For example, when Henry Glassie recorded Theresa Rooney singing "The Wild Rapparee" in Ballymenone, County Fermanagh, in 1972, he was aware that rapparee stories and songs were performed almost exclusively among republicans as thinly veiled commentaries on the just cause of the IRA in post-Partition Northern Ireland (1982:109–110). Likewise, in her dissertation Margaret Steiner noted how Catholic singers in Newtownbutler, County Fermanagh, avoided singing about tories, rapparees, and highwaymen in the company of Protestants for fear of seeming to support armed struggle carried out by the IRA (1988:113). In my own experience in Aghyaran, County Tyrone, people made direct comparisons between the outlaws of history and the modern IRA. As Charlie Lunney explained, "Well they were out of circulation by my time! But I heard them talking about Proinsias Dubh, singing on Brennan on the Moor in Segronan. There were always rebels in this country, you see." To this Mickey Byrne added, "Aye, well, it's the same as the present day Troubles, you know. That Proinsias Dubh, he was the same thing as the present IRA" (Cashman 2000d:64).

Packy Jim thinks otherwise. True, there is a structural similarity—both Proinsias Dubh and the twentieth-century IRA volunteer were proscribed outlaws whose actions had political implications. But as Packy Jim observes, "Proinsias Dubh never gunned down a neighbor for being a Protestant." Indeed, according to the legends, he never gunned down anyone at all. To paint the modern IRA man with the same brush as Proinsias Dubh is, for Packy Jim, a stretch. From his perspective, making this rhetorical comparison depends on a false analogy and must borrow from the outlaw's heroism rather than stand on the IRA volunteer's own virtues, which are more equivocal. Outlaws do provide a way to think about republicanism and violence, class and justice, past and present, but Packy Jim's versions of Proinsias Dubh stories acknowledge the contingency and complexity of such a thing as community, especially in the midst of sectarian conflict, among those of roughly the same socioeconomic class. In any case, Packy Jim's Proinsias Dubh stories set out some of the parameters for his own internal debate about history and politics, particularly the place of armed struggle and its effects on community. To better appreciate what is at stake for Packy Jim in the politics of representing what may broadly be called the Troubles—stretching from Plantation to Partition to the present—consider his stories of local sectarian and political conflict.

The Troubles, Justifications, and Complications

Although Packy Jim entertains revisionist accounts of the past that diverge from a more mainstream, less complicated nationalist vision, he recognizes that from Plantation forward there was across Ireland systematic and institutional oppression of Catholics at the hand of central authority in Britain, and he appreciates that later nineteenth- and twentieth-century nationalists had legitimate cause to seek independence. Casting across the local landscape for evidence, Packy Jim has referred often to a mass rock in nearby Cloghore where Catholics would have gathered to worship in the open in the wake of Anglican confiscations of Catholic churches and of Penal Laws proscribing unlicensed priests. Packy Jim also took me to the remains of a wide road stretching a quarter mile from nowhere to nowhere else near his home, a vestige of the Famine (1845–1852) when the British government refused to supply relief aid except for feeble food-for-labor schemes. Perhaps most unjust was the institutionalization of the landlord system in which dispossessed Catholics were in a position of having to rent land—land they had previously owned—from their Protestant supplanters. Over time, not every Catholic was a landless laborer or a poor cottier, nor was every Protestant a wealthy landowner, but dispossession conflated religion, politics, and class in such a way that the sectarian divide and open conflict were unavoidable. The landlord system also came with significant collateral damage, not only ensuring sectarianism and endemic Catholic poverty but also helping to shape Catholics into the kind of helpless and hapless subjects a colonial system requires for its own justification. As Packy Jim explains:

> In the last century, if you repaired about your house or repaired it any much they could raise your rent. Made the Irish very, very, very, very leery to do much of repairs about their work. They'd rather let the place go there, and be shabby looking—an old doughal maybe right in front of the door, what they call a manure heap out of the byre. Do no repairs, because sometimes you had to watch the bad neighbor maybe more than

the landlord if he says such-and-such'n a one's repairing the place. And
somebody come around—an authority—and see that you'd improved
your holding in a considerable amount, they could have jerked up your
rent.

Then that led to the mentality: "We'll do nothing. We'll let the place
be as it is. We'll change nothing"—as the saying goes—"If we're going
though some place up to our knees, we'll go through it before we'll fix
it!"

It led to a bad mentality among the Irish, like. Oh, aye, that was a
common thing, too.

As much as the system created subalterns, it also allowed if not invited landlords to become tyrants. Affluent men with few checks or balances, landlords
followed their own conscience, or lack thereof, in deciding the fates of their
tenants. Even worse were the absentee landlords interested only in profit and
their land agents tasked with squeezing the tenantry for as much financial gain
as possible. Packy Jim continues:

Or *bad* landlords, like, there were all classes: there were bad, good,
and middling. But oh, largely they were a *bad* set. They were a bad set, the
landlords. No one to tell them what to do—what do you expect? Do you
understand, the temptation was there and no one to tell you, to tell you,
to gainsay a *word*.

Joe McGrath told me that, uh, his mother was reared out there, back
of the hill out there, in an old house in the middle of the moorland—
Frank McCanny's. There was Rosie McCanny and there was Biddy
McCanny and Kate McCanny and Frank McCanny—four of a family.
This would have been back, we'll say, uh, 'round eighteen ninety, when
they were young girls—youngish girls, teenage girls, early teens or whatever.
They would have been what you'd call reasonably good-looking women,
young women.

And, uh, the shooting season commenced in August, 'round about
the twelfth of August the shooting season commenced. These gentry was
out shooting grouse, I suppose, and they were from all over the place—
England and here and there and where not, you know—a bundle of them,
maybe seven or eight of them going along and their gamekeepers with
them.

And sometimes they might maybe get dry or something like that.
They would call maybe by the house, by some house for a drink of water

or something. But he said that when they found them boys coming close, the girls was put to the room and the door was closed.

And again, if I'd have been any good, I'd have queried Joe farther. I never was no good at asking questions. I listened to what I heared, but it's a long time since he told me that.

So like, there was lustful people in high places. And the ordinary peasantry—as the saying goes—were more or less like kids, and if some lustful man—as the saying goes—took a fancy for this girl—twelve, thirteen, fourteen, or whatever—he could use her and you couldn't say, "Don't do it." That's the meaning I took out of it.

But he told me that they were put to the room when them boys were coming close, like in case they would happen to come in, like, you know— "Could you give us a drink of water?" or something like that, or maybe light a pipe, or something like that. And you couldn't say, "Don't come in," either, you understand.

Christ, Joe McGrath told me that.

But over in England, these landlords were just acting the cunt with the English people just the same. It was no better *there*. Oh, not at all, no, no, it was a landlord system there, too. They would have been just suffering, too. Oh aye.

And then people was living in fear and dread. You'd have a good landlord—he's one of the best—but in a lock of years he'd be dead. What'll the son be like, do you understand? You were in that, you were in that dread.

Oh, it was a, it was a, it was a good day that the rear of that was seen. I would think, aye. Would be, aye. (November 16, 1998)

Note that Packy Jim resists any accusation of Protestants as being somehow inherently lascivious, unscrupulous, or greedy. Moreover, at the end of his disquisition he backtracks to underscore his earlier point about the iniquity of the landlord system as an institution. Vulnerable to the capriciousness of this landlord then the next, the Irish tenant is in the same boat as the English one. While mostly Catholic, the Irish tenantry also included a significant number of Protestants, and as Packy Jim declared later, "You know a lot of Protestant people didn't like the landlord either. Oh, indeed they did not. Got the same treatment as the Catholic."

The primary local example is William Graham, landlord of Tievemore, Grouselodge, and Scraghey until his death, in 1908. Universally despised then and now, he never married but is said to have fathered several children. A widely known anecdote has Graham raising the rent on one of his Protestant tenants three times in the same day. In Packy Jim's words:

> Aye. Bill Graham. He was a man of evil repute and very harsh. He was, aye, he was. Both immoral and cruel as a landlord, the landlord of three townlands. And he was a lady's man, an immoral man that had a mistress or so, and he didn't, uh, balk at pitching you out if you weren't able till pay the rent. He didn't mind what your religion was. That didn't come into the question.
>
> So there was people up in Tievemore Brae the name of Read [also spelled Reid]. And this Read man, he was summoned by Graham to build his haystack for him. And, uh, it failed. And he had to go back and rebuild it again. And then Graham come and he riz his rent.
>
> Well, I'll quote a figure—as the saying goes—it's not a correct figure, but an old-time figure. We'll say that his rent for the year was two pound. Ah no, we'll say his rent was two pound, four *shillings*.
>
> And Bill Graham comes to Read, and he says, "I'm raising your rent. I'm going to make it two pound, *six* shillings." And away he goes.
>
> But then, he comes back again around later in the day, "I'm going to raise your rent again. I'm going to make it two pound, *seven* shillings."
>
> So Read didn't say much, but he says, tells him, "I suppose I'll hardly be seeing you the day more." That wasn't a big thing to say. "I'll hardly be seeing you the day more."
>
> Your man walked away.
>
> But 'round about bedtime, the knock come to the door again, and he opened it, and it was Bill Graham again.
>
> "I couldn't," he says, "go to my bed," he says, "contented after that remark you made to me. I'm raising you another six pence." So he must have took that as some sort of a back-handed insult.
>
> That's the story from the Reads, like, you know.
>
> He was a bad boy. Wasn't he?
>
> "After that remark you made, I couldn't go to my bed content. I'm raising you another six pence." That's only, I'm only quoting, like, a figure. I don't know what the man's rent was.
>
> But he was a bad boy. He was a bad boy. (March 18, 1999)

For Packy Jim and many others, Graham is emblematic of everything that was despicable about the landlord system: the rules were inequitable and arbitrary, the enforcers despotic and capricious. Once again class emerges as the more important divide; in the case of Graham, a Protestant landlord mistreats his Protestant tenant with no regard to his religion.

That said, while the system was corrupt because the prospect of fair play depended on the individual landlord, Packy Jim nevertheless gives credit where it is due. According to him and others, the Leslie family, who owned Lettercran and most of Pettigo's hinterlands, were consistently reasonable over the generations and rarely evicted tenants or charged more than what the holding was worth. Historically, the Monaghan-based family served in high positions of the Church of Ireland, firmly supported the Jacobite cause, and just as firmly opposed Oliver Cromwell. They even produced Sir John Randolph (aka Shane) Leslie, Third Baronet, who converted to Catholicism, spoke Irish, supported Irish Home Rule, and transferred his estate to a son who then conferred ownership of Lough Derg to the Roman Catholic Bishop of Clogher. Not unlike the earlier Anglo-Normans who were said to have become "more Irish than the Irish themselves," the Leslies figure in local folklore as the most sympathetic landlords that an otherwise loathsome colonial system could produce. They are the exception that proves the rule.

Even if certain landlords deserve praise, Packy Jim finds it understandable that both Catholics and some Protestants remain bitter about the landlord system as an institution. Likewise he understands and to a large extent shares Catholic animosity toward the excesses of successive British regimes. The picture is more complicated when moving from the macro level of colonial power dynamics to the micro level of neighborly relations carried on across the sectarian divide. Although Packy Jim considers Catholic–Protestant neighborliness and cooperation, or at least tolerance, as the standard rather than the exception over time, he nonetheless acknowledges that issues at the macro national level have many times poisoned affairs at the micro local level. In other words, institutional oppression and resistance to it have had parallel vernacular expression in face-to-face conflicts that stemmed from and gave rise to increased sectarian hostility.

The eighteenth century saw occasional alcohol-fueled faction fighting between Catholics and Protestants in Tievemore. Tensions rose again on July 12, 1795, when Protestants running the ferry concession on Lough Derg capsized the boat, drowning over seventy Catholic pilgrims; the boatmen were drunk and rancorous as a result of their annual celebration of King Billy's victory at the Boyne. The nineteenth century saw both the rise of violent agitation by Catholic Ribbonmen and a group of Protestant bigots on Drumawark Hill smashing an ancient cross that guided Catholic pilgrims to Lough Derg. Sectarianism being the great shame of Irish history, these are events that

Packy Jim acknowledges but does not wish to dwell on or narrate at great length.

It would seem that resistance to institutional oppression is a justifiable decision to make but a very difficult goal to achieve: Proinsias Dubh and a litany of nationalist martyrs are proof. How this resistance plays out at the local and interpersonal level is often the stuff of tragedy. On the one hand, Proinsias Dubh managed to stand up to an iniquitous system without taking life, but of course he met his end on the gallows without effecting any lasting change. On the other hand, the IRA may have fought—and killed—its way to the negotiating table and attained many of its goals, but at what costs, be they political, economic, social, or soteriological? Are the grave costs to neighbors and strangers alike—indeed to the possibility of peace, reconciliation, and community—surmountable? Forgivable? Given such a fix, people must decide how to proceed, weighing among other things whether clear oppression and defensible ends justify violent means.

Packy Jim's father socialized and was friends with Protestants throughout his life. In his youth he attended the same school and went mumming with them, and in adulthood he ceilied with them at night and traded agricultural and skilled labor with them during the day. Tommy McGrath was also a member of what Packy Jim terms the Old IRA during the Irish War of Independence (1919–1922). With those facts in mind, I asked Packy Jim if he saw any inconsistency here, to which he replied:

> No, the point of the IRA was putting an end—as the saying goes—to British rule, which it did in this part of Ireland. But it didn't mean that you were against your Protestant neighbor, even you—as the saying goes—even if you don't agree on, on the united Ireland idea.
>
> Well then your Protestant neighbor, they weren't maybe involved with politics. They couldn't help it. If you were associating with them, as you would be if you were close to them, well, maybe that Protestant house was as good to go into—as the saying goes—as your *Catholic* house. (August 21, 2007)

Again, Protestants as a category of people are not the enemy, even though individual Protestants and Protestant organizations may stand in the way of nationalist aspirations. Once the landlord system was fully dismantled by the early twentieth century, the older institutional enemy remained: the British government that continued its interference and preserved the legacies of colonialism. In Packy Jim's view, Tommy was not necessarily wrong to volunteer in the struggle for Ireland's independence from Britain, a just cause given past exploitation. A major complication, however, was that the main enforcers of the union with whom one had daily contact were local Protestant members of the B-Specials or B men.

Established in anticipation of Partition, for the purpose of combating republican insurgency in Northern Ireland and incursion from the Free State, the B-Specials were a part-time reserve force with military organization, training, and ordnance, and they drew membership almost exclusively from the local Protestant population. Nationalists saw the formation of the B-Specials as nothing more than an excuse to arm Orangemen, and indeed this fully volunteer organization did attract staunch unionists and loyalists. But more alarming for even the least political Catholics, the B-Specials were a grave threat to the delicate balance of interaction, cooperation, and reciprocity that governed local daily life in spite of the historical sectarian divide.[2]

When your Protestant neighbor dons a uniform, straps on a rifle, stops you at the foot of your lane, asks your name, and searches your person and property, he has made a series of decisions that privilege the institutional authority of the state at the expense of local community. Electing to police his Catholic neighbors, he safeguards Protestant entitlement and dominance. And yet, however committed one might be to ending British rule, when the fighting starts, is someone like Tommy McGrath to fire upon his Protestant neighbors? This was exactly the situation he faced in early June 1922 when nonlocal IRA forces had amassed in Pettigo, and the B-Specials were tasked with engaging and dislodging them. When these efforts were inconclusive, the British army stepped in with a larger force, including artillery. Back in Pettigo's hinterland along the Lettercran road, people were seized by the fear that events were spinning out of control and that a stand must be made. As Packy Jim describes that period:

> Along the border there, from Pettigo out there till Cloghore, or near Cloghore, the B men was ranged on the far side about all of them Protestant houses over there. They were ranged *there*.
>
> And then there was the Sinn Féiners ranged on this side, and there was a lot of shooting done back and forth, from side to side. Nobody really killed but, uh, of course people was keeping a wary eye. You weren't going out into the open. If you went across a field, or anything in the Lettercran braes, you were liable to be fired at, a danger that you could be hit and wounded or killed.
>
> It lasted for two or three days, but uh, the real heat of the battle and the worst of it was in *Pettigo*. There was a nest of the Sinn Féiners about Pettigo. *Hundreds* of them I suppose.

And the British army, they come into Pettigo, and they took Pettigo. They took the village of Pettigo and occupied it for a week or so. Took Pettigo. That was after the State come into operation. It would have been illegal, illegal, I suppose, for them to do it, but they done it anyway, and drove the nest of Sinn Féiners out of it.

That was the time that boy was shot, that Patrick Flood, the fellow on the back of Frank Gorman's out there on Drumhariff. He was shot, but I think he would have been maybe a bit drunk, too, I suppose. He was called upon to surrender but he wouldn't surrender. So then there was nothing else for it, only be shot, you understand. That's the story. He belonged to that house there in Pettigo the McGoldricks has now. He was a member of that Flood family, had a shop and a public house. Brother of, he was either a brother of Paddy Flood's or an uncle of Paddy Flood's.

Aye, there was Dessy McCanny, I think, shot too that time when they were redding them out, when they were pushing them out, when the army come in. And one of them was Deasley, and one of them was Kearney. Four IRA men killed in that. And I think there was maybe one casualty that was reported. There was some one casualty on the other side, driving an armored car. But the boys had to clear then. They had to clear out of it then, and bailed away by Donegal town, and away here and away there. They fled, the IRA boys fled.

But the Brits took Pettigo and they held it for a while. But that, at that same time then, on out the border I suppose, maybe they were dreading something, maybe that the Sinn Féiners would maybe go till make an attack to take Fermanagh, or take a part of Fermanagh or something like that, and of course the idea was "Not an Inch," you understand.

But all them boys was all out there, all out there, I suppose, for miles and miles away, about every house and behind hedges, firing at houses in the State. The State crowd was at the *same* thing.

Sure they're like, I mean, Daddy and [Uncle] Hughie was on that old Sinn Féin thing, but it was, it was desperate, like. The bullets didn't even fit the rifles, so there was boys wrapping twine around to get them to fit the barrel.

Oh, they spent a night or two out there about Lough Veenagreane, out there on that *safe* side away from Fermanagh. Tried to sleep, and not fit to sleep, back to a ditch, you know, on like that.

Daddy went in one morning, during the month of June too, early June, first week of June. But he went in one morning, middling early anyway, with the hope that he would spend the day in bed, spend the day in bed in his own house. And uh, Eleanor McCrory was there and some more people that was down near the road had moved back to James's place.

But uh, he was aiming till have a, have a snooze in bed. And up in Fermanagh, up there was what they call a Sinn Féin judge. He was Monaghan. I forget his name, but he was Monaghan anyway, and was he a Sinn Féin judge. And he was an old boy, maybe seventy-six or seventy-seven. And uh, he had no need, I suppose, of taking off to go to the State, but for safety's sake, he took away to the State, too. I suppose in one way, he was an important man, for he was putting up to be a judge, you see, in what they call the Sinn Féin courts. And this old boy was lying in bed, in Daddy's bed. I don't know where he went after that, but uh, he wasn't going to go into the bed then anyway and this old boy there.

He come, I suppose, in the nighttime, too, this old boy. He was a kind of a vet, a farmer man and a sort of what you'd call a cow doctor. But he was this, too, as well. Like they were trying to outlaw courts in the north, and if two neighbors has a quarrel of some description, take it to the Sinn Féin Court and don't go to the legal court. And he was a judge in a Sinn Féin Court, so he had fled, and uh, that was that.

But oh, it was hot for a couple of days at that time. Oh, it was real bad June of 1922 with the B men just taking shots. Anybody that was seen on the far side, on the State side, was going to be fired at and that was that. With the intention that they would kill you if they could. It didn't matter a damn who you were or what you were. You had to keep under cover. You couldn't be seen out. It didn't matter a damn whether you were a civilian or not.

And then, there was two women shot in the back of the chapel there, back of Lettercran Chapel there, not far behind Lettercran Chapel on that lane. They were belonging till an organization, a women's republican organization called Cumann na mBan.[3]

And they were in Cumann na mBan, and them Protestant people down there had fled across till the north and into Fermanagh. They had fled across. Well then they had hens, and they had calves to be fed and hens to be fed, maybe dogs and things like that, and an odd time under cover of darkness, they would, uh, come back again under cover of darkness to milk the cows, feed calves, feed a dog or something like that.

And this old lassie was Stewart, I suppose from up, higher up there, but they had give her quite a bit of a searching—too much of a searching, believed to be, just a bit *overdone*. And this Stewart woman would have been a married woman, maybe, in her fifties or sixties, and them two lassies in their twenties. Then when she got back then till her own side again, to the Fermanagh side, she complained about the McGrath lassie and the McMeel lassie giving her this searching, and maybe asking her who she was and knowing who she was. The UDR [Ulster Defence Regiment] sometimes had that unmannerly habit, too, asking Catholics that they knew, "What's your name, sir?" That's very insulting.

So anyway, she tells about this, and this man, Willie of Skea, says till himself, "Well, I'll fix that. I have to go over there too. If I meet them pair I'll fix them." Do you understand? So he was going or coming, and he met them on the lane. He had a revolver in his pocket, and he fired at them—it was behind the chapel there, up there between it and Lanty's. So he shot one of them in the thigh, and he shot the other in the arm—two single shots—and went about his business and back into the North.

But uh, they were wounded anyway, and I don't know who come on the scene or—aye, the [school] mistress [Susan McMeel], she was fit to walk. She was fit to walk alright. She was wounded in the arm. But the other lassie [Bridget McGrath] wasn't fit to walk. So I suppose she was stopping up in McGrath's. Aye, she was stopping up in McGrath's, Big Joe's.

So she made her way up and said, "We've been fired at" and "Willie of Skea's fired at us." The daughter of that place wasn't able to walk, and they went down then to the road then, or down to the lane where she was lying and carried her up. Some two or three of them carried her *up*, old father I suppose or somebody else.

So then when night come then, there was neighbors got, and they got a door, an office house door. And uh, I suppose they done like the coffin long ago. They maybe bored holes in the door, you know, and put in the stick underneath and the rope business, you know—roped the two sticks to the door. Then four people carry it. She was got on the door, and they carried her out over Crocknacunny, going out by Lough Derg, out to the far road, and got her into Donegal Hospital. Carried her that way. I think my daddy was there. Like the—now and again then it would change, four carry for a while and then four more and four more and on like that. Under cover of darkness, too. Oh, it was a difficult job, like, you know. But they carried her on the door, but the mistress, she was fit to walk like. She was shot in the arm, she was fit to walk. But the other lassie had to be *carried*. Don't know whether the bullet lodged in her, lodged in her or not, or had to be took out—I don't know what way. But I knowed her. I seen her many time after. It didn't kill her anyway.

That Susan McMeel was from County Monaghan. She was a schoolteacher in the school down there, from County Monaghan, and the other lassie was a local, Bridget McGrath, daughter of John McGrath, lived beside the chapel there. She become a Mrs. Greene. I knowed her. I knowed her a bit. Didn't know her too well, but I knowed her a bit. Biddy Greene.

Who, I asked, was Willie of Skea?

Willie Johnston, Willie Johnston. Skea is a placename, a townland name just over the border in Fermanagh. But he was originally a Donegal man and a Lettercran man. Brother of Lanty Johnston's I think.

Oh, I knowed him, too. I seen him a couple of times. I seen him here in this house, going away by there to Duffy's to bore calves. I seen him oncest anyway, Willie Johnston of Skea. I did.

But there was talk about retaliation for the shooting of these, uh, two girls, who could have been both shot dead, and half lucky to be wounded. And uh, word was spread, sent out then by the Protestant crowd: "If Willie of Skea is shot dead, there'll be seven Catholics shot in his place."

That was the word that the other boys put out: "If he's shot there'll be seven Catholics shot in his place."

So I suppose that stopped that. (August 20, 2007)

With neighbor fighting against neighbor along sectarian lines, community had broken down, in some ways irrevocably. Later Packy Jim reviewed the names of Protestant families who left and those who stayed—recalling about an equal number of both—and he noted that the demographic shift of Protestants moving out of Donegal, as well as northern Catholics moving in, lasted until the 1940s. By 1954 the Orange Lodge in Tievemore had been abandoned, and a decade later dwindling Protestant numbers led to the closure of the Cashelinny Orange Hall and the nearby Anglican church on the Lettercran road. The demographic shift was both sudden and gradual, but the six months or so after the summer of 1922 were the most tense. Neighbors fired nightly shots to advertise their intention to defend themselves. Some Donegal Protestants intimidated Fermanagh Catholics into selling to make room for them and the rest of the Protestant exodus.

The basic facts of Packy Jim's account of the border battle and its aftermath comport with historical accounts,[4] but of greater concern here is how Packy Jim carefully represents these events and qualifies the motivations and actions

IRA memorial, Pettigo

of those involved. He does not assign blame to either side and in fact takes all
points of view into account. True, the British occupation of Free State territory
was illegal, but then the British did have a legitimate concern that republican
incursions into Northern Ireland were imminent and that those wishing to
remain British citizens were in danger. Packy Jim underscores how the Irish
resistance was more desperate than heroic: the bullets were the wrong caliber
for their weapons; Tommy was less interested in fighting than in a chance to
sleep, which was also thwarted. We might expect Patrick Flood to be cast in a
more heroic light in that he was the one local IRA man to be killed (the others
came from County Tyrone), but in this unverified and perhaps unverifiable
account he is wandering inebriated rather than mounting serious opposition.
His death was senseless, but seeing things from the British army's point of view,
Packy Jim acknowledges that he would not surrender "so then there was nothing
else for it, only be shot."

From Packy Jim's perspective, Willie Johnston's actions were not justified—
"It was an extreme reaction, it was sharp, he could have killed them!"—but he
is also willing to entertain the possibility that the young women of Cumann na
mBan were not necessarily innocent in their unmannerly treatment of an elder
neighbor. As he observes, "You see, you don't know, there's two sides to stories.
The firing of the shot and this and that and thon, do you know, was vicious, but
you don't know the tale that the Stewart woman told or what she had done to
her." It is also interesting that Packy Jim assigns to McMeel and McGrath the
officious formality of asking a neighbor for a name, which is something that
Catholics usually complain about concerning their experiences with B men
and later the Ulster Defence Regiment, both quasi-military forces manned by
their Protestant neighbors. At any rate, Packy Jim does not exploit the shooting
as evidence of typical Protestant perfidiousness or as justification for further
violence. Rather, he wants us to understand the incident in the context of both
the IRA and B men firing at civilians and combatants alike from positions on
either side of the Termon River, up and down the Lettercran road from Pettigo
to Cloghore. In Packy Jim's ideal world, neither side would have resorted to
violence, but violence and paranoia were nonetheless rampant during that
heightened period of military and paramilitary mobilization.

Despite the posturing and intimidation in the summer of 1922, no major
sectarian or political violence took place in the Lettercran–Pettigo area for
many decades after the border battle. Tommy supported the anti-Treaty side,
associated with the Fianna Fáil party, which did not accept the compromise of
partition as a stepping stone to an eventual united Ireland. But he took no part
in the ensuing Irish Civil War that pitted pro- and anti-Treaty forces against
each other. Furthermore, Éamon de Valera's provocation of the Economic

War in the 1930s moved Tommy to vote Fine Gael (historically the pro-Treaty party and de Valera's main competition) for the rest of his life.[5] Packy Jim maintains that by the time he was a young boy, there were few if any sectarian flare-ups, in large part because of the demographic shift. The "deep" or most staunchly loyalist Protestants had all sold out and bought new homes and farms in Northern Ireland, particularly in north Fermanagh, whereas the Protestants who stayed were typically those least invested in politics and most integrated with local Catholics. While these Protestants were more out-numbered than before Partition, Packy Jim maintains that they were not suddenly any more vulnerable. "They were neighbors. We didn't think of them as Protestants, we thought of them as neighbors." Unfortunately the peace was not to last.

The causes of the reemergence of the Troubles at the end of the 1960s are manifold. Systemic discrimination against Catholics in Northern Ireland led to public demonstrations, peaceful at first, inspired by the civil rights movement in the United States. These demonstrations were met with disproportionate and often violent opposition both from loyalist vigilantes and paramilitaries and from official state forces including the majority Protestant Royal Ulster Constabulary (RUC, police), B-Specials, and the Ulster Defence Regiment, which replaced the B-Specials in 1970. Once both Catholic and Protestant rioting spread beyond local control, the situation was militarized and arguably compounded by the introduction of British troops and the imposition of direct rule from London. Tensions and violence escalated in response to draconian anti-terrorist legislation including imprisonment without trial, the British army fatally shooting Catholic protesters during Bloody Sunday in 1972, and increasingly apparent collusion between the police, army, and loyalist paramilitaries. In this context, the IRA, which had dwindled in numbers and significance, was in the midst of a resurgence followed by a split between the Official IRA, which remained committed to nonviolent political action, and the Provisional IRA, which espoused armed struggle against British rule in Northern Ireland and assumed the role of defending the Catholic community. Nearly four thousand people were killed and countless injured or bereaved over three decades of political violence.

Living in the Republic did not insulate Packy Jim or his neighbors from the Troubles, for in Lettercran they were surrounded by Northern Ireland on three sides. Because the IRA took advantage of the opportunity to strike from and retreat into the relative safety of Donegal, the British army made regular incursions, wittingly and unwittingly, across the border that essentially runs through Packy Jim's front yard. Indeed, more than once British soldiers searched his property, and more than once Packy Jim happened upon evidence of local IRA activity such as a stolen vehicle intended for a car bomb, suspiciously disguised from airborne surveillance. In order to stem paramilitary traffic, the British army blocked or cratered cross-border roads, as it had done toward the end of the Irish War of Independence in the 1920s and during an IRA border campaign in the 1950s. Riddled with overland smuggling routes, however, the border remained particularly porous in places such as Lettercran even with the paved roads severed. Whether staying close to home or venturing into Tyrone for socializing and shopping, Packy Jim witnessed an extensive and at times intimidating military buildup.

> Every road you looked on the border, going or coming in the daylight, you were liable to see troops, British troops, and you were liable to be stopped by the UDR on the road, or the police on the road, or the British Army. There were three crowds could have stopped you—policemen, UDR men, and Brits.
>
> And uh, in the early stages when I was going away here and there and thonder on bicycles into the North, I wouldn't have been giving a damn if there were a crowd of five hundred of them on the *road*. It wouldn't have annoyed me in the slightest *bit*. And then, as time wore on then, I got as afeared of them—as the saying goes—if I seen them, it was like meeting *ghosts*, and say it that way.
>
> But they paraded through the, through the country, looking in waste houses to see if there was anything in it. Or see if there was any signs of occupation by the IRA, like any signs of occupation that they had been in it. There was ones in here counting the number of mugs, judging to see if I was entertaining any crowds, aiding and abetting, you understand.
>
> Oh Lord, aye, surely.
>
> And then there was helicopters flying in the sky. Well, there were days when you could have seen five or six helicopters flying across here and there and thonder and soaring and soaring and soaring. I seen a helicopter one time away up there and she soaring for maybe an hour. And up and down, and like that again. I seen them going up and down the border there. I suppose maybe at that particular time, there'd have been a policeman maybe in helicopter, you know, that knowed the area. British helicopters, and they were *flying* way up there like *hell*, way by and out of sight.
>
> And I think it was—as the saying goes—thinking to trap you. Maybe perhaps they were foolish enough to think there were a couple of IRA boys in here, with some explosives or something with them, and they

would be foolish enough to say, "The helicopter's away, we can make a run for it." And if that had been the case, they mightn't have been half roads down the meadow when the helicopter come back again, trying to see would there be any move, I would think. That was what that was, flying away by and then coming down again.

See, any house like this, an occupied house on the border, or if it was unoccupied for that part of it, it was better still—it was *suspected*. And if it wasn't an occupied house it was suspected *stronger*.

Then the Guards, they started coming here then and visiting here as regular as the clock. I seen them turning on that street at twelve o'clock in the night, and I seen them turning on that street there afore daylight in the morning, the Guards. Indeed they did often. (August 20, 2007)

For Packy Jim, the Old IRA was justified in its armed struggle against the British, though it found itself in an impossible situation when faced with the prospect of fighting its Protestant neighbors. The Provisional IRA of the 1970s through 1990s expanded its targets from British soldiers to the RUC, B-Specials, and UDR, organizations comprised of local Northern Irish Protestants. Engaging in a war between neighbors, the Provos crossed a line, in Packy Jim's view. While Packy Jim's ideological sympathies remained with the civil rights campaign and abstractly with Irish nationalism, his more immediate sympathies were with the victims of political violence he knew personally, Catholic and Protestant. For example, Fermanagh UDR men such as Johnny Barton and Stanley Marshall narrowly escaped assassination attempts by the IRA, and their colleague Gerry Coulter led a life of constant vigilance.

He lived there closer to the border, back there in Fermanagh, Gerry Coulter. He was a UDR man, and he had a place then, up fairly close to the border that come out toward the top of the hill, and down in like that till it.

Well, he used to have his rifle with him, like, when he was, like, to fire back if there was an attack. Gerry was prepared—as the saying goes— to swap shots with them.

But he was a pretty well liked man, and he was no way—as the saying goes—over officious or anything like that. He was a likeable personality. Of course, whoever was going to shoot him was going to come from a distance, I suppose. If that was going be the case, then they wouldn't be particular about his *personality*.

But he was being a brave man, like, and taking the chance for you didn't know where somebody was going have a crack at you. I would say he was, he was a valiant man. He was. (November 16, 1998)

For a Catholic, this is a fairly sympathetic portrait of a UDR man, doing his duty ethically and courageously despite being surrounded by an enemy committed to ambush and assassination. This is a perspective more in line with revisionist rather than nationalist historiography. Packy Jim's sympathies, however, are primarily personal rather than ideological; they are not with the UDR as an institution or unionism as a political platform but with an individual in a marginal position doing the best he can. Packy Jim also mentions here one aspect of why the recent Troubles became so vicious—"whoever was going to shoot him was going to come from a distance." Locals provided information and remain accountable to this day, but typically both republican and loyalist violence against neighbors was committed by outsiders brought in for the job. Packy Jim remembers a litany of victims from Aghyaran, County Tyrone, Catholics and Protestants—McHugh, Shanaghan, and Dolan; Pollack, Bogle, and Kerrigan. In a long reflection from 2007, note Packy Jim's ecumenical stance, his sympathy with victims on both sides, and his willingness to find fault with all parties—loyalists, republicans, and the forces of the state:

There was a fellow shot there in Corgary. Big Mick McHugh was shot there when he was going till his work one morning in Corgary. He was driving, he was driving a forestry lorry, for the forestry crowd. And uh, I would know or say, I suppose, what the, what the UVF [Ulster Volunteer Force, a loyalist paramilitary group] said was right. The UVF, do you see, he'd be different places here and there and thonder in his work, with a lorry. The UVF blamed him for picking up a bomb, ready to explode, in his lorry, and taking it on down the road, and leaving it some road convenient where it could be taken to Castlederg. He was blamed for that. And most probably, he was doing that too. He wouldn't have been maybe in what you call the IRA, but he would have been a, he would have been a supporter.

So uh, I don't whether they threatened him or not. I can't tell you whether they threatened him or not, what happened. That's about 1973. But he was working on the forestry and he was driving the lorry and he lived up a long road, up a steep road, up a steep hill way up there. I think I knowed the house he lived in. And in the dark—it was in the wintertime—when he come out to the main road, the wee by-road run out to the main road, he was halted there. And he was shot dead in the lorry in the morning in the winter months.

And then the woman, then, she had to have a sale then. I suppose the farm was sold, but she sold out, and I think she went and lived in Castlederg. And uh, I don't know who owns the land now, I couldn't tell you. But he was shot.

That was one that was shot, then *Paddy Shanaghan* was shot. Oh, he got a bad doing. Paddy Shanaghan got a wild bad doing too, afore he was shot, like intimidated and stopped maybe three or four times in one day. And he sold *An Phoblacht* newspaper at the chapel on Sunday. And he'd have been a member of Sinn Féin. But uh, I wouldn't say ever he shot anybody. I would swear he never shot nobody.

He was working on the, whatever you like to call it there, DOA [Department of Agriculture] on the roads, and he had a farm of land, and a good farm of land, to manage as well. And working on the DOA. He had no time. But he was very, very interested in ceili dancing and followed up ceili dancing a lot. In other words, he was what you might call, uh, *quite* a bit of an *Irishman*.

But for whatever reason or another anyway, uh, all the policemen and all the B men in the locality and far and wide got the belief that, uh, Paddy Shanaghan was enemy number *one*. And it was known that sometimes he could be maybe stopped as often, maybe, as five times in *one day*. And the house was raided regularly, and there was even boards lifted up on the loft, look on the ceiling and under. And uh, furniture, wardrobes, and things like that, and drawers, emptied out, never bother to put in again or replace. And that was the harassment that went on and on and on, for a long, long time. And of course they knowed that he was threatened, that his end was coming near. And there were one day he was putting up a lean-to shed some road or another, and some of them come on the job, on the spot, like—I don't know, police I suppose was at it and the UDR—but they says till him, "You're only wasting your time at putting up that shed *sir*. You're soon going to be a dead duck." He was told that, "You're wasting your time." So that was it.

And there were sometimes when he'd go to go out at night there, they would be about. There was a lane, two high ditches on the sides of the lane, and there'd be rocks left on the lane, you know. And he'd have to get out of the car and put the rocks back in the ditch again to get away on. The harassment was *wild*.

So he got shot, when he was going till his work one morning. It went that way that there were lots of people who wouldn't, like, go to work, and nobody near wanted to work with him. He had to be on his own. They weren't going to take the chance. They didn't know when the attack was going to be launched.

They fired at him one night. He was going away some road or another. The mother was away some road or another, but he was going till a dance some road or another. And uh, in the dark, he went out of the house and he was fired at twice, I think. Then he maybe escapes into the fields.

So that was a couple of months later, and then they had another, another attempt made down at this waste house there. Fired when he was going by, fired and shot him in the neck. Lord save him.

I *knowed* that fellow. Used to be by here, time and again. Like, a bicycle he used till, uh—he had a car on the street there for a while. He had a car on the street there for about a month one time. It wasn't right for the North, missing MOT [Ministry of Transport roadworthiness certification] or some damn thing that was in vogue or something like that. He used to ride a bicycle up from home to here and then away on the car, that way. He told me at the time—I suppose maybe it was true—he had a girlfriend about Donegal town. But he was the big dancing man anyway, followed up the ceili dancing.

So uh, anyway, he was a *right* sort of a boy.

But uh, anyway, I was going down to Castlederg, and uh, I met Lawrence Duffy there at Luddy's Lane. And he stopped me and he says, "Shanaghan got the works." Oh, I heared it on the wireless before and I was judging it about "Prominent Sinn Féiner shot in the Castlederg area." I was suspecting it. But Lawrence Duffy said, "Shanaghan got the works, yesterday morning."

So *knowing* him, and *liking* him well enough, I decided that I'd go till his *funeral*.

So uh, anyway, I headed off for the funeral on the bicycle, and uh, going down there by Duffy's, I seen one helicopter flying, and then I seen two helicopters flying. And I says to myself, "What do you make out of this?" This was the funeral day, but I took the cold feet, at that time, and I went up to Willie Dolan's. Aye, she [Mrs. Dolan] was going to the funeral alright, "Get in with me." So I got into the car with her. And we headed down to Killeter, turned and headed out for Aghyaran. We met a big bus coming, an empty bus coming in from Gortnagross. It was out with a busload of *police*. Then, we went out the length of Charlie McHugh's. The helicopter had taken off there, off the field there beside Charlie McHugh's. There was three policemen standing in the road there, and there was about seven in the field just in back of Charlie McHugh's. So uh, that was looking—as the saying goes—like something.

Landed up to the chapel, parked the car and got out. Big, big crowd there—as the saying goes—the biggest big crowd ever you saw. Was ahead of the funeral getting the length. Hadn't long to wait. The helicopter come flying along, above the hearse, keeping pace with the hearse. A police car either in front of it or behind it—I don't mind which. But then when the, when the uh, funeral come fairly close till the chapel, along there, coming along the bottom road there, close to the chapel, it veered away. But then the police car still come on.

So then I didn't very well *see* because with the old crowd in front of it, big, big crowd along in front of the chapel, but uh, the police car—I think it was in front of the hearse—it driv away on. And then the coffin was taken out of the hearse then and carried into the chapel, and Mass began, and then after the Mass was over then, the removal then till the graveyard. I didn't want to be keeping Willie Dolan's woman standing too long, like, so uh, when the thing was over—like the rites was over, or the prayer or whatever—I headed then back to get down till the front of the chapel again. Well, if there was one policeman there—and they were at different places that I didn't see—there could have been about two hundred policemen at that fellow's funeral that day.

Hell. Damned the like of it ever I saw!

Aye, and you could hear walkie-talkies going this and that and thon. Maybe they were looking, maybe they thought that there would be other, maybe, prominent *personnel* about the place that they would arrest. I don't know what, but jimmity Christ, anything like what, what policemen I never saw. I'm damned but between here and there and thonder, there could have been two hundred. And was there any call for it? I'd never saw *nothing* like it. There'd be funerals about Aghyaran yet, and there might be less mourners about them than there'd been policemen at thon. It was an *eye-opener*. Was there any call for it or not, I don't know.

And then that day Pollack's sheep was supposed to be put out on the road that day, or let out on the road, like, *willfully*. Pollack—forget his first name—Pollack had five sons. He had one son I know in the UDR, and he was killed—William Pollack. He was killed. He lived down there in the new house there at Glashagh, beside Glashagh Pub. And he had got a trailer to draw something some road or another, some stock. And he was, the trailer was *booby-trapped*, and when he was lifting the trailer up to attach it till a yoke, the bomb went off and it killed him. William Pollock was killed there by a booby-trapped trailer.

He was a son of Andy Pollack's. And Andy Pollack was a neighbor of
Shanaghan's. And uh, William Pollack was killed maybe several months
afore Paddy Shanaghan was shot, maybe three, four, five months.
Somebody, some Catholic body, was shaping to sympathize with Andy
Pollack about the death of his son in accident. And Andy Pollack says
till them, "They're over with you every Sunday at Aghyaran [Catholic
church] that knows a lot about that." He put no more questions till the
man, but that was the answer. "Yous has them about Aghyaran chapel
that knows quite a bit about it." And it was . . . taken that he was alluding
to Paddy Shanaghan.

   ·   But unless that Paddy Shanaghan was a fingering man, that there
was a shooter coming from a distance, and that he was taking them
around and showing, "There's a UDR man lives in there, or two, and
somebody lives in there"—whether he was at that job or not, that is hard
to know. But uh, he definitely wasn't a shooting man. But he was alluding
to Paddy Shanaghan.

But *why* were they so heavy-handed with Paddy Shanaghan, when
there was so many other young Catholic people in the locality that might
be stopped and questioned, that they *weren't* persecuting? *Why* were they
so heavy-handed with *him?* That's a mystery. But they were heavy-handed
with him, and very heavy-handed. That's all I know.

Well the way of it was in them days there was no young Catholic
that wasn't suspect. The Protestant people in them areas that was bigly
threatened, every Catholic was suspect and every Protestant was far from
stupid.

But they were heavy-handed. Any Catholic at all that knows anything
can tell you that there was nobody as, uh, leaned on as him. John Corey
was in with ones like that and got maybe a rough time. Paddy O'Donnell
was in, ones like that. But uh, they didn't get the rough time that
Shanaghan got, I doubt.

But he didn't die a coward anyway. He was, he maintained, "I done
nothing wrong, I was no way"—as the saying goes—"abusive to anybody.
If they want to shoot me, they *can* shoot me. I'm never going to *budge*."
That was his, and he had said, too, to somebody, "My only hope is, that
whatever time I *get* it, that my mother doesn't be with me."

Packy Jim continued with several additional accounts of Patrick Shanaghan's
harassment, then related that the Pollacks now have the land Shanaghan
worked. This led him to recall other examples of the Pollacks being unlucky. In
addition to William Pollack killed by the trailer bomb, several other family
members died early or otherwise tragically. The UDR connection prompted

me to ask about Willie Bogle, who was shot, presumably by the IRA, at the post office in Killeter in 1972. He continued:

> That's right, Willie Bogle, coming out of that shop door. He was coming out of that shop door. He was shot in front of his wife and children. He was a UDR man, too. Aye, he was. I didn't know him either. I didn't know him. He was a UDR man. That's right, he was shot in the door.
>
> Then there was a girl killed then, later on then again, a Dolan girl killed then in a car bomb explosion. A week or two later there were a Dolan girl killed then. After posting the last three or four or so of her wedding invitation cards away in the post office. Kathleen Dolan. She was crossing over the street again and off it went.
>
> A lot of people think there was a connection, that this was retaliation, like. And maybe. But then, that loyalist crowd wasn't much into making bombs. They never claimed it. And don't you know there was more nor one IRA bomb passed through Killeter on the way to Castlederg. It never will be known for sure. But that could have, could just as easily have been—as the saying goes—a *botched job*. Oh, you don't know, now.
>
> No, those were *wild* dark times. (August 20, 2007)

Dark times indeed. Castlederg alone suffered over seventy IRA bombings directed against government and police facilities and Protestant-owned businesses, and in the broader Castlederg–Aghyaran area the IRA killed twenty-eight local Protestants—twenty of them, like Pollack and Bogle, in the UDR or RUC, full-time, part-time, and reserves. In our 2007 conversation Packy Jim recounted most of the local Catholic victims of the Troubles though he leaves out Dermot Hackett, who, like Shanaghan, was killed by loyalists who appear to have been assisted by the Royal Ulster Constabulary and/or British army.

Being an acquaintance, Shanaghan attracts the most attention in Packy Jim's recollections, but the emphasis is not on the justness of the republican cause for which he may be seen as a martyr. Like UDR member Gerry Coulter, Shanaghan is in a marginal position doing the best he can; he is heroic not for his particular politics but for standing his ground in an impossible situation. In a time and place where all young Catholic males are suspect, Shanaghan openly promotes Irish culture particularly through dancing, and he broadcasts his politics selling republican newspapers and volunteering for Sinn Féin. None of this is illegal, even if it may be inadvisable in the face of sectarian intimidation and institutionalized discrimination. Such a symbolically rich target—a young ceili dancing republican, every bit the Irishman—is irresistible to the authorities, and their heavy-handedness with Shanaghan, before and after his death, is further indication of just how "bigly threatened" was the Protestant establishment and state forces by what he represented.

Tyrone republicans who have discussed Shanaghan with me emphasize—as does Packy Jim—that he was not a member of the IRA, underscoring his innocence. But Packy Jim is the first person in my presence to consider, though not commit to, the possibility that Shanaghan provided the IRA with information. In doing so Packy Jim is assessing a possible cause for Shanaghan's excessive and prejudicial harassment by the police and army rather than impugning the reputation of a man he admired. Likewise, Packy Jim is willing to entertain the feasibility that Mick McHugh's assassination by loyalists was not an arbitrary act in that McHugh may have been involved with the IRA, and he introduces the possibility that the tragic 1972 bombing in Killeter that killed Kathleen Dolan was a republican accident rather than a loyalist retaliation. Packy Jim's searching but inconclusive accounts are not typical of how fellow Catholics in the area have spoken to me about the deaths of Shanaghan, Dolan, and McHugh. Ambiguity and the possibility that blame may be mutual or at least complicated is certainly not the spin *An Phoblacht* would put on such events.

Asked directly about his politics, Packy Jim says, "I suppose I could think of myself as a nationalist and not a republican," but the labels are insufficient for representing his more complicated position. He would be labeled a "nationalist" by virtue of being born a Catholic, regardless of his personal views on the prospect of a united Ireland or how it might be achieved, so the conventional designation is largely insignificant. Like the neutral angels, Packy Jim takes no sides among the available options, but not choosing, of course, is a choice. This unorthodox position contributes to Packy Jim's marginalization among fellow nationalists, just as the angels' fence-sitting led to their exile. Perhaps the one thing in common between the British government, loyalists, and republicans—the available sides to take—is the willingness to pursue their goals through lethal force, but here Packy Jim is no longer willing to be a fence sitter. Still an admirer of Proinsias Dubh, the mature Packy Jim is all for standing up for what is right, but internecine bloodshed is the line neither he nor his heroes will cross. Once that moral principle is established, Packy Jim is free to entertain and even sympathize with different perspectives, without necessarily agreeing with them, always underscoring complexity.

> Things are looking better, but there's still a lot of bitterness and animosity there. And the Protestant mind is, a large amount of them, "We want to live our own way in our own country. We don't want to be ruled by Dublin." It's just like somebody forcing you to go to somebody else's house to live. We'll say you had a brother or a sister or a cousin—no, I'm

not going to go there, I'm going to live in my own place. I suppose if you were born a Protestant, and particularly a Protestant in one of them large Protestant areas, *you could not help but have that same attitude.*

No, you can't blast, you can't bomb a million and a half Protestants into a united Ireland. That's not the way you're going to do it.

Then, I suppose Catholics was getting a bad showing with housing and work and things of that kind, but there was, uh, rich Catholics, fairly wealthy Catholics, professional people in the North, and all you had to do if you wanted to get—as the saying goes—a good chance for your children: join the Unionist Party. And that was as good as if you changed your religion, understand.

But then the curious thing about it was, there was plenty of Catholics in Northern Ireland and they were more unionists than the unionists themselves. That's the case, too—piles and piles of them—so there's such a thing as Catholic unionists.

Oh, it's always more complicated than the stories you get. (June 27, 2009)

Packy Jim likens the Protestant aversion to a united Ireland to his own experience of not wanting to be moved to a cousin's home, relinquishing autonomy, after his mother's death. He notes the existence of Catholics voting with unionists for reasons of financial security. Whether shaped by self-interest or the influence of environment, people make understandable decisions even if they may not be your own. Bombing people into joining you, however, does not stand to reason, and any story that begins to justify this is suspect for Packy Jim. During an earlier conversation, I had asked him if his views on politics, nationalism, and the IRA had changed over time.

It would, it would have changed a lot. As a kid you have notions about being the hero, you're filled up with all them books and stories about bold rebels, the Wild Geese and all that. But the reality, you just—I would be what you may call disaffected.

Tommy would have liked till have seen a united Ireland—say it that way—he'd have had that attitude of mind. For my part, the son—as the saying goes—I couldn't have cared less. What I'd have been more interested in: if they could come till an *amicable* settlement in Northern Ireland between the parties. Well that fitted me—as the saying goes—that fitted me nicely.

But, like I never was asked for any help or any aidment or any abetment, but it would have been rather reluctantly that I would have been prepared to aid or abet what you would call the Provisional IRA. I never was asked to, nor I wouldn't have wanted to. And that was that. I never was in the position where you could, for this here was—with helicopters and soldiers—this place was well enough watched.

But I think that there's a good system in Northern Ireland now, a very good system that should please *most* of the people. It's not bad. It never was a hair better, I think. Now, there's a handful that it doesn't please or never will please, them boys that they call the Continuity IRA and the Real IRA—all the hardliners. They'll be putting off bombs maybe in ten or fifteen years from now. But uh, any person, fair-minded person, thinks that is a good system.

Big Joe said—when the IRA started blasting and blowing in the North in nineteen seventy or seventy one—he said they should have left it to the *civil rights people*. Big Joe was right. He said the IRA should have, never should have dipped in because that civil rights campaign was being highlighted *around the world*. And for a long, long time, a lot of what was going on in Northern Ireland was *unknownst* to the British. The British wouldn't have knowed very much about it, you understand, until it was highlighted by TV and all the rest of it.

I don't know whether that was a good idea or not—that blowing and blasting that they were at—that was *their* notion. But—as the saying goes— what was it doing, only making it very difficult for the rest of us. (August 13, 2007)

Republicans—whether the Provisional IRA until their 2005 decommissioning or later dissidents who continue in armed struggle—have the capability of not just destroying property but also of taking human life and reshaping the political landscape. This observation, however, does not address the question about whether such power should be exercised. For Packy Jim the answer is no. It is possible that real progress toward greater equality for and political representation of Catholics in Northern Ireland would not have been possible without the threat and exercise of violence. Then again, perhaps the progress may have been slow but nonetheless inevitable with world attention to the situation raised by the civil rights movement through the media. Packy Jim does not know which is closer to the truth, but he is satisfied that the legal and political system in place now is as fair as could be expected and that there is no longer a convincing case for armed struggle as there may have been earlier.

Today in Northern Ireland it is no longer clearly the case that acting morally includes breaking the law as it was in the time of landlords and Proinsias Dubh. Of course, the libertarian border mentality continues, and neither Packy

Jim nor his neighbors see much shame in breaking minor laws relating to customs and excise, committing arguably victimless crimes such as illicit distillation or otherwise taking advantage of weaknesses and loop holes to game the system. But then again, even after the recent international financial turmoil and its local repercussions, times are not nearly as straitened for someone like Packy Jim as they were in the 1930s through 1950s, so in the interest of survival there is no longer as great a need to outflank rules and authority as there once was.

At a time when most but not all of the conflict in Northern Ireland has shifted from the realm of bombs and violence to the realm of symbols and discourse, there remains for Packy Jim—as much as for Northern Ireland's politicians and commentators—a great deal at stake in the politics of representing the Irish past. Sectarianism is the result of the original sin of dispossession and colonialism—fingers may be pointed and blame assigned—but such a simplistic, binary Catholic versus Protestant worldview simply does not fit Packy Jim's experience on the ground among neighbors where class is often the more relevant issue. If the idea and practice of community has a fighting chance at survival, the sectarian vision of the world is well worth complicating—as do the figures of Proinsias Dubh, Renardine, Piaras Grás, even the Protest Ascendancy Armstrongs and Leslies. In speaking of the Troubles, giving it shape through narrative, Packy Jim represents the exercise of power by others—loyalists, republicans, state forces—and how he does this is itself an exercise in power in the contemporary competition over memory and meaning.

Doing the Best

Packy Jim brings to the table a tension between submission and transgression, between exercising autonomy and following received rules, established in his early days when the stakes were relatively low. By his teens, Packy Jim had developed a more mature and trickier worldview in which the postulates that rules-as-rules are inviolable or that authority is not to be challenged are not considered specious so much as they are not even considered. Given the myriad case studies that the political history of the Irish border provide, a mature Packy Jim reviews available sources to sort out legitimate and illegitimate forms of compliance and resistance, and here, especially in the context of war, the stakes are considerably higher. Of Proinsias Dubh and his form of resistance, Packy Jim says, "When he died, he wouldn't have been damned for it." He is less sure about the men who killed Pollack and Bogle, Shanaghan, Dolan, and McHugh. Support for armed struggle—whether bolstered, questioned, or undermined through commemorative discourse—can be a matter of life and death. Connecting armed struggle to a glorious tradition of heroic rebellion is what in large part allows dissident organizations such as the Real IRA and the Continuity IRA to continue drawing what support they have for their ongoing campaigns of bombing and assassination.

In boldly rehearsing history as he sees it—indeed, as he thinks we need to see it—Packy Jim does not replicate the more ardent received nationalist narratives. Packy Jim emerges from his disquisitions as clearly more a pragmatist than an ideologue, attuned to ambiguity and complexity but equally committed to his own moral compass. He is firmly on the side of local community at the face-to-face micro level rather than on the side of any particular paramilitary force or nation-state at the abstract macro level. It may not seem possible at first to draw connections between UDR man Gerry Coulter, Sinn Féin activist Patrick Shanaghan, and highwayman Proinsias Dubh, but in the context of Packy Jim's larger repertoire they are all, regardless of their personal political affiliations, people in marginal positions standing their ground. On the border such figures are worthy of contemplation, sympathy, and emulation. Or paraphrasing what Packy Jim says about himself, each one was doing his best on the edge of a complicated world, his own boss.

4

Place, History, and Morality

Packy Jim's personal narratives demonstrate that one way to think through the tensions that animate the self and shape society is to contemplate everyday practices—illicit distillation or marriage, for example—that may give rise to the declaration of an orientation: "it's a bad thing to be too scrupulous" or "was I to be such'n a fool?" Another option we have seen is thinking vicariously through the actions of a well-known local figure or an established religious, historical, or (oral) literary character who has made choices in the face of fundamental tensions—the neutral angels, Henry David Thoreau, or Proinsias Dubh, for example. Such stories may focus on the actions of others, but they provide individuals with positive and negative exemplars, contributing to the development of worldview and subjectivity. In addition to debatable practices and exemplary figures, another complementary catalyst to memory and past–present evaluation—another resource for constructions of self and society—is place.

In Packy Jim's everyday conversation and wider narrative repertoire, one of the strongest themes is the deep resonances of certain places he associates with past happenings and the relevance of these happenings to choices to be made today. These meaningful places include the more intimate settings of everyday life. Recall Packy Jim's gesture to the lasting imprint of Frank McCanny—"sitting in that corner there, in the chair *there*"—speaking words that shaped Packy Jim's perspectives for a lifetime. More typically locations farther afield—the site of an unjust eviction, out there, on the mountain, in Carrickaholten townland—compel narratives of the past with enduring meaning in the present.

Investigating testimony from Ballymenone, County Fermanagh, Henry Glassie contends that history is the essence of the idea of place (1982, especially chapter 31), and his work demonstrates the centrality in Irish oral traditions of a commemorative genre traditionally known as *dinnseanchas* or "place lore." Through dinnseanchas ordinary people—not least Packy Jim in Lettercran or Hugh Nolan in Ballymenone—inscribe the landscape with meaning. In the process, history—the amalgam of past precedents relevant to the present—becomes organized in the mind largely in terms of where rather than when. Likewise, through narrative, places become sites of memory that invite the initiated local to draw connections between then and now, those people in the past and ourselves in the present.[1]

Paying attention to such places and the stories associated with them continues the tradition of folklorists and cultural geographers engaged in what Kent Ryden (drawing on E. V. Walter, drawing on Ptolemy) calls *chorography*: mapping the invisible landscape of the local imagination, demonstrating how people transform arbitrary space into meaningful place. The promise of chorography is to offer a more emic perspective on insiders' senses of place and to reveal, more generally, that sense of place is simultaneously a way of thinking about the world and those who inhabit it (Ryden 1993).

For Packy Jim in particular, his immediate physical surroundings serve as a vast mnemonic device for archiving legendary stories that join and amplify his personal narratives in mapping the boundaries of his moral universe. Many of Packy Jim's emplaced stories serve as morality tales about humans interacting with other humans in the social realm. Characters serve as exemplars of values worthy of emulation or as exemplars of questionable, even damnable, values. The places where significant human dramas unfolded—and continue to unfold, both in memory and in narrative performance—comprise a landscape of moral testimony. As Keith Basso has observed in his examination of Western Apache place lore, "geographical features have served people for centuries as indispensable mnemonic pegs on which to hang the moral teachings of their history" (1996:62).

Furthermore, Packy Jim's immediate physical surroundings serve as a vast mnemonic device for preserving stories that establish propositions about the nature of this world and of life itself—what is knowable, known, or presumed. On this point, Tim Cresswell has observed that place "is not so much a quality of things in the world but an aspect of the way we choose to think about it—what we decide to emphasize and what we decide to designate as unimportant" (2004:11). As such, place is not just a thing in the world but a way of knowing or "as much about epistemology as it is about ontology" (2004:12). Layered with years of sentiment, association, and narrative, Packy Jim's physical surroundings, then, comprise a landscape of not only moral but also epistemological and existential testimony.

Basso uses the term "place-world" for a site of such manifold personal and potentially collective significance. Drawing from Bakhtin's notion of the chronotope (1981:84–258), Basso characterizes a place-world as a site where time and space merge, where aspects of the past may be conjured as the needs of the present demand (1996:6, 62). Likewise, "place-making" through narrative is a widespread strategy for constructing history, for fashioning novel usable versions of what happened in a given place (1996:5–8, 32–33). Every place-world— developed through an accretion of association and narrative—manifests itself as a possible state of affairs. Whenever these constructions are accepted and circulated as credible and convincing—or plausible or provocative—they enrich the common stock on which everyone may draw to contemplate past events, interpret their present significance, and imagine them anew as changing wants and needs dictate.

For Packy Jim, one such place-world is the spot on Lough Mulken Hill where in 1848, at the height of the Famine, Peggy Roe McGrath died attempting, in vain, to save her younger brother, Patrick, from exposure. This location stands in for Packy Jim as a daily, physical reminder of the prospect of tragedy in the world and of the human virtues of fidelity and sacrifice. While folklorists may identify the stories associated with such places as historical legends or as dinnseanchas, Packy Jim is more invested in the business of recounting, rather than labeling, these narratives. Most crucially for him, such stories serve as equipment for living in the present (Burke [1941] 1973). That is, for Packy Jim, moving physically or imaginatively through the landscape—considering numerous meaningful sites—invites narratives that amount to a meditation on proper behavior in the social world. Moreover, these stories, archived in a landscape of testimony, provide Packy Jim with the most extensive indications of what he, or any of us, can expect life to have in store. While the activity of place-making may not be unique to Packy Jim, the specific place-worlds he selects to emphasize and conjure through narrative provide a critical insight into his values, identity, and worldview.

Consider further the case of seventeen-year-old Peggy Roe McGrath and her fourteen-year-old brother, whose frozen bodies were found on a lonely hillside less than a mile from Packy Jim's home. In Lettercran and surrounding areas, this tragic end is well known. To unravel questions of when, where, how, and why, we can turn—as have many others—to Packy Jim, who takes care to tend the memory of those events. In a version of the story from November 2011, Packy Jim starts with orienting context, including an explanation that the Roe ("red") McGraths are a different branch of the family from his own Bán ("fair" or "white") McGraths. From there he explains what drew these youngsters to walk eight miles from home:

Well, the fairs in Castlederg were very big occasions, any time of the year—spring, summer, autumn, or winter—where there could be maybe hundreds or maybe thousands gathered for a lock of hours. In other words it was a kind of *social* occasion as well as being an occasion where you could have sold stock or hire yourself off or anything like that. It was a *social* occasion.

But these young people wanted to get to the fair, and the father was going to the fair as well. I suppose we may presume that the three of them went away to the fair together in the morning.

And, uh, I suppose there was a storm blowing up, but when they went away the storm was still far away. And the days was short. And, uh, as night was starting till approach, these two kids left on their own, without their father, come up the road walking several mile till the Blacktown, and when they reached Ardgolan Glen—to say it that way—up at the Buffer's, that's where their padroad cut across the moorland, two mile again, or more, till their own place.

At this point in the telling, with the complicating action established, Packy Jim speeds his delivery, shuts his eyes tight, bobs his right knee, and winds his right hand in a fitful circular motion. He begins to emphasize with volume and pitch the key words and images—showers, dark, light, nighttime, cold. Moreover, he transforms his telling from exposition to something more subjunctive. Similar to Basso's Western Apache place-makers who dramatize how things "might have been," switch to present tense, and use quoted speech to de-emphasize pastness (1996:11–13, 23–28), Packy Jim shifts into a kind of speculation, knitting facts and likelihoods so that we may better imagine the unfolding tragedy from the perspectives of the victims.

It would have been getting *dark*, and the storm was then, I suppose, about *on* them. And it come on, first it come on with thunder and lightning and hail *showers*. And then it changed then from that to a fully blown snowstorm after *that*.

And they were out on the mountain and it got *dark* and they had no *light* and the *pad*road couldn't be *seen*. And, anyway, the place got snowed *over*.

Perhaps when they went to that town they got nothing to *eat*. Maybe they'd ate nothing from the morning and then it was—as the saying goes—*nighttime*, hours and hours later.

Hunger.

Cold.

Fear of being *lost*.
TERROR.

Whereas at the beginning of this section Packy Jim's pace quickens to mirror and vivify the growing sense of panic of the lost youths, by the end he shifts tack with a series of dramatic pauses and short, even one-word, sentences that sum up the "emotional core" (Coffin 1957) of the moment—hunger, cold, lost, terror, with greatest emphasis on the last. If this section were a musical score, it would have progressed from bars of half and quarter notes to bars of eighth and sixteenth notes, then slammed up against a slow, punctuated series of whole notes and rests, the piano's sustaining damper pedal pressed to the floor—*TERROR.* Emotional core established, Packy Jim proceeds with further developing events, continuing to intone the key words, images, and endings of complete thoughts.

> And they wandered this road and *that road.*
> And, uh, the cub was giving up that he could go no farther, and I suppose com*plain*ing about it that he could go no farther. She had some kind of a coat or petticoat on her and I suppose she was about finished *too.* So she took off her garment and she put it around the *cub.*
> And they landed at this spot where, I suppose, *neither* of them could see, they could go no *farther*, nor didn't know what road to *go.*
> So they laid down on the, on the *snow* and—the two beside the other—and *there* they laid until they died, maybe one o'clock or maybe two o'clock in the morning till—as the saying goes—the life went away. And then, probably then, when the snow was over they were practically snowed over—I think it could have snowed maybe half a foot of snow, something like that, a good amount of snow.

For Peggy and Patrick the action has concluded, but Packy Jim continues, first with an aside—calling a reliable witness to verify that the winter storm in which they died was indeed treacherous—then with a chronology of how Peggy and Patrick were found.

> And Big Joe McGrath said that old McCanny—that would've been his grandfather—was down at that house where James Hegarty used to live at, uh, John—what do you call it?—John, John *Sproule's.* He was living down that house on the burn side, the house where Hegarty got flooded out of—you might of heard tell of that place, maybe you were at it, the walls of it. So he was living there and *he said* really and truly it was a *bad night*, the night that they got lost.

So *then* that was Friday, Friday night. Saturday morning—I suppose they died on Saturday morning, one or two o'clock or whatever, probably the cub died first and probably she died next.

And then, uh, the father come home some time the next day then, when the weather'd have cleared, and then the family, they weren't there. *Where did they go?*

Then there was a search got up then. And, uh, probably, probably on Sunday, maybe the search was got up on Sunday. And Monday.

But on Tuesday there was a man there from Lough Nageage, out there from Lough Nageage, was on the search. He was Stewart from Lough Nageage. And he was at the head of the search—uh, there could have been maybe fifteen or twenty or maybe more searching the area, like, that was knowing they would have been *on* to head for home. But it was Stewart of Lough Nageage that got them. *He got them.*

At this point, Packy Jim pauses, perhaps visualizing the pitiful scene that Stewart and the search team must have come upon. Then he reiterates Peggy's sacrifice, speaking in a reverent hushed tone:

And then, when they were got, they seen that she had her petticoat and maybe a little shawl around the young boy.

So it was believed that the young boy give up first, being a wee bit, four years younger or so, he'd be a little bit weaker. But that was the way they were *got*: she had the clothes 'round him. (November 18, 2011)

Even here the story does not end, for loose ends and questions remain. At this point in the telling, I waited for a couple beats then asked why the father, James, or Jimmy Roe, had not returned with Peggy and Patrick. To this Packy Jim replied that we will never know for sure. But he did speculate that the father must have taken shelter in a house on the road Friday night or else he would have perished as well. In the narrated event, this deepens the father's sense of guilt when he returns home the next day to find his children missing; in the narrative event it deepens our sense that the father is at least in part to blame. Indeed, in the first version of this story I recorded, in November 1998, Packy Jim mentions that the father was said to have been fond of drink and that this may explain why he stayed longer in the fair; that, however, was the only time I heard him mention this possibility. Whatever the reason for their separation, all of my recorded versions of this story include, usually as a coda, the image of James Roe McGrath—stone cutter and mason by trade—inscribing a headstone for his children. He gets no farther than "In Loving Memory" before being overcome by emotion, and the stone remains unfinished to this day.

Usually offered as an aside in the middle of the story or sometimes as an additional coda at the end, other pieces of complicating drama concern the father and amplify the gratuitousness of the tragedy. Apparently, Peggy and her brother took a more hazardous overland route home because her father forbade her to take a more traveled road that would have led her near the house of a young man of reportedly dubious reputation, who had wanted to elope with her. In fact, Patrick was allowed to the fair in part as a chaperone for Peggy, to help ensure that she did not stray from the approved path. As Packy Jim explained in a previous conversation:

> Well then, they could have come another way. But then on that road down there, there was a man lived—he was McGrath too—called James Davy McGrath. And he had been a sweetheart of this girl's, and the marriage was broken up because they had, uh, the father had a grudge against this chap.
>
> So then she was forbidden then to go in that direction lest they would meet or have any converse or anything like that. She wasn't to meet him *no more.*
>
> He was even supposed to say that he would rather see his daughter *dead* as married to James Davy, who was supposed to be what they call a small thief, you know, a petty thief. That's what he was supposed to be. I think that was the grudge that they had against him.
>
> Oh, I think that was right enough. He was supposed to say that he'd rather have his daughter dead as married on James Davy, and he *did* see her dead, *too.*
>
> That was the old story. I think it's right enough, too. (November 16, 1998)

Nothing doubles down on tragedy quite like the theme of star-crossed lovers and particularly star-crossed lovers faced with uncompromising parents. Over time several local accounts have focused attention on this twist to the tale. Pettigo policeman James Donoghue published a lengthy and rather florid poem titled "The Ballad of Peggy Roe" in the December 1935 *Garda Review* (reprinted in Hilley 1999:60–64).[2] The vast majority of the twenty-five eight-line stanzas deal with the yearnings of Peggy and James Davy (here named Padraig) to be together (e.g., "With her restless soul calling out to the East from a heart bereft of joy / Till in night's release her dreams found peace in the arms of her mountain boy"); their hopes being dashed by Peggy's implacable father (e.g., "My daughter fair will never I swear, a moonlight robber wed / No, never I vow, right here and now, I'd rather behold her dead."); and her lover's frantic search for Peggy on the moorland (e.g., "Where, where cruel snow is my own Peggy Roe / O cold desert, where is my love?"). The final stanza includes the death scene and suggests again that Peggy died trying to save her younger—here unnamed—brother:

> Bare, frozen and still on the cold lap of earth and Carrickaholten her bed,
> To the broad light of day on the wasteland she lay, stretched frozen-limbed,
>> motionless, dead.
> And clutched at her bosom, companioned in death, his head pillowed deep
>> on her breast,
> In her great mantle clad, the tender young lad lay peacefully taking his rest.

The star-crossed lovers theme and the father's interdiction that forced the siblings to the mountain route also feature prominently in the compressed ten sentences of a commemorative plaque recently placed at Lettercran Chapel. Likewise, both elements of the story feature in a pair of relatively recent local history articles. One, "The Story of Peggy Roe" by Charles McGlinchey, appeared in the 1996 volume of *Aghyaran* (the parish magazine of Packy Jim's neighbors across the border in County Tyrone). Another is an anonymously authored chapter, "The Tragedy of Peggy Roe," in the 1999 book *Lettercran: An Illustrious Past, an Uncertain Future*, edited by James Hilley. Both accounts acknowledge consulting with Packy Jim.

In another medium, local historian Danny Gormley of Ederney, County Fermanagh, with the help of videographer Noel Grainger, interviewed Packy Jim for a 1994 video in private circulation titled "The Snow Storm of 1848: A Tragedy Remembered." Packy Jim's version of the story on this video includes all the elements, in the same order, as the versions I have recorded, with one exception. He mentions that an older woman living nearby had heard the cries of the children and left out a shovel of embers as a beacon, being unable to brave the storm herself. The video also includes a section in which Danny Gormley and the late Mickey Hegarty exhibit and discuss the aluminum Celtic cross they constructed and placed at the location where Peggy and Patrick were found, a site now in Carrickaholten Forestry, maintained by the Northern Ireland Forest Service. The cross replaces two stone slabs that were laid at the site not long after the tragedy but have since subsided and become overgrown. The cross includes a plaque reading: "Two children died on this mountain in a snowstorm. They were Margaret McGrath, aged 17, and her brother Patrick, aged 14. Their bodies were found at this spot on 18/1/1848."

If we want to appreciate the relevance of this place-world to Packy Jim or to others, it seems natural to search for meaning in the story texts, as told

Memorial cross for Peggy and Patrick McGrath

in numerous versions, with all their associated asides and codas. But of course the meaning, function, and affect of any given narrative can be as various as the discursive contexts in which it is deployed. Depending on who's speaking to whom, when, where, how, and to what ends, the story of Peggy Roe could serve equally well as a relatively neutral chronicle of past happenings in a particular locale, or as a more charged story of desperation during the height of the Famine, or as a warning for parents both lax and iron-fisted, or as an indictment of societal norms concerning familial and gender relations, or as a singer's gloss on similar tragic events in a popular local ballad such as "The Little Penknife." In telling the story to me, Packy Jim's rhetorical intent and by extension the text differed only slightly from context to context. The first time I recorded the story it emerged during an open-ended interview in which we poured over an Ordnance Survey map of the area. Place may have brought the story to mind, but once he launched the story, the emotional impact revolved around the senselessness of the tragedy and the moral righteousness of Peggy Roe's actions. At other times, Packy Jim rehearsed the story to provide background for his account of a later encounter with the ghosts of Peggy and Patrick (discussed in chapter 5); to offer a gloss on the less virtuous behavior of teenagers today, in comparison to Peggy Roe; in response to my requesting local history to enlighten visitors I had brought to meet him; and finally in response to my direct request for him tell the story on a video made for my teaching purposes. The prompt for each recorded version was either external, to greater or lesser extent from me, or internal, from him responding thematically to preceding conversation. But each time he included the same elements, in the same order, and the impulse for telling the story was commemorating both tragedy and virtue.

We can review emphases and surmise intended meanings from the texts themselves and from how they are shaped and used in context, but I am also in a position to ask Packy Jim directly: why are you drawn to the Lonely Hill and to the story of these McGrath youngsters?

> Because. It's so sad. Sad, sad, *sad*. That's the appeal it would have with me, and put it that way.
> No, it's *heart*breaking, like, the more we're told, this is a world of miseries and suffering and bad things happening to good *people*.

So you can relate, I ask.

> Well . . . I never had a sister died, or a child died, but I know the kind of world we're living in.

Like, we have to live our lives, and suffer—as the saying goes—so
many miseries that's in it. And then, at the end of the day, and if you
get older—as the saying goes—you're seeing it more clearly, you suffer
the death then—as the saying goes—do you understand.

But for it to come to them so young—no, couldn't be more of a
tragedy. But that's—as the saying goes—that's the world we're living in.
(August 31, 2007)

The story establishes and reminds Packy Jim of the prospect, maybe even
inevitability, of tragedy in this world. He knows the kind of world we are living
in, as illustrated so well by this story. One begins to sense the existentialist's
stance on events as arbitrary, even meaningless, unless and until one imposes
meaning on them. As usual, one imposable layer of meaning for Packy Jim
reflects a vision of one's moral responsibility to others.

When I asked if anything else makes this place-world resonant for him,
Packy Jim pointed out what for him is most obvious but cannot be overlooked:
Peggy's sacrifice. As Packy Jim contends, Peggy's giving up her outer garments
in trying to save her brother's life is evidence that she was "something of a
saint." As a boy, Packy Jim recalls, he considered Peggy a role model.

If Peggy Roe McGrath is readily cast as an exemplar of self-sacrifice, altru-
ism, and familial duty, Packy Jim is not alone in seeing pedagogic potential in
this story. For example, a late nineteenth-century schoolbook that Packy Jim
owns and occasionally reads for entertainment includes a lesson titled "A Sister's
Love," inspired by the story of Peggy Roe. ("A Sister's Love" is also the title of
the Peggy Roe McGrath plaque at Lettercran Chapel.) In addition, my former
County Tyrone neighbor Danny Gallen has an undated taped copy of a radio
interview with the Lettercran-born local historian John Cunningham. At the
culmination of the program, the radio announcer sums up in didactic terms
for children the significance of Peggy giving her petticoat and shawl to her
brother:

On the Lonely Hill she had tried to save his life by giving up everything
that could have saved her own. . . . Most boys and girls agree that the story
deserves to be preserved in a book where they can read it often. They
may not have occasion to give their lives to save the lives of others, but
in smaller matters they will often be able to relieve the distress of others
by giving up some comfort of their own. When such occasions come,
perhaps they may sometimes think of Peggy Roe McGrath.

Certainly a book is one option for preserving the story of Peggy Roe as homily,
and now there are several written and audio-visual representations, from the

The view toward Carrickaholten, now covered by forestry

nineteenth century to the present, to choose from. For Packy Jim, however, reader though he may be, the landscape—traveled in mind and body, made meaningful as place through association and sentiment—remains a primary archive for stories worth knowing.

Whereas the story of Peggy Roe offers both the compelling pathos of tragedy and an uplifting, redemptive portrait of moral behavior to be emulated, certain sites on the landscape serve as continual reminders of the darker side of human behavior. One advantage place-worlds have over published representations is that—being conjured orally, customized for specific face-to-face interactions, not necessarily open to all—there is greater potential for personalization and revision, greater candor or secrecy.

One need not range far from the Lonely Hill to encounter a place-world that reminds Packy Jim of humanity's fallen nature and particularly of treachery and the cardinal sin of avarice. In the same townland of Carrickaholten, the moral themes of biblical stories about Cain and Abel and about Jezebel resonate powerfully at a certain site where a man, evicted through the duplicity of his brother and sister-in-law, was forced to build a makeshift sod house. This he later abandoned to emigrate to Australia sometime in the 1860s. A house that no longer stands—like the emigrant long dead and his descendants scattered across a far continent—is a significant absence that creates its own presence in a landscape of moral testimony.

The circumstances leading up to the Carrickaholten eviction are not widely known today, and Packy Jim fears that circulating the story without sensitivity could cause offense. Some stories are tellable but not to all or at least not without care, especially when the descendants of those portrayed are still living. At Packy Jim's request, I have changed the names and omitted other identifying markers. I also quote alternately from more than one version of the story for the sake of clarity and coverage. I start with a telling from August 2007.

There was a *dirty* story in our *own* country, not a mile, not a mile from where you sit, concerning two brothers, and one brother's *wife*.

They lived up there in that house up there that you pass when you come in here, where you see [. . .]

Danny McFadden, they called him. And he married a lady called Cassie McCrory, and the two went up there to *live*.

And then, out the lane a wee bit farther—by that sharp turn in the lane there, where the sally bushes is—was another farm and another house and another brother, *Barney* McFadden. And we may presume a wife and maybe a family.

So Cassie, and the man I suppose, thought, "We haven't a big enough farm. We could do with a lot more land. We haven't near enough."

So they cooked a *plot*, that they would have a go at removing the brother from his place, then they'd get it.

Well the *brother* was a man that was out *shooting*, as they called it, *poaching*, you know—hares, rabbits, grouse, and all them things. All was the landlord's property and a tenant dare not kill *one* of them. If you were out with your greyhound or whatever at it, that was all right, but if you were *caught*, it was a breach of the *law*.

So Barney McFadden was caught poaching, and he got a fortnight—or something like that—in jail.

And he was put into jail for his poaching business, and uh, we'll say, for example, he was to get out on a *Friday*—out of jail on a Friday, land home on a Friday.

So they [Danny and Cassie] had a stack of turf of their own—some road or another, not far away—a turf stack of their *own*. So they lit the turf stack and burned it on the Friday night to get it blamed on *him*.

But then unfortunately for them, he didn't get out until the next day. It was the next day he got *back*. So that *fell through*. I don't know what proceedings was taken, but that *fell through*.

Then they hatched another plan. They had two plots of lint—Barney had a plot of lint, Danny had a plot of lint.

Lint was a thing that you grew, and then you threshed it, and it was great for putting on the roof—thatching roofs—because it lasted for a very long, long, long *time*—maybe thirty years or *more*.

So anyway, possibly the two plots of lint wasn't put in maybe in the one week. Could have been maybe a fortnight or three weeks between the planting, which when the lint would grow up would show up in the crop, like, you know—the *earlier* crop, the *later* crop. (August 31, 2007)

Here I switch to an earlier, slightly more elaborate version of the story, picking up at the same point in the action. Note Packy Jim's return to direct discourse in dramatizing Cassie's scheming, a narrative strategy not unlike that of Basso's (1996) Western Apache place-makers bringing past action into the present. As Gary Butler (1990:118) and Elliott Oring (2008:154) observe more generally, quoted speech and dramatization are common rhetorical techniques in the performance of legends and other stories that make claims to truth.

So they'd both patches of lint, and Cassie, she says till her man, "Right, me and you will go up the hill, to the hollow that's on the hill, and you lie down there. I'll take a couple of stripes of this lint with me. I'll tie your two hands like that behind your back, tie your feet at the ankles, and I'll go away and I'll leave you. And then after a time, then I'll get a search up. And I'll be out of course myself searching, and I'll get you. Well, then you say then, you met your brother on the mountain, and yous had a tussle, and he tossed you—he overcome you—he tossed you. He tied you up with these two stripes of lint, and he left you to die. That'll be a case we'll have again' him!"

So, she did get out and about, and whatever other folks was around about on the search as well. I suppose she got him herself. Them that . . . as they say, *them that hides knows where to FIND.*

So Danny was *got* and his story was:
"I was out on the hill.
I met my brother.
We had a tussle.
He overcome me.
He tied my hands to my feet, and I suppose he left me here to die.
Only by good luck I was *got*."
That was the *story*.

But it went to the *law*, took it to the *law*. I suppose, well, Barney was denying it, naturally enough, when confronted.

And the *law* in them days wasn't so very slack. They took a sample of
your *woman's* lint, and they took a sample of the *brother's* lint, and the two
didn't correspond. It would have been planted maybe a fortnight to one,
and it would be a fortnight or three weeks earlier than the other, do you
know. They didn't correspond, and I'm damned but they lost that. That
fell through. That was made out to be, you know, a *scheme* or a *fallacy*.

But, them two plans not working, they must have tried some other
plan. What that plan was I don't know, but it finished out that Barney
had to leave his house on the lane side, go away about a quarter of a
mile away—it wasn't a far flit—into the County Tyrone.

And he built himself a wee hut of a house with sods out on the
Carrickaholten side, up there where them big bushes is growing tall now,
and spent three years there in a sod house.

And then him and the wife then made it away then on a cheap, on a
cheap trip to Australia. Away till Australia—emigrated till Australia—aye,
on a free emigration or a cheap emigration till Australia.

But, uh, Cassie did succeed in that. And that's how that farm comes
to be the one farm today, Barney's and Danny's.

Oh, *damnable*. (November 16, 1998)

In versions of the story from May 1999 and November 2011, Packy Jim adds
that Danny and Cassie ended their lives in great debt. Moreover, he mentions
that at the time of these deeds the story circulated widely enough for the local
priest to speak out from the altar against the perpetrators, cursing their crimes
as sinful. As Packy Jim sums up their moral failings: "Old greed. Old greed.
That's what was at the back of it. Damnable, deadly sin. *Avarice*, a lust for
worldly things! That's what did them in."

Although Packy Jim acknowledges that Cassie and Danny were in these
schemes together, he consistently portrays the woman as the greater instigator
and mastermind. Note also that in the first sentence he introduces this "dirty
story" as one about two brothers and one brother's *wife*, using greater emphasis
and volume in intoning "wife," which comes at the culmination of the sentence.
The first instance of direct discourse—"We haven't a big enough farm"—
seems to be attributed to Cassie, with a supposition that Danny is in agreement.
Plotting the second scheme to evict Barney is rendered speculatively but entirely
in reported speech, quoted from Cassie's mouth. Indeed, when Danny is
"found"—"them that hides knows where to FIND"—he speaks for himself in
direct discourse for the first time. But as Packy Jim performs it, Danny expresses
himself staccato in short, simple sentences as if trying to remember his wife's
instructions. Indeed, his speech matches her scheme bullet point by bullet

point. But the law is not "so slack" in comparing the length of the flax stalks from the two farms, and it is consistent and telling that Packy Jim says that they "took a sample of your *woman's* lint" rather than "Danny's lint" or "Danny's and Cassie's" lint. Indeed, in the end, Packy Jim says that Cassie, rather than Danny and Cassie, succeeded in evicting Barney.

Arguably Danny is the more despicable of the two schemers, having betrayed his own brother. But in rural Ireland, as elsewhere, there is also an already established sexist framework in which Cassie is likely to be understood as an untamed shrew, a tricky and rapacious Jezebel. Danny is to blame for not reining her in; he has failed in his masculine role. But Cassie is perhaps all the more deviant for wanting to wear the pants in the family. Such a framework may help explain why she may be portrayed by generations of storytellers as the more culpable of two guilty parties.

It is difficult to say for sure what, if anything, this characterization of Cassie McFadden as villain says about Packy Jim's attitude toward women, and misogyny is too serious a charge to be leveled without hard evidence. There are, of course, fully realized misogynists in the world—as well as fully realized racists, xenophobes, and so on—but most people cannot be labeled categorically as either misogynist, racist, xenophobic, or not. Any fear of and hostility toward difference is an ideological stance and behavioral option open to everyone (and probably taken by most people at some point given certain circumstances). I suggest, however, that doing so is contextually determined rather than categorically consistent, more often than we think.

For all we know, Packy Jim's characterization of Cassie McFadden may be accurate, though of course this cannot be proved, and historical accuracy is not our primary concern. More likely perhaps, Packy Jim's characterization is faithful to the story as he received it from others, notably his mother. Of course, coming from his mother does not prove or disprove misogyny either, and as always with storytelling there is room for shaping received wisdom to meet personal need or orientation. Likewise, there is room for shared expectations and habitus to skew both the received and re-created narrative in a misogynistic direction, shifting blame as it were at least partly from the individual to society.

The ambitious, man-manipulating female protagonist is no doubt well established, from the Bible (Eve, Jezebel) to Shakespeare (Lady MacBeth, Gertrude) and beyond (Scarlet O'Hara, Livia Soprano). Still, a repertoire-wide perspective on Packy Jim is relevant here. As I have shown, there is evidence that he is not categorically hostile toward or threatened by women. Certainly he holds particular female characters in contempt, especially for immoral behaviors. But note also his attachment to his mother, as well as his sincere admiration of Peggy Roe as heroine and exemplar of moral behavior. Consider his stiff critique of the Church for its negative attitudes toward and repressive treatment of women. Granted, his most praiseworthy women do seem to fit a certain mold—nurturers, from Peggy Roe, to his mother, to Holy Mary, Mother of God—and that mold is a well-established aspect of the gendered status quo.

Packy Jim is not actually on trial for misogyny—at least this is not my intention—but one cannot help but see a connection here between not only Cassie McFadden and Eve or Lady MacBeth but also between Cassie and other women in Packy Jim's wider repertoire of traditional and personal narrative. By the same token, one cannot help but see a connection between these bad women and bad men in Packy Jim's wider repertoire. Of course, gender cannot be ignored, and it is likely the case that in Packy Jim's mind women who fail as selfless nurturers are particularly despicable. But for Packy Jim a major common denominator in immoral behavior—committed by women and men—is selfishness, greed, and a willingness to use treachery to get ahead at the expense of others in a world of limited good.[3]

Packy Jim calls this lethal combination "ambition." As he begins a December 1998 version of the eviction story, "She was very ambitious and the man be'd to be as *bad*." How interesting that in Packy Jim's worldview, ambition is a moral failing in the same constellation with the sins of avarice and deception. Ambition as bad simply does not compute for a number of Americans and, I am sure, for a number of Irish men and women as well. But I relate; I feel that I know where Packy Jim is coming from. The merits of ambition and competition were often a point of contentious debate between me and my father—both a good man and a good capitalist, confident in the American dream and unlimited opportunity. But Packy Jim's experience has been nothing like my father's, and so he has internalized instead a vision of a world of limited good where the advancements of one person often entail the diminishment of others (see in particular chapter 7).

In November 2011, having recently reviewed all previously recorded conversations, I pressed Packy Jim on his views regarding ambition. I suggested that many people, not least in the United States, value ambition, and I wondered if he thought that ambition is inherently a bad thing.

> Well, it's alright if you could gain and get what you wanted—as the saying goes—cleanly and honestly and without—as the saying goes—clipping somebody else's wings. When you're young, I mean, it's all right when you're young—or even when you're not so young—to have an ambition if you have a family to leave it till. But when you come till, we'll say, fifty-five or sixty years of age and you've damned the one at all to leave anything till, I think it about time to—as the saying goes—to forget about ambition, when you've nobody to leave it till. (November 15, 2011)

For Packy Jim, ambition leads to material gain; there is an "it" produced that will be left to some but not others, rightly or wrongly. Seeking a way to be in agreement with me, qualifying his position, Packy Jim allows that ambition serving a higher cause—such as financial security for one's family—is permissible. He cites his parents' struggles to make and save money, to leave something to help him in the future. Striving, however, should not be for the sake of gain, in and of itself. Striving and gain, beyond a certain point, is questionable, possibly immoral, because ambition leads to competition and competition involves winners and losers. More simply, ambition leads to competition and creates losers where there had been none before. So, to act morally one cannot advance one's own interests and livelihood while impeding or precluding the interests and livelihoods of others.

As a follow up I asked whether it is possible to avoid such conflicts of interest altogether, to which he replied, "It's rare enough, I suppose." So ambition remains suspect, I pressed. "It does. It does. I have my doubts. You chat about ambition . . ." Here Packy Jim launched into two unpublishable anecdotes about a local cattle dealer who got ahead at the expense of his neighbors, including Packy Jim's parents, with shady deals and broken promises of payment. I responded by making a connection from the ambitious cattle dealer to Cassie and Danny McFadden, both scheming to prosper at the expense of others. From there I made a connection to Packy Jim's previous accounts of Lucifer as the personification of ambition run amok. Packy Jim nodded vigorously. "That's right, that's right," he said.

I further made a connection to a book I had given Packy Jim as a gift, Michael MacGowan's *The Hard Road to Klondike* ([1962] 2003), the autobiographical account of a Donegal emigrant who survived the cut-throat, profit-driven world of mining and prospecting camps across North America of the late 1800s. I even took off on a tangent describing the major plot points of the HBO series *Deadwood*, which evokes an even starker cut-throat, profit-driven world. Circling back—a bit regretful for having monopolized that part of the conversation—I tried to summarize my point: "Anyway, so given what you've told me about ambition, and where it gets you, what, uh, what it does—can do—in the world, it seems to me that that world of *The Hard Road to Klondike*, or *Deadwood*, that would be something like your worst *nightmare*." Packy Jim erupted with a surprised laugh, then added, smiling and in rapid fire, "Aye! Aye, aye, aye, aye, *aye*. So. That's so, that's so, that's *so*!"

Packy Jim is clear in his thinking about ambition, which developed long before my presence. But in an effort to be reflexive, I have to consider that my status as an American and a descendant of Irish emigrants may have been relevant to our present and previous conversations. In Packy Jim's world, ambitious people leave for Scotland, England, America, Canada, and Australia either to make their fortunes or to fail. Those who never leave may be judged as lacking in ambition, especially when compared to the few who do well enough to return. A popular cycle of jokes and anecdotes about Americans and especially the obnoxious Returned Yank—the Irish emigrant who returns to boast of success—certainly speaks to the ambivalence and sensitivity of those left behind (Cashman 2008b:124–129). While I hope I am not guilty of the worst excesses of the Returned Yank, the fact of my Irish Americanness remains, and Packy Jim may be all the more motivated, consciously or unconsciously, to mount an implicit defense of his staying put. Stories of overweening ambition cast as moral failing would readily serve that function. When his mother cried at hearing his plans to emigrate to Scotland, Packy Jim sold his suitcase and stayed home out of a sense of filial duty. He is not one to turn on his own family as a more ambitious person might, as Danny and Cassie McFadden did.

Barney McFadden's sod house in Carrickaholten may be long gone, but that place-world nonetheless stirs Packy Jim to evaluation and knowledge. The wages of sin—ambition, greed, betrayal—are inscribed in the landscape. With a proposition about humanity's darker side established, Packy Jim knows what is possible and what he may expect from life in dealing with others. By extension, through a negative example, Packy Jim is reaffirmed in a moral code founded on obligation to others, especially kin, and including an imperative not to out-strip one's neighbor in social advancement and material wealth. In not striving beyond what is necessary to live, one hope is to avoid exacerbating a status quo in which there is already a stark contrast between the haves and the have-nots. There will always be landed gentry on the hill, rich merchants in the town, and well-to-do politicians in far-off cities, but among one's own neighbors of small farmers and laborers—neighbors of roughly the same socioeconomic class—excessive striving is a threat to shared equalitarianism and community equilibrium.[4]

Of course, the stories surrounding Peggy Roe McGrath and the McFadden eviction are not the only emplaced stories that map for Packy Jim a range of moral codes, ideological orientations, and existential variables to contemplate. Other examples of place-lore or dinnseanchas are relevant to previous and sub-sequent chapters, so they are addressed more fully there. Note, however, the range of themes to which additional place-worlds bear witness for Packy Jim: the tragedy of accidental or otherwise needless deaths; infidelity and betrayal within married and other close relationships; the complexity and calamity of sectarian division; the depredations, indifference, and self-interested or seem-ingly arbitrary directives of ruling elites; the scandal of neighborly material conflicts leading to violence and even murder; and as always for Packy Jim, the tension between rule following and transgression. With the exception of emplaced stories about needless deaths—these underscore the arbitrary and ultimately tragic nature of life—the majority of these stories serve as a personal social critique, focusing attention on human behavior that may be judged worthy of emulation or, more often, the opposite. Taken as a whole, these emplaced stories testify to, as Packy Jim says, "the kind of world we're living in." Moreover, Packy Jim derives from these stories support for his own moral code and the conceptual materials for constructing a self, grounded in a sense of place. Packy Jim's personal identity is locally sourced and assembled, founded on values indexed throughout his surrounding landscape.

5

Place, the Supernatural, and Cosmology

For all the perspective that emplaced historical legends offer us on Packy Jim, his moral orientation, epistemology, and cultural and historical surround, there are other stories—no less deeply rooted in place—that point us in other directions. Specifically, my chorographic approach to landscape, narrative, and memory so far has not yet embraced stories of supernatural encounters. I am thinking about his stories of supernatural encounters right here at this very door, out there at the end of the lane, over where the lough meets the sluice gate, and so on. Neither has this chorographic approach accounted for Packy Jim's most expansive conceptualization of place, which extends beyond the here and now, a sense of place that is perhaps best discerned through stories of supernatural encounters.

The stories that I want to investigate here are ones Packy Jim "credits." That is, Packy Jim makes a distinction between what he takes to be factual stories of supernatural encounters (my focus here) and fictional stories that feature the supernatural but are told primarily for entertainment, negotiating belief, or social control (addressed in the next chapter). When asked if he had ever had a firsthand experience with the supernatural, Packy Jim was quick to say, "Oh, thank God, no!" So none of Packy Jim's stories are first-person memorates. But the legendary accounts he passes on are ones that come from what he takes to be credible sources and that meet his standards for coherence and internal logic. Furthermore, they both shape and articulate that part of his worldview concerning the supernatural generally and core conceptual fields including cosmology, teleology, and eschatology.

Looking to these stories as a whole, the supernatural figures include wraiths (locally pronounced "raths"), ghosts, and fairies. Differences between these beings can be delineated as we progress, but according to Packy Jim the common denominator is that they are all spiritual beings who can take physical form temporarily in this material creation. Moreover, they all belong primarily in an immaterial spiritual world Packy Jim refers to as "beyond" and "parallel to" this one. In certain places and at certain times, however, these spiritual beings make their presence known. Having crossed a boundary, wraiths, ghosts, and fairies may be out-of-place in this material world, yet their presence confirms a sense of place that includes both this world and the next. Moreover, signs of the Otherworld in this world point to a divine plan.

Part of that plan is the inevitability of death. Eventually we all cross that ultimate border between life and death, but some have warning of the day when that journey will begin. Throughout Ireland the banshee (*bean sí* or "fairy woman" in Irish) is the best-known harbinger of death (see Lysaght 1996). As Packy Jim describes her, "You see, the banshee is a spirit, associated with the fairies. It never had a body, but sometimes it can appear as a little old woman combing her long hair, sad and weeping, weeping bitterly." In some cases, the banshee is heard to cry out near the home of a person fated to die. In other cases, she wails and keens at the site of an impending death. Such was the case in 1913 when Tommy Haughey and Dennis McGrath heard the banshee the night before two Haughey children drowned in Lough Veenagreane. Packy Jim also relates the widespread belief—reflecting the banshee's origin in earlier Celtic mythology—that this spirit is connected in particular to old Irish families rather than to those of later English and Scottish Planters (see Lysaght 1996:56–60):

> See, they were the old Celtic race of people, too, the Haugheys. The banshee always keens for the Macs and the Os, people with the old Celtic names: O'Haughey, McGrath, and the like. Earlier the Haugheys had dropped the O from their name, but they were the same race of people the banshee follows. Oh, there's something to that, now.
> (December 1, 1998)

Messenger from the fairy Otherworld, intimate with the "old Celtic race of people," the banshee serves in many ways as a conceptual bridge between the worlds of human ghosts and alien fairies. There has long been in Irish folklore a lingering conflation of the fairy Otherworld with the pre-Christian Celtic concept of Tír na nÓg (Land of the Young), a timeless land where souls of the dead live in perpetual youth. As I will show later, it is not too far a step to further connect this older sense of the Otherworld with the later Christian vision of Heaven, Hell, and Purgatory.

The other well-known harbinger of death is the wraith, which like the banshee is a boundary-crossing spirit. As Packy Jim explains, wraiths are most closely associated with ghosts because both are temporary, visual, and even physical manifestations of a person's soul, independent of his or her body. The difference is a matter of timing. In his words:

> A wraith is a ghost of a person that you see afore they die. They're not dead. The spirit moves away from the body, some fashion or another. Like, the more a person's living, you could [still] see the wraith. And if the wraith's coming to you, they're going to be here living for a long time. And if the wraith's walking away from you, their death's supposed to be close. (August 15, 2007)

Over time, Packy Jim has told me stories of three wraiths seen in his townland, including one man who was seen by his neighbor walking toward him, carrying a lap of hay into a byre. The sighting was unremarkable until the neighbor discovered that the man in question was actually away at a fair that day. The neighbor was unsettled but took comfort in the fact that the wraith was approaching rather than walking away. Although the mysterious sighting took place around 1940, the man with the lap of hay did not die until 1982.

In another chilling account of a wraith, Packy Jim describes how a local man, who had emigrated, returns home:

> There was another old story—Paddy Morris told it, too—about some boy that was up Tieveeny Lane, and he'd been in America for maybe thirty or forty years.
>
> And it was give out that he was coming home on a certain date. We'll say, for example, the tenth of October: "He's coming home on the tenth of October."
>
> And there was a few locals—this was a thickly populated place at the time—a few locals in to welcome him, welcome him *home*.
>
> So, around about six or seven o'clock or thereaways, he did come in. And, I suppose, there was some talk, like, some talk or another. But there was no, like, uh, idea but he was real and he was there in the flesh and this and that and thon.
>
> But he was a *pipe* smoker, and he pulled out his pipe, and he filled the pipe, and he lit the pipe.
>
> But when it was all over and done with, they remarked that he had held the pipe in some kind of a *peculiar way*—now Owens's Packy could tell you that story better nor me.

But after a time, he riz and he walked out.

And seemingly, like, I mean, it wasn't in a place where there was any rocks or obstructions—you could see a person going away for a long, long distance. So after a time, they went out to look, and he was nowhere to be seen. That was the *rear of him*.

And the next word come home out of America was: your man was *dead*. (March 18, 1999)

Yet another wraith sighting comes from even nearer hand, within feet of Packy Jim's own door:

Well then, for good measure, there was supposed to be a wraith seen at this house *here*, away back by a previous occupier of this house, away back around about nineteen hundred and seven, or nineteen hundred and eight, or nineteen hundred and nine.

The woman of the house that was here, before my father and mother came to it—Mary McGrath, Pat McGrath's woman—she was supposed to look out *there* from that half door.

And down *there* at the end of that ditch there was a very large ash bush that grew *there*, a very big bush for a mountainy part—it was cut by the man in nineteen twenty-four for to keep the fire going in there, turf was scarce.

And she looked out in the evening time.

And there used to come a lady visiting here—she was called Margaret *McGreece*.

And your woman looked out, and at the root of that bush, standing there, within less nor a stone's throw of the door, doesn't Pat's woman see Margaret McGreece. She was supposed to be standing at the root of this ash bush down *there* at the corner of the street.

And when she didn't come in, or when she looked again and she wasn't there, well, you'd have knowed that there was something wrong. Only later did she hear the news: Margaret McGreece had died, died suddenly.

So that was one, like, that I had heared—as the saying goes—inside this house here when I was a young boy.

So that was—as the saying goes—close for comfort, *too* close for comfort.

Whether that story was true or not, I don't know, but she was seen *there* by Mary Hilley.

Aye.

That's a long time since I heared that. That was Frank McCanny's
story, I think. I don't forget it, but thanks be to God it doesn't annoy
me much anymore, do you understand? But when you're a *young boy*,
honest to God, after night in them days, I couldn't have went out of
that door there. If I was going to make my water, I would be damn sure
to be on this side of the door. (August 15, 2007)

According to Packy Jim, it is safe for me to use Margaret McGreece's name
because there are no close living relatives who might be upset. Generally the
wraiths and ghosts of near neighbors are a sensitive topic, and at his request, I
cannot name most of those involved in these stories. Or as Packy Jim puts it
more directly, "Oh, Jimity God, you wouldn't want to be telling that one. I'm
telling it to you, but they would split you, about the road, if they heared that
one." Understandably, no one living wants to hear about sightings of his or her
wraith, and bereaved relatives could be troubled by the idea that their loved
ones' souls are not at rest.

A soul wandering, out of place, not at rest, is the essence of a ghost for Packy
Jim. That is, in his view, all humans have spirits that reside within our bodies and
endure after death. Some spirits or souls—he uses the terms interchangeably—
will leave the body before death temporarily as wraiths, but most souls leave
the body after death to go to Heaven, Hell, or Purgatory, depending on the
deceased's behavior during life. In a very few cases, an unfulfilled or frustrated
spirit will remain suspended in this material creation and be visible at least to
some as a ghost. A person who dies by suicide, murder, or tragic circumstance
is the most likely to haunt this world, often at the location of his or her untimely
demise.

Such is the case for the ghosts of Peggy and Patrick McGrath, who are
reported to have appeared at the lonely spot where they perished in the snow.
As Packy Jim remembers their first sighting:

Way back about eighteen fifty-five or eighteen sixty, there was cattle in
Carrickaholten and there was a bull with them. And these boys would
have been down about Lettercran there. He was Morris, a young chap,
Morris, and another neighbor, Haughey.

And they went out with a cow to the bull. It was in the dusk of the
evening, like. And they stopped when they got the length of the cattle,
and they laid down on a knoll, I think, or something like that, until the
bull would bull the cow.

And in the dusk, they thought they seen, like, the forms of two people coming, like, walking close to the other in the *distance*. It would have been about four or five years after these people was lost.

So, uh, of course it was an era when ghosts was the big, big thing all over Ireland.

So the one says to the other, "If it happened to be their *ghosts*, would you be *afraid?*" And the other be's, "Ah, damned a bit."

So just when they looked again, they were coming up quite close till them, within a stone throw of them.

So they took to their beaters and they never cried halt 'til they landed at home in Lettercran, I suppose left the cow there.

That's an old story about that, of one of the times they were seen. (November 18, 2011)

In the same manner, for over two centuries, several have claimed to encounter a ghost at Cushey's bridge in Cloghore townland, said to be the site where associates of the eighteenth-century highwayman Proinsias Dubh shot and killed a Protestant gentleman named Glendinning. More recent ghosts include that of a young woman accidentally drowned at another local bridge and that of a creamery manager who haunts his former home where he committed suicide in the face of mounting debt.

During one interview on an appropriately dark and stormy November afternoon in 2011, Packy Jim recounted a string of seven stories about ghosts said to haunt locations in the nearby vicinity. These accounts include too many identifying details to quote at length, with or without pseudonyms. But together they underscored the conception of ghosts established so far—unfulfilled disembodied souls, often lingering at the locations of their tragic deaths, having failed to fully make the ultimate transition from this material world to an afterlife located elsewhere. To this set of understandings, Packy Jim's string of ghost stories added the proposition that a troublesome ghost can be removed from this material world through an exorcism performed by a Catholic priest. Although Packy Jim reviewed the theories of local skeptics—including his father—who dismiss ghostly sightings as the delusions of the mentally weak or intoxicated, he maintained his belief in the core elements of most of these stories, bolstering them with biblical references and with similar ghost stories from across Ireland that he has read in *Ireland's Own*. Testament to the power of place-worlds, this string of stories ultimately leads Packy Jim to remark, as he had on previous occasions, that as a young boy he knew so many haunted locations across the landscape that traveling anywhere at night was a "crucifixion" and the "worst of all gauntlets to run."

It left you that if you were out in short days—it was dark when you were making your way home—it left you in a great, great *torture*. I was at different times caught out late at night on my way home, when damn all I could do only *come on*.

And then there were a ghost *here*, and a ghost *there*, and ghosts *thonder*!

And Christ, you couldn't come off the road either, you had to go the road, you couldn't be circuiting a way around and take—as the saying goes—you were taking pot luck.

Oh God, it was a wild, it was a *wild hardship*, till you got hardened up, like, after a time, whatever length of time that took that you didn't give a damn, like. Aye.

Oh, God of Almighty! (August 15, 2007)

Packy Jim's observations here suggest that there is room for different types and intensities of belief, especially during different phases of life, and I will return to this point in the next chapter. For now I can say that on that cold, wet November afternoon, Packy Jim's ghost stories and his childhood reminiscence of the "gauntlet" had effectively transported me to a ghost-haunted world, one not entirely relegated to the past. A faint clouded-over sun had set by 4:30—which is to say, before I began the muddy tramp back to my car, on a route that took me past more than one place-world Packy Jim had just conjured. Although I do not hold an uncomplicated belief in literal ghosts, it is safe to say that the right experience would un-complicate things for me rather immediately. I made the trek back in record time.

To this general profile, let us add a closer look at Packy Jim's most elaborate ghost story. First heard from Frank McCanny and recounted by other neighbors, the story of Bob Goudy's ghost is one that Packy Jim believes to be factually true and one that, being a part of his active repertoire, I have recorded on six occasions. The first recorded version I have, below, came during a string of stories about happenings in his townland, in anticipation of our walking out to visit these sights for me to take photos.

Up there, on that rock up there, that Carrickanowen rock, there was an old house there—thatched house—and it originally belonged to people the name of McGrath. And then people the name of Johnston got into it then, and they owned it for a length of time, and it finished up again that it was McGrath's *again*, and it's still McGrath's.

But Bob Goudy, he would have been a man from the County Tyrone country, as far as I know, and he would have been a poor man with a wife and some family. And he'd have been a youngish man in his early thirties and one of them homeless people known as, what they call, *squatters*. I presume a squatter, there.

So this man, woman, some family lived there, way back about, uh, before seventeen ninety-eight we'll say, about the mid-seventeen hundreds or there-a-ways.

And, uh, he *died* there. He went out one day—some business—and he took ill and he was got dead, lying on a rock outside the house.

And he was a Protestant man, and he was taken away till Carn Graveyard, which those people had taken over at that time, like, it's a mixed graveyard, Catholic and Protestant. And he was buried there.

Oh, the story is true.

So, uh, then, the wife lived for some time then, I suppose, hard put about. Wherever she moved to, no history doesn't record. But she was there, we'll say, for the fall and a few months.

So, anyway, this boy used to . . . well, they would have been living in poor conditions, the kids and the wife lying, I suppose, on the floor on *straw*. You know, like, poor primitive conditions of maybe two hundred years ago.

But *this boy's ghost* used to come, and somebody seen it, probably maybe the wife recorded it. But, uh, the childers, like, when they'd fall asleep, and their legs maybe would become exposed, you know, in cold weather, that he was seen till arrange clothing over the kids. His ghostly figure was seen to arrange clothes over the kids' feet or the kids' *body*.

That's part of the old story.

So, in any case, the woman left and went elsewhere, and her kids, and another man came on the scene named McSorley. He was a Catholic, and he belonged to a secret society called the Ribbonmen. He was a Ribbonman, so perhaps he was on the run from the English authorities. And perhaps he was a Tyrone man too—it's a Tyrone name largely.

And he came to it, and he was a big man and a strong man and a bit of a *boxer*. In other words, a character that didn't give a damn who he met, he feared *nobody*.

So he was living there in this place on his own. He had a rush candle on the hob, as they called it—sort of a place at the side of the fire—burning. And this figure came in the dark, at dusk, and it moved up the floor and it blew out the candle and it moved to the one *side*.

So he lit the candle again, according to the story, and the figure riz and moved forward, blew it out again. Second time, I suppose. We'll say the second time, anyway.

So your man lit it again, and he said, "Better not make that a habit," like, you know.

But no good, it was put out again. So he [Goudy] made the lunge for the boy [who] riz and blew it out again. So he made the lunge for him with his fists, like, to *hit him.*

And he claimed that when he hit him—there's what they call a wool sack, filled with wool, you know, it's soft and you can push into it with your fist or the end of a stick a little bit.

But he felt something, and that was the way he explained it: It was like hitting a bag of *wool*, a wool sack. And when he got the stroke back, it was like a *sledgehammer BLOW*, that way, from the ghost.

So presumably, that fight did not last too long, it was an unequal contest. Nobody said that, but I'm presuming it didn't last long.

And *then* the story that old Frank McElhill told here, from the Shanaghy country, was that, uh, McSorely was a broken man, and in less nor a year he was a *dead* man in some graveyard, as a result.

So I don't know *who* come after that, I'll not tell you. In these old mountainy parts, there was always somebody keen for a house and a roof and a place where they could grow a lock of spuds. *Somebody* must have come, and *this boy* must have been giving trouble still.

So they applied till our P.P. [parish priest] of—this parish used to be called Templecarn, it's now divided in two. We'll call this section of it now the Lough Derg Parish.

So they applied till the P.P of the parish till exorcise the ghost. And uh, the name of the parish priest, as far as I know, was Father Ryan, Father Neal *Ryan.*

So he said a Mass, presumably in Lettercran Chapel, or if Lettercran Chapel wasn't built at the time—I think it was built in eighteen thirty-four—there was a little lean-to that done for a chapel up on the far end of the graveyard.

But he said a Mass there, and old Charlie McCrory, a man who I knowed here in my younger days, his uncle, Tom Haughey, clerked the Mass. And after that, then, they left and they headed for the rock up there. And they exorcised the spirit, and they put it into the hole in the rock.

So that was *that*, anyway, on then till some time about the mid-eighteen hundreds, there was a big mansion of a two-story house built with a slate roof on it, what you photographed there some time ago. *It* was built there, and people the name of Gallaghers lived in it for a period of time. And then they left it, and it was people the name of Croziers lived in it for a length of time. And then they left it, and then the son of the builder, uh, went out to the back of the hill there and married a lady that lived back there called Rosie McCanny and they set up house *there*.

And according to the story that Big Packy McGrath told *me*—who was a considerable amount of a historian, too—that there was supposed to be rumblings and chairs rattling and strange noises about the new house, too. The chairs *rattling and RUMBLING*.

And they were attributing to the fact that maybe perhaps the ghost of Bob Goudy—that was put into the rock some, we'll say, two hundred yards below it—still wasn't—as the saying goes—properly *settled*.

That's the rear of that, like. Big Packy's dead now, but boy, I heard Big Packy at that, too. Like, I have a brave memory, and things like that'll fasci*nate* me. And God, you'd never forget it. No, you don't forget it.

But it's *true enough* now. That priest, Father Neal Ryan, exorcised that ghost. But seemingly it's not always permanent, as far as I'm told. No, not always permanent. (March 18, 1999)

Here we have a story of a frustrated soul, out of place, clinging to his last worldly abode. The ghost poignantly carries on his mortal fatherly role, then lashes out violently at interlopers who succeed his wife and family, to the point that he has to be exorcised. Interestingly, the exorcism of the ghost into a hole in a cairn of rocks proceeds with the perhaps unspoken understanding that this unhappy soul takes up space—indeed, he causes physical damage—and must be put in his proper place beyond. The cairn itself is reminiscent of burial mounds and other archaeological sites associated in folklore with the fairies and understood to be portals into the Otherworld, including the world of the ancestral dead. Goudy's later escape to haunt the house nearest the site of his former home casts the larger story as one of conflict over where the ghost—unfinished in his transition—ultimately belongs.

Other ghosts, on the other hand, appear content, even relieved, to complete their journey to the other side. Packy Jim tells another story of a neighbor who saw his brother, ten years dead, hurriedly walk past his door smiling to himself and muttering, "I'm away now, I'm away now, I'm away now," at which point he disappeared. Packy Jim interprets this—as do others—as a soul who has finally completed his time in Purgatory, off to meet his reward in Heaven.

Having crossed the ultimate border between life and death, ghosts and wraiths may persist on the wrong side of the divide between this world and the

The cairn into which Bob Goudy's ghost was exorcised

next. Fairies, on the other hand, seem to maintain outposts in this world and make frequent use of portals between their world and ours. Although Packy Jim considers the majority of his stories about fairies to be fictions best suited for children—many of them entertaining fantasies from and mementos of his mother—there are a handful of encounters with fairies at local sites that he considers genuine.

The nearest example of a fairy outpost and portal is Meenabol bush, a lone thorn tree near the shore of Lough Veenagreane where in the mid-1800s Packy Jim's great-grandfather, Hughie Bán McGrath, heard fairy music. Packy Jim warns that, whether you believe in fairies or not, you are best to tread lightly in such a place or to avoid it altogether, for the fairies are no more tolerant of intruders than Bob Goudy's ghost. As Packy Jim says,

Packy Jim at the fairy bush in Meenabol

I wouldn't let someone interfere, nor *I* wouldn't interfere with that
gentle bush, in case of some bad luck, maybe fall and break your leg or
maybe take some kind of an illness. You wouldn't know. You could
maybe damage that fairy thorn and *nothing* would happen, but you're
not going to take the *risk*. No, you wouldn't take the *risk*. It's too
dangerous. (August 15, 2007)

Packy Jim's most memorable and repeated example of bad luck befalling
those who interfere with the fairies came to him at a wake in Killeter more
than forty years ago. There he met but had trouble recognizing Johnny Neddy
McMenamin, one of his more distant relatives from Meenamullan in County
Tyrone. The word at the wake was that this man had cut down a fairy thorn
tree to clear one of his fields, and overnight his jet-black hair, beard, and eye-
brows fell out. Packy Jim was unsettled to see that only a few short wisps of
downy white hair had grown back on top of his head, while his face, like the
face of a young boy, was completely clear of any whisker shadow. Packy Jim
often follows and supports the veracity of this local story with another he read
in an *Ireland's Own* about a County Limerick farmer who became ill, along with
his family, after he leveled the remains of an Iron Age ring fort, considered to
be a home of the fairies.

While Packy Jim offers such stories as evidence of the continuing existence of fairies in recent times, his most intricate, nonfictional story about the fairies is his account of their origin. That story can be used to different rhetorical effects in different conversational contexts including—as we have seen in the 2002 version—establishing a proposition about the nature and pervasiveness of wickedness, declaring personal orientations to the world, and connecting thematically from mythic narrative to personal experience to critique of present-day society. Regardless of immediate performance contexts, illocutionary forces, and perlocutionary effects, however, all of Packy Jim's versions of the story draw their authority from their foundation in Judeo-Christian teleology, cosmology, and eschatology—established ideas about why we are here, how the universe is designed, and how it will all come to an end. This story is a primary vehicle for establishing, expressing, and contemplating worldview. Most relevant for the present argument, this story also serves to reconcile the disparate strands and characters discussed thus far in this chapter by tying them together—ghosts and fairies, humans and supernatural others, the material and the immaterial—into a broadly coherent but ultimately mysterious system.

Regarding Packy Jim's 2002 version of the origin of the fairies, discussed in the introduction, the audience likely had a primary effect on his using the story for double duty. Present were myself, my wife, with whom Packy Jim had spent relatively little time, and my mother-in-law, whom he had not met before. Establishing a presentation of self would be a natural inclination for any storyteller encountering a new audience, even if the immediate conversational thread—in this case, accounts of the fairies—did not necessarily foster personal narrative. An earlier version I recorded in 2000, however, comes during a one-on-one recording session, following a discussion of ghosts and his making a connection between ghosts and fairies as spiritual beings that can occasionally take material form. I asked Packy Jim directly for the origin of the fairies story, having heard him tell it previously when I was not recording. He offered the following, which sticks closely to the outlines and imagery of subsequent versions but focuses more on the eschatology and cosmology established by the War in Heaven, a system that simultaneously accounts for all spiritual and material beings—past, present, and future.

Well, God made Heaven and he made nine batches of angels, and they were termed "nine choirs"—that's my mammy's story as I heared it in me youthful days—and they were placed outside of heaven, like—you know?—on what they call a probationary period.

And there was no two of them the same; there were a difference between them like the stars in the sky. But the greatest angel of the lot was called *Lucifer*, now known as Satan.

This is the curiosity about religion, what some things . . . what religion has to say: I suppose, uh, we need not liken, liken, liken angels to humans, but we must—as the saying goes—for to put the point over, I must—as the saying goes—say it this way:

He took it in till his *head* that he was as good as *God*, do you understand? He was so *great*, he was so *POWERFUL*, that he took it in till his head that he was as good as *God*.

And then he organized some type of rebellion *against* God with the idea of over*coming* God, and got an immensity of angels to *follow* him. I suppose thousands of *millions* of *billions* of *TRILLIONS*, probably.

Well then, the good angels took God's side, and they were led by an angel called Blessed *Michael* the *Archangel*. They were on *God's* side.

And *then*, at that point then, *Satan* and his cohorts, as they say, were over*come*. And *Hell* was made, and *he* was put into Hell—him and all his angels was put into Hell—to suffer torments for their *insults*.

Well *then*, seemingly in the *middle* somewhere, there was an allotment of angels, didn't take God's side, they didn't take Satan's side, they remained *neutral*. And *they* were supposed to be known as the *fairies*, and they were cast on this earth *here*. With great power, *too*, do you understand. They weren't taken into *Heaven*, they weren't taken into *Hell*, because they'd taken *no sides*. They were the *neutral* angels.

That's the old *story*.

That's the old story that my *mother* told me. I think I heard it from Master Cunningham at school, too, if I'm not making a mistake; Master Cunningham one time said that, *too*. But I, like, it's a story I was *fascinated* by. If I was to live to be three *hundred*, I'd still *mind* it, do you understand.

Whether it's *real*, whether it's *not*, but I doubt it's at the roots, it's at the roots of our religion, if you go *deep*.

Well *then*, the good angels was taken into *Heaven*, at that point, and there was a *place* in Heaven for *every* angel. The *neutral* ones had become known as the *fairies*, and the devils went to *Hell*.

So *then*, God took it in till his head *again*—and putting it the rude way again—that, uh, it would be too bad for to have the place not half *full*. "I'll go about it again and I'll make another creation, but *it*'ll be a different *creation*."

And then this universe was made, and human beings were made— Adam and Eve to start off with. The human race were made. And then they were to live, as the saying goes, the good life—and say it that way— and *not* to die. You were to be taken from this world without suffering the *death*. And breed and breed and breed and breed, and cover the world over, and increase and multiply, and then when your station on this earth was over, you went into Heaven, and that went on, and on, and on, and on, and on, and on until Heaven was again *full*, that every place in Heaven was occupied. And then, at that point *then* [*claps his hands*] everything finished then. This place . . . come till an *end*.

That's the STORY.

I think, like, I mean, if you chat to a theologian, or you chat a, I think, any reasonably—to say it that way—educated clergyman should be fit to tell you the same as I'm telling you, and I'm *no* clergyman.

But uh, this place is supposed to go on until there's so many souls saved to occupy them places that were lost, and then this creation comes till an end.

That's the *story*, I think.

That's . . . I think even a Protestant theologian—any *Christian* theologian—will tell you the same thing as I'm telling you.

But my mother Maggie Gallagher was the first that I heared at that, and I think Master Cunningham was the next that I heared at that, too. Oh, that's going till the root of the faith. (July 4, 2000)

According to Packy Jim, then, the fairies are refugees from the original war in Heaven between Lucifer and God. In the beginning there was no material creation, only God, Heaven, and spiritual beings, the angels. After defeating Lucifer and his rebel angels, God cast them out of Heaven, creating the first new place, Hell, as their prison. In a sense, God then started a new project with yet another new place, this time a material creation—the earth, a home for humanity. But the angels who took neither side in the rebellion were a lingering problem; they were neither good enough for Heaven nor bad enough for Hell. These neutral angels he cast to the earth where, diminished in status but clutching residual powers, they became known as the fairies. Suspended between Heaven and Hell, the fairies are doomed to share earth with humanity, a punishment in that there is no one they envy more. For if we follow God's law on earth, at death our souls ascend to Heaven to take the places vacated by the fallen angels. Once Heaven is filled to capacity with deserving spiritual beings, time and this material world will end and the Heavenly Kingdom will be complete. Until this time, peevish, harassing fairies express their resentment, having forfeited the opportunity we enjoy to transcend the material world and become one with God.

For my purposes here, one thing to take away from this origin myth is that it establishes a system in which all spiritual and material beings play a role. That is, here is a grand narrative with a beginning-middle-end trajectory into which all the characters discussed so far fit. In a sense, ghosts and fairies are the out-of-place leftovers, the remnants and remainders that point to the very existence of the system. In being out of place in this world, signs of the Otherworld nonetheless point to divine order; they are the exceptions that prove the rule. Wraiths and banshees evidence the spiritual world and our inevitable crossing from this world to the next. Ghosts represent something like the cross current of an eddy in the flow of deserving souls from this material creation to Heaven. The material creation of the earth is a testing ground for humanity, a place apart where we either fail or succeed in returning home to Heaven, thereby filling the chasm left by the sin of pride and the original rebellion against God's intended hierarchy and cosmological order. And as we toil we are surrounded by harassing fairies, something like flunkies from God's original test; like ghosts, fairies serve as proof that we must conform to God's will or suffer similar exile and untenable suspension between worlds.

If, however, ghosts and fairies, wraiths and banshees, seem to comprise a coherent system, individual encounters nonetheless point toward mystery. On the one hand, Goudy's ghost and the fairies who took revenge for the loss of their tree seem to be endowed in narrative with psychological realism, a reasonable, emotional motivation for causing trouble for interlopers. But on the other hand, we cannot predict whose wraith will wander and how, whose death will be foretold and when, who will see whose ghost and where. We cannot know when fairies will let their music fill the night air or when they, like dispossessed bandits, will raid our hearths and homes. Individual encounters come as a shock while pointing to a larger system that we cannot entirely know or control. Cosmology, God's order of things, can be grasped in outline, suggested by uncanny events. The eruptions of ghosts and fairies into our world are not breakdowns in the system, flaws, or glitches; rather, they are design features. In the end, however, the system allows for mystery rather than mastery.

Bringing us back to where we started, the ultimate order of things, evidenced by supernatural encounters, shrouded in mystery, undermines a narrow sense of place that includes only the here and now. Ghosts, wraiths, and fairies may be nothing new in the study of Irish folklore or, more broadly, European folklore. Yet so far I have approached the topic not searching for a perspective on belief but rather building on what we have already established about Packy Jim's sense of place. Certainly his local historical legends tied to place provide many revealing dramas about social behavior and offer us a glimpse into his moral perspectives. I find it thrilling to think of landscape and place as a vast mnemonic device for contemplating morality. And yet emplaced stories of the supernatural bursting into everyday life revolve around location and dislocation in telling ways. Emplaced and displaced, material and spiritual beings interact in narratives revealing a broader sense of place that extends beyond immediate visible surroundings and shifts our focus from the here and now to the immaterial and visionary. Likewise, exploring this strand of Packy Jim's repertoire extends sense of place inquiry from its customary associations with morals, values, and identity to the broader issues of cosmology, teleology, and eschatology.

6

Belief and Skepticism

On a blustery gray February day in 1999—early in our recorded sessions—I reached Packy Jim's place, eager for more conversation, an hour earlier than my usual arrival around noon. He was in the process of making tea. Waiting for the turf to flame up and boil the water in his soot-darkened kettle, Packy Jim told me of his latest affliction. He lifted his shirt to show me a rash on his chest, and recalled going to see Agnes Lunney in Segronan townland, County Tyrone, for a cure. Agnes, Packy Jim told me, inherited the cure for shingles from her mother in the countryside near Ederney, County Fermanagh.

During his visit, Agnes had mixed something green—herbs, Packy Jim presumes—into butter that she then used as a topical ointment three times, saying, "In the Name of the Father, and of the Son, and of the Holy Spirit" with each application. She then sent him home with three pats of the specially treated butter, wrapped in paper, and a photocopied instruction sheet with hand-written times for application:

USE TONIGHT BEFORE_____6 p.m.
AGAIN AFTER_____12.30 a.m.
TOMORROW NIGHT BEFORE_____6 p.m.

Her verbal instructions were to rub one pat upwards on the rash while invoking the Trinity, followed by making the Sign of the Cross, then to repeat this sequence with the other two pats.

Packy Jim said he felt better now with his rash in retreat, thanks be to God. Then he followed Agnes's final instruction by throwing the unused ointment, along with the instruction sheet, into the fire. As the paper lit and the remaining nubs of butter sizzled, I started to reach for the day's finding list in my pocket notebook (it concerned the Troubles and local history), but I left it there, sensing that perhaps Packy Jim already had an agenda for the day. He mentioned that the water in St. Patrick's Well in Magherakeel, County Tyrone, is known to have healing powers, which reminded him of his mother getting relief there and at Knock for her sore hip.[1] And we were off. The rest of the day's conversation ranged over cures, holy wells, ghosts, fairies, and more generally over the mysterious side of life.

The time was right to delve more deeply into what Packy Jim believes, does not believe, or entertains concerning that which may be deemed supernatural, numinous, otherworldly, or simply—noncommittally—mysterious or "queer." Declarations, discussion, and particularly narrative concerning the mysterious side of life all point to a significant portion of Packy Jim's worldview. One thing is clear: Packy Jim believes. He believes in his guardian angel and the power of prayer. He believes that humans can channel divine power to heal others—through the ritual application of medicinal plants God left for us, through the wells the saints blessed in His name—even if he does not consistently follow every tenet of the earthly institutionalization of Christianity. He believes in spirits and supernatural forces, even if he does not credit every story—or every element of every story—told about them.

For the possibility of ghosts, Packy Jim looks to biblical evidence, particularly to the resurrection of Christ.[2] He is particularly attentive to the account in the Gospel of John in which Christ, post-Resurrection, takes on material form—as ghosts and fairies do, according to Packy Jim—to satisfy the doubting Apostle. Packy Jim uses Christ's exhortation to Thomas—"Blessed are they that have not seen, and yet have believed" (John 20:29)—to endorse his own faith in ghosts despite not having seen one himself.[3] Bob Goudy remains his most elaborate local ghost story, and this one validates and is validated by several sightings of other local ghosts and wraiths. To explain why not everyone has seen ghosts or wraiths, Packy Jim cites his mother's understandings that certain people—children, those born at night, those born into certain more sensitive families—are more likely to see them.

Asked about fairies, Packy Jim says directly, "Some might laugh, but I believe that the fairies exist. That's what I think. That's what a lot thinks." He connects them to foundational Judeo-Christian myth, as we have seen, and for local evidence he turns to Meenabol bush, where his great-grandfather heard fairy music, and to his cousin who lost his hair after cutting down a fairy thorn. *Ireland's Own* magazine provides him several other stories he counts as evidence of the fairies, including the story of a disbelieving County Limerick farmer who, despite warnings, quarried stones from a fairy fort and took ill along with the rest of his family in the 1920s.

I would be inclined to credit that as genuine, surely. That they took the bad flu and wouldn't mend and couldn't mend, and the neighbors advising to not touch it, and he scoffed at that and said, "Now we're in the twentieth century." I would be inclined to think that could be right enough alright. Aye. (August 31, 2007)

To explain why the fairies seem scarce today, Packy Jim turns again to his mother for a historical explanation: the fairies still exist but their power was greatly curtailed by the Catholic clergy in the century before last, the century of Maggie's own childhood.[4] The banshee is less often encountered now, he explains, because she follows the old Celtic aristocratic families, of which there are few left due to war, emigration, and diffused bloodlines over time. Packy Jim has no problem reconciling archaeological explanations for megalithic tombs, stone circles, and ring fort foundations with the folk belief that these are homes of the fairies and portals to the Otherworld: "They're the work of Stone Age man, surely, but them boys [the fairies] took them over later." Packy Jim also expresses belief or at least entertains belief in witchcraft and black magic, premonitions in dreams and therefore predestination, and jinxed roads (not necessarily connected overtly to the fairies). All of these beliefs are tested and affirmed by stories he mentally collects and shares with appreciative, broad-minded audiences.

Back on that February day when Packy Jim completed Agnes's cure instructions, half an hour into our recorded conversation, Packy Jim followed a brief fairy story from his mother with a rare story of the supernatural from his father:

Well then, Daddy had a tale from maybe the early eighteen hundreds, before eighteen fifty, a tale concerning the Lettercran area, down there in Letter—in *Crilly* townland. Down on Carrickahony Rock before Willie John Simms's. Down there in the hollow, there's a valley, and in the middle of the valley there's a long rock running called Carrickahony Rock, a limestone rock.

And in the evening after sunset, they could hear a noise—on the calm evenings, a noise, like—and it resembled a hammer hitting on the stone like that. Chop. Chop. Chop. Chop. *Chop.*

Well, in them days, it was very common to hear the stonecutters, the stonecutter's hammer going on the chisel—cutting stones, dressing quoins, and making them things there and all sorts of things out of *stone.* Only that this was a *limestone* area, so there was no stone being cut about it.[5] But this was "chop, chop, chop" all the *same.*

And after a time it got to be know as the *Hammer* Man.

The only thing about it was nobody was seen either, but you'd stand and you'd listen to it and you'd *wonder.*

And it become known as the "Hammer Man."

So, after some period of time, whether it was after *months* or after *years,* I don't *know.* Presumably after maybe two or three years, this *Johnston* man lived in the area, and he addressed it from some distance away. He *addressed* it. And the way he addressed it was:

"If you're a *good* thing, in God's name *continue.* And if you're a *bad* thing, in God's name *discontinue.*"

And, it *never* was heared again.

That is an old story. True or false, that's my daddy's story. And it was known as the *Hammer* Man. And I suppose there's nobody could tell you a haet about it in this old world we're living in now, only *me.* And I have it from *Daddy.*

The last time I heared that tale told is nearther on fifty years nor forty years since I heard it lastly. But, uh, I'd never forget it. I'm fascinated by that little tale. Gives me a *thrill.*

That's what intrigues me, like: I'm *fascinated* about the spirit world, and all that. *Bigly* fascinated about it. (February 18, 1999)

Here at the end, Packy Jim recalls that although it has been decades since he last heard anyone else speak about "The Hammer Man," the fact that he still remembers the story underscores that he is—and always has been—interested in the "spirit world" and more generally in mystery. In a sense, his coda steers this otherwise generically conventional account of a supernatural encounter toward the goals of personal narrative. The coda offers a presentation of self, one that affirms what sort of person he is by virtue of the sort of stories that fascinate him. Moreover, this story—like Packy Jim's seeking out a cure with both natural and supernatural elements—speaks again to the issue of belief.

I say that it is clear that Packy Jim believes in God, ghosts, fairies, and cures—he tells me so—but it is also clear from *how* he tells stories that he does not fully believe every claim about supernatural happenings at home or abroad nor does he believe in every official claim made by his long-established and formalized religion. As Timothy Corrigan Correll concluded from his review of nineteenth- and twentieth-century documentation of narratives and beliefs concerning fairies and healers in Ireland, "traditions of belief and traditions of disbelief were competing discourses that came into collision, interpenetrating and modifying each other in a dialectical relationship that informed individuals as they negotiated their own attitudes" (2005:1). Having inherited stories

revolving around mystery, Packy Jim has inherited also those competing discourses over belief—rationalism versus supernaturalism in terms used by Gillian
Bennett (1999) and by Diane Goldstein, Sylvia Grider, and Jeannie Thomas
(2007). In telling these stories, he joins in a generations-old, society-wide delibera-
tion. Depending on the internal coherence of a given story, the reliability of the
source, the context in which it is told, Packy Jim is at turns convinced, skeptical,
or willing to entertain but not fully committed to firm belief in accounts of
queer happenings. So whereas we might assume a spectrum of belief, ambivalence, and disbelief across a population as a whole, we can also glimpse such a
range in the repertoire of one person who negotiates—story by story, context
by context, however idiosyncratically—his or her own place on that spectrum.[6]
Moreover, complete belief or disbelief is both rare and often irrelevant to
whether a story gets told and retold. Stories of queer happenings circulate—
and Packy Jim helps circulate them—because of, rather than despite, debates
over their authenticity.

Returning to "The Hammer Man," note that up until Packy Jim's coda,
the story shows all the hallmarks of a legend, understood by Linda Dégh as a
debate about the truth of a given set of narrated events and, more generally,
about belief (2001:97; cf. Dégh and Vászonyi 1976). Throughout "The Hammer
Man," Packy Jim makes several bids to qualify the story as true, even if by the
end of the story—"true or false, that's my daddy's story"—plausibility remains
an open question that invites further discussion. Interested in how legends
are framed as plausible, true, or untrue, Elliott Oring (2008) has compiled a
thorough catalogue of the most common rhetorical devices for making truth
claims in legends, many of which feature in this story, the place-based legends
told as morality tales in chapter 4, and throughout Packy Jim's repertoire. Most
immediately evident in "The Hammer Man" is attribution to a reliable original
narrator, Packy Jim's father, Tommy McGrath.

Over several conversations, Packy Jim has characterized his father as less
likely to tell stories for their entertainment value, much less so than his mother.
Being the most skeptical member of the family, Tommy regularly sought rational
explanations for others' purportedly supernatural experiences. For example,
differing with Maggie over the existence of wraiths and ghosts, Tommy maintained that a neighbor who claimed to have seen his dead brother was simply
old, doting, and given to drink, and therefore not to be believed. We cannot
know if Tommy told "The Hammer Man" as true or as true in certain contexts.
But if "The Hammer Man" is "Daddy's tale," as Packy Jim reiterates, this is
tantamount to claiming that it comes from a reliably skeptical source, so disbelief
should be suspended at least temporarily. If Tommy McGrath told it—rather
than a more credulous or garrulous type, or a more random and distant friend

of a friend—then "there may be something to it." This phrase—"there may be
something to it"—is the common, vernacular phrase Packy Jim and his neighbors use for holding open the door to belief.

Looking to other authenticating devices noted by Oring and others (Dégh
and Vászonyi 1976; Ballard 1980; G. Bennett 1999; Correll 2005), we see that
Packy Jim offers several details grounding the story in local place (in Crilly
townland, down on Carrickahony Rock, near a neighbor's still-standing house)
and in local customs (such as stonecutting being a part of everyday life in the
local past). These details ground the extraordinary in the ordinary, framing it
in fact and routine. The age of the story, from the early 1800s, bolsters the sense
that "there may be something to it," for if the story has survived this long it is
worth considering. Note that Packy Jim also anticipates and discounts alternative explanations (cf. Oring 2008:136, 144–146). Although a chopping sound
would have been familiar to locals at the time of the narrated events, Crilly
townland, Packy Jim tells us, was not an area for stonecutting. So the phenomenon requires another explanation, and a supernatural explanation fits after
Johnston invokes God to address the mysterious force and in doing so put a
stop to the eerie sounds.

Although Packy Jim has heard stories of Catholics, especially priests, succeeding in controlling the supernatural where Protestants have failed, it is
worth noting that Johnston is a Protestant. This part of the story has double
significance. First, Packy Jim and his Catholic neighbors consider Protestants
as a group to be generally less inclined to believe in fairies, ghosts, or spirits
than themselves, so if a presumably sober and critical Protestant is willing to
entertain the possibility of supernatural agency—enough to call it out—then,
again, "there may be something to it." In a sense, any Johnston would be seen—
in the local, sectarian-inflected ecology of belief—as a more reliable corrobo-
rating witness to a supernatural event than many Dolans, Duffys, McHughs,
McMenamins, or McGraths, Catholics all. In addition, the detail of Johnston
commanding the unknown force to quit "in God's name" underscores the
common belief that invoking the Christian God by name or through prayer is
an effective protection against any threatening spirits or forces, no matter who
invokes Him. This is commensurate with the cosmological hierarchy established
in Packy Jim's account of the origin of the fairies, and we will see this belief in
the power of God's name at work in Packy Jim's account, below, of a man saving
a bride from fairy abduction.

In addition to discounting alternative explanations and building plausibility
through familiar local detail, Packy Jim also establishes himself as a reliable
narrator by highlighting what he does and does not know. In metadiscursive

asides, in this story and others, he often says things such as "whether it was after *months* or after *years*, I don't *know*. Presumably after maybe two or three years . . ." In doing so he telegraphs that he is unwilling to make up or give false information, but for the sake of furthering the story, he is willing to make some presumptions, underlined as such. This move is quite explicit in his account of the origin of the fairies in the introduction. This is a matter of Packy Jim displaying good judgment, a critical stance, and a commitment to the truth (cf. Oring 2008:135, 148). Moreover, as we have seen before, Packy Jim makes effective use of quoted speech in "The Hammer Man" ("If you're a *good* thing, in God's name *continue*. And if you're a *bad* thing, in God's name *discontinue*.") and of phonetic imitation ("Chop. Chop. Chop. Chop. *Chop.*"). Both quotation and mimesis persuasively add to a sense of immediacy, realism, and verisimilitude (cf. Butler 1990:118).

That being said, Packy Jim stops short of using every potential rhetorical device noted by Oring and others. After he has made his case—based on direct and indirect evidence, bolstered by rhetorical devices that authenticate as much through style as content—Packy Jim does not commit himself fully to the story as absolute nonfiction. Like Jenny McGlynn of County Laois, interviewed by Patricia Lysaght (1991), Packy Jim does not always fully believe stories that he nonetheless tells. Like McGlynn, Packy Jim will tell stories about which he is unsure in such a way that presents the evidence as he has it and leaves the door open to belief. While authenticating devices invite audiences to suspend disbelief for most of the story, by the end the audience must decide for themselves about the truth of the narrated events. If "there may be something to it" is the typical local phrase for inviting belief, note the understatement in that phrase, the guardedness, the room left for ambivalence in the midst of competing discourses of belief and disbelief. Whatever the listener may decide, however, Packy Jim lands hardest and last on what the largest number of people might agree on—true or false, the tale is fascinating, the ongoing debate intriguing.

If "The Hammer Man" is a strange one-off story from Packy Jim's father, for Packy Jim and others the fairies are a perennial topic for reveling in those things that are fascinating but often inconclusive. As Angela Bourke observes, "The essence of fairy-belief is ambivalence" (1996:12). When the topic of conversation shifts toward fairies, Packy Jim does not typically launch into a version of the origin of the fairies because it is assumed knowledge—nonfictional context for a host of other stories. As an outsider, I can ask for the origin story in my role as folklorist. Or as an insider Packy Jim can choose to rehearse or simply reference the story as a gloss on human nature, in his role as vernacular social critic, as we saw in the introduction. But with fairies on the table, Packy Jim is more likely to tell a suite of three stories featuring the fairies, which I have recorded together, usually in the same sequence, on five occasions. Discussion of fairy mischief, during a visit in 2002, prompted the following:

Well, the fairies have been said to do a good turn, too. There was a story about a woman who was in a *starving* condition, some road down in the Castlederg area—we'll say about Blane or around there, in that area. This was *Famine* times.

And she was sitting by the fire one day, and this little man came in, and he had some, he had some oat*meal* with him. And he give him—or he give *her* the oatmeal. He told her he knowed she hadn't ate for several days, and he says, "I'm giving you this and you needn't be afraid of it," he says, "for *that* is the top grain of *Croghan*."

There's a hill down there not too far from Castlederg called Croghan Hill, which is very fertile *land*.

Well, she was hesitant to take it because some sixth sense was telling her this isn't a *normal* individual, do you understand? She was hesitant in taking it.

Then he says, "My good woman, you needn't be afraid of taking that and eating it, for that's the top grain of *Croghan*."

And *that* is a story from my *mother* that she got from *her* mother, old Cecily Moss, a story from the century before the last, way back in the Famine times in the eighteen forties I suppose. Rightly or wrongly, true or false, many a time I heard my mammy at that.

Aye. "That's the top grain of Croghan."

Well, then there's a story in Segronan, then, the man in Segronan in the Famine times that was scarce of *grain*. Oat bread was the common staple diet then when the spuds failed. And his . . . like my turf here being at near an end, his sheaves of *corn* was near at an end.

But one day he went out till his office house and he found a full good size of a sheaf of corn lying there. And he take it in and thrash it and process it to get it into meal, you know, and make some little bit of bread.

And then again, he went again and there was another, and he started to think that was funny and how did this come about? So he says till himself, "I'll find out what's at the back of this."

So he lay in some hidden place in the house to watch. And this little chap come in—small little boy, if you like, a toy man, I suppose, you could call him. And he had a straw across his back like, you know, a single stalk with maybe nine or ten or twelve grains on the head of it. He had that across his shoulder, and he dropped it down like that, and he says, "Oh, but I'm *tired*," and went out.

And another boy come in and he dropped another, his stalk of corn on top of the first one, like, and, "Oh, but I'm *tired*."

So your man being impatient and a bit bad tempered, started to get ragged about it. And this next chap come in and dropped it where there was others, and he says, "Oh, but I'm *tired*."

And out your man jumps, "Oh, the De'il [Devil] *stint* you," he says, "to be tired carrying *nothing!*"

And that was the rear of it. They finished with him. That finished the corn coming.

That's a story Johnny Duffy told me down there in Segronan, as he has heared it from older folks. And it may be right, or it may be wrong, but that's the way I've *got it*.

Aye.

"Oh, the De'il stint," he says, "to be chatting about being tired, carrying nothing!"

Well, then, uh, there was the *other* story that Mom had, about this boy. He was a peddler, they called him, and he was selling little wooden noggins that took the place of *bowls*, like, you know, for drinking soup out of or having a sup of water or a sup of milk, in *wooden* bowls, they called them *noggins*.

So this boy—there were a nickname on him—they called him Nick the *Nogginweaver*.

So he was jogging along on the road one night in the dark, going from one place to another, and suddenly, by the roadside, he hears,

"Where's *my* horse?"

"Where's *my* horse?"

and "Where's *my* horse?"

Several voices, one after another: "where's my horse," and "where's my horse," and "where's my horse?" And as soon as the word was said, the horse seemed to be there and away he galloped.

So your man says till himself, "By God, I'll have a go at it, too," and he says, "Where's *my* horse?" And he had it no sooner said nor he was on a horse, and the horse was away along with the rest. Across, across the country for a number of mile, and they landed at some sizeable house.

And uh, the next place Nick the Nogginweaver found himself was—there was couples across and backs, you know, the back to bind the

couple, like up there, you know, high up, on the *roof*, supporting the
roof. [*Packy Jim points to the open underside of his roof to indicate the horizontal
joists spanning the ceiling, connecting the rafters.*]

So the next place Nick found himself was sitting on the back, like
that, and underneath there was a wedding feast going on, underneath,
like, you know.

And these boys be'd to be beside him too, and he heared them
talking till the other about what they were going to do: *they were going
to steal the BRIDE.*

And one of the fairies was going to go down to the table, and he was
going to have a straw in his hand, and he was going to tickle the bride's
nose, like, run the straw up her nose a bit, to make her, you know, *sneezy*.
And the bride would sneeze, and if nobody in the company said, "God
bless you," that was okay. He'd have a go at it again. She'd sneeze again,
nobody would pass any remarks, that was okay. And then the third time,
then, he'd tickle her nose again, and nobody said, "God bless you," then
they had her.

So he was listening to this, and then he was paying attention. So
she sneezed after a time, nobody passed no remarks. After a time she
sneezed again, nobody passed no remarks, and then she sneezed the
third time, nobody passed no remarks. So then he knowed then they had
her. So sooner nor let them have her, he says, "God bless you." As soon
as he says, "God bless you," down he fell, smashing and destroying *all.*

So he come down, and the fairies were away, and he was down in
the middle, making a *destruction* on the table, and say it that way.

But I suppose then, well, I suppose then when he related his
experience, he was the Good Samaritan. He was a *hero* of the incident
rather than the *bad boy*, aye, for saving the bride.

Nobody passed any remarks. The next time he says, "Well I'll save
you," he says, "God bless you." And down he come.

That's an old story. Wasn't *that* a great . . . *yarn?*

That's a story of my mother's *too*. I heared that as a young boy, and
I heared it many and many a time. And if I was to live till five hundred
years of age, I would *still* mind it. It's just solid rooted in my memory.
Oh, God aye. (July 12, 2002)

In all three stories the fairies give to or take from humans—or try to—and
though they have power, even magical power, they work within certain social
and divine limitations. Despite their customary jealousy and harassment of
humanity, the fairies in the first two stories "do a good turn" by providing for

people in a time of deprivation, and they act positively or negatively based on the level of reverence and appreciativeness from their benefactors. While humility, gratitude, and trust are rewarded in "The Top Grain of Croghan," bad manners break the spell in "Segronan Fairies." Contrasting with the first two stories, the fairies in "Nick the Nogginweaver" are back to their usual mischief and avarice. They seek to take for themselves someone representing the best and most promising in human society, someone who could rejuvenate fairy society, presumably through interbreeding, thereby helping their chances for salvation at the Final Judgment. This is not to be as Nick breaks the spell by invoking God, who had expelled those neutral angels in the very beginning and who would seem to have little interest in welcoming them back.

In terms of form and style, "The Top Grain of Croghan" is the shortest, least complicated, and most similar to fairy legends told as true. Yet here and in other recordings it does not stand alone but rather serves as a catalyst for "Segronan Fairies" and "Nick the Nogginweaver." Whatever truth claims the story makes might be understood best in light of the other two stories that follow. As Oring (2008:141, 152) points out, accompanying legends can modify—supporting, deflating, or complicating—the truth claims of a legend that might be understood differently in isolation. Even before launching into the second story, Packy Jim concludes "The Top Grain of Croghan" with a statement of distancing ambivalence—"rightly or wrongly, true or false."

Although the first two stories incorporate local place names and details that could add to a sense of veracity, there are few other authenticating devices that stand out. Packy Jim points to his mother and grandmother as the source of "The Top Grain of Croghan" and a contemporary, Johnny Duffy, as the source of "Segronan Fairies," but he does not commit any of those narrators to believing in the narrated events. All three stories make extensive use of direct discourse, and each one culminates in a repetition of maximally quotable speech—"That's the top grain Croghan," "The De'il stint you to be tired carrying nothing," "God bless you." As we have seen, quoted speech, attribution, and incidental localizing detail can contribute to the truth claims of legends, but here there are counterbalancing elements that suggest efforts to suspend disbelief more for the sake of entertainment.

Note for instance the prominent threefold repetitions in "Segronan Fairies" and "Nick the Nogginweaver"—three fairies in succession exclaiming, "*Oh*, but I'm *tired*"; three voices calling out, "Where's my horse?"; three unblessed sneezes necessary for a successful abduction. In this part of the world at the present time this narrative convention is much more characteristic of fictional wonder tales, both migratory and homegrown Märchen that Packy Jim heard as a child and read versions of in his school readers and in the story books that circulated through his home. Essentially Packy Jim—and presumably those he heard the stories from—embellishes "Segronan Fairies" and "Nick the Nogginweaver" by borrowing the threefold narrative device from a fantasy genre. In so doing these two stories may telegraph to the initiated their fictional status but in such a way that a child—who has not yet internalized knowledge about different generic conventions—would not appreciate.

Other aspects of style underscore the fictional status of Packy Jim's suite of three fairy stories. As Gillian Bennett points out in her study of urban English-women's accounts of ghosts, those narrators who told polished, linear, and well-organized stories—not unlike Packy Jim's here—were the least likely to entertain a sincere belief in ghosts (1999:121). Drawing from Bill Ellis (2001), Oring, too, notes differences in narrative style that indicate whether a legend is told for fun or as true (2008:140, 145–46). Those told as true proceed in a looser, more circular, searching manner—lingering on description, detail, and particularly evaluation—while often inviting discussion. Packy Jim's three fairy stories are much more tightly ordered and, in their polished coherence, relatively closed off to further discussion. Incidentally, they are structured and polished to the point that each version I recorded is very much like another. Admittedly, here we are presuming to some extent that Oring's model is universally or at least widely applicable and that the communicative conventions of Bennett's population are similar to Packy Jim's. But if that evidence were not enough, note that Packy Jim concludes "Nick the Nogginweaver," the last and most elaborate story, with, "Wasn't *that* a great . . . *yarn?*" Even more so than "tale" or "story," in the vernacular of Packy Jim and his neighbors, a "yarn" is associated with embellishment, exaggeration, and fiction.

Even if Packy Jim volunteers few direct truth claims about these three stories, form and style matter—as Dell Hymes reminds us (1981, 2003)—for they convey meaning as much as content does. That said, unlike Hymes, working with historical materials, I am in the comparatively enviable position of being able to consult my source, to ask whether I have interpreted correctly—to his mind at least—the clues that he has embedded throughout his narratives. At the end of a two-week summer visit in 2007, I began to ask Packy Jim about all the stories I had heard him tell on multiple occasions. The goal was not to record additional versions but rather to elicit further exegesis through both indirect and direct questioning. When starting a conversation about "Nick the Nogginweaver," the issue of belief was not at the top of my agenda, but I nonetheless happily followed Packy Jim to the topic. I began with a very general question:

RC: What's the significance of that story for you?

PM: Well, when I heared Mammy at it so often, like it got rooted in there, rooted in my memory. That is the kind of story she would tell *me*. So I was slightly fascinated by it as a young boy. That kind of a way. Aye.

RC: So, to you that story is sort of a . . . a memento of your mother, in a way?

PM: It would be. Aye, it would be.

RC: Right. I see. But it—as a young boy—it would have captured your imagination because it . . . ?

PM: Oh, I believed it for a length of time. I would have believed that it was real, a really and true fact. Oh God, you would surely.

RC: The imagery is very captivating.

PM: Aye, that's right. The tickling with the straw. The tickling with the straw, and if she didn't, if she didn't get a blessing they had her.

RC: Right. . . . But later on you would class that as a fictional story?

PM: You would surely. You would, certainly you would. Or, well, I suppose something like that could have happened, like, it could have happened a way far back in the past. Aye, could have happened, I suppose.

RC: Mmhmm.

PM: But that story I would just kind of think is a *tall yarn*.

RC: Mmhmm. Well then how would you compare that story with say, you know, the one Johnny Duffy told you about the fairies in Segronan, the "Oh, but I'm tired," that one? Or this, uh, "no fear of that, this is the top grain of Croghan" story?

PM: Aye, aye, aye. Aye, aye.

RC: How would you compare Nick the Nogginweaver to those other ones? Would they all be . . . ?

PM: All in the *same class*.

RC: Would they be?

PM: All in the same class, surely. Aye.

RC: Okay.

PM: All in the same class. Aye.

RC: So you would, they would have been believable stories to you at a time, but now you're skeptical about them?

PM: I would be skeptical, I would be skeptical, surely. Oh God, very much so, I doubt.

RC: Mmhmm.

PM: That was Johnny Duffy told me that one. That was a new, that was one of the *last* I heared like that one. Mammy and Daddy was dead you know at that time, quite a while, when Johnny Duffy happened to bring that up some way or another. About this old boy in Segronan that had, was on the bare board, had nothing.

At this point Packy Jim recapped another version of the "Segronan Fairies,"
concluding with a final evaluation in a slightly bemused yet doubtful tone,
"Oh, I don't know." I then asked whether he believes in his mother's and
grandmother's story "The Top Grain of Croghan." The answer was the same,
"I would be skeptical," followed by another short recap of that story. It occurred to me then to ask:

> RC: And do you suppose she [Maggie] took that to be a nonfictional
>   story, a true story?
> PM: Oh, she would have taken it to be fictional, too. Mammy would
>   have taken it to be fictional.
> RC: Oh, is that right?
> PM: I would say she would. I would say she would. Just a bit of
>   diversion for me as a young boy.
> RC: Right.
> PM: Just telling it as an old tale, sort of thing.
> RC: So it's, for your mother and maybe for your grandmother, telling
>   those sorts of stories was for entertainment's sake?
> PM: Aye, largely I would say, I would think so. Maggie Gallagher—as
>   the saying goes—lived on to very nearly, well on to near the end
>   of the twentieth century, and Maggie Gallagher—as the saying
>   goes—wasn't—as the saying goes—she wasn't living away back
>   in the century before. She was very, very modern. Very, very
>   modern type of person. The more maybe she didn't keep a
>   modern house or this or that or thon.

As Packy Jim characterizes it, belief evolves over time with childhood being
generally a more impressionable, credulous phase and adulthood being generally
a more skeptical, critical one commencing after one has "hardened up a bit."
He also implies a similar evolution for society as a whole—people of the modern
age are rational and discerning, less likely to believe every account of queer
happenings—and he makes this point more explicitly later in the same conversation. Similar to reminiscences in the previous chapter, Packy Jim recalls the
torture of "being caught away in the distance and you had to come home in the
dark past some of these places" associated with ghosts and fairies. Eventually
for him and for most—though not for everyone—the fear gradually subsided.

> RC: So what made the difference?
> PM: Well, as time wore on—you were out a bit more and a wee bit
>   more and a wee bit more—it just wore off and wore off and

wore off. And finally it was nonexistent. And you get a sense,
like, of which stories was genuine and which ones just old talk.
And in them days there was an awful lot of talk.

RC: Mmhmm.

PM: That was the way it was. And then we're told, then, that there
was people that lived away back long, long, long ago, like old
Barney McHugh, and he was doing a job for my grandfather in
the wintertime, and my grandfather had to leave him within a
stone throw of his own door. Back at his own door, within a
stone throw of it, because he was so afraid of ghosts, and him
maybe seventy years of age or maybe more. So seemingly he
never got rid of it. Aye. Oh, it's true. That is true. (August 31,
2007)

For Packy Jim, progress toward adulthood can be characterized in part by a
desensitization to childish fears but also by a burgeoning critical perspective
that allows him to better discern the truth of a given narrative on its own terms
and in the context of a wide range of other stories heard over a long period. For
him gaining greater communicative competence in telling and receiving legends
was an integral part of achieving greater sentience. But maturity is not simply a
matter of putting away childish things. He still performs his mother's, grandmother's, and Johnny Duffy's stories artfully and with pleasure as mementos of
the past. Moreover, he remains open to old and new testimonies of supernatural
events. Each new bit of narrative or purportedly experiential evidence has the
potential to fine-tune his beliefs even today.

As Packy Jim represents him, Barney McHugh, the fearful old man from
his grandfather's time, is not someone who failed to mature. Rather, he is indica-
tive of an older, premodern generation who would have heard and believed
far more supernatural stories than Packy Jim does. Packy Jim's theory—that
the further back you go the more childlike and credulous people were—is an
iteration of the ontogeny-recapitulates-phylogeny vision that Sigmund Freud
co-opted from now discredited biological theory. The original idea is that each
individual organism develops in stages that mirror the evolutionary history of
the species as a whole (and vice versa, according to Freud). Applying this to the
mental development of humans, Freud considered the projections and wish
fulfillment fantasies of children to be analogous to more primitive and superstitious stages of humanity ([1927] 1961:43; cf. Gould 1985:156–158). Unlike Freud,
Packy Jim does not go so far as to consider supernatural beliefs and, more
broadly, religion to be a mass neurosis that humanity will eventually outgrow.
But he does share with Freud a belief in a parallel between the individual's

lifecycle and the historical evolution of society, both of which can be distinguished by analogous intellectual transformations from undiscriminating credulity to more sophisticated discernment.

That being said, as Bourke (1996) argues and as Correll's (2005) historical review of varying levels of belief in fairies over time suggests, each generation tends to overestimate the credulity of their forebears. Whether seen as an age of unquestioning belief or, indeed, as a time when there really were more otherworldly things to believe in, the past serves as a removed but relevant realm into which we project the pure, untainted versions of ideas or realities that are much more complicated, muddied, or uncertain in our own present world.

With this in mind it is interesting to note that, in his commentary on the fairy story suite, Packy Jim volunteers the possibility that such narrated events could have been possible in the far distant past. In doing so he reiterates his mother's belief that the fairies had more power in the past but now they appear more in fiction and fantasy than in person. This vernacular theory comports, however literally, with Max Weber's concept of the disenchantment of the world at the dawn of modernity ([1904–1905] 1976). To Packy Jim's mind, Maggie was firmly a part of this modern disenchanted world; she was no backwards country rube despite uncharitable interpretations of surface appearances. Though she may have believed in the existence of fairies and ghosts, like Packy Jim she was not entirely credulous. Like Packy Jim, Maggie was invested in evidence and credible sources. She had the communicative competence to recognize whether a story was told for fun or as true, and if told as true whether it could be believed. It is quite possible—as David Hufford (1995) and Diane Goldstein (2007) argue—to be a believer in spirits and a rational, even skeptical, actor in the world. Even with the frightening personal sensation of being under the control of a mysterious force in personal narrative 8—an experience that could easily be interpreted in a supernatural frame, as have many who experienced sleep paralysis (D. Hufford 1995)—Packy Jim, believer in spirits, nonetheless rationally assesses his context and concludes that the monster is only the memory of a dream inspired by his anxiety over helplessness.

Take for another example a story Packy Jim would not have fully appreciated, or told, as a child. It speaks to the development of his skeptical adult mind and to his present position as what Goldstein calls a "rational believer."

Well, I'll tell you another story, too—about the water horse—while I'm at it. There was a woman out on Carrickaholten townland, and she was called Mrs. McPeake—P-E-A-K-E.

And, uh, periodically, she used to take some clothes that she had down to the lough on Carrickaholten called Lough na Bui. There was a little strand there, and the water was shallow, and if it was middling warm, well, the water would have been a sort of a lukewarm.

I suppose she was washing them—soap wouldn't have been very plenty, for sometimes they used to use a little lime, burned lime, till, till mix with the clothes, burned lime.

But, uh, she was washing them *there* anyway.

And this water horse—according to the story—made a tear out, and he grabbed her and he pulled her in. And that was—as the saying goes—the end of Mrs. Mc*Peake*.

So, uh—this is an old tale, it's a peculiar one, too—seemingly down here in your throat, on each side of your throat, there's two little things, they call them *lights*. I presume they're what they call the *tonsil* glands. But they chatted about the lights, and they were down here, and there wouldn't be a big affair *altogether*.

So, like I was a young boy at the time, but I had a bit of shrewdness about me. But the story was told, this woman was eaten completely, that there was nothing to be seen on the sand, only her *lights*.

And I imagine, by God, yous be'd to have brave—as the saying goes—*eyesight*, when they could see her lights! For I imagine the lights wouldn't have been a big *affair*.

So *that* was the story of the woman that disappeared and the water horse that ate *her*. Aye.

The story so far is an amalgamation of what Packy Jim had heard as a boy from his parents, Frank McCanny, and other visitors; this is the local lore. To Packy Jim's maturing mind, however, not everything added up. In another version of the story (from August 2007), he expresses his doubt about the supposed evidence of Mrs. McPeake's demise: "They'd be to be very expert people when they went to look—as the saying goes—when they knowed what the tonsils was." This detail that only her lights remained is vivid and memorable but also sug- gestive of past storytellers' *efforts* to be vivid and memorable. Not to mention, one has to accept the existence of the water horse—a mythical underwater monster associated with the fairies in Irish and Scottish folklore, said to inhabit lakes such as Loch Ness. True, Packy Jim believes in the existence of fairies, then and now. But apart from this story, he had never heard of water horses and had no reason to believe in them, whereas "there may be something to it" when countless internally and externally consistent stories from credible

sources circulate about ghosts, fairies, and other supernatural figures and
forces. Too good to be true, the story about Mrs. McPeake edges toward implausibility for Packy Jim, but complication follows, including plausible vindica-
tion of Packy Jim's skepticism. He continues:

> Then, years and years and years passed. That century went out,
> and another century come in. And on about nineteenth hundred and
> seventy-four, or so, Danny Nolan [a requested pseudonym] bought a
> place up there—that place you come through—off James McGrath.
>
> And he was getting some renovations till it, and among other things,
> he was getting the river *redd*—the Lubog [pronounced LOO-boge], as they
> call it, *redd*. And Pat Duffy [another requested pseudonym] was employed
> with a digger to redd the Lubog, I think he redd it in about a fortnight
> or so—Sunday and Monday and every day when the weather was *dry*.
>
> But there was a *loop* in the Lubog—the Lubog took a turn like that,
> like a *loop*. So Pat Duffy said, when they come to the loop, that they
> would open it on straight, like, to give the water maybe more *power*. It
> wouldn't go around the loop; they'd open it straight and connect *up*
> again.
>
> Well then, when they were going through that—it was only a lock of
> yards altogether—Danny was standing there, but uh, they picked up some
> bones, maybe a thigh bone and a skull or something that they seen on
> the . . . on the, uh . . . as the digger, you know, lifted them out the earth,
> you know, throwing to the one side.
>
> So they examined it, and they seen that it was the remains of a *human
> being*. So, they said to themselves, what would they do? This would be a
> long time ago, that this happened.
>
> "Ah, we'll cover it up and we'll say nothing about it." You know?
> Sensible enough idea.
>
> But then, Danny Nolan, then, was intrigued about the matter, and
> he says till himself: "The first time I meet Packie [not Packy Jim] or Joe
> McGrath, I'll make an inquiry: Did anything *untoward* ever happen
> around here?" You know.
>
> So he stated his story to him about that. It was a hush-hush thing,
> in case these boys would be out and raising up a fuss about nothing—
> police, you know?
>
> So they studied, the McGraths, and they come up with a *theory*. The
> theory could be very far wrong, but uh, more nor likely it's quite right:
>
> Mrs. McPeake would have been a *poor* woman.
>
> She'd have been got *dead* in bed in the morning.

Her people had no *money*.

But her people would have been a little bit, maybe, *smarter* or brighter nor their neighbors. They didn't want to have the bother and expense of a wake or a priest or anything like that, so they concocted this cock and bull story.

They took the woman away under cover of darkness, and they buried her there, which wasn't too far away, and then they spun the yarn, then, about her going to the lough and washing the clothes and the water horse coming out and *eating* her, leaving only her lights.

And in simple—*them old times*, I imagine that'd have been around about the 1740s, maybe, or the 1750s—some of them two decades. But people were *steeped* in superstition. They were very *simple minded*, and they would have drunk a story like that. They would a lapped it *up*.

That's the McGraths' theory, and I think that they are right. That was the remains of Mrs. McPeake that was buried there, and she would have been got dead, and they would have buried her out there to save them the expense of the wake and funeral. (March 18, 1999)

Interestingly, in a third version of the story (August 31, 2007), Packy Jim tells it backward in a sense. As in a detective story, he begins with the discovery of a skull and bones, then works backward through local memory. He underscores the McPeakes' poverty by citing his father's memory of seven ruined wattle houses built by squatters at the foot of Meenashamer Hill where the McPeakes had lived. Packy Jim then traces the evolution of Joe and Packie McGrath's theory for how Mrs. McPeake's remains came to rest near the Lubog. In advocating the theory, Packy Jim debunks the "cock and bull story" accepted by his more credulous forebears: "Aye. No such a thing as water horse. But long ago, way back about two or three hundred years, you would have believed anything."

According to the debunking explanation that Packy Jim accepts, the McPeakes had good or at least strategic reasons for telling an untrue story about the supernatural. Other common reasons for doing so include controlling others, especially children (cf. Glassie 2006:298). Packy Jim's mother warned him about the nightly appearances of the ghost of a man named Bob Barr, and his father told him that he had seen a mysterious coffin floating on the surface of Lough Veenagreane. Packy Jim recalls that it was not until he was fifteen or sixteen that he realized—and confirmed with his parents—that those stories were made up to keep him home at night and away from the dangerous shores of the nearby lake where three children had drowned in recent memory. Such realizations and confirmations were watershed moments in Packy Jim's

adolescent reorientation toward belief, his evolving reconciliation of faith and
critical acuity.

Part of this reorientation involved, again, a growing awareness of how
storytelling works and a greater communicative competence as both teller and
listener. Exaggeration or indeed wholesale fabrication are, of course, liberties
taken for the sake of entertainment, and as Packy Jim witnessed over countless
late night ceilis, those who earn a reputation for a way with words accrue very
real social status and benefits. Becoming something like a connoisseur of supernatural legends, Packy Jim came to appreciate an artful but implausible narrative
overreach when he heard one. As a coda to one version of his story about Bob
Goudy's ghost, Packy Jim recalls:

> But there was a man, Paddy McGoldrick, lived down there at the road
> there. He'd have heared the story when he was a young boy. And there
> was, there's always smart alecks doctoring things. But I suppose he
> heared somebody, some smart aleck who, uh, added their touch to it.
>
> But your man [Goudy] died, and he was a Protestant man, and the
> Protestant graveyard was out there, Carn Graveyard. That'd have been
> maybe three hours' walk. Carrying a corpse would have taken a long
> time. A day's walk, you might say.
>
> Well, "God," Paddy says, "after they buried him and come home
> again, Goudy was sitting in the corner smoking and a sleeved waistcoat
> on him!"
>
> Daddy used to say there wasn't much use in burying *that* boy.
>
> "God," he says, "when they come home from the funeral, he was
> sitting in the corner smoking and a sleeved waistcoat on him!"
>
> So that was putting it a wee bit too *far!* Aye. (July 4, 2000)

Thus far, we have considered whether or not Packy Jim believes in particular
spirits and queer happenings based on the stories he knows, tells, and evaluates.
We have witnessed his negotiating discourses of belief and disbelief, finding for
himself a place—indeed, more than one place—on the spectrum between the
two. But of course, as the first story about the Hammer Man demonstrates, belief
is not always—in fact, is rarely—a simple yes or no proposition. The survival
and popularity of supernatural legends owes everything to the very wide gray
area of ambivalence wherein arguments are made for and against the accuracy
of a given account or the existence of a given supernatural being or force, even
if the arguments are rarely conclusive.

While it does matter ultimately to Packy Jim whether or not ghosts and
fairies exist, it is possible that in telling specific stories, the question of belief or

disbelief is not always the most relevant one. Whether or not Packy Jim or his audiences understand his suite of three fairy stories as fiction or nonfiction, these stories nonetheless provide useful models for thinking through, for example, neighborly values, reciprocity, and civil behavior. This comports with Conrad Arensberg's early assertion (1937) that in stories about the fairies, human values and behaviors are projected into the parallel fairy world, considered and evaluated, confirmed or challenged. This also comports with Angela Bourke's notion that regardless of the issue of belief, fairies (and perhaps by extension ghosts and wraiths) are "good to think," in Lévi-Strauss's memorable formulation. That is, fairy legends provide a grammar of ideas and a virtual reality within which to contemplate real-world issues and tensions (Bourke 1996:12–17). What Bourke says of fairy legends may apply more broadly to supernatural legendry:

> It may in fact be more useful to imagine not that people in rural Ireland remember and tell fairy legends because they believe them, but that they tell them (and sometimes believe them) because they remember them. That is to say, being able to find one's way around such an intricately interconnected set of narratives as fairy legend provides may be a valuable intellectual practice in itself. (1996:16)

In a complementary move, drawing from Marilyn Motz (1998), Patrick Mullen (2000) understands belief less as something you either do or do not have and more as a process of knowing and a way of making meaning. Belief is like place in that it is more verb than noun, as much concerned with epistemology as with ontology. It is a valuable intellectual practice compellingly conducted through storytelling and discussion. As Packy Jim demonstrates, belief as practice may be unfettered in ranging beyond the here and now, but it remains subject to rules of evidence and rational thought. Discussion and debate have the potential to move one's estimation of a given story—and the realities it signifies—out of the broad gray area of ambivalence toward firmer belief or disbelief. So Packy Jim is in the business of rehearsing the old stories, testimonies of mystery, because true or false—or something more complicated—these stories question the reliability of perception, the nature of knowledge and knowledge-production, and ultimately the shape of reality. Such stories are enticing, intriguing, and "good to think," even for the skeptic, even if rejected at the end of the day.

That being said, note that in this and the previous chapter, the discussion has been limited to beliefs that might be termed folk, unofficial, or vernacular. As Patrick Mullen (2000) and Leonard Primiano (1995) note, distinguishing folk belief and folk religion from other categories of belief and religion is notoriously difficult and fraught with hierarchical assumptions and privileging. Packy Jim, however, is unconcerned with such distinctions. It would be wrong to assume some separation or indeed competition in his mind between belief in fairies and ghosts on the one hand and in God, Christ, saints, and angels on the other hand. To Packy Jim they are all interrelated and accounts about them are mutually reinforcing. Packy Jim sees Bob Goudy's ghost taking form to battle McSorley the Ribbonman as the same phenomenon as Christ's spirit joining with his "glorified body" in the upper room in Jerusalem after the Resurrection. Spirits, whether fairies or the souls of humans, have the power to take on material form; they are all part of the same system. While technically unorthodox from the perspective of the Church, Packy Jim is satisfied that scripture and Catholic tradition underpin the origin of the fairies, and by the same token evidence of the fairies bolsters rather than calls into question Christian cosmology and eschatology.

Packy Jim's version of Christian cosmology and eschatology is not part of the broad gray area of ambivalence; this is fundamental reality and essential truth. But as a rational believer he no more accepts everything his church teaches than he accepts everything proposed by local supernatural legends. Packy Jim is particularly well aware of the manmade and variable nature of institutionalized religion. The 1992 omission of the existence of Limbo from the official catechism of the Church causes Packy Jim consternation in that it calls into question the larger system. "You might as well say, Hell—forget about it. It's not there. Heaven—forget about it. It's not there." Moreover, like the many changes brought about by the Second Vatican Council, the decanonization of certain saints such as Saint Christopher, and the recent retranslation of the English-language missal, abrupt changes to the catechism and liturgy reveal to Packy Jim just how constructed and seemingly arbitrary are many of the trappings of his church. This opens the door to all manner of reasonable questioning and rational theorizing that ultimately rejects unthinking orthodoxy.

At the end of our first recorded session—a point at which Packy Jim seemed most keen to sum up his way of thinking before I departed, not knowing if and when I would return—he asked rhetorically whether earthquakes, hurricanes, and droughts today are a punishment from God. These would happen regardless of our presence, he reasoned:

> Because these astronomers has seen on Jupiter or some of them outside
> planets, they have seen volcanic eruptions and mighty storms. And
> there's certainly no human beings there to permit sin—as the saying
> goes—to be either good or bad. No.

And some people would think that the Famine in Ireland was a punishment on the people for maybe their immorality, and this and that and *thon*. That may have been, but that's questionable. That's *questionable*. I think it's questionable.

So what then do we make of, like, the punishments that was meted out to the children of *Israel*, as stated in the Bible, punishments for their sins and their disobedience? Like the seven plagues in Egypt, and Sodom and Gomorrah and the destruction of Sodom and Gomorrah, and the seven plagues of Egypt, and this Noah's flood that they talk about, and all them things.

Can we take that at—as the saying goes—can we take those things at face value?

If there wasn't a human being on the face of the world to commit sin, and we'll go further—if there wasn't an animal or a bird or a little thing in it—would there not be terrible earthquakes? Would there not be volcanic eruptions? Would there not be droughts? Would there not be floods? (November 16, 1998)

Once the door is open to rational doubt, fundamentalism becomes less tenable and scripture begs alternative explanation. Take for example his deliberations over creation as depicted in Genesis.

I couldn't believe that this old world or universe was made in seven days, or six days. I wouldn't like to take that in at all. That covered millions of years, it did. Couldn't take that in at all. No, I suppose the Creator done it some way, but he didn't do—it wasn't a one-week job.

Sure, isn't it well enough known and can be, can be—as the saying goes—*argued*—or whatever way you like to put it—that it can't be contradicted that it's there for millions of years. Sure that's, the Church of Rome or no other church in the world can say against that.

But to get seven days or six days, first and foremost, that has to be a manner of speaking, that, that's just—as the saying goes—a way of putting it. (August 17, 2007)

Here we come to the limits of literal interpretation and to the possibility of metaphor and allegory. In this vein, Packy Jim deals with the conundrum of all of humanity issuing from only two people: "As far as Adam and Eve is concerned, I think that Adam and Eve was not a man and a woman, but Adam and Eve was men and women. That's what would be my idea." Likewise,

Packy Jim appreciates that in actuality neither God nor Satan has a sex, but that language and society invite us to speak of them in gendered terms even as this distances us from actuality. Recall how in his account of the origin of the fairies Packy Jim was so careful to hedge and qualify his speech as metaphorical, "putting it the best way I can," thus highlighting the limitations of language to convey ultimate realities.

How can one both believe and disbelieve? Part of the answer lies in a better understanding of one's means of expression, both its affordances and limitations. Consider Packy Jim's contemplation of two hagiographic stories about St. Patrick's exploits in the local area.

> Then there was that story about Lough Derg and Saint Patrick, and Saint Patrick slaying that *serpent*, that serpent that was attacking and killing livestock and killing humans and ravaging the country *around*, before Saint Patrick's time.
>
> He came on the scene, and he was supposed to kill the serpent, and the serpent bled so much blood that, uh, the water of the lough became red and, uh, "derg" then was the old Gaelic word for red. And it become known, then, as Lough *Derg*.
>
> Well, Johnny Cunningham [a local historian], he wrote a story about Lough Derg, a book about it I have it in the house if you're interested in it, any time I'd give it to you.
>
> Well, *he thought*—that was only thinking, of course—that a *famine* or a *pestilence* could've been working in the area, killing people like, as either of the two can. And he chatted about, like, the way he termed it, an *allegorical* tale, and that that could have been the *monster*—a pestilence or a famine working locally—that that story about Lough Derg, he termed it an allegorical tale. It's a big word, like, but it refers to—as the saying goes—a sort of double-meaning thing, this or *this*.
>
> And do you know what it is but *Johnny Cunningham could have a POINT*.
>
> Aye.
>
> But there's the thing about that, uh, Saint Patrick's Well there [in Magherakeel townland, County Tyrone]. There was a monastery there beside that well down the road there, a bit from it—you might see the butts of the walls of it there when you go by Paddy McFadden's, it's there to be seen. And I don't know what order of monks they were— damn me if I know—but, uh, some important man, *clerical* man—like an abbot from some other place or a *head* abbot—could've come there and stopped a lock of days, and it's possible that that's the well that they

lifted the water from, that they carried the water from that well *there*. And he'd go there, and he'd bless that *well*.

Well, he'd be a man—as the saying goes—that'd be a stranger to the *locals*, and maybe a bit higher in rank nor the ordinary clerical monk would be, and that them people, then, telling it from father to son to grandson and on down, that he got *confused* with Saint *Patrick*, do you understand.

But it's said, and it's believed, that there's a cure in that well. That well was blessed by somebody.

But that's only a theory, again, that *I* have, that it could be some *other* important cleric that blessed it. It is possible. Aye.

But now it's said that there's a cure in it. It's said that that well is a good well. (March 18, 1999)

Faced with unlikely events in otherwise locally accepted and officially sanctioned hagiography, Packy Jim's first proposition is that allegory accounts for the fantastical and perhaps familiar element of hero combat with a serpent or dragon. The theory that the ravaging serpent offers a figurative way to express the horrors of famine and pestilence comports with folklorists' interpretations of myth and legend as conveying nonliteral truths.[7] Packy Jim neither accepts the story at face value nor dismisses it as patently false. Rather, he entertains the more complicated notion that the truth of the story is metaphorical rather than literal and that the characters involved stand in for ideas worth thinking.

In the second story attributing the cure in a Magherakeel holy well to Saint Patrick, Packy Jim does not doubt the cure that has relieved many, including his mother. He believes in cures and miracles, but he also entertains the euhemerist's notion that mythical events and characters are often embellished distortions of historical events and characters. Packy Jim shares with storytellers in Bally-menone a sense that their communities were too insignificant to have attracted so great a figure as Saint Patrick,[8] and he reasons that, great though he was, Saint Patrick was a mortal man and unlikely to have been to every place that claims a connection. Other lesser-known missionaries would have done the work in humble Magherakeel, though Saint Patrick eventually got the credit. Here Packy Jim explains remarkable but questionable narrative elements not by virtue of generic conventions such as metaphor and allegory but through an appreciation of the dynamics of memory and oral tradition over time, including the tendency to concentrate the actions of many into that of one character and to attribute those actions to the most recognizable or famous character.[9] In other conversations, he has doubted local lore maintaining that at this well Patrick summoned and converted the local pagan chieftains as he had at the

Packy Jim surveying Crilly

Hill of Slane in County Meath—a place of greater power and importance—
and he discounts the motif that Saint Patrick personally created the holy well in
Magherakeel by striking a rock with his staff. For the ultimate source of that
detail he points to the story of Moses doing the same thing to persuade non-
believers of God's power (Numbers 20:11). So Catholic believer though he is,
Packy Jim entertains the notions of traveling motifs and oicotypes as would a
folklorist faced with multiple versions and variants of essentially the same story
localized in numerous places.[10]

Perhaps more fundamentally Packy Jim can both believe in core numinous reality yet doubt the generic conventions and exigencies of hagiographic
narrative—and even the official teachings of the Church—because he has a
sophisticated understanding of the relationship between the sacred and the
profane, one not unlike that of Mircea Eliade or Max Weber. For Packy Jim,
priests may be able to exorcise ghosts, for example, but in doing so they are
channeling divine power, the same divine power that lay people, such as Agnes
Lunney, may channel to heal others. It is not that priests and the rites of the
Church are unnecessary. At times they claim or are granted too much authority, but they are essentially conduits for and reminders of the sacred in this
quotidian, profane, and inevitably unreliable world. As it is for Eliade's conception of *homo religiosis*, for Packy Jim outbreaks of the sacred in this profane
world—hierophanies—point to ultimate reality (Eliade 1959). At the same

time, Packy Jim is sophisticated enough to realize that our understandings and commemorations of such hierophanies are always circumscribed by our human temporality, means of expression, and social structures.

There is a parallel dynamic at work in Weber's notion of routinized charisma. In his terms, charismatic authority—the authority based on the radical genius, often understood as divinity, of figures such as Jesus—is ultimately untenable. Charisma and the original inspiration for belief—often understood as revelation—will be succeeded by efforts to traditionalize, rationalize, bureaucratize, and codify, as is common in the institutionalization of religion ([1904–1905] 1976; [1922] 1964). But, as Packy Jim appreciates, those layers of routinization are not the "really real," as Clifford Geertz terms it (1973:112, 121, 124). They are the trappings of the profane world whose authority is relative because they are constructed and circumscribed. So for Packy Jim, the Church is venerable and necessary for educating humanity about the gospel and Christian faith, but it remains a second-order manmade institution that is limited—as are all human faculties—in its ability to grapple with, contain, or even relate first-order revelation. The Church provides us manners of saying and thinking things—whether through narrative, symbol, or ritual—but we are limited to the metaphorical "as if" in our conceptualization of and communication about the sacred. This does not amount to a hostility on Packy Jim's part toward organized religion, its hierarchy of clergy, or its tools of communication—narrative, symbol, and ritual. Rather, Packy Jim has matured through a willingness to question, to the point that he maintains a healthy skepticism for the things of this profane world while holding to a firm belief in the sacred, a belief buoyed by narratives—however imperfect or circumscribed—of the numinous experiences of others.

Such orientations and perspectives resonate in Packy Jim's account of one particular miraculous outbreak of the sacred in the profane world. After discussing the Garden of Eden story as metaphorical rather than literally accurate, then describing the end of the world—"I would say the end of the world, as John's Jimmy said, will be some big change"—Packy Jim recalled everything he could about the Marian apparition at Fatima.

There was two sisters and a cousin of theirs in Fatima, in Portugal. If I'm not making a mistake it was a boy and two girls—brother and sister, maybe, and a cousin—and they were sent till herd goats or sheep on some little hill in the distance on which *bushes* grew. One of the bushes was an *oak* bush.

And they were doing this herding for the parents. And suddenly, suddenly there was a rattle of *thunder* and, uh, just in the oak bush, no bit away from them, a big, big, big, big, big, big *ball of LIGHT*, around like that in the branches of the bush. And in the middle of that ball of light was a *lady* standing.

And she *spoke* to them.

I don't mind now the words that she spoke to them, but they kneeled down. They took it for granted very, very quickly that that was the Blessed Virgin. And I think that she told them to say some prayers, kneel down and say the rosary and say some prayers, but the interview that she give them was very short. But she told them, "I'll be here again this day [in a] *month*."

So they went home and they told the story about this rattle of thunder, this big ball of light in the bush, this lady appearing—they told it—and then that she'd be back again that same *time*, same day next month, which she was.

And that went on and on. There was some chat between them and they had to kneel down and say prayers. Neighbors come and neighbors looked, but the bush was there but damned all they could see at all, do you understand. But they could see the children and they knowed that the children was talking to somebody, but they could see nothing.

So, uh, she appeared six times to them from April to October, and she said that she was going to show a miracle on the last month that she would appear, which was October. And, uh, it was 1917. And she told them that two of them would soon be dead and would be in Heaven with her, but one of them was to remain in the world for a long, long, long time, and she's not that many years dead yet.

So, uh, October come along anyway, and it was raining cats and dogs. And there were people coming early in the day or earlier in the night before from all directions until there was thousands gathered, thousands of people.

But, uh, it was remarked—a lot of them had come and journeyed till it was wringing with the rain, wet—but it was remarked that the sky cleared and the sun come out, but then when you looked away in the distance it was still raining in the distance two or three mile away still letting down. But the sun come out, people's clothes started to dry and feeling—as the saying goes—they were feeling good. So, uh, finally she *come*, anyway, but, uh, again the time she come, there was lots of people got fed up waiting and there was a good deal of people moving off in different directions, moving off, but there was still a lot *there*.

But, uh, the miracle, anyway, *was* or it did be that the sun was in the sky to be seen. And the sun started waving and dancing about like that,

walking about and big long spikes of light of different colors skating
away from it in all directions, scooting away from it, red and blue and
orange, on like that. And it was dancing about. And the people got
scared, scared the wits out of them, and they threw themselves down
on the ground—as the saying goes—and they, and they begged *to* God *for*
MERCY.

Then after a minute—as the saying goes—all become *still again*, and
the Blessed *Virgin* appeared, and that was the end of the story.

Well, I read about it, a little pamphlet about it, but Christ of
Almighty maybe it's fifty years ago, so like, uh, you don't mind all the
details. But that is, that's the rough part of the story.

She had told them, *too*, sometime during the session that the present
war would soon end. That was the First World War, which ended on the
eleventh of November 1918. And she said if the world wouldn't pull
itself together—to say it that way—to become a better world, another *war*
was to *follow*, which come in nineteen years later. She told them that, and
that two of them would be dead and that they'd soon be in Heaven and
one of them would be in the world for a long time. And she entered some
nunnery, and she was a nun for the remainder of her days, and she's not
that wild long dead. I think she lived to be way over ninety years of age
before she died.

Aye, it's a great place of pilgrimage, and there's a big, big cathedral
built about it, and it's a great place for people going. It's what you may
call one of the famous Marian shrines, Fatima in Portugal. Like Knock
or Medjugorje or Guadalupe in Mexico.

Oh that was true enough all right.

I read a fairly brief outline of it in a, in an *Ireland's Own*, wrote by that
Englishman, John Macklin, that, you know, prints them stories. It was
something similar to what I'd read in the booklet. The *first person* that I
heared talking about Fatima was Black Johnny Corry, way back about
nineteen forty-one. He was telling it here, he was in the smuggling line,
dropping things here for people to collect. That was the first that I heared
talking about it, Black Johnny Corry, as far back maybe as nineteen forty-
one or nineteen forty. But then I read a booklet about it at a later date.

Oh it was quite true, quite true all right.

But this sun started walloping about like that in all directions with
spikes of light shooting away from it in all directions and the people got
terrified. They threw down, threw down their, dropped down on their
knees and begged God for forgiveness. They thought it was the end of
the world.

Oh aye.

And there was some kind of a *secret*, some kind of a secret that was to be made known to the world in nineteen sixty. And this secret was, uh, written on a paper and put in a sealed envelope and given to the pope. And the pope was supposed to turn *pale* when he read it. Apparently she was to have made some kind of a hideous prophecy believed to be concerning some major disaster that would strike this world. But that there was *no* . . . the pope never said nothing, kept quiet about it. But he was supposed to turn pale when he read it. I heared that. Nineteen sixty, they were all preaching way back at that time that this was going to be known—whatever the hell it was about, like—it was going to be known.

But the pope, he kept mum about it.

Oh I heared that.

That's true. That's true. (November 16, 2011)

Although Packy Jim's account differs in some details from print sources concerning the Marian apparition at Fatima,[11] essentially the story revolves around a hierophany and prophecies of future events that, when fulfilled, further authenticate the divine nature of the apparition. In the face of the otherworldly dancing of the sun, the gathered people witness true power and fear the end of the world. The pope, too, blanches at the Virgin's unspecified prophecy about traumatic events to come, presumably concerning the End Times. Indeed, the pope cannot handle the truth—or thinks that the faithful cannot—and keeps it a secret, allowing room for conspiracy theories. The content of such theories does not matter in that the more important effect of keeping secrets is the suggestion that the pope's authority is merely bureaucratic and temporal. While the sacred reveals itself and conveys important information to the lowest and least powerful—peasant children herding sheep and lay pilgrims from all walks of life—the pope, the ruler and figurehead of the Church, is somehow threatened by the very power that he and his institution are meant to intercede with and purport to represent. Miracles and revelation are first-order numinous experience, and in the face of hierophany the Church may lack authority and relevance. Its attempts at containment may confirm its profane, incomplete, and second-order nature.

As a narrative, Packy Jim's account of the Fatima apparition follows the now familiar conventions of supernatural legend, employing authenticating devices that mount a rhetoric of truth, inviting us to contemplate whether this world and the next really are as we assume. Through attribution to reliable sources, descriptive details, direct speech, and explicit declarations of truth, Packy Jim vouches for these events as accurate, extraordinary, and meaningful.

Stories framed by truth claims—ranging from full belief (Fatima), through ambivalence (the Hammer Man) and skepticism (Saint Patrick and the serpent), to full disbelief (the fairy suite, Mrs. Peake)—bear witness to Packy Jim's locally and collectively informed but ultimately personal positions as a rational believer. Taken together, these stories of supernatural events offer direct insight into Packy Jim's worldview, particularly into his conceptions of the sacred and the profane and of their interrelationship.

7

Community
in a World of Limited Good

How do you know when you are finished conducting ethnographic fieldwork? One answer is something of a cliché: you are done once you can predict what your interviewee is going to say. I thought that I might be nearing that point in November 2011, but then Packy Jim told me a story about an instance of witchcraft that took place not far from his home. It was a story that I had never heard him tell and that was in fact relatively new to him.

The story is a localized version of a migratory legend—common in Ireland, known also in Britain, Scandinavia, and other parts of Europe—in which a person transforms into a hare to steal milk from a neighbor's cow. In doing so the witch magically acquires that cow's dairy output and particularly the butter-fat content necessary for churning butter, traditionally a reliable source of income. Upon discovering the witch in the form of a hare, the cow's owner shoots the hare, often with an improvised bullet, possibly with magical properties, such as a silver coin. The witch's identity is revealed once he or more usually she transforms back into human form with a tell-tale wound. Among other things, the story is proof, if needed, that Packy Jim's narrative repertoire is not static, that he actively seeks out and incorporates stories that not only stir his interest but also confirm, elaborate, or challenge what he takes for granted.

The conversational context for Packy Jim's witch hare story was in some ways artificial in that we were not having an entirely open-ended chat. As I had in 2002 when videoing his version of the origin of the fairies, I asked him in November 2011 for stories I already knew he had while making a video for teaching purposes, a kind of greatest hits collection, volume 2. The topic at hand was, again, the fairies—always a favorite among American college students eager for accounts of the supernatural. First I prompted Packy Jim by asking about his great-grandfather hearing fairy music at Meenabol bush, then as we proceeded I gave him the space to transition to other stories along similar topical lines or I prompted him for specific stories when he came to the end of a thematic thread. Eventually Packy Jim shifted from stories about the fairies that he takes to be nonfiction into the three stories I have come to think of as the "fairy suite"—"The Top Grain of Croghan," "Segronan Fairies," and "Nick the Nogginweaver." Although Packy Jim understands the fairy suite to be fiction, the motif of fairies attempting to "sweep" or abduct the youthful bride in the final story seems to have prompted him to bring up a traditional belief in changelings—old, worn out, cranky fairies left in the place of young children, brides, and other valued humans who are taken away to the Otherworld. Although Packy Jim had no local examples of suspected changelings to narrate, he had read about them in *Ireland's Own*, and he holds open the possibility that such abductions occurred in the past.

Packy Jim lingered on the theme of covetousness, whether that of the fairies whose society parallels our own, or the envy and greed of our more immediate human neighbors. Without rehearsing the full story, he mentioned the familial treachery behind Barney McFadden's eviction from Carrickaholten as an example of damnable covetousness (see chapter 4). Then he struck out into what to me was new territory:

> Well then, there was another thing then. There was what they called the *witches*. Witches in old Ireland were said to be pretty common, were said to be pretty common in England and European countries as well, *witches*.
>
> And that was using the black *art*. Whatever way it worked, you got to use the black art and, uh, you could have changed yourself into the shape of a *hare*. And, uh, that may be one way that you got the milk.
>
> Probably another way that you got the milk was you walked in the dark of the night to the people's byre with a little container with you, and you took a little stroan of milk from each of the two or three or four cows that was there, into your container, and you took it home with you. And by means of that, it meant that when them people went to churn their milk they had a very bad, poor return for their milk. They had little or no butter. But when you went to churn your drop of milk you had the full of the tub of butter.
>
> Oh, that was—I doubt there was something about that, too.
>
> So, uh, anyway, this is a story of Willie McHugh's that I heared, uh . . . Well, you'd want to keep quiet about it, too.

Up to this point, Packy Jim had introduced a set of traditional beliefs and purported practices involving witchcraft, said to be common in the past in Ireland and beyond. From this prologue he proceeded to name people involved in a local occurrence of milk-stealing witchcraft as told to him by his friend and distant neighbor Willie McHugh. More importantly perhaps, Packy Jim named the protagonists' second- and third-generation descendants and more distant relations still living in the area, noting that they might not appreciate his committing the story to print. With Packy Jim's permission I quote the rest of the story below, omitting identifying geographical information and using pseudonyms to disguise the protagonists. As he shifted from prologue to the story proper, Packy Jim sat on the edge of his chair, straightened his back, and began to rub his hands back and forth on his knees. Taking his time with the set up, descending in volume then punctuating the end of his lines with emphasis on key images and ideas, Packy Jim continued to build tension throughout with dramatic pauses and shifts in volume and tone.

> Denny Byrne
> > or his woman
> > > or the both
> > > > was supposed to be *witches*
> > > > taking the milk off, away from neighbors' *cows*.

So Willie McHugh's story is: old Robert Harrison who lived out there, him and his sister Kate—lived there, brother and sister—and, uh, Denny Byrne was known to be dangerous for taking the, taking the milk off your *cows*.

And old Robert Harrison had a muzzle-loading *gun*.

And he had *powder*, but he had no hail [shot]. He had powder, no *hail*.

Well, you put in the powder—there was a cap that was put in or some damned thing, and then there was the powder put in, and then there was some piece of paper put in, and then the *hail* was put in, and then there was another piece of paper put in, in front, and then you were ready then for your *shooting*.

So. He had no hail for his gun.

So. He decided on another method.

He put in his cap, he put in his powder, he put in a piece of paper, and he put in a silver threepenny bit, and he put in a piece of paper again, and then he was ready for *action*.

So according to the story, he was outside about the door, he had his cow or his cows in the *byre*. I don't know whether he was looking out for this, looking out for this outfit or not, anyway—I don't *know*. But begod he sees the hare going out of the byre *door*.

He races for his *gun.*
He fired at the *hare.*
The hare give a *screech,* but she *went ON.*
AND.
The next thing happened, the doctor was summoned from
Castlederg and he landed up there to treat Denny Byrne for a, for a
wound somewhere, on the body.
If you're interested in that story more fully—maybe you are and maybe
you're not—if you contact Willie McHugh, he might be able to—as the
saying goes—picture the thing quite differently.
But *that* is the story that he fired at the *hare,* the hare give a *screech*
but went on, and then the next day the doctor from Castlederg was
summoned up to treat Denny Byrne for a wound on his body somewhere.
That's the story, and I didn't hear that one until of late, inside
maybe the last twelve or fourteen months. Willie McHugh—as the saying
goes—told me that story. Well *that* was *news to ME.*
Willie McHugh doesn't tell *lies* or anything like that. Well he heared it
from his daddy or old James McHugh or people that lived in the locality.
(November 18, 2011)

When Packy Jim finished, I wondered aloud whether the doctor found a silver
coin in the wound, imagining its potential as an additional piece of evidence
and knowing that this motif is present in other versions of the legend (see Ní
Dhuibhne 1993:77). He did not recall hearing that detail. Either this motif of
the tell-tale silver coin found in the witch's wound was not a part of Willie
McHugh's telling or it did not stick in Packy Jim's memory, which seems im-
probable. Packy Jim then reiterated his main authenticating device—attributing
the story to a credible source, emphasizing that neither Willie nor the rest of his
family tell lies. Unfortunately I have not been able to ask Willie McHugh further
questions. Even if Willie had told the story as codology—as a test of gullibility,
which is possible but unlikely in that he and Packy Jim are close friends—the
story corroborates for Packy Jim a widespread older belief specifically in dairy-
stealing witchcraft and more generally in neighbors pilfering each other's luck
and prosperity through supernatural means. These supernatural means include
intentional uses of "the black art" (witchcraft) and the evil eye—the not necessarily conscious ability to inflict harm or bad luck through an envious glance at
the belongings or loved ones of others.

Packy Jim had occasion to tell his witch hare story a second time during a
more open-ended chat two and a half years later. Again he held open the door
to belief, this time with the additional authenticating power of the proverbial

saying: "Oh I doubt [think] there was something about it. As they chat about, there's hardly ever—as the saying goes—smoke without a *fire*." Here again the conversational surround—that which came before and after the story—builds a context of association, amplifying themes and conveying meaning through relation.

While walking to Packy Jim's house in June 2014, I saw a notice on a gate that declared tests were being conducted to determine the feasibility of erecting electricity-generating windmills in the area. Naturally enough, I asked Packy Jim about the notice once I arrived. He had complaints about the company involved being misleading to him and to others, but his main focus was on the awkwardness and even open conflict stirred by the possibility of one neighbor getting a greater windfall than the next. Apparently it takes relatively little for people on adjoining land to object and wreck a neighbor's deal with these wind farm companies. As Packy Jim assessed the situation, resuming his role as vernacular social critic:

> Old jealousy, because somebody's getting a couple of quid out of it. Oh now, I'm telling you, *old jealousy*, that's the Irish for you! It's running away from father to son, to grandfather to great-grandfather, all the way back for a thousand years, I would think, running through the blood stream or the genetics or whatever the hell you like to call it. That's what I would think.
>
> Maybe it's only an old pishtreog [superstition] but they chat, too, about the evil eye, about this jealous look taking the luck out of—maybe you have a nice couple of pigs doing wild well and then one of them takes ill and dies. They chat about this being over the evil eye, a person admiring and coveting your pigs, giving them a look.
>
> And even you don't mean to or even you don't *know* you have the evil eye, it has its effect, do you understand.

Without my prompting, Packy Jim had made a connection to the evil eye. From there he continued with a couple sensitive stories of ill will between neighbors competing for fortune and profit in a world of limited good, and he took every opportunity to lambaste the unfortunately plentiful sort of people who would prefer to see their neighbors "going downhill rather than up." With the evil eye on the table, Packy Jim again searched for illustration in narrative and landed on the story of a local man, Black Henry McCutcheon, who was accused—unfairly, according to Packy Jim—of having the evil eye and being the cause of livestock dying, particularly calves and milk-giving cows.

Evidence for McCutcheon's culpability was circumstantial, based on his habit of strolling through fields—perhaps surveying neighbors' animals—rather than taking established paths and main roads. He was remarked to be an oddity in other ways as well: unmarried, socially awkward, jobless and idle, and too much under the thumb of his parents and later his sister. (Similarities here to his own reputation, among less charitable people, are not lost on Packy Jim.) Lacking hard evidence but believing the rumor all the same, one man, Dody McGoldrick, dug two false graves to look like the burial of calves in an effort to convince others—and perhaps McCutcheon himself—that McCutcheon had the evil eye and was responsible for these fabricated deaths. The fact that accusations were false, according to Packy Jim, only serves to underscore the lengths to which people will go in the inevitable competition between neighbors. This theme he further elaborated by discussing how a relative of one of the people involved in the evil eye story got rich informing on smugglers to the authorities—a dangerous bid to profit at the direct expense of neighbors and a clear violation of the border's (ideal) libertarian, equalitarian, anti-authoritarian, and solidary ethos.

With neighborly discord, jealousy, and treachery a clearly established theme, Packy Jim launched into a version of his story about Denny Byrne the witch hare, which was similar to the one from 2011 quoted above. In 2014, however, he followed his witch hare story with a newly remembered childhood memory:

Ah, there was an old woman up there, up there in Fermanagh—Mrs. Turner, Mrs. Margaret Turner—and she was blaming, uh, a local, uh, that lived nearby for, for, for being a witch. She was Monaghan, Miss Monaghan, Alice Monaghan, Alice the Baffler. Whether she imagined it or not, I don't know.

But, uh, she used to keep a turkey cock, and me and Mammy used to be up a time or so with the hen to roost her. And she took a fancy for Mammy. I mind her—tea was scarce at the time in the State—I mind her giving Mammy a good big present of tea, maybe half a pound of tea or so. Far, far more nor Mammy sold half crown for the turkey anyway.

But she said about this lassie, she was looking over the half—"I was looking over the *half door*," she says, "and this old hare jumped on the, jumped up on the wall in front of the street, and it stuck out its teeth at me."

And she says, "I called '*hares and witches and dirty butter!*' and it jumped off and run away again!"

Aye. "*Hares and WITCHES and DIRTY butter!*"

Aye. I mind her telling that to Mammy, old Mrs. Turner. (June 18, 2014)

According to Packy Jim, Mrs. Turner's recognition and declaration of witchcraft, accompanied by her chant-like anti-charm "hares and witches and dirty butter," was enough to safeguard her milk and prosperity from what she took to be her neighbor's attempts at theft. Apparently knowledge, and not violence alone, is a key to disarming one's secret enemy. Just as Margaret Turner undermines Alice Monaghan by exposing her secret, Dody McGoldrick wants all in the locality to know of Henry McCutcheon's supposed power so that, in knowing, neighbors can take precautions, not least further shunning and stigmatizing of McCutcheon. When Robert Harrison learns the truth about Denny Byrne, confirmed by the wound and the doctor's visit, his knowledge backed by the threat of violence ensures that Byrne will not try the same trick again.

Note that I am treating in the same category Packy Jim's two witch hare stories and his evil eye story—and to some extent the nonsupernatural story of the man who informed on his neighbors' smuggling, and even the contemporary gossip and wrangling about wind farms—because Packy Jim does: they all speak to the same constellation of concerns. A large part of this constellation consists of anxieties over the conflict of economic interests and the balance to be struck between personal gain and community well-being.

Drawing from a broader but similar corpus of stories concerning witchcraft, the black art, fairy theft, and supernatural aggression in Ballymenone, County Fermanagh, Henry Glassie adduces a set of principles concerning prosperity and profit in particular (1982:527–551). The basic local understanding is that making a living requires intelligence and hard work, but this is not enough to make one rich. There are two paths to wealth, both of which require something more. One path involves evil, specifically witchcraft, which may be characterized as the use of magic to circumvent hard work and intelligence, gaining an easy profit at the expense of your neighbors. The other path requires luck and the continued application of intelligence and hard work during the good times that are not necessarily deserved or earned but bestowed by God nonetheless.

If the first path springs from greed, envy, spite, and the willingness to opt out of community, the second path comes with the obligation of generosity to one's neighbors so as not to cross or join paths with the witch. As Glassie observes, the witch "is a projection, proposed out of fears within to mark the acceptable limit of success" (1982:548). To be a witch is to steal and to advance one's interests at the expense of others, disrupting community equilibrium. To be a member of community is to give, to share the profits of and extend the circulation of luck. Note that Mrs. Turner is the opposite of her witch nemesis in giving Packy Jim's mother a great quantity of tea in a time of scarcity, in being open-handed beyond the obligations of their economic transaction.

Glassie further observes that the anxiety over profit revolves logically around the dairy. Milk is the product of God-given natural resources, and the butter churned from it is sold for a profit to outside parties—not unlike the wind-powered electricity sold to urban suppliers. With butter, the ideal counterbalance to the destabilizations of profit is to share this gift within the community in symbolically crucial acts of hospitality and reciprocity, blunting the excessive gain of a purely self-serving, profit-driven enterprise. As yet there is no equivalent line of reasoning or ritual to settle the current wind farm wars, but whether one reaps profit from wind or from rain, grass, and cows, Glassie observes that profit in itself is not considered wrong:

> The land's bounty is evidence of God's goodness, and success in extending it into profit can be read as a sign of His support. . . . People are free to pursue profit so long as they negate the witch's traits of spite and greed by remaining "harmless" and generous, "good" so long as they uphold neighborliness: so long as they, as they would say, "fear God and harm no man." (1982:549)

So the sin is not profit per se but that profit is ill-gotten and selfishly used. It is "dirty butter" from which nothing good can come, and it connects conceptually to other forms of ill-fated profiteering. The two-faced man who sold information about smugglers to the police died with tens of thousands of pounds in the bank, but the money was unlucky and eventually given away to distant relatives. Cassie and Danny McFadden framed Barney McFadden to take over his land, but the priest cursed their sins and their fortunes dwindled to penury and debt. Land stolen in conquest, held fast through the mechanisms of injustice—military occupation, Penal Laws, rack-renting, gerrymandered electoral districting—became the stage for centuries of compounding tragedy, all but foreclosing the possibility of community. In reaction, the outlaw—inadequate for effecting political change but symbolically resonant—strikes a blow for justice by robbing the profiteering landlord class, inevitably sacrificing himself for the collective. It is tempting to cast our most recent global financial crisis in terms of so much dirty butter while we await our Proinsias Dubh. Suffice to say that in the witch hare legend and related stories the mercenary logic of capitalism and self-interested individualism find significant resistance.

We have seen this theme in Packy Jim's repertoire before. Roused by the place-world of the sod house built and abandoned by Barney McFadden, Packy Jim recalled the unfolding of his unjust eviction, then railed against "old greed," "a lust for worldly things," and, notably, "ambition." In a world of limited good, one person's advancement entails the diminishment of others unless precautions are taken, unless generosity to one's neighbors is constant and unstinting. Striving and profit are permissible but within limits. The path of the witch, however, is beyond the pale. Indeed, the deep-seated anxiety over ambition has roots in the outcome of the War in Heaven with the fall of the Angel of Pride and the origin of the fairies.

The witch hare legend and associated stories speak to another related anxiety as well: having secret enemies among those with whom you regularly interact and customarily trust. Such an anxiety may have special resonance along the Irish border. While there is evidence that belief in witch hares stretches back to the medieval era in Ireland, Éilís Ní Dhuibhne (1993) demonstrates that the documented twentieth-century distribution of the corollary migratory legend told by Packy Jim corresponds to areas on the denominationally mixed edge of the sixteenth- and seventeenth-century Plantation. That is, judging from sixty-three versions of the witch hare legend collected by the Irish Folklore Commission (IFC), mostly in the 1930s and '40s and as late as 1975, the legend survives most strongly in areas that are divided between Catholics and Protestants such as the northern border counties of Donegal, Cavan, and Monaghan. (The National Folklore Collection, the current repository of IFC materials, has less information for Tyrone and Fermanagh, but the story is documented there as well.) Indeed, in most of the versions Ní Dhuibhne discusses, the witch who uses magic for easy profit is old, female, and Protestant, whereas a younger male Catholic commits the violence that reveals the witch and breaks the spell. As such, Ní Dhuibhne's compelling argument—drawing from Bengt af Klintberg's (1978) assertion that the survival of migratory legends depends on their sociological relevance—is that "the legend is a useful vehicle for feelings of resentment directed at people of a minority religion or social group" (1993:78).

Key here is the concept of projection. For the sake of argument, a Catholic may be hostile toward a particular Protestant or Protestants in general, but in a plural society with community as the shared ideal, such hostility is inadmissible to others and perhaps to oneself. Therefore one denies that hostility while projecting it on to a Protestant, cast in the role of witch, the one who attacks and threatens community (cf. Rieti 2008:43). There is no reason, however, that this Catholic–Protestant polarity cannot be reversed.

Having concentrated their efforts on Irish-speaking and recently Irish-speaking areas, the Irish Folklore Commission had closer ties, better access, and greater commitment to Catholic informants. It is perhaps no surprise that the overwhelmingly Catholic-supplied texts feature Protestant witches as symbolic representatives of a resented minority group. One issue, however, that makes social life conceptually complex along the Irish border is that both Catholics and Protestants can be considered a minority or a majority relative to each other, depending on whether one considers demographics on a local, regional, national, or all-island scale. Protestants may be in the majority in parts of Tyrone, Fermanagh, and Donegal—until recently in Pettigo and for the time being in Northern Ireland—but they are the minority on the island as a whole. Likewise, Catholics may be in the majority in more marginal places such as Lettercran, Aghyaran, or Ballymenone but they are outnumbered certainly across Northern Ireland and closer to hand in villages such as Killen and large swathes of North Fermanagh. Following Ní Dhuibhne we might expect that any given person said to be a witch is consciously or unconsciously cast as the representative of a resented minority group, but whether that person is a Protestant or a Catholic probably depends on storytellers' and audiences' perspectives on demographic superiority and other forms of dominance in a given local area. Which group is the detested minority is fluid.

In each of Packy Jim's witch hare and evil eye stories, supernatural aggression occurs across denominational lines. On the one hand, the witches Byrne and Monaghan are Catholic, whereas the victims-turned-vanquishers are Protestant—a reversal of the pattern established by the greater number and geographic range of Ní Dhuibhne's examples. On the other hand, in the conceptually parallel story involving the evil eye, Black Henry McCutcheon is Protestant and his accuser and most of his neighbors are Catholic, confirming the pattern Ní Dhuibhne encountered in the IFC materials. This see-sawing of polarities does not call Ní Dhuibhne's work into question but rather is commensurate with the demographic patchwork quilt of Packy Jim's world situated at the collision of Donegal, Tyrone, and Fermanagh.

At least in the limited sample from Packy Jim's repertoire, the victims of supernatural aggression can be either Catholic or Protestant, but if the victim is Protestant, the perpetrator will be Catholic and vice versa. If af Klintberg is correct that migratory legends circulate and survive if they speak to cultural, socioeconomic, and political tensions, Packy Jim's three accounts of supernatural aggression seem to resonate with anxieties about the Other, specifically having secret enemies among neighbors from the "other side of the house." Indeed the border is a place where the ideal of neighborly reciprocity and mutual support regardless of one's religion—in other words, community—is threatened by secretive, exclusive societies such as the Orange Order and the Ancient Order of Hibernians. This is a place where in the very recent past one's neighbor may have opted out of community by leading a double life as an informer or as a loyalist or republican paramilitary or indeed by serving as a part-time policeman or soldier, enforcing the will of the state at the expense of local autonomy and solidarity. Having a secret enemy may well be a universal fear regardless of place and time period, but this is likely to be compounded in a milieu where, although lip service to community is paid through daily politeness in mixed company, one remains aware that the truth beneath the surface may be utterly at odds with appearances.

Of course, one issue that cannot be ignored is gender. Ní Dhuibhne observes that, "as is general in witch-hunting syndromes, the resentment focuses on the most vulnerable and also most despised representative of the minority group, the solitary, usually old, woman" (1993:78; cf. Lysaght 1994:223). This argument parallels Richard Jenkins's (1991) conclusion that stories of supernatural aggression by female witches, violently put in their place by men, illuminate tensions in power relations between the sexes. Given the materials Ní Dhuibhne and Jenkins explore, the gendered aspect of their arguments is convincing, but if we look only to Packy Jim's stories, gender differentials do not seem relevant. Robert Harrison and Denny Byrne, protagonist and antagonist, are both men; Margaret Turner and Alice Monaghan, protagonist and antagonist, are both women. There may be an age differential between *Mrs.* Turner and *Miss* Monaghan, but it is the reverse of what we might expect from the pattern Ní Dhuibhne illustrates where the witch is the older and, it is assumed, more stigmatized character. Likewise in the stories about witchcraft collected by Glassie in Ballymenone—including the witch hare legend—the characters at odds are quite often the same gender but the opposite religion, shifting the emphasis onto tensions in cross-denominational neighborly relationships rather than gendered familial ones (1982:527–551). Again, none of this undermines Ní Dhuibhne's or Jenkins's arguments about the witch hare story carrying messages of sociological relevance and projecting anxieties from everyday life into folk narrative. A battle between the sexes is clear in Ní Dhuibhne's and Jenkins's materials, but the witch hare legend also offers itself as a conceptual model for thinking through other problematic relationships. As Glassie argues, legends about supernatural aggression speak to anxieties over "any social relation that can become saturated with guilt and confusion" (1982:781).

In Packy Jim's repertoire and in Packy Jim's world, the more pressing relationship saturated with guilt and confusion seems to be that between neighboring Catholics and Protestants struggling with the ideal of community in a world of limited good. In a context such as the Irish border, there is clear sociological and psychological relevance to narratives that stage age-old conflicts between neighbors, and sometimes their resolution. Such repeatable, transposable narratives speak to deep-seated concerns while shaping conceptual frameworks that guide how people perceive, think, and behave. While Packy Jim's recently acquired witch hare legend reminds us that no storyteller's repertoire is static—and that while ethnographic fieldwork must end, it is never in fact complete—this story and related ones also invite a more explicit examination of something that has been implicit throughout this book so far: worldview.

8

Worldview

The concept of worldview can be problematic and nebulous. But shaped to fit a particular project and speak to specific materials, "worldview" remains a useful label for a constellation of interrelated frames of mind, orientations, assumptions, beliefs, and convictions about the nature of life, time, the sacred and profane, space and place, self and others, society and humanity. One question not yet addressed is whose worldview we are discussing.

Packy Jim's worldview, of course, is our focus, but to what extent can we say that his worldview is also representative of the collective, shared by others in his immediate vicinity, in the north of Ireland generally, throughout the island, or across northern Europe? As Gregory Schrempp observes,

> Though it is possible to talk about the unique worldview of a particular individual, it is probably fair to say that, considered in its long-term history as a concept, "worldview" tends to have a collective orientation. Even when the focus is a particular individual, the worldview in question often turns out to be a variant of more broadly-shared traditional themes. (1996:21)

Here I am not making direct claims about the worldview of any individual except Packy Jim. That said, in a world where our mouths are full of the words of others, where sense-making is achieved through bricolage and appeals to shared tradition, Packy Jim's worldview is bound to articulate the personal and the collective at the one time. The exact proportions cannot be quantified exactly, but I repeat: let it not be said that privileging one individual as a focus for study is too small a scale, the details too microcosmic, the stakes too low. As Lauri Honko observes, the only way we can learn and substantiate anything about worldview or tradition or indeed culture is through engaging with individual human minds, their articulations and artifacts (1998:70–71).

We cannot say, for example, that the worldview of Menocchio, the sixteenth-century Italian miller investigated by Carlo Ginzburg ([1976] 2013), is exactly the same as that of his neighbors in early modern Montereale. Departing from church teachings, Menocchio declared, for example, that the universe had formed from chaos as cheese forms from milk, with angels spontaneously emerging from the mass as do worms. His casual blasphemy and his unorthodox vision of the creation were not seen as merely idiosyncratic but rather were determined by Church inquisitors to be sufficient heresy for his execution. Nevertheless, Menocchio came to his eccentric, even anarchic, beliefs in reaction to the same conditions as his neighbors, thinking through the same official catechism, oral traditions, and popular literature in circulation among them. Certainly many of his contemporaries would have made more conformist uses of the available pool of tradition, but everyone was working with similar available resources in the lifelong process of developing a worldview.

One might wish for more microhistories like Ginzburg's before making pronouncements about sixteenth-century Italian worldview, but Menocchio's articulations of mind alone—often nonconformist reactions to nonetheless collective conditions and ideas—express a self while throwing his world into sharp ethnographic relief. Likewise, elucidating Packy Jim's worldview simultaneously speaks to an individual subjectivity (the term implies a viewer) and to shared realities of life on the Irish border (a world), past and present.

Aspects of Packy Jim's worldview have emerged gradually from his reminiscences and repertoire of traditional narratives, and these aspects bear reiteration in an effort to sum up, to see the forest for the trees. Packy Jim's worldview becomes all the more apparent when we turn to comparative work.

My former field site in Aghyaran, County Tyrone, lies just to the north, jutting west while Lettercran juts east, the two interlocking in a mirror image, yin and yang, sharing a border. Aghyaran is home to many people Packy Jim regularly interacts with, including those to whom he is related. The testimony of hundreds there, ranging in time from 1998 to 2007, is clearly relevant for delineating the idiosyncratic and the generally shared in Packy Jim's worldview.[1] Furthermore, Lettercran is only thirty miles by road north of what may be the most thoroughly ethnographized locale in Ireland: Ballymenone, County Fermangh (see chapter 1, pp. 32–33, for the situation of Lettercran, Aghyaran, and Ballymenone relative to each other). Derived from the songs and stories, customs and material culture of the people of Ballymenone, Henry Glassie's "epic of common life" serves as crucial evidence for setting much of Packy Jim's worldview in sharp relief. So far I have referred somewhat sparingly to Glassie's work (1975, 1982, 2006), but now we are more informed and in a better position to appreciate the comparison and contrast that follows.

Reading Glassie's work as an extended treatise on worldview, I observe
that many of Packy Jim's basic postulates about self, society, right and wrong,
the natural and the supernatural are similar to, if not the same as, those of
Ellen Cutler, Michael Boyle, Peter Flanagan, Hugh Nolan, and others in
Ballymenone — people from a previous generation who nonetheless overlapped
in time and nearly in space with Packy Jim. The comparative exercise should
lend considerable support to the idea of shared regional culture that extends
beyond a particular field site. At other points of comparison, I notice divergences
that inevitably arise from variation in sociocultural context and changing times.
I am working, after all, with a man living in the next county two decades after
Glassie was in Ballymenone. At still other points of comparison, I must recognize
that Packy Jim's subject position, experiences, and personality account for differences from what may be posited as collective norm along the western Irish
border that connects Donegal, Tyrone, and Fermanagh.

Using a comparative perspective where possible, the broad scope of Packy
Jim's worldview is discernible from the details, and one could start almost
anywhere — with handed-down stories or those of personal experience, with
accounts of childhood dramas, of outlaws and landlords, or of ghosts and fairies.
Note that the witch hare case study of the last chapter points us in two directions
in the delineation of worldview: convictions (and sometimes unresolved debates)
related to the supernatural and belief, and convictions (and sometimes unresolved debates) related to the ethical and moral exigencies of living among
others in a society situated in historical context. More broadly we can think in
terms of the sacred and profane. Disentangling these two strands in Packy Jim's
worldview is ultimately impossible — for him, social and divine order ideally
reinforce each other — but for the sake of a linear review, let me first examine
those aspects of worldview concerning the supernatural and belief.

The Supernatural, Belief, and Worldview

The term "supernatural" presents some difficulties that Packy Jim himself
registers. Literally meaning "above nature," the term implies two realities: a
knowable, predictable natural order (including such things as the laws of physics
or the inevitable rotation of the earth on its axis as it orbits the solar system) and
a realm of mysterious beings, forces, and events that are governed by other
unknown laws if they are governed at all. Packy Jim does not claim to be "one
of the greatest Christians going," but he does believe that a natural order exists
and it has an author: God. He also holds open the possibility that certain individuals can transform themselves into the form of an animal and steal the profit
from a neighbor's dairy. Likewise, he believes that the immortal souls of the

departed may return to this earthly plane, that his guardian angel has saved his life more than once, and that angels banished from Heaven for want of loyalty have roamed the earth and may continue to do so. By extension, he keeps an open mind about extrasensory perception, ley lines, and all manner of "queer things" he reads about in magazines. None of these things follow the known laws of nature, but according to Packy Jim they, too, exist and share the same divine author.

Are there really two sets of rules (one governing the natural, another the supernatural) or only one set of rules (God's rules) that establish a coherent system, only part of which humans mostly understand? Packy Jim leans toward the latter understanding.

In the context of a longer discussion about ghosts, for example, Packy Jim read to me an article in *Ireland's Own* about "the ghost chicken of London." According to the article, Sir Francis Bacon (1561–1626), advocate of the scientific method for the delineation of natural laws, experimented with freezing meat for preservation. Many chickens met their untimely ends interned in a snow bank, and ironically perhaps, Bacon died of pneumonia in the process of his experiments. More remarkably, for centuries people have reported the apparition of a plucked chicken running about frenetically flapping its featherless wings in the square outside Bacon's former home.

Packy Jim professes neither belief nor disbelief in this story. It provides him fodder for contemplating whether nonhuman animals have souls, and it invites him to contemplate the nature of the supernatural. Specifically, he takes exception to the article coming under the heading "Tales of the Natural and the Supernatural." For him the implied juxtaposition is a false one: "The natural and the supernatural—as the saying goes—they must be connected some way or another." It is a pity that Bacon did not live longer to continue his empirical investigations, but then again some things are beyond human methods of explanation. Mystery, however, does not shake Packy Jim's belief that the so-called supernatural is not above or beyond the natural but simply another part of God's all-encompassing order.

Perhaps "numinous" or "transcendent" or "supranormal" would be better terms (cf. M. Foster 2009:15–17), but as it is, "supernatural" is the term Packy Jim has at his disposal for everything from wraiths and banshees, to Marian apparitions and holy wells, to the power of prayer and the triumph of Christ's resurrection. We may note, in such a range, ideas with Christian and pre-Christian origins: things that the Church professes (prayer, the Resurrection), others that it does not officially acknowledge (wraiths, holy wells), and others it actively rejects (unsubstantiated apparitions, any and all fairy lore). But in the same way that Packy Jim appreciates the natural and supernatural as part of a

continuum, he has no problem making connections between official and vernacular religious belief. Indeed he actively seeks to understand one in terms of
the other. As we have seen, Packy Jim cites the Bible's account of Christ's taking
on material form before his followers at Pentecost to bolster the plausibility of
Goudy's physicality as a ghost, such as when tucking in his children or striking
Ribbonman McSorley. More generally, for Packy Jim scriptural appearances
of the Holy Spirit lend credence to the potential materialization of a range of
spiritual beings, as much as handed-down accounts of ghosts, wraiths, and fairies
lend credence to official Church teachings. He is not concerned that official
catechism fails to cover the full range of things he has come to believe or at least
entertain, but many core Church teachings, nonetheless, anchor his worldview.

Throughout his life as a regular Mass-goer, Packy Jim has professed his
Christian faith countless times in the form of the Nicene Creed. He believes "in
one God, the Father Almighty, maker of heaven and earth and of all things
visible and invisible." That last phrase holds a key for Packy Jim. God exists,
and God is the creator of all things known and unknown. Packy Jim's belief in
God as the author of all things complements his corollary belief that there is an
underlying consistent system connecting all, whether or not we fully grasp it. In
line with the worldview of Ballymenone articulated by Hugh Nolan, we must
die knowing that we cannot know all; faith is necessary where evidence is lacking
(Glassie 2006:334). Yet even though the system admits mystery, not mastery,
Packy Jim is satisfied that we are allowed enough glimpses into the really real,
enough revealed truths, to know that nothing supernatural is arbitrary.

In Ballymenone, legends of the saints discovering and passing on cures —
relieving bodily pains and worldly anxieties — were taken as sure signs of God's
existence, God's love, and a divine plan inherent in creation, discoverable by
those who walk in God's ways (Glassie 2006:261–267). For many in Aghyaran
the cures available in Saint Patrick's well (Magherakeel townland), Saint
Davog's well (Crighdenis townland), and Father McLaughlin's well (Slievedoo
townland) fulfill a similar function, bolstering belief. Here I say "belief" rather
than "faith" because, if faith is belief despite the absence of proof, God-given
examples such as efficacious cures are taken as compelling evidence. In such
cases, belief is rationally held. Packy Jim, too, finds evidence for his beliefs in
God and divine order in such things as local healing wells and Agnes Lunney's
handed-down cures.

Perhaps the greater or at least more elaborate source of Packy Jim's belief
in an underlying all-encompassing system, however, is a story so important that
we have already examined it twice: the origin of the fairies. The story is substan-
tiated by references to the War in Heaven in the Book of Revelation and lent
further credence in historical time by encounters with the fairies taken to be

genuine. Packy Jim marshals the story to a range of contemplative and rhetorical ends, but as we saw in chapter 5, it is particularly illuminating for answering questions about why we humans exist, how the universe is designed, and how it will all come to an end. In terms of cosmology, the failed rebellion of Satan, the Angel of Pride, is the catalyst to God's elaboration of the cosmos into Heaven, Hell, and earth, the first material realm, established for newly created humanity. Earth provides the stage for millennia of social dramas involving people coming to terms with living together; this material creation, in other words, is the stage for history. Human teleology is at base a challenge to follow God's moral laws well enough on earth that after death our souls may transcend the material world and take the places in Heaven forfeited by the rebellious and neutral angels. Following this vision of human teleology, eschatology is straightforward: history and this material world will come to an end once enough deserving souls have filled Heaven to its original capacity. Taken together, this is the profoundly ordered vision at the base of Packy Jim's worldview.

Contemporary secular thought in the West, heavily influenced by existentialism and the postmodern rejection of grand master narratives, is in many ways a project for dealing with the arbitrariness of life and for delineating codes for ethical conduct in the absence — or refuted presence — of sacred eternal laws.[2] Packy Jim's faith in profound order of divine origin is arguably not modern from this narrow perspective. Nevertheless, it would be a mistake, from any perspective, to understand Packy Jim's beliefs as divorced from reason or shackled by unthinking compliance with tradition. Tradition itself is nothing if not the dynamic and creative recycling of the past to meet present needs. Of course, people may engage more or less with precedent, creatively recycle with different ends and results, and hold different worldviews. But Packy Jim is no less of his moment than the trendiest critical theorist, who may be surprised to find that as a man of faith Packy Jim follows reason to come to many deeply relativistic conclusions.

Chapters 5 and 6 revolved around a range of legendary supernatural stories that Packy Jim frames with truth claims ranging from full belief to ambivalence to skepticism to incredulity. Supernatural stories taken as reliable and literally true are fewest in number but have survived the long process of Packy Jim's maturation. Similar to observations by Tommy Lunny, Peter Flanagan, and Hugh Nolan of Ballymenone (Glassie 2006:296–298), Packy Jim notes that he came to his present critical perspective only after considerable time and experience, having "hardened up a bit." Today he can laugh at the idea of ghosts and water horses in certain locations, just as Hugh Nolan did, both of them realizing that such stories were told by adults to control children. Likewise, Packy Jim can believe in fairies but still appreciate his mother's tale of Nick the Nogginweaver to be a fiction, a gift of entertaining diversion to him as a child, an enduring memento of her love. On the other hand, certain stories are harder to classify. There was no stone-carving industry in Crilly, so the sound of the Hammer Man could not be explained away as human, and the sound, which everyone heard, finally ceased after the right man invoked the name of God. A supernatural explanation remains possible, even likely. Alternative theories have not been exhausted, however, and the door remains open to debate within certain standards for proof and plausibility.

Over time Packy Jim has developed a communicative competence that alerts him to moments where received narratives temporarily or permanently swerve between nonfiction and fiction in terms of generic convention and performance style. These moments include artful but dubious narrative overreaches, such as fanciful embellishments of Bob Goudy's irrepressible return or the too-good-to-be-true polish and repetitive three-fold structure of the fairy suite. Packy Jim is alert also to matters of logic and probability that may unravel truth claims, such as the unlikelihood that anyone would have seen, much less recognized, Mrs. McPeake's "lights," and the implausibility that such an observation would lead naturally to suspicion of a water horse as the culprit. Like a detective deliberating various suspects' motivations, Packy Jim imagines the conscious concoction of a cover story for Mrs. McPeake's disappearance and cost-saving disposal. The forensics uncovered in the bog in recent times lends support to Packy Jim's doubts.

In other cases, Packy Jim is, like a folklorist, alert to the implications of oicotypes when he notes motifs he knows to be migratory, such as Saint Patrick, Moses-like, creating the well in Magherakeel by striking a rock with his staff. When the dynamics of folkloric replication and circulation are most apparent, Packy Jim—like Jan Vansina (1985)—begins to doubt historical accuracy. This could not have happened in the same way in all these places, so the story must have traveled, he reasons. Nevertheless, like Américo Paredes (1961) and Brynjulf Alver (1989), Packy Jim maintains that inaccurate stories may convey nonliteral truths and ideas worth contemplating. So Packy Jim eschews the literal when it is implausible but nonetheless entertains metaphorical and allegorical readings of, for example, the fantastic elements of hagiography (Saint Patrick battling the serpent) or indeed of the creation story in Genesis (seven days, Adam and Eve).

Packy Jim may trade in stories of the supernatural, including those about which he is skeptical, but he repeatedly scrutinizes each one. A kind of legend connoisseur, he evaluates any given story piece by piece, as a whole, and in comparison to all other like stories that he knows. In the process, he is deeply invested in reliable sources (his father is all the more trustworthy for being a skeptic, his friend Willie McHugh would not lie), credible evidence (he saw John Neddy's fairy-blasted bald head himself, the possibility of ghosts and fairies comports with the Bible), and logical consistency (the idea that natural disasters are punishments from God for sinful behavior is undermined by the fact that such things occur on far-off planets without human wickedness). Packy Jim, in other words, has all the hallmarks of what Goldstein calls the rational believer.

Indeed, by appealing to reason and consistency, Packy Jim comes to remarkably skeptical and relativistic observations about the chief representative and arbiter of the supernatural in his world: the Church. He has no doubts about the eternal fundamentals of Christian morality, cosmology, teleology, and eschatology, and he appreciates the need for the Church, clergy, liturgy, and sacraments as a source of spiritual education and a conduit for the sacred in everyday life. But the worldly and continually revised trappings of a fallible Church cause him to question institutional authority and in many cases to keep his own counsel.

As Packy Jim's extensive account of the Fatima apparition attests, first-order numinous revelation in this material world in historical time lifts a veil, confirming sacred power and eternal divine order. Although the pope blanches at the Virgin's prophesy that he will not reveal, radical, staggering, mind-boggling hierophany cannot be contained. In the end the Church may be inspired by first-order revealed truths, but there is no getting around the fact that the Church is a manmade second-order institution, circumscribed by human limitations. The Church provides shared narratives, symbols, and rituals that serve as evocative metaphors but cannot completely, transparently convey the really real. There is a parallel here to Packy Jim's distrust of language— indispensable but inherently limited—for communicating ultimate realities. Like the second-order institution of the Church, language only allows us to speak and comprehend metaphorically, analogically: "as if," "as the saying goes," "to put it the best way I can." There is for Packy Jim something like a *langue* and *parole* relationship between the divine order of the supernatural and its worldly, corrupted implementation, representation, and routinization.

Here we come to a natural transition from the sacred to the profane, from the realm of the supernatural and eternal to the realm of history and human interaction. Consider first what might safely be said about Packy Jim's worldview at this point: God exists and nothing is arbitrary. The natural and supernatural are part of the same system, and all is profoundly ordered. Certain aspects of the supernatural divine order are revealed from time to time, in one place then another. Other aspects are beyond human comprehension. While all may be revealed after death, we must die not knowing. Comprehensible or not, certain things are definite. Humans have souls, and transcendence of one kind or another is inevitable at the end of life. More broadly, time itself is finite, an attribute of the material world, and it progresses toward an ultimate goal of atonement and restoration that will bring humanity, history, and this material world to an end. Packy Jim's conviction that the supernatural is quintessentially a realm without arbitrariness offers a profound contrast to his understanding of the worldly and manmade as quite the opposite—constructed, tendentious, unstable, and ultimately arbitrary.

History, Morality, and Worldview

Packy Jim, professing the Catholic faith, knows that because God exists and loves us, we are compelled to follow his greatest commandment, articulated by his Son, to love our neighbors as much as ourselves. We have free will, so nothing stops self-interest from trumping our sacred obligations. When we fall short—and it is human nature to do so, to sin—there are consequences, but forgiveness is freely available to those who repent. History is comprised of countless social dramas in which people fail or succeed, in small and large scale, to follow God's will, to act morally. As we have seen, Packy Jim's immediate surroundings are a vast mnemonic device for remembering such social dramas, legends told as morality tales, set in a familiar landscape.

Chief among these is the story of Peggy Roe McGrath, sacrificing herself in the hope of saving her brother, following the model of Christ, who sacrificed himself for all humanity. Peggy Roe is remembered as "something of a saint," an exemplar for Packy Jim and for many. The lonely spot where she died is an ever-present reminder of human virtue, the adherence to sacred moral law. Not far away is another locale that stands in for the opposite: pernicious human vice. Cued by the former sites of lint fields and a hastily constructed sod house, the unjust eviction of Barney McFadden—"a dirty story in our own country"—features a man and his wife driven by ambition and avarice to betray a family member, take his land, and force him into the desperation of squatting and the exile of emigration.

Recall Packy Jim's more general ambivalence about ambition. Grounded in the social charter of sacred myth—the disastrous rebellion of the Angel of Pride—Packy Jim's apprehensions about ambition color all his narratives that revolve around a lust for power or worldly things. Ambition within limits, allows Packy Jim, is justifiable. Providing for oneself and one's family the basic needs and, with luck, a little comfort is an obligation, but unchecked ambition leads to selfishness, greed, and betrayal. Ambition begets competition that creates winners and losers where in an ideal world there would be only equals getting by together in reciprocal generosity.

Drawing from stories as varied as the folktale of Willie the Wisp to legends of heroic rebels to memories of a local rich man who despaired of wealth and ended his own life, Glassie identifies a fundamental principle of Ballymenone's worldview as "Satan's Wager." When people compete for worldly stakes, they may win but their victory will be followed by defeat. Packy Jim dramatizes a similar perspective in the story of the unjust eviction when the local priest rails against Danny and Cassie McFadden's moral crimes—sins—and in the end the couple's short-term gain is no profit at all. God's will is done, and one message is clear. There is a right and a wrong, and the unrepentant will reap what they sow, sometimes in this life, always in the next.

If ambition is suspicious, the fact of profit brings anxiety to a head. Even today in Aghyaran and Castlederg, in Lettercran and Pettigo, some people who accept money for goods or services will offer back a "luck's penny"—a coin or two that shares a small symbolic amount of profit with the customer, keeping it in circulation, blunting the unlucky negative reciprocity inherent in capitalism. The anxiety over profit implied in such a custom runs conspicuously through Packy Jim's legends and anecdotes about human interaction, as much as it does through his accounts of supernatural aggression. This calls into question, again, how neatly we can separate the sacred and profane, the supernatural and natural as separate aspects of Packy Jim's worldview.

In the last chapter I showed how Packy Jim's conceptualization of witchcraft and supernatural aggression is very close to that found in the evidence from Ballymenone (Glassie 1982:530–538, 544, 547–551; 2006:297–299). In both places, local stories and practices point us to a shared concern with the potential destabilization to community wrought by profit often intuited as a species of theft. In contemporary Aghyaran this concern echoes in the non-supernatural stories about a certain recurring character type, the competitive farmer-capitalist who sacrifices neighborliness in his feverish pursuit of wealth. In anecdotes told about the neighbors at wakes and ceilis, this capitalist drone is made fun of for having no regard for traditional norms of sociability and generosity, having adopted the creed that "time equals money" identified as American, modern, and/or urban (Cashman 2008b:173).

Casting farther in space and backward in time to late nineteenth-century Ballyvadlea, County Tipperary, Angela Bourke (1999) notes that the striving upwardly mobile ways of Bridget Cleary were perceived by her family and neighbors as privileging short-term personal gain over long-term familial and communal stability. Perhaps people in this time and place had little vocabulary for conceiving and expressing these views other than that of the fairy faith. Bridget Cleary's ambition and independence were taken as evidence of her association with the fairies and supernatural profiteering, and this fueled the abuse that ended in her death. Such preoccupations with legitimate and illegitimate ways of creating profit, ambition, and getting ahead seem to have been around for some time and not just on the Irish border.

More broadly the evidence from Lettercran, Ballymenone, Aghyaran, and Ballyvadlea alerts us to a longstanding postulate of rural agrarian and pastoral Irish worldview that this is a world of limited good, decidedly different from the American dream of unlimited opportunity. Keeping luck or fortune circulating through neighborly generosity—long-term stability through reciprocity—is the ideal. The self-serving actions of the witch—short-term personal gain at the expense of others—are the opposite, and in contemporary comical anecdotes the suspiciously similar actions of the modern farmer-capitalist are risible while inviting serious ambivalence and implicit condemnation. For Packy Jim and for many, it seems that if ambition is worrisome, profit is more so, and both are provocative and potentially threatening in a world of limited good.

We may advance in our examples from the family circle (Peggy Roe and her brother, the McFadden triangle) to broader networks of neighbors (Denny Byrne and Robert Harrison, Dody McGoldrick and Henry McCutcheon, Alice Monaghan and Margaret Turner) as widening arenas for dramatizing and contemplating both moral and immoral interactions. Widening the frame to society as a whole, similar issues arise from the human dramas set in motion by conquest.

Self-interest, competition and conflict, theft and illegitimate profit, resistance and violence all compound threats to the ideal of peaceful, equitable social interaction. After all, Ireland is Britain's first and possibly last colony, and in the rush to exploitation that is colonial expansion—as much as in resistance to this expansion—God's commandment to love one another falls on deaf ears. While morality and community remain central concerns, our focus in delineating Packy Jim's worldview necessarily shifts to his contemplation of history and politics.

In Packy Jim's repertoire, a range of heroic rebels and outlaws introduce the prospect of resistance to colonial oppression. Particularly in Packy Jim's boyhood and adolescence, these figures—manly, courageous, and not a little stylish—filled his fantasies with models for standing up to injustice. His favorite fictionalized literary rebels, the Wild Geese—Irish Jacobites, noble in defeat, fighting the good fight on the Continent—join in concept with domestic Robin Hood–like outlaws, the romantic Renardine of "The Mountains of Pomeroy" and the highwayman William Brennan of "Brennan on the Moor." A local boy reared next door in Cloghore, Proinsias Dubh stands above them all.

In the wake of defeat and dispossession, Proinsias Dubh is forced into outlawry by circumstances beyond his control, in a context where acting morally and enforcing justice includes breaking the law. Note that he is not a sectarian-minded Catholic avenger. Proinsias Dubh is at the height of his power nearly a century after King Billy's victory at the Battle of the Boyne, nearly a century and a half after the devastation of Cromwell, and nearly two centuries after Elizabeth I's successful experimentation with Plantation. By Proinsias Dubh's time, Protestants are already firmly established as weft in the Irish social fabric. There is no sending them home, for they are home. Having inherited their privilege of land tenure—established in conquest, maintained by anti-Catholic (and anti-Dissenter) Penal Laws—the gentry may be Protestant, but not all Protestants are the enemy. Most Protestants are among Proinsias Dubh's comparatively modest neighbors, some of them are truly poor, and a few of them are in his gang. The class hierarchy is founded in sectarian division, but the real enemies are those at the top of the corrupt land tenure system, not one's working-class Protestant neighbors.

Of course, the outlaw who would redistribute wealth from the illegitimate rich can hardly do so without the threat of violence. Remarkably, however, Proinsias Dubh obeys the commandment not to kill. His prominence in Packy Jim's repertoire—and in the collective repertoire of Ballymenone (Glassie 2006:283–288)—owes much to the fact that he points to a moral form of resistance, justly redistributing profit in a world of limited good, without taking human life. As such, Proinsias Dubh vaults over sectarianism and outflanks the conundrum of whether the ends justify the means when the means include killing. More class-warrior than Catholic avenger, Proinsias Dubh as exemplar enjoys an enviable moral clarity that cannot be claimed as easily by others willing to mount armed resistance to the colonial establishment.

Consider for comparison that in Ballymenone, historians such as Hugh Nolan and Michael Boyle carefully juxtaposed battle tales to illustrate the fix that binds the people of the North (Glassie 2006:275–282). At the Battle of the Ford of Biscuits, the men of Ulster stand up to invasion and decimate an English army encroaching from the south. The slaughtered army, it turns out, was comprised of Irish conscripts. The victory is both tragic and short-lived, for Plantation follows regardless. Centuries later in what is known as the Mackan Fight, Protestants celebrating the victory of King Billy threaten to burn the homes of their Catholic neighbors, and the Catholics arm themselves in resistance. Violence erupts, Protestants are killed, and one Catholic is sentenced to hang while others are exiled to Australia. "In fighting they win; in winning, they lose" (Glassie 2006:276). Such stories were sometimes told as parables to the young men of the IRA who made the bombs. Oppressed, one may have an obligation to stand up for one's rights, but neighbors and innocents die when people resort to armed struggle in their own land. Such stories require men of

violence to think twice, to be aware that when they disobey God's commandment not to kill, victory cannot be separated from defeat. One's immortal soul
hangs in the balance.

The fix illustrated by these stories finds resolution in Ballymenone in a
singular story also elevated and immortalized in song. Decades after the Mackan
Fight, the landlord of Swanlibar moves to raze a Catholic church—the Swad
Chapel—but Catholic women gather in prayer and Catholic men converge in
the thousands, armed with agricultural implements. The chapel is saved when
the landlord backs down and soon after dies in his bed, naturally or perhaps
by the will of God. The victory is ideal in that it is bloodless. If the landlord dies
it was not by human hands. More importantly the enemy faced by the Catholic
assembly was the profane tyrannical landlord, not their Protestant neighbors.
The logic of this resolution—the way out of the fix—is similar to that running
through Packy Jim's accounts of Proinsias Dubh. Just resistance applied to the
authors of injustice is rare and nearly impossible but all the more celebratory.

That said, Packy Jim's tales of Proinsias Dubh are not entirely the same in
concept or rhetoric as Ballymenone's Swad Chapel drama. The heroic outlaw in
Lettercran—as much as in Ballymenone, Aghyaran, and throughout Ireland—
inevitably goes down in defeat. His victories are minor and short-lived, and like
the victors of the Ford of Biscuits or the Mackan Fight, Proinsias Dubh ultimately
does nothing to halt the oppression of the larger system he resists. In the outlaw's
legacy there is no equivalent to the saved chapel or the defeated landlord.

More troubling, there is no exact equivalent to the Swad Chapel drama as
hopeful ideal in Packy Jim's wider repertoire. Especially when turning attention
to the Troubles, Packy Jim's worldview concerning the moral fix that binds the
people of the North is bleaker for these lacks. The sad fact is that in Packy Jim's
world the past is replete with sectarian faction fights, drowned pilgrims, and
smashed crosses. Frustration and rage are understandable, but finding a proper
target for pushing back without threat to community, without breaking sacred
law, is impossible. Perhaps the British army invading Pettigo in 1922 is a legitimate target; the incursion offers the Old IRA a chance to face the forces that
would defend the original theft of Plantation and prolong the legacy of colonialism. But the reality is that the other side includes one's Protestant neighbors
armed as B men, swept up in the paranoia of ambush and secret enemies. What
is arguably a justifiable act of armed resistance descends into desperation,
confusion, and neighbors battling neighbors.

The anxiety and deep pessimism over the prospect of community despite
the sectarian divide finds articulation even in stories that are not concerned
on the surface with the moral conundrum of armed struggle. Whereas previous
research into the witch hare legend explored the symbolic implications of older

Entrance to the Carn graveyard

female witches and younger male victims, in Packy Jim's repertoire witches and victims differ by sectarian affiliation, not gender or age. The same is true in Ballymenone. The most troubling relationship—given form in supernatural narrative—is that between neighboring Catholics and Protestants, struggling with the ideal of community in a world of sectarian tension and limited good.

Ours is a fallen world, and human nature is disposed toward sin. Both postulates are central to Packy Jim's worldview, deriving as much from received theology as from evidence about human interactions in the local past. There are glimpses of righteousness in the devotion and self-sacrifice of Peggy Roe, in the nonviolence and generosity of Proinsias Dubh. But the greater number of Packy Jim's personal and legendary stories reveal a preoccupation with ambition, betrayal, injustice, and the contravention of God's moral law. The scale may shift back and forth from the micro level of the family circle and neighborly network to the macro level of the nation and human society more generally. But inviting evaluation of the morality of human behavior is the conceptual and rhetorical common denominator of all these stories. Taken as a whole, such stories suggest that prospects for peaceful coexistence are bleak, but for Packy Jim the tumult of social drama nonetheless clarifies certain understandings and ideals.

In the profane realm of history, defeat is constant (cf. Glassie 2006:275, 282, 288). As it is in all versions of millennialism, true and lasting justice is not to be found in this world but rather is deferred to the next world. Complete passivity, however, is untenable for Packy Jim, and the urge to resist injustice is understandable. Knowing the human propensity for exploitation, Packy Jim challenges Christ's metaphorical injunction to turn the other cheek, at least in day-to-day interpersonal dealings. Departing from official teaching, this part of his worldview has been conditioned by bitter experience begetting a mature refusal to suffer abuse while stopping short of physical violence. For Packy Jim, legitimate resistance is behavioral (cutting ties with the smart alecks and high flyers) and verbal (fighting words with words when necessary, as he is exceptionally well equipped to do). In the realm of national politics, it seems that the stakes are higher, and nonviolence bolstered by the Golden Rule unequivocally applies. Packy Jim observes that armed struggle most often compounds injustice, and taking human life cannot be excused by the logic of ends justifying means. At this macro level of human affairs, "Do unto others as you would have them do unto you" and "Love your neighbor as yourself" are not mere platitudes but rather the main platforms in Packy Jim's political worldview. Given the impossible fix of the Troubles, concern for one's neighbor—Catholic, Protestant, or Dissenter—trumps all other compulsions and desires.

Worldview, Collective and Singular

Packy Jim's stories of the local past elucidate that portion of his worldview concerning morality and his understanding of human nature. Clarity about certain aspects of right and wrong and about our capacity for both, however, does not imply that Packy Jim rigidly applies a moral litmus test to every aspect of human behavior. This is also the man who tells us that it is a bad thing to be "*too* scrupulous," an attitude that is widely shared.

Throughout I have referred to a border mentality, a libertarian and antiauthoritarian worldview broadly held over time by Catholics and Protestants living along the simultaneously arbitrary yet long-established boundary between Ireland's two states. This border mentality does not involve an amoral free-for-all but rather reserves the individual's right to follow his or her own moral compass when evaluating and selectively complying with legislation and other restrictions that are imposed from above or from afar. Thoreau's notion of civil disobedience is perfectly at home here, but as we saw when Maggie McGrath finished her poitín distillation then found absolution through a loophole, disobedience is typically quiet, under the radar, and more a matter-of-fact exercise of autonomy rather than an overt show making a point.

This border mentality has long been enacted through everyday practices such as illicit distillation, smuggling, tax evasion, and collecting agricultural subsidies or dole money in both the north and the south. Furthermore, these transgressions have long been commemorated in popular narrative such as Packy Jim's anecdote about Cassie Pat Suzanne making a mockery of the Crown court when charged with complicity in cattle smuggling. Such extralegal border practices are celebrated as survival skills, victories in gaming the system, and assertions of local and individual independence. Judging from Packy Jim's repertoire and from a broad range of border folklore, it seems that no one in his world admires those who follow rules for the sake of following rules. The ultimate authority of the state—either state, any state—is questionable, and inflexible ideologues are typically less popular than clever pragmatists.

This border mentality is essential context for understanding Packy Jim's personal balance of conformity and resistance, and it maintains a revealing conceptual distinction between two fundamental categories. On the one hand is the realm of morality—a code of conduct that is of sacred origin and holds true regardless of what anyone else says or does—and on the other is the realm of ethics—typically comprised of church- and state-imposed strictures that are manmade, change over time, and may be seen as fungible and negotiable. Packy Jim's worldview, then, comports in terms of its dynamic with that of his neighbors by reserving a limited category of clear moral laws but foregrounding individual autonomy and free will when evaluating for oneself the vast gray area that extends beyond the bounds of morality. Shaped by this contrarian relativizing border mentality, Packy Jim is very much of his time and place, but where he draws the line on a case-by-case basis between right and wrong, conformity and resistance, is tellingly idiosyncratic, revealing a particular individuality. Or in his own words, "I suppose I must be a person that, in some fashion or another, I'm very much like the thousands around me, and in other ways I must be very different."

Even among a generally contrarian, freedom-loving crowd, part of what makes Packy Jim stand out is his willingness to tilt with militant nationalism and Roman Catholicism, the two ideological poles around which much of the discourse of his world revolves. Compared to his largely republican Fianna Fáil- and Sinn Féin-voting neighbors, Packy Jim goes against the flow with his middle-way nationalism that supports self-determination and opposes colonial exploitation but draws the line at violence in deference to the greater good of local community regardless of religious or political affiliation. This position is commensurate with his father's and uncle's retreat from armed struggle after serving in the Old IRA. This position is also commensurate with the just resistance morality of Proinsias Dubh stories, a cycle of narratives that features a clever pragmatist and sustains an aspirational fantasy about social justice rather than advocates a particular political ideology. However morally coherent

Packy Jim's politics may be, he has been insulted and seriously harassed—particularly by younger republicans—paying a price for his political iconoclasm. He stands his ground nonetheless.

Likewise, while Packy Jim is no heretical Menocchio, he is a relative maverick in his views on the organized part of organized religion. If the manmade church can reverse itself on Limbo, declare poitín-making a reserved sin one decade and never mention it the next, and change course in liturgical matters more than once during his lifetime, Packy Jim cannot help but question institutional authority, witnessing orthodoxy as malleable and transitory.

Popular attitudes purportedly founded on Church teachings are likewise suspect. Lettercran, no less than Aghyaran next door, is a part of Ireland where a considerable number of people believe or at least entertain the idea that the untimely death of the actor Dermot Morgan was divine punishment for his role in the arguably blasphemous BBC comedy series *Father Ted*. For Packy Jim, a man who holds open the possibility that fairies are a part of the divine order, such gossip is superstitious nonsense.

Lettercran is also part of the electoral district with the second highest percentage of votes against the successful 2015 referendum to make same-sex marriage constitutionally legal in the Republic of Ireland. Among his devout Catholic neighbors in a socially conservative milieu, Packy Jim is rare for holding a live-and-let-live attitude toward homosexuals, supporting the inclusion of married and female Catholic priests, and questioning literal, fundamentalist readings of scripture, among other things. Such positions are becoming more and more popular in Ireland as a whole today, but many would be surprised to find support for such positions from a man of Packy Jim's generation and background. Note that there is no evidence in Glassie's accounts of such overt interrogation of Church orthodoxy among Ballymenone's Catholics in the 1970s and '80s, and I noted very little two decades later in Aghyaran, except among a small and relatively quiet minority of young adults, typically those who have spent time away for work or education.

Packy Jim's peripheral social position has perhaps the most profound effect on his worldview. Self-aware and keenly attuned to received hierarchies of social status, he has transformed social distance into the intellectual distance necessary to become both native ethnographer and vernacular social critic. Most notably, Packy Jim's subject position increases his empathy for the people most often marginalized in his world—fellow bachelors, the poor, women, homosexuals, Protestants. All are to some degree the victims of grand master narratives proffered by transitory manmade ideologies that have become doubtful for Packy Jim over time. Young urban cosmopolitans did not invent nor do they have the monopoly on progressive thinking concerned with equality and social justice.

Bearing witness through folklore to propositions about the sacred and profane, Packy Jim is to Lettercran—in some ways—what Hugh Nolan was to Ballymenone: an elderly bachelor of modest means who is gifted enough to theorize and articulate the human condition as it is shaped in a particular moment and part of the world. Of course, Lettercran and Ballymenone differ in circumstance, and Packy Jim McGrath and Hugh Nolan differ in generation, experience, preoccupation, personality, and voice. But how interesting that both trade in similar supernatural and historical narratives—about fairies, witchcraft, Proinsias Dubh—that point to similar conceptions of cosmology, teleology, eschatology, history, society, morality, and community. How interesting that both mount comparable critiques of modernity, hold sacrosanct the commandment to love, and tell history as a series of morality tales conceptualized in spatial rather than temporal terms. If we gather in supporting evidence from the likes of Michael Boyle, Peter Flanagan, and Ellen Cutler of Ballymenone and from the likes of Danny Gallen, John Mongan, and Cissie Dolan of Aghyaran, a sense of shared regional culture along the western Irish border emerges. Much of Packy Jim's worldview registers as cultural, traditional, collective, shared.

On the other hand, many of Packy Jim's habits and stories are unique, and much of his worldview appears to part ways with that of his neighbors, near and far, past and present. This becomes most apparent when setting Packy Jim's evidence in relief. For example, the number, structure, and rhetorical functions of Packy Jim's personal narratives are not surprising if the point of comparison is social life in the contemporary United States, the field examined by sociolinguists and folklorists such as Linde, Labov, Shuman, and Stahl (Dolby). But the fact of Packy Jim's many personal narratives—let alone their content—is remarkable when the more relevant point of comparison is Ballymenone or Aghyaran, where the genre is considerably rarer. It is difficult to say whether Packy Jim's worldview is more individualistic or simply self-aware compared to that of his neighbors, but we can surmise that he envisions the social world as comprised of independent protagonists, of which he is one, engaged in narratable interpersonal dramas. Packy Jim's is not a universal conceptualization. More integrated, less atomistic models of personhood and society may be found in, for example, many Native American autobiographies (Brumble 1988:3–5, 108–117, 145–147).

Apart from the relative abundance of Packy Jim's personal narratives, their thematic content reveals a certain preoccupation with undeserved ridicule and disregard, which inevitably has an effect on his worldview. Consider that nothing in Glassie's accounts suggests that Hugh Nolan faced the level of stigma and harassment that Packy Jim recounts and deplores. Nolan, too, would have been considered marginal by high society, but he was characterized by his neighbors as a saint and a star, a widely celebrated curator of community memory. While Packy Jim seems to enjoy a similar status among a small group of friends, such status is not universally conferred and does not come without the counterweight of the disregard and mistreatment that features in almost half of his personal narratives. To be sure, Packy Jim has his quirks and foibles, as we all do, but the collective judgment of the "high flyers" can be merciless, casting him as the epitome of all that is old-fashioned and backward. In this sense, Packy Jim is less like the integrated eccentric Peter Flanagan—Ballymenone bachelor gossiped about for his courtly manners, fastidious dress, and artistic temperament—and more like the respected historian Hugh Nolan if Nolan were transported a generation into the future when priorities and sensibilities have irrevocably changed and such talents as Nolan's are no longer as adaptive or highly regarded.

Part of Hugh Nolan's genius—continuing in the tradition of local wits before him, such as Hugh McGiveney, George Armstrong, James Quigley, and John Brodison—was the ability to lighten the world's burdens by making a joke of drudgery and misfortune through absurdist exaggerations in comic anecdotes and tall tales. This was the gift, too, of Pat McMenamin, known as the Buffer, whose self-effacing yarns about making the best of a bad situation Packy Jim recounts. But where Nolan and his neighbors continually swapped over a hundred such stories, Packy Jim has offered me only the one cycle of tall tales from the Buffer, and he does not invent such stories about himself. Confounded by the adversities of this world, Packy Jim more typically turns to outrage rather than irony. As he explained to me early in our acquaintance, "The abuse that I got and that old smart chat jokes at my expense—you know you can make a dog cross, well the same can happen with a human."

While differences in personality, the product of nature and nurture, must be accounted for, if Hugh Nolan found himself in Packy Jim's shoes—in a world where the rustic bachelor is often derided and abused as a scapegoat in the ever-accelerating mad rush toward the modern—it is just possible that he, like Packy Jim, might be more tempted by outrage and despair, less able to sustain himself with humor and absurdity. As it is, whether context or personality accounts for the differences, the range of Packy Jim's coping mechanisms is comparably narrower, his worldview less than sanguine.

Of course, Hugh Nolan was no stranger to lamentation. After a striking account of technological advancement bringing comfort while doing nothing to halt social and moral decline, he proclaims that "the greatest change in my lifetime has been that people has lost all respect for authority, civil or divine" (Glassie 2006:134). As Glassie observes,

> This is Hugh Nolan as Jeremiah, the worried old man as prophet. He said it in his way, calmly and clearly, but he had read the signs and seen the future. If people lose respect for the system that enacts and enforces the secular law, which in the midst of Ulster's Troubles they are bound to do, and if they lose respect for the sacred law that undergirds order, then society is doomed and a chaotic war of all upon all will come to the land. (2006:134)

While there is no literal chaotic war of all upon all waging in Lettercran at present, Packy Jim's bleak view of weakened interpersonal, marital, and community bonds fits Nolan's prophetic vision. Moreover, Packy Jim's detached and sometimes agonistic orientation to authority, civil and divine, suggests that in some ways Packy Jim's world is the future Nolan envisioned. Packy Jim and Hugh Nolan share a quite similar moral compass based on sacred teachings, even if Packy Jim may be more willing—or, more accurately, compelled—to critically evaluate and selectively comply with the manmade aspects of church and state strictures. Either the border mentality observed in Packy Jim's testimony is stronger more generally in present-day Lettercran—located as it is on the border itself—than it was in Ballymenone of the 1970s and '80s, or it is stronger with Packy Jim than it was with Hugh Nolan, Michael Boyle, Ellen Cutler, and Peter Flanagan as individuals. The truth is likely a combination of these possibilities—spatial, temporal, and personal. In any case, Packy Jim's unresolved ambivalence over authority, civil and divine, stands out conspicuously as a defining tension in his mature, complicated worldview.

Think back to Packy Jim's version of the origin of the fairies and the imaginative world it opens up to him. The angels had a choice to make in the war between God and Lucifer. This parallels humanity's situation in the subsequent material creation. Packy Jim would agree with Peter Flanagan's observation:

> You're sittin on the fence when ye start off in the world. Ye can go to that side, or ye can go to that side. Ye can go forward; ye can go back. With the result: at the same time He has left you in that position, He has filled you with grace and courage to exercise in the right way. But He wants to *see* what are ye made of. (Glassie 2006:175)

We come provided, blessed by God, with free will and the capacity for endurance through wit and bravery. The burden, however, is on each of us either to follow the commandment to love or to stray to another, easier path. For Packy Jim, it would seem, the burden is more involved still, complicated by an unsteady faith in manmade laws and ethics, compounded by bitter experience and a basic distrust of human nature. Peter Flanagan concurs, "There's too many villains and bad people all around. We are persecuted with bad people" (Glassie 2006:176).

Certain moral laws are clear—love thy neighbor as thyself, honor thy mother and father, thou shalt not commit adultery, thou shalt not commit murder—but beyond those, there is a vast expanse of personal decisions to be made about right and wrong, about what side to take, about how conformist or nonconformist to be. Recall one of Packy Jim's personal foundation myths, the epic tale of skipping school, his first major experiment with transgression. It was a nightmare of misadventures and bad choices. He can laugh now at his overwrought younger self who had little sense of proportion, but the burden of choice remains a fact of everyday life. Interestingly, in Peter Flanagan's version of the War in Heaven, the fairies are those rebellious angels who sided decisively with Lucifer (Glassie 2006:301–302), whereas in Packy Jim's version, they are the neutral angels, the fence-sitters who took neither side and paid the price. Packy Jim is perhaps equally risk averse as the neutral angels, making considerable sacrifices to avoid vulnerability and betrayal in interpersonal and romantic relationships. Perhaps these neutral angels better parallel Packy Jim's, Peter Flanagan's, and Hugh Nolan's shared vision of the human condition: equipped with free will, burdened with choice.

Clear from the fairies' origin story is that the angels who rallied with Blessed Michael the Archangel made the correct choice, coming down on the right side of the fence. With this sacred precedent in mind, convinced of God's goodness, Packy Jim would like to think he would have made the same decision were he in the same position, forced to choose. An upstanding man who prefers the sheltered life—who fears change and roaming far, who would happily submit to his parents' governance were they still alive—Packy Jim identifies with those who obeyed the Father, who were entrusted with the mysteries revealed only by the Mother of God, who cleaved to the original plan. At the same time, the death of his parents denied Packy Jim the equivalent on this earth of such an ideal sanctuary. For Packy Jim, the original plan of carefree submission to parental order was terminated as fatefully as humanity's fall from grace with the expulsion from the Garden of Eden. Like all of us, Packy Jim was left to endure through bravery and wit. As such, he can identify equally with the neutral angels in that their burden to choose is his as well, everyday, doing the best, his own boss.

Everyone can use a helping hand over the course of a lifetime, making sense, distinguishing right from wrong, choosing a path. Tradition provides Packy Jim the handed-down raw materials, the means for both thought and expression, to face those fundamental existential tasks. And as much as tradition is a resource, it is also a process of meaning-making, a process discernable among large populations over time as much as throughout the lifetime of an individual. Tradition—"volitional, temporal action" and "the means for deriving the future from the past" (Glassie 2003:192)—is also an apt name for Packy Jim's lifelong discursive cultivation of a simultaneously idiosyncratic and collectively shaped worldview.

Tracing the contours of worldview, gleaned from a range of people's self-expression, is worth the effort. We start necessarily with a singular person and specific texts, noting patterns and connections, and the task only deepens while the rewards multiply with comparative research. As Alan Dundes observed, if worldview is as pervasive as we imagine, one could start looking for it almost anywhere—kinship systems, agricultural practices, grammar. But folklore offers a privileged vantage point because implicit principles of worldview are often most explicit in folklore, itself a kind of auto-ethnography (1980a:70). Contextualized rigorously in the social world and personal history of specific individuals, and traced in its rhetorical uses and aesthetic achievements in face-to-face interpersonal communication, folklore is our best window into worldview. For me, delineating worldview remains the most important objective. Understanding the world from the perspectives of others is the fundamental goal of ethnography and the ultimate promise of studying folklore.

Afterword

Real Folklore

In the beginning, people in Aghyaran sent me across the border to Packy Jim, telling me that he was the man for "real folklore." What real folklore might mean is a question only indirectly addressed in the preceding pages. Of course, folklore has been variously defined and redefined by scholars, artists, travelers, and state functionaries for ages, even before William John Thoms coined the term in 1846 as a catch-all for popular antiquities, customs, and oral traditions. How best to define folklore remains a question worth asking, though it is not my goal here to answer it once and for all, were that even possible. Instead, let me begin a final meditation grounded in particularities encountered during fieldwork.

Knowing the complexity of both positive and negative associations with the word "folklore," I consciously did not use it in my first encounter with Packy Jim. I first identified my interest as any local stories—whether comic, historical, or mysterious—that might give me some insight into his part of the world, past and present. Even then I did not intend to restrict my research only to narratives in certain genres on a limited range of topics. Certainly I used the survey of topics in Seán Ó Súilleabháin's *A Handbook of Irish Folklore* (1942) as a valuable resource for questions, but my first attempts at conversation were geared mostly toward building up necessary context and inviting Packy Jim to point me in the direction of topics that attracted him. As it turns out, and as my Aghyaran neighbors already knew, local stories of history and mystery are exactly what arouse Packy Jim's curiosity. As he says himself, "I'm bigly interested in old history and queer things."

When I first used the word "folklore" during our second visit, I was clarifying my presence and my interests further by explaining that I was a graduate student in a folklore department working on a dissertation. Despite my halting account, Packy Jim's impulse was to be helpful. "Oh," he said, "you're interested in folklore. Wait till we see now . . ."

With that, Packy Jim stood and reached into a nook under the half loft to retrieve a well-worn school reader with a duct-taped spine. He proceeded to read me stories based on translations from Irish into English—first about the ancient warrior Fionn Mac Cumhaill traveling from adventure to adventure in disguise, another about his son Oisín returning from the fairy land of Tír na nÓg, then another about how the boy Setanta became Ulster's champion Cúchulainn, and finally one about a woman who paid a price for losing patience with her goose that laid golden eggs. He recalled the basic plot of the Battle of Ventry in which Fionn fights the King of the World and his champion Dealbh Dura, though the full text, he regretted, was in another school reader he could not locate. As a whole these were mostly adaptations of heroic tales originating in the pre-Christian Ulster and Fenian Cycles, plus one wonder tale or Märchen. To the antiquarians of the nineteenth century, the luminaries of the Irish Literary Renaissance, and the professional folklorists of the twentieth century, the heroic tales would have counted as authentic voice-of-the-nation folklore, while the wonder tale would have exemplified Ireland's unique contribution to an international heritage of oral literature. It is no wonder that they were selected for his reader at a time when schools were a primary organ of the nation-building project in a newly independent Ireland.

As the conversation unfolded, Packy Jim mentioned that it was a pity I had not been here to listen to Sam Baxter, a man who died in 1950 at the age of one hundred. Baxter was known for his broad repertoire of wonder tales, including Ashy Pet Jack, The King of Ireland's Three Sons, The Black Thief of Sloan, and The Hound, the Hawk, and the Filly. Moreover, he remembered that his father told a version of Huddon, Duddon, and Donal O'Leary, a tale that Hugh Nolan of Ballymenone worked into an epic of neighborly tensions in a tight-knit community (Glassie 2006:234–244). Still, Packy Jim could not remember full versions of any of these. While these adventurous trials and moralistic lessons offer him fond reminders of his childhood imaginary life, they have little daily currency in his adult mind. I said I was interested in folklore; he went to his book trove to offer me some. But if this is the stuff of real folklore—old fictions from the ancient fantastical past—Packy Jim of the present has less interest than one might expect.

It is not the case that Packy Jim has had no exposure to "real folklore." His neighbor told wonder tales; his mother told fairy legends. Indeed, I recently discovered that Packy Jim's maternal grandfather, Patrick Gallagher, was singled out by earlier collectors. Between 1928 and 1931 the Royal Irish Academy (RIA) in collaboration with Dr. Wilhelm Doegen, director of the sound department of the Prussian state library, made an audio record of regional variation in spoken Irish. Styled Pádraig Ó Gallchobhair on their forms, Packy Jim's grandfather was identified as one of two remaining Irish speakers in Aghyaran, County Tyrone. Gallagher/ Ó Gallchobhair was transported from his home in Tulnashane to the Letterkenny Courthouse, County Donegal, on October 5, 1931. There Doegen's assistant Karl Tempel recorded him on shellac disk as Myles Dillon of the RIA provided the prompting. Among the well-annotated online recordings and transcripts of Packy Jim's grandfather are a mildly sectarian anecdote, the beginning of a love song, a formula tale, and a version of an international folktale, "The Two Sinners" (ATU 756C), all in Irish (for the audio, see http://www.doegen.ie). Packy Jim was delighted to hear his grandfather speak from my laptop and he vaguely recalled hearing an English version of "The Two Sinners," but apparently these stories do not speak to him as much as the other stories, mostly legends, treated here. Although "real folklore" by most conventional definitions, Patrick Gallagher's oral traditions do not inform Packy Jim's current repertoire any more than the Anglophone wonder tales of his earliest memories.

If we follow the old distinction between types of storytellers and narratives in Irish tradition, the *scealaí* specialized in *scealaíocht*: longer, often multi-episodic stories of heroes, mythological beings, and magical happenings. The *seanchaí*, on the other hand, specialized in *seanchas*: shorter, realistic, and usually single-episode stories including accounts of locally and nationally relevant past events.[1] These are not terms that Packy Jim uses, but clearly his tastes and talents run toward seanchas. But just as peasant society (it seems) and later folklorists (definitely) regarded the scealaí more highly, Packy Jim equates real folklore with scealaíocht, and telling scealaíocht is not his primary interest or strength.

At any rate, Packy Jim and I were not using the term "folklore" to mean the same thing. While Packy Jim's usage is narrower, mine does not simply add seanchas to scealaíocht. I would add a range of vernacular custom and material culture in a broad concept of folklore, but were I to focus solely on verbal folklore I would also include recurring narratives of personal experience, several comical genres such as tall tales and local character anecdotes, and indeed just about any genre of conventionalized verbal expression, whether oral or literary in origin, that is meaningful to a given individual. There is more to be said about this particular vision of what might constitute real folklore, but let us step back for broader perspective.

Packy Jim listening to the 1931 recordings of his grandfather in 2014

Essentially, most previous scholarly attempts to define folklore have sought common denominators among folklore forms—that is, among the range of things considered folklore by the people accustomed to using that word. At different times, some scholarly definitions have emphasized traditionality or continuities in thought and expression, while others have emphasized artistry and aesthetic concerns. Some scholars have been more invested in defining folklore by its mode of transmission (through oral tradition or via imitation of example), while others have focused on the social base of folklore (any and all cultural forms popular among a non-elite social stratum, such as the peasantry or subaltern classes more broadly conceived). Elliott Oring reviews several definitions—such as Richard Dorson's "the hidden submerged culture lying behind the shadow of official civilization" and Dan Ben-Amos's "artistic communication in small groups"—and he concludes that one definition accounting for all conceivable examples of folk and lore, shifting targets themselves, is not particularly desirable nor indeed possible. Instead, Oring offers us an orientation, noting that, whatever they study, folklorists are typically concerned with those things in the world that reflect the communal, the common, the informal, the marginal, the personal, the traditional, the aesthetic, and the ideological. Such an orientation—an interpretive lens—allows us to think of folklore "less as a collection of things than as a perspective from which almost any number of forms, behaviors, and events may be examined" (1986:18). Specifically, Oring's formulation invites folklorists to consider relevant forms of expression that are not commonly found on prescribed lists of canonical folklore forms. Note, however, that Oring's orientation locates and privileges efforts at meaning-making, facilitated by the term "folklore," among folklorists more than "the folk."

Dorothy Noyes also departs from previous common denominator definitions to situate the invention and application of the term "folklore" in the broader history of ideas that has shaped Western modernity. She offers us a succinct definition of folklore as "a metacultural category used to mark certain genres and practices within modern society as being not modern" (2004:375). By metacultural category, Noyes refers to a culturally circumscribed concept—grounded in certain times, places, and agendas—for thinking about the nature of culture. She goes on to characterize seven overlapping conceptions of folklore used by academics and nonacademics over time: folklore as survival, national tradition, oral tradition, face-to-face culture, community culture, cultural resistance, and market niche. (The last one—less obvious than the others from its label alone—refers to a strain of contemporary cultural production, notably by the heritage and tourism industries, that recycles old forms to new purposes, specifically the commodification of authenticity, a marketable rarity set in opposition to modernity.)

Using Noyes's terms, we can see that Packy Jim's received notion of "real Irish folklore" closely matches the Romantic nationalist conceptions of folklore as national tradition and as survivals from a lost golden age, perspectives that view folklore as the building blocks of shared heritage in the construction of an authentic nation-state. My usual default notion of folklore, on the other hand, is closer to some of Noyes's other overlapping categories: folklore as oral tradition, face-to-face culture, community culture, and, in many instances, cultural resistance (i.e., folklore as counterhegemonic culture).

It makes sense that Oring and Noyes would approach the slippery term "folklore" by skirting a definition of the presumed stuff of folklore while shifting attention to the politics and rhetorics of the users of such a term. The term originates with literate social elites, and it has been imposed on real-world phenomena as part of a particular intellectual tradition for comprehending reality. Of course, scholars have not been the only ones using the term since it began to circulate. Reflexive intellectual history such as Noyes's also opens the door to appreciating how in many cases the people traditionally thought to have folklore have co-opted the term, and related ones, to their own strategic needs concerning economic viability, social integration, and counterhegemonic resistance. Both scholarly and vernacular conceptions of folklore have implicated a series of binaries—such as tradition versus modernity and authenticity versus fraudulence—that we would do well to interrogate. Contemplating folklore as a metacultural category is absolutely appropriate and necessary because the term comes with ideological baggage we need to appreciate and navigate.

That said, some of the more extreme hand-wringing about the evils of Romanticism and the "invention" of folklore—including calls for the abandonment of the term "folklore"—strike me as overreactions threatening to throw the baby out with the bath water. Rewriting one of my favorite exchanges from Tom Stoppard's *Rosencrantz and Guildenstern Are Dead* (1967), I have mentally condensed more than one conference panel exchange and faculty meeting debate to:

> ROSENCRANTZ: I don't believe in it anyway.
> GUILDENSTERN: What?
> ROSENCRANTZ: Folklore.
> GUILDENSTERN: Just a conspiracy of ethnographers, then?[2]

My point is that folklore may be a loaded term imposed on reality, but it is imposed nonetheless on observable phenomena. Folklorists did not somehow invent folklore out of whole cloth. There is such a thing as traditional, vernacular, expressive culture that provides people, including Packy Jim, an invaluable resource for conceptualizing their world, resisting some aspects, embracing others. People with fewer resources who are disappointed by their social position are often some of the most talented at asserting agency and attaining forms of compensation through the creative recycling of available and inherited expressive culture.

With Packy Jim as the primary example before us, we encounter a man who came into a mature, collectively shaped yet idiosyncratic worldview by mastering what many metropolitan elites may consider the relics of obsolete discourse: myths, legends, tall tales, jokes, anecdotes, comic and tragic folksongs. Like folklore, these generic terms, too, are etic labels of convenience—faulty like all labels are—imposed from outside Packy Jim's world and not always perfectly fitted to his emic terms and concepts. Here I find myself paralleling Packy Jim, frustrated at times with the limitations of language but trying "to put it the best way I can . . . as the saying goes." As best I can, I have owned my roles and agendas in conducting fieldwork with Packy Jim and in representing his words and perspectives here in print. Whatever one makes of my commentary, at the end of the day, Packy Jim repeatedly tells these stories one may label "folklore," and they perform for him crucial intellectual work. There is nothing obsolete in Packy Jim's bricolage of tradition marshaled to personal ends.

I am not concerned that Packy Jim and I do not share a conception of real folklore. I can use other terms to discuss with him that which he finds most meaningful. Persuaded by Oring's preference for an appreciation of the folklorist's orientation over the futile quest for watertight definitions and canonical lists, I do not spend much time trying to distinguish between that which is and is not real folklore. More importantly, how I define folklore depends greatly on context. If I am teaching an introductory folklore class to undergraduates, unpacking the implications of a potted definition — "folklore is traditional, vernacular expressive culture comprised of verbal, customary, and material forms" — is a fine place to start. But when fieldwork allows me to engage with an interestingly complicated storyteller such as Packy Jim, my attention shifts to — and I might define at least a branch of folklore as — whichever genres of conventionalized verbal expression are most demonstrably meaningful to that storyteller as an intellect and a personality.

Oral provenance and transmission is not necessarily a sine qua non for folklore. Note that the very first text I quoted from Packy Jim in this book is a poem, "An Old Woman of the Roads," by a published author, Padraic Colum. The poem did not spontaneously emerge from the anonymous happy dancing throng once seen as the primal font of oral tradition (Gummere 1907). Rather, Packy Jim had memorized it from a school reader, and he remembered and recited it many decades later because it speaks to him of the value of staying put, sheltered in domestic security. I treat the poem here as folklore because it is meaningful to Packy Jim; it is one small part of the vast intertextual web that constitutes his sense of self and his perspectives on the world. The same applies to his accounts of historical fiction he has read, such as *A Swordsman of the Brigade*, and to his versions of songs learned from print or radio such as "Brennan on the Moor." For Packy Jim, texts memorable and meaningful enough to shape his repertoire, persona, and ultimately worldview are just as likely to come from an *Ireland's Own* as from a face-to-face ceili. By way of contrast, consider the heroic tales and wonder tales Packy Jim read to me. No definition of folklore I ever encountered or could conceive of would exclude such stories, and the fact that Packy Jim read literary adaptations word-for-word from print does not categorically disqualify them as folklore for me. Nonetheless, they neither feature prominently in this book nor are treated as folklore here because they are neither meaningful to Packy Jim nor part of his core repertoire.

The better I came to know Packy Jim over time, the more I shifted from a collecting model of fieldwork to a more reflexive and dialogic model. In doing so I better appreciated in context the stories that resonate for him and why, and I came to understand how texts from genres as seemingly disparate as myth and personal narrative perform complementary work in the process of subject formation. Even when stories come with tale type and motif numbers, on some level all expression is autobiography.

Different contexts necessarily beget different definitions of folklore. Real folklore in this context—a performer-centered ethnography—might best be understood as any conjunction of individual creativity and talent with larger resources and conditions. Rare accomplishments though these instances are, folklore is not a limited commodity consisting of fragments from residual culture destined to obsolescence. Real folklore, rather, is an achievement, "a momentary fulfillment of what it is to be human," in Glassie's words (2006:415). We all have this potential, but the artful, incisive interweaving of past and present, the ready-made and emergent, the traditional and individual, is nowhere better achieved than in the words of Packy Jim McGrath.

Acknowledgments

I could not have written this book without years of patience, assistance, and trust from Packy Jim. My deepest and most sincere thanks go to him for his friendship, and I hope that the preceding pages do him justice.

This book also depends on the help of many others. I am grateful for the insights, hospitality, and friendship of Danny and Susan Gallen, who regularly hosted me on my return visits to Ireland, as did Jim and Sarah Falls, and Danny and Marian McHugh. Like Danny Gallen, Danny Gormley and Charlie Hilley kept in touch and provided invaluable information for better understanding the world they share with Packy Jim.

After a long period when I felt forced prematurely to write conference presentations and publish chapters and articles based on ongoing fieldwork, my colleagues at the Ohio State University kindly reviewed my earlier work and gathered to help me conceptualize this book. I thank Dorry Noyes in particular for organizing that work-in-progress event, for her careful critical reading, and more generally for her tireless efforts as both boss and colleague. Other valuable contributors to that event included Barbara Lloyd, Kate Parker Horigan, Cassie Patterson, Martha Sims, and Sabra Webber. Ohio State colleagues Pat Mullen, Amy Shuman, and Margaret Mills graciously read preliminary parts of the manuscript and made many valuable comments and suggestions for development. Larry Syndergaard, God rest him, and Richard Green provided useful historical references to the fairies in Ireland and across Europe.

Henry Glassie read an incomplete draft at an inopportune time, and his advice was indispensable for the final push. The tremendous debt this book owes to Henry's work in Ballymenone should be readily apparent, and I thank Henry effusively for his unequaled perspective and long friendship. Gearóid Ó Crualaoich read the first full draft and helped me make further connections within and beyond the materials. Gearóid launched me into this folklore business, and I cannot thank him enough for his inspiration and generosity.

Among the Irish folklore establishment, I want to thank—in addition to Gearóid—Linda May Ballard, Jonathan Bell, Seamas Ó Catháin, Diarmuid Ó Giolláin, Lillis Ó Laoire, Ríonach Uí Ógáin, and Mervyn Watson for correspondence, encouragement, and their exemplary scholarship. Críostóir MacCárthaigh, a first-rate scholar and archivist at the incomparable National Folklore Collection at University College Dublin (UCD), deserves special thanks for his manifold assistance and hospitality. Bairbre Ní Fhloinn, Kelly Fitzgerald, and Barbara Hillers were also welcoming and helpful when I conducted research at the NFC in June 2014. These Dublin-based folklorists—Ríonach, Críostóir, Bairbre, Kelly, and Barbara—along with the Cork-based folklorists Stiofán Ó Cadhla, Ciarán Ó Gealbháin, and Clíona O'Carroll, joined me in presenting a double panel on Irish folklore studies at the 2014 American Conference for Irish Studies held at UCD. I benefited greatly from their perspectives, as well as from those of fellow attendees Guy Beiner and Deirdre Ní Chonghaile, and I look forward to future correspondence and collaboration. Éilís Ní Dhuibhne has been particularly discerning in her critique of my previous work, a generous sounding board, and an inspiration for many aspects of this book.

My life is enriched intellectually and socially by everyone mentioned above and additionally by Brandon Barker, Dick Bauman, Brent Bjorkman, Katey Borland, Erika Brady, Danille Christensen, Jeff Cohen, Robby Dobler, Tom DuBois, Michael Evans, Ann Ferrell, Michael Dylan Foster, Lisa Gilman, Diane Goldstein, Jason Baird Jackson, Jon Kay, Greg Kelley, John Laudun, Jim Leary, Carl Lindahl, Tim Lloyd, Moira Marsh, Dave McDonald, John McDowell, Mustafa Mirzeler, Galey Modan, Tom Mould, Elliott Oring, Jim Rogers, Jack Santino, Patricia Sawin, Jennifer Schacker, Greg Schrempp, Pravina Shukla, Steve Stuempfle, and Sue Tuohy.

I thank my three anonymous reviewers and the able staff of the University of Wisconsin Press—Sheila Leary for initial discussions and encouragement and for later publicity, Raphael Kadushin and Amber Rose for handling the acquisitions phase, Adam Mehring for overseeing the editing schedule, Sheila McMahon for exceptional editing, Carla Marolt and Terry Emmrich for excellent visual work, Andrea Christofferson for marketing, and Dennis Lloyd for running the show. Dan Connolly masterfully constructed another impressive subject index helping readers connect dots and make cuts through sometimes challenging material. Any faults in the type and motif indexes are my own.

Rob Vanscoyoc did an outstanding job with the initial phase of transcription, battling through an unfamiliar vernacular, suspending disbelief, and reveling in the occasional absurdity of the monumental task. I also thank him for his friendship and our diversions away from screens and out of doors.

For financial assistance that supported my fieldwork I thank the Department of Folklore and Ethnomusicology and the College of Arts and Sciences at Indiana University, the Academy for Irish Cultural Heritages at the University of Ulster, the School of Social and Behavioral Sciences at the University of Alabama at Birmingham, and the College of Arts and Sciences at the Ohio State University. At Ohio State, Valerie Lee and Richard Dutton were particularly supportive, using their administrative powers for good. At Indiana University, Diane Goldstein and John McDowell were generous in helping to protect my time in the final push toward publication.

My daughters, Maggie and Nora, have grown to astonishing heights in the long process of my researching and writing this book. They, too, count Packy Jim as a friend and have added many of his stories to their own repertoires. There is hope for this thing we call folklore and for the future of its study. Lorraine, my partner in all things intellectual and playful, this book is dedicated to you.

Appendix: Transcription Style

Throughout this book I have used complementary but distinct styles for rendering different types of speech quoted from Packy Jim. One- or two-line comments from Packy Jim are embedded in my prose, framed by quotation marks per journalistic and literary convention. Longer commentary, extending beyond a couple lines, is transcribed word for word in a block quote. Typically, short block quotes from Packy Jim consist of remarks or informational statements that emerge in the natural give and take of conversation. Attention here is more on content than on style of delivery. For moments of dialogue, such as the conversation between Packy Jim and the journalist Miriam O'Callaghan at the end of chapter 1, I have adapted this block quote style to indicate who is speaking as in a play script.

The majority of transcribed quoted speech here, however, consists of extended stretches of discourse where Packy Jim has the floor mostly to himself and is engaged in contextualizing, performing, and retrospectively commenting on longer narratives. In these longer stretches, Packy Jim takes responsibility for a display of communicative competence, in Richard Bauman's terms (1977, 1992, 2004), achieving at various points what Dell Hymes calls a breakthrough into performance (1975). In full storytelling mode, form, function, and meaning interrelate—style matters as much as content with one complementing the other—so my rendition of Packy Jim's words invites a modified ethnopoetic treatment.

The point of ethnopoetic transcription is to reflect message-relevant aspects of orality specific to a given speech community and/or performer, translating performance style into print (Tedlock 1992; Duranti 1997:122–161). One goal is to have speech look on the page something like it sounds in person. That said, there is no one correct way to achieve this goal; it depends both on discernable communicative features and on those aspects of communication one pursues for analysis. Folklorists, linguistic anthropologists, sociolinguists, and conversation analysts have developed intricate and illuminating systems of icons and orthographic marks for conveying a range of the linguistic and paralinguistic features of communication. In this book, however, I am most interested in broad expressive fidelity, and like Bauman, I am wary of "loading the printed text with so much formal furniture that it is inaccessible to the reader" (1986:ix).

My aim is not to provide a full ethnopoetic score that is detailed enough to allow readers to recapitulate almost every aspect of a given performance (cf. Fine 1984). Rather, I want to use print conventions to preserve an impression of language as it is spoken, particularly those moments where—through parallelism, pacing, intonation, and volume—Packy Jim pushes beyond prose toward poetry, beyond informational discourse toward artful expression.

To that end, I am influenced by Henry Glassie's transcription style in his books treating Ballymenone, County Fermanagh, which is in turn influenced by Tedlock (1972, 1983) and Hymes (1981). Like Glassie (1975, 1982, 2006), I use blank space on the page to indicate pause, pacing, and relative silence. I render the beginning of quoted stories flush left then break into indented paragraphs as the storytelling develops. Especially in Packy Jim's more expository, less adorned contextualizing introductions to stories, a longer uninterrupted paragraph may unfold. As he gains momentum, however, I listen for dramatic pauses, changes in pitch and volume, and formal devices such as parallelism in order to make decisions about organizing speech on the page. A line break and new indentation indicates a brief meaningful pause that signals a completed conceptual element in the sequential progress of a narrative. In addition to brief pauses, repeated particles such as "so," "and," or "but" and parallel constructions provide additional clues for line breaks because they often announce transition or a shift in orientation. Any decision to skip to the next line and indent, then, is a balance struck between breath pauses, sense pauses, and formal features, which often coincide but not always. A line space indicates a longer, usually dramatic pause of three or more seconds. A stair-stepping arrangement, adapted from Glassie (1975, 1982, 2006) and Tedlock (1972, 1983), indicates a tension-building descent in pitch level, though not necessarily volume, as in,

> So Danny was *got* and his story was:
> "I was out on the hill.
> I met my brother.
> We had a tussle.
> He overcome me.

> He tied my hands to my feet, and I suppose he
> left me here to die.
>   Only by good luck I was *got*."

The above passage also points to other significations of prosody. Italics indicate emphasis, a stress in intonation that identifies a word of primary relevance to a given passage. In the example above, the repeated emphasis on "*got*" bookends and emphasizes the manner in which the character Danny was discovered, the point of this passage. Stress in intonation can but does not always overlap with an increase in volume, which I denote with all capital letters in a word or syllable. So Packy Jim raises his voice, in imitation of the loud person he quotes, in the line "'HE WOULDN'T BE WORTH A *DAMN*!'" Note, however, that beyond the increased volume throughout the line, he reserves the greatest emphasis for the italicized "*DAMN*," underscoring the profane hostility of the person he quotes.

Given the combined use of italics and capital letters to offer a better sense of how the original sounded, the exclamation point after "*DAMN*" may seem superfluous. In general, for ease of accessibility, I have used punctuation in the same ways that it is used to render dialogue in literature—commas indicate a pause in thought and timing, often separating clauses or lists; periods indicate the completion of a thought, though this is true here whether or not the thought is a grammatically complete sentence; colons precede an enumeration or elaboration; question marks identify an interrogative statement and usually indicate a slight elevation in pitch. As in print, exclamation points here convey strong feeling but may appear on their own without being preceded by italics or capital letters where they are not warranted. An exclamation point on its own conveys strong but not necessarily the strongest feeling, which may be indicated by a combination of italics, capital letters, and exclamation point, as in "*DAMN*!"

Other punctuation is relevant as well. In some cases, em dashes indicate the end of a false start and point to a change in direction, a common phenomenon in oral communication. More often em dashes set off coherent asides—clauses that modify or clarify the preceding statement before proceeding, as this one does—serving where a period would be too strong and a comma too weak. When em dashes set off brief summations they serve much the same function as parentheses. But listening to the natural flow of speech with all its tangents, false starts, and embedded clauses, I "see" dashes that leave a mark but still connect horizontally and sequentially, rather than parentheses that throw up vertical subdividing walls. Ellipses serve like commas to signal an internal pause in a line, but ellipses typically signify a longer pause in which Packy Jim is taking time to think before continuing, or in some cases, usually at the end of a line, he is trailing off without completing his thought.

Bear in mind that in spoken language, very few people speak in complete, grammatically correct sentences. The fact that I have not corrected Packy Jim's grammar in my transcripts should not reflect badly on him but rather reflect that oral discourse is simply a different mode of language than is found in writing. A run-on sentence, for example, does not mean that Packy Jim is a bad or un-educated speaker, only that a given thought is richly complicated and must extend to achieve full expression.

Occasionally I interrupt longer ethnopoeticized stretches with one or two words of clarification in brackets. In places where longer explanation and contextualization are required, I break from the quotation, skip a line, shift to the left margin, provide my editorial commentary, then skip another line and return to the ethnopoeticized block quote. Although I interrupt some longer block quotes several times or for relatively lengthy comments, I always offer the recording date at the conclusion of the stretch of speech being quoted.

Approximating pronunciation in transcribed speech can be a sensitive matter, so I have attempted a balanced approach. The goal is to be faithful to Packy Jim's use of language, while forestalling an evaluation of him as less sophisticated when judged unfairly by foreign sociolinguistic standards. Wanting to avoid potentially insulting conventions characteristic of "stage Irish" eye dialect, I have used standardized spelling in many cases regardless of actual pronunciation. In doing so, I render speech as, for example, "queer" instead of "quare," "women" instead of "weemin," "of course" instead of "of coose," "fellow" instead of "fella," "my mother" and "by Christ" instead of "me mother" and "be Christ." Likewise, I do not drop the "g" in the present parti-ciple "ing" as Packy Jim does in pronouncing it, and I render the "mighta been" heard in person as "might have been." In these cases, I have obscured Packy Jim's pronunciations so as to avoid obvious pitfalls of misjudgment by the casual reader.

That said, Packy Jim's Ulster Hiberno-English makes perfect sense on its own terms, and overall my editing of his language is quite minimal. So when Packy Jim says "again'," "'round," or "'em," for example, I do not alter the rhythm of his speech by rendering these as "against," "around," or "them." Nor have I substituted "heard," "afraid," "arose," or "drove" for his usages of "heared," "afeared," "riz," or "driv," which are part of the wider local vernacu-lar. There is nothing to gain and much to be lost from jettisoning poetic collo-quialisms such as "thon" and "thonder." Likewise, I have not changed perfectly good northern Hiberno-English and Ulster-Scots terms such as brae, oncest, or redd, but the glossary of such terms after the preface is intended to help non-Irish readers. In some cases, a standard word or phrase such as "idiot" or "by God" is pronounced locally in a way that has already given rise to an easily recognized and nearly equally standardized spelling such as "eejit" or "begod." In these cases, I privilege Packy Jim's pronunciation through spelling because it is widespread, easily deciphered, and unlikely to cause offense.

Notes on the Recitations, Songs, and Traditional Stories

These historical and comparative notes on the primary texts recorded from Packy Jim follow the order in which the recitations, songs, and stories appear in this book. Citations below that include "NFC" or "NFCS" refer to volumes and page numbers of the main manuscript collection or schools' manuscript collection, respectively, of the National Folklore Collection, formerly the Irish Folklore Commission (IFC), at University College Dublin. I am grateful to Professor Ríonach Uí Ógáin, former director of the NFC, for permission to search the collection and cite materials here. Motifs discussed come from Thompson (1960), and migratory legend types come from Christiansen (1958) and Almqvist (1991a, 1991b).

"An Old Woman of the Roads" (xviii)

Having memorized this poem from a school reader as a boy, Packy Jim recited this—one of Padraic Colum's most popular and frequently anthologized poems, from 1907—nearly verbatim. His only deviations from the original were reversing the order of "white" and "blue" in the final line of the third verse and omitting Colum's fourth verse:

> I could be quiet there at night
> Beside the fire and by myself,
> Sure of a bed and loth to leave
> The ticking clock and the shining delph!

Written from the perspective of a Traveler (Tinker being the older, more pejorative term) the poem can be read in a nationalist light with the landless Traveler standing in for all Irish people in the wake of the broad dispossession of colonialism. Likewise, the yearning for ownership and landed stability in the form of a modest yet tidy, well-appointed home echoes a preoccupation with respectability among the rising Catholic middle class of the period. The old woman's Catholic piety—and the fact that Padraic Colum was one of the few Catholic associates of the Irish Literary Revival—likely would have complemented the political and class themes to make this poem a natural choice for school readers in a newly independent Ireland. At the time Packy Jim recited this poem—the first text I ever collected from him—I mentally noted that he has everything the old woman desires. I did not appreciate, however, how well this poem captures his high estimation of autonomy and domestic security, and his commitment to staying put, all of which is elaborated in several of the personal narratives he would eventually share and repeat.

The Origin of the Fairies (13–15, 156–158)

The idea of the fairies as fallen or neutral angels—motifs F251.6 and V236.1—has a long history and wide European and even North American distribution. Richard Firth Green (forthcoming, chap. 1) cites a number of twelfth- and thirteenth-century French, German, and English sources of pastoral (as opposed to scholastic) theology that identify the fairies as neutral angels who may be considered less demonic than the fallen angels who had sided boldly with Lucifer. This pastoral theology, then, softens the official Church line that fairies were demons and thoroughly evil. Green further traces the idea of more and less culpable classes of devils to the third century. Perhaps such notions allowed for the clergy, closer to the common people, to rationalize, co-opt, or absorb popular traditions about the fairies as less than completely evil, but this never became officially sanctioned Church teaching. In Ireland, Ó hOgáin (2006:208) cites fifteenth-century manuscript evidence for the connection between fairies and neutral angels, and William Wilde ([1852] 1972:125) specifies the ninth-century Book of Armagh and the fifteenth-century Book of Lismore. Rieti (1991:21–24) notes the belief in fairies as neutral angels in Newfoundland, a place of significant Irish immigration; MacDonald (1994–1995:43) notes the belief in Scottish sources; and Evans-Wentz ([1911] 1990:85, 105, 130, 154, 205, 241) notes the belief in Celtic regions beyond Ireland, particularly Scotland and Wales. Christiansen (1971–1973) discusses variations on the folk idea of the fairies as fallen or neutral angels farther afield in Europe, especially in Scandinavia. The idea missing from Packy Jim's account—that fairies want to interbreed with humans and increase the amount of human blood in their veins, in the hope of returning to Heaven at Judgment Day—is conveyed by a migratory legend (type 5055 in Christiansen 1958 and type 5051 as suggested by Almqvist 1991a:271) with examples in Ó hEochaidh (1977:35, 261, 373), Ó Súilleabháin (1967:83), and Ó Catháin (1985:79). For published versions of the origin of the fairies collected and discussed by folklorists in Ireland, see William Wilde ([1852] 1972:125), Lady Jane Wilde (1888:37–38), Wood-Martin (1902:5–6), Christiansen (1971–1973:96–97), Ó hEochaidh (1977:35), Ó Súilleabháin (1977:44–45; 2011:153–156), Ó Duilearga (1981:253), Lysaght (1996:44), and Glassie (2006:301–302). Glassie (1982:779–780, n. 5) offers a thorough annotation of additional published Irish versions. Some of the few English-language versions of this story as elaborate as Packy Jim's can be found in the NFC (for example, NFC 220:101–106 from County Wexford and NFC 1242:347–348 from County Mayo).

"I See His Blood upon the Rose" (43)

Packy Jim recited Joseph Mary Plunkett's poem—published in 1916 and later in Packy Jim's school reader—for my recorder on April 8, 1999:

> I see his blood upon the rose
> And in the stars that glory in his eyes
> His body gleams amid eternal snows,
> His tears fall from the skies.
>
> I see his face in every flower.
> The thunder and the singing of the birds
> Are but his voice, and carven by his power
> Rocks are his written words.
>
> All pathways by his feet are worn
> His strong heart stirs the ever-beating sea
> His crown of thorns is twined with every thorn
> His cross is every tree.

Packy Jim's rendition was accurate word-for-word except for the second line, which was originally published as "And in the stars the glory of his eyes." One of the architects of the 1916 Easter Rising, Plunkett understood that the insurrection had little chance of military success but was convinced that the emergence of an independent Ireland required a blood sacrifice. Scheduling the Rising for Easter was a conscious symbolic choice, and like fellow organizer Patrick Pearse, Plunkett modeled his inevitable martyrdom on that of Christ, elevating the nationalist cause beyond mere politics. For Packy Jim, the poem is not only a religious meditation, with or without political associations, but serves most often as the centerpiece and anchoring text in a repeated personal narrative about his early vulnerability and mistreatment.

Daily Prayers (45)

Both of Packy Jim's daily prayers are fairly common and part of the official catechism of the Roman Catholic Church. The text of Packy Jim's guardian angel prayer is:

> Angel of God, my guardian dear,
> To whom God's love commits me here,
> Ever this day, be at my side,
> To light, to guard, to rule, to guide.
> Amen.

His daily prayer for the intercession of the Virgin, like that of Anglophone Catholics worldwide, is:

> Hail Mary, full of grace,
> The Lord is with thee.
> Blessed art thou among women
> And blessed is the fruit of thy womb, Jesus.
> Holy Mary, Mother of God,
> Pray for us sinners,
> Now and at the hour of our death.
> Amen.

Paddle Your Own Canoe (55–56)

According to the *Oxford English Dictionary*, to paddle one's own canoe, figuratively speaking, is to be self-reliant, minding one's own business, and making one's own fortune. Wolfgang Mieder (2001) discusses Frederick Douglass's use of the proverbial phrase to characterize himself as a self-made man in his third autobiography, published in 1893. According to the etymologist Barry Popik, the couplet Packy Jim has taken as his motto (Love many, trust few / And always paddle your own canoe) was printed in American newspapers at various times between 1826 and 1866 and has been popular in autograph albums since at least 1879 (see http://www.barrypopik.com/index.php/new_york_city /entry/love_many_trust_few_and_always_paddle_your_own_canoe/). A basic Google search indicates that the couplet remains widespread as a popular dictum, epigram, or motto on social media sites such as Facebook and Twitter. Incidentally, the actor Nick Offerman (channeling aspects of his former television character Ron Swanson) has written an often amusing but sententious autobiographical ode to self-reliance titled *Paddle Your Own Canoe* (2013).

The Buffer (71–72)

Packy Jim's version of the Buffer's unexpected flight to Scotland, motif X1852 (Boy shot from cannon), is also quoted in Cashman (2008b:120–122), where analysis focuses on the management of reported speech and the generic complexity of a tall tale repurposed for a local character anecdote. The other examples of the Buffer's expressive lying—the creel of leopard's blood, the pickpocket disappointed—have not been published. The notion that tall tales and expressive lying more generally can be a means of elevating one's social status regardless of one's material circumstances is born out in Bauman (1986, chap. 5; 2004, chap. 5) and Mullen (1988, chap. 8), all of which treat the Texas storyteller Ed Bell. Glassie (1982:49–50, 737–741) offers exhaustive treatment of the form and function of tall tales—known as "pants" in Ballymenone—and of published collections and examinations of the genre in Ireland and beyond. Cashman (2008b:61–62, 117–123, 189–193, 264–265) covers similar ground with some updating and significant attention to the generic conventions and expectations of tall tales and expressive lying, known locally as codding or codology.

Cassie Pat Suzanne (81–82)

The relevant motifs here are J1190 (Cleverness in law court) and J1300 (Officiousness or foolish question rebuked). This story conforms exactly to the generic conventions and expectations for local character anecdotes as they are told at wakes and ceilis in Aghyaran, County Tyrone. For more on the form, function, and meaning of this genre, see Cashman (2008b:6–9, 94–106). Compare Packy Jim's anecdote about Cassie Pat Suzanne with John McShane's anecdote about the smuggler David Logue getting the better of the Crown prosecution during cross-examination (Cashman 2008b:183–185).

"Fontenoy, 1745" (87)

I recorded Packy Jim reciting Emily Lawless's poem about the Battle of Fontenoy three times (March 18, 1999; August 13, 2007; and November 17, 2011), and there was remarkable consistency from version to version. Compared with the original published version (in Colum 1922), Packy Jim makes only occasional substitutions, such as "vanquished men" for the original "banished men" at the end of the first stanza, or "that" for "which" in the fourth line of the second stanza. The full text from my second recording (August 13, 2007, the clearest audio of the three) is below. Note that Corca Baiscinn, in the second verse, is an area in southwest County Clare that many of the Wild Geese (Irish Jacobites) left to join Irish brigades in France and Spain after the defeat of 1690.

> Oh bad the march, the weary march, beneath those alien skies,
> But good the night, the friendly night, that soothes our tired eyes.
> And bad the war, the tedious war, that keeps us sweltering here,
> But good the hour, the friendly hour, that brings the battle near.
> That brings us on to battle, that summons to their share
> The homeless troops, the vanquished men, the exiled sons of Clare.
>
> Oh little Corca Baiscinn, the wild, the bleak, the fair.
> Oh little stony pastures whose flowers are sweet if rare.
> Oh rough, the rude Atlantic, the thunderous, the wide,
> Whose kiss is like a soldier's kiss that will not be denied.
> The whole night long we dream of you, and waking think we're there,
> Vain dream and foolish waking, we never shall see Clare.
>
> The wind is wild tonight, there is battle in the air.
> The wind is from the west, and it seems to blow from Clare.
> Have you nothing, nothing for us, loud brawler of the night?
> No news to warm our heartstrings, to speed us through the fight?
> In this hollow star-pricked darkness as in the sun's hot glare,
> And sun-tide, moon-tide, star-tide, we thirst, we starve for Clare.
>
> Hark yonder, through the darkness with distant rat-tat-tat,
> The old foe stirs out there, God bless his soul for that.
> The old foe musters strongly, he's coming on at last,
> And Clare's brigade may claim its own wherever blows fall fast.
> Send us, ye western breezes, our full and rightful share
> For faith, for fame, for honor, and the ruined hearths of Clare.

This is the first movement of Lawless's poem, "I. Before the battle; night." It is not clear whether Packy Jim does not remember the second movement—"II. After the battle; early dawn, Clare coast"—or if it was not printed in Packy Jim's school reader.

"The Mountains of Pomeroy" (88)

Set to the tune of a traditional air, the lyrics of this song were composed by George Sigerson (1836–1925), a nationalist doctor, scientist, politician, and poet from near Strabane, County Tyrone. It was first published in Ralph Varian's *The Harp of Erin* (1869:229–230), then widely anthologized and later commercially recorded. I taped Packy Jim's version in our first recorded session (November 16, 1998):

The morn was breaking bright and fair,
The lark sang in the sky,
The maid she bound her golden hair
With a blithe glance in her eye.
For who beyond those gay green woods
Was awaiting her with joy?
Oh, who but her gallant Renardine
On the mountains of Pomeroy.

An outlawed man in a land forlorn,
He scorned to turn and flee.
But he kept the cause of freedom safe
Upon the mountains high.

Full often in the dawning hour,
For oft in the twilight brown,
He met this maid in the woodland bower
Where the stream comes foaming down.
For they were faithful in their love.
No words could e'er destroy.
No tyrant's hand touched Renardine
On the mountains of Pomeroy

"Dear love," she said, "I'm so afraid
For the yeoman's force and you.
They've tracked you through the lowland plains
And all the valley through.
My kinsmen frown, when you are named.
They would your life destroy.
Beware," they say, "of Renardine
On the mountains of Pomeroy."

"Fear not, fear not, sweetheart," he cried,
"Fear not the foe for me.
No chain shall fall whate'er betide
On the arm that will be free.
But leave your cruel kin and come
When the lark it is in the sky
And it's with my gun that I'll guard you
On the mountains of Pomeroy."

The morn has come, she arose and fled
From her cruel kin and home.
And bright the wood and rosy red,
And the tumbling torrents foam,
But the mist came on and the tempest roared
And did all around destroy,
And a pale drowned bride met Renardine
On the mountains of Pomeroy.

Again, Packy Jim's substitutions that deviate from the original text are minor. In the third verse, Packy Jim has "No tyrant's hand touched Renardine," whereas Sigerson wrote no tyrant's "law" touched him. In the fourth verse, Sigerson's maid fears the "foeman's force" whereas Packy Jim sang of the "yeoman's force." Either term is appropriate in that the yeomanry—voluntary military units drawn from the Protestant population—would have been the outlaw's chief "foeman." In the fifth verse, Packy Jim inserts a redundant "it" after "lark" that is not in Sigerson's original.

"Brennan on the Moor" 88–89)

The full text of Packy Jim's "Brennan on the Moor" (recorded on November 16, 1998) is:

It's of a famous highwayman
A story now I'll tell.
His name was Willie Brennan
And in Ireland he did dwell.
'Twas on the Kilworth Mountains
He commenced his wild career
Where many a wealthy gentleman
Before him shook with fear.

Brennan on the Moor,
Brennan on the Moor,
Bold and yet undaunted
Stood young Brennan on the Moor.

A brace of loaded pistols
He carried night and day,
And he never robbed a poor man
Upon the king's highway.
But what he'd taken from the rich
Like Turpin and Black Bess
Sure he always did divide it
With the widow in distress.

One night he robbed a packman
By the name of Peddler Bawn.
They traveled on together
'Till the daylight began to dawn.
The peddler seeing his money gone,
Likewise is watch and chain,
Yet once encountered Brennan
And robbed him back again.

When Brennan saw the peddler
Was as good a man as he
He took him on the highway
His companion for to be.
The peddler threw away his pipe,
His bag without the least delay,
And proved a faithful comrade
Until his dying day.

One day upon the highway,
As Willie he sat down,
He met the mayor of Cashel
A mile outside of town.
The man he knew his features.
"I think, young man," said he,
"Your name is Willie Brennan.
You must come along with me."

Then Brennan's wife being gone to town,
Provisions for to buy,
When she saw her Willie taken
She began to weep and cry.

He says, "Give me that tenpenny."
As soon as Willie spoke
She handed him a blunderbuss
From underneath her cloak.
Then with the loaded blunderbuss
The truth I will unfold
He made the mayor to tremble
And robbed him of his gold.

One hundred pounds was offered for
His apprehension there,
And he with his horse and saddle
To the mountains did repair
Where cavalry and infantry
To take him they did try.
He laughed at them with scorn
Until at length to say
That by a false-hearted woman
He basely was betrayed.

In the County Tipperary
In a place called Clonmore
Willie Brennan and his comrade
They did suffer sore.
He lay among ferns,
Which was thick upon the field,
And nine wounds he did receive
Before that he did yield.

Then Brennan and his comrade,
Seeing they were betrayed,
They with the mounted cavalry
A noble battle made.
He lost his foremost finger,

Which was shot off by a ball,
So Brennan and his comrade
Were taken after all.

So they were taken prisoners,
And in irons they were bound,
And both conveyed to Clonmel Jail,
Strong wall did them surround.
They were tried and then found guilty.
The judge made this reply,
"For the robbing of the King's highway
You're both condemned to die."

When Brennan heard this sentence
He made this brave reply,
"I own that I did rob the rich
And did the poor supply.
In all the deeds that I have done
I took no life away.
The Lord have mercy on my soul
Against the judgment day."

"Farewell to my loving wife
And to my children three,
Rightwise my aged father,
He may shed tears for me.
And to my loving mother
Who tore her locks and cried,
Saying, "I wish you, Willie Brennan,
In your cradle you had died."

The author of the song is unknown, but it was quite popular, with countless broadside printings in Ireland and Britain, from the 1840s. Much later, Burl Ives, Ed McCurdy, and the Clancy Brothers and Tommy Makem recorded versions during the Folksong Revival of the 1950s and '60s. Cashman (2000b:200–203) offers historical, literary, and folkloric sources concerning William Brennan, as does Graham Seal (1996:72–76, 215–216). Jürgen Kloss (2011) collects an impressive amount of material on the history of the song itself.

Proinsias Dubh (90–94)

The memory of Proinsias Dubh in next-door Aghyaran, County Tyrone, is consistent with Packy Jim's cycle of legends, though no one I have met in Aghyaran can tell as many well-elaborated Proinsias Dubh stories as Packy Jim. Likewise, Packy Jim's Proinsias Dubh closely fits the outlaw's profile in nearby Ballymenone, where he is known as Black Francis. His cunning methods for robbery and the redistribution of wealth, his chivalric defense of the vulnerable such as Miss Armstrong at Lisgoole, and his inevitable capture and clever last words are all remarkably similar (Glassie 1982:116–119, 132–136; 2006:283–288, 472–473). The relatively short distance between Lettercran and Ballymenone is a factor. Although I have given Packy Jim books by Glassie that include discussion of Black Francis, note that Packy Jim told me all of the legends about Proinsias Dubh reproduced here before I began giving him books. Not included in the Ballymenone accounts are discussion of Proinsias Dubh's birth in Cloghore, identification of him as a McHugh, a description of his appearance, his early enlistment with the Achesons, and the Achesons' treachery and the servant girl's coded tip-off, a traveling motif attached to other outlaws (see Cashman 2000b:213, n. 17). Although the transcribed series of Proinsias Dubh stories from November 16, 2011, is extensive, it leaves out two legends that are also part of Packy Jim's repertoire. The first recalls a heroic escape by Proinsias Dubh's colleague Supple Corrigan.

> Supple Corrigan was chased by a man on horseback—a Captain Barton maybe—some road up there in Fermanagh way up toward the Lisnaskea country. And they come to the river, a good sizeable river, but he was said to be very supple and good, like, an athlete. He jumped the river. And the horseman, he didn't care to face it in case of jumping in. And I think maybe Corrigan could have trained a gun on him by this time from the, from the opposite bank.
>
> So, uh, the horseman following him was supposed to say, "That was a brave good jump you made." And Supple Corrigan said, "The Devil stint it," he said, "I had a long enough run at it!"
>
> I think that's true enough, too.
>
> "The De'il stint it, I had a long enough race at it."
>
> So he made his escape for that time, some middling river, you know, that would have been deep. Aye. (November 18, 2011)

This story of the enormous leap (motif F1071.2.1) is also told about Corrigan and a Lord Belmore in Ballymenone (Glassie 1982:128; 2006:284, 473) and elsewhere in Fermanagh (Livingstone 1969:131). Other heroic outlaws are credited with this running leap over water, either on foot or on horseback, including Daniel O'Keefe (Marshall 1927:62) and Dermot Buckley (O'Leary 1946:184), both of County Cork. The other legend not included in the series from November 16, 2011, concerns the rumor that Proinsias Dubh buried but never recovered a large portion of his treasure on a hill above Killeter, County Tyrone. Packy Jim takes this to be "an old paxity," a word learned from his mother, meaning a falsehood or tall tale.

> And then they told—but that's only an old, an old, an old *paxity*, anybody would know that it was a paxity. But he had a foal's skin, he had a foal's skin of gold *sovereigns*. That's a foal that—a young horse or pony that dies and his skin is taken off, skinned. And it was hid on Leitrim Hill down there, about a mile from Killeter.
>
> And there was something about it, when he hid it, that you could see this point here and that point there at sunset, two steeples lined up and the sunset on a certain *day*. Like, in other words, giving a descriptive *marking* of where this foal skin of gold was hid on Leitrim Hill up *there*.
>
> There was an old chap lived out in Shanaghy there. He heared all them tales, and he used to go, or went a few times to search, to look, in the hope—he was a poor body, you know—to recover Proinsias Dubh's foal skin of sovereigns. And uh, Neil McElhill might be fit to tell you a bit about that, or he might not.
>
> But uh, it would be very, *very* hard to believe that Proinsias Dubh had that, had gathered that amount of money, that it would amount to, we'll say, a bucketful of gold sovereigns or *more*, and that he would hide it down *there* so far away. Why hide it down *there*? I would say it was only an old paxity.
>
> But Neil's Frank, as they called him—that's going back seventy years ago or so—made a few forays in that direction, to try to recover Proinsias Dubh's gold, but he didn't manage it. No, nor nobody ever will.
>
> But I'd be afraid I wouldn't take it serious. That's an old paxity I doubt. I wouldn't like to believe it. (August 13, 2007)

While Packy Jim doubts the veracity of this story, unrecovered buried treasure is a common motif in legends of Irish outlaws in general and this outlaw and his associates in particular (for example, see Glassie 1982:106–107, 128; 2006:284). For treatment of the many recurring patterns in Irish outlaw lore with discussion of their symbolic resonances and rhetorical uses, see Cashman (2000b, 2000d).

Bill Graham (99–100)

A common way for Irish folk tradition to convey the villainy of the landlord class and to underscore the inequality of the landlord-tenant relationship is to portray landlords as sexual aggressors preying on the most vulnerable—young female servants and tenants—or generally living outside of normal sexual propriety, taking mistresses or fathering children out of wedlock. Séamus Mac Philib explores this phenomenon by focusing on legends of *ius primae noctis*— landlords claiming the right to sexual relations with new brides on their wedding nights—and by identifying international parallels to stories of landlords' sexual lasciviousness (1988, 1994–1995). Such stories may have shaped the popular portrayal of the landlord Bill Graham and certainly informed the custom of hiding young women from hunting parties for fear of "lustful people in high places," in Packy Jim's words. Graham's reputation as a scoundrel is further accentuated by his malicious overreaction to the mildest hint of insolence from Read, perceived as a challenge to his absolute authority. The fact that it makes no difference to Graham that Read is a fellow Protestant impresses Packy Jim further that Graham was a petty tyrant with no loyalties beyond his own self-interests. Relevant motifs in Packy Jim's accounts of local landlords include Q326 (Impudence punished), W127 (Petulance), and W151 (Greed), and secondarily or by implication T471 (Rape), T481 (Adultery), and T640 (Illegitimate children).

Peggy Roe (126–131, 148–149)

A local story of actual past events, rather than a localized migratory legend, the story of Peggy Roe is popular for including certain widely dispersed, compelling motifs. The emotional core of the story—and the climax of James Donoghue's "The Ballad of Peggy Roe" (1935)—is encapsulated in the image of the two frozen corpses with the younger brother wrapped in Peggy's arms and outer garments. Here motif W28 (Self-sacrifice) is applicable, as is T89.2 (Woman sacrifices self to save beloved), although the beloved here is kin rather than a romantic partner. The tragedy of youths dying before they have reached their full potential is underscored by their restless ghosts returning to the site of their deaths years later, motifs E275 (Ghost haunts place of great accident or misfortune) and E411.10 (Persons who die accidental deaths cannot rest in grave). Motif T80 (Tragic love) is also an important element given that Peggy tried to make her way home via a less direct and more exposed route, obeying her father's command that she no longer go near the home of her former boyfriend James Davy McGrath. This star-crossed lovers theme certainly draws out

Donoghue's "The Ballad of Peggy Roe" and another locally popular ballad, "The Little Penknife." Although not part of Packy Jim's active repertoire, he is familiar with and knows some of the stanzas of this ballad, having heard it sung by the late Johnny Corry from Segronan townland, County Tyrone. In the song a coachman falls in love with a rich farmer's daughter. The farmer accuses the coachman of theft and has him hanged. The daughter commits suicide. Both Packy Jim and Johnny have drawn connections for me between the song and the story of Peggy Roe, particularly the parallel themes of the father's prohibition, the male lover's reputation tainted by accusations of being a thief, and the female lover's death. For liner notes and a commercially recorded version of Johnny singing this ballad, see James Foley et al.'s "Harvest Home: Songs and Crack from West Tyrone" (1991).

Carrickaholten Eviction (136–138)

This is another local story of actual past events, rather than a localized migratory legend. It includes, nonetheless, motifs of wide interest and dissemination. Motifs K2211 (Treacherous brother), K2212.2 (Treacherous sister-in-law), and K2155 (Evidence of crime left so that dupe is blamed) are all pertinent in this "dirty story" of Danny McFadden and his wife, Cassie, trying to frame Danny's brother Barney. Motif Q552.3.5 (Punishment for greed) relates to Packy Jim's observation that—though victorious in getting Barney evicted and taking over his land—Danny and Cassie ended their days in poverty, denounced by the priest and ostracized by neighbors.

Wraiths (146–148)

The emigrant from Tieveeny Lane returning as a wraith and prefiguring news of his death in America very likely has analogues in the NFC collections that, unfortunately, I have not had time to locate. Ó Súilleabháin's *A Handbook of Irish Folklore* suggests as much by including questions about the dead seen in distant places, including the wraiths of emigrants seen back home at or just before the time of death (1942:249). Likewise, an anonymous reviewer notes that in Scandinavian tradition there are accounts of wraiths (*fylgje*) sighted at home when emigrants die abroad (Kvideland and Sehmsdorf 1991:81). Motif E555 (Dead man smokes pipe) may suggest possible connections between this and other local or migratory legends. On the whole, Packy Jim's accounts of local wraiths, including that of Margaret McGreece and of the absent neighbor seen carrying hay, are consistent with the common representations of and beliefs about wraiths in Irish tradition. Several widespread traditional motifs are pertinent: E323.6 (Appearance of wraith as announcement of person's death), E574 (Appearance of ghost serves as death omen), E721 (Soul journeys from the body), and E723.2 (Seeing one's wraith a sign that person is to die shortly).

Ghosts (148–153)

Two dozen motifs from Stith Thompson's index are applicable to Packy Jim's ghost stories—mostly designated with E, concerning the dead, and a couple with F, concerning marvels. These can be reviewed in all their detail and relative distinction in the international motif index that follows the references. As mentioned, the sighting of the ghost of Peggy Roe and her brother at the spot where they died is consistent with narratives and beliefs about restless ghosts (motifs E275 and E411.10), as is Packy Jim's mention of Glendinning, the man shot by the Achesons whose ghost haunts the bridge where he fell. In fact, all the tragic ghosts Packy Jim mentions are tied to the locations where they died by accident, murder, or suicide. Bob Goudy's ghost is perhaps the most tenacious, resisting attempts to exorcise him. Packy Jim is not the only one who tells the story at length. At http://www.storyfinders.co.uk you can find, under the Castlederg group, audio of Patrick John McGoldrick telling Pat O'Loughlin, a local folklore collector, his version of the Bob Goudy ghost story. Differences are minor. For example, McSorley is married and he challenges the ghost to combat (motif E461.1) after it repeatedly extinguishes his wife's candle. After the fight, McSorley takes to his bed and dies shortly thereafter, whereas Packy Jim has him lingering to die within the year. The climactic description of the fight—McSorley feeling like he was punching a bag of wool while receiving a heavy metal blow in return—is almost word for word in both versions. Patrick John McGoldrick ends with the exorcism into a rock and does not include the poltergeist disturbance that took place years later suggesting that Goudy had escaped. Incidentally, at the same website, Patrick John McGoldrick also has a version of the witch hare story set in the foothills of County Tyrone's Sperrin Mountains rather than in the immediate local area.

The Hammer Man (163–164)

Motif F382.3 (Use of God's name nullifies fairies' power) is relevant here, though it is unclear from Packy Jim's story whether the Hammer Man is understood to be a fairy, a ghost, or some other supernatural force or figure. In Ireland, conflation of the worlds of the dead and of the fairies is common, and some posit a belief in fairies as being in fact the souls of the ancestral dead (see, for example, Lysaght 1991). Whether the story concerns a fairy, a ghost, or some other sort of revenant, Johnston's appeal in the name of God clearly suggests a hierarchy of supernatural instrumentality with the Christian deity at the top. For Packy Jim, the nature of the Hammer Man remains a mystery but one that does not actually beg too rigid a distinction between types of supernatural being.

Top Grain of Croghan (168)

Bo Almqvist (1991a:272) observes that migratory legend type 5080 (Food from the fairies) is quite rare in Ireland. Ó hEochaidh (1977:153–155, 337–343) includes two stories of meal or bread freely given by the fairies to humans who have to overcome great trepidation in order to partake, even in time of famine. A third legend, titled "The Fine Grain of Mullach Chruacháin," does not parallel exactly the plot of "The Top Grain of Croghan." The former focuses on a fairy paying back the human who loaned her meal, whereas the gift from fairy to human in the latter is unexpected and freely given despite the human's inability to reciprocate. The two stories, nevertheless, share a motif in the fairy's reassurance that the meal offered is good quality and from a place locally associated with the fairies: "It is better than anything you gave me—this is the meal we call the grain of Mullach Chruacháin!" (Ó hEochaidh 1977:153). In a similar formulation, Katharine Briggs quotes the reciprocating fairy—in a Scottish version set down by John Francis Campbell—as exclaiming, "Braw meal, it's the top pickle of the sin corn," or in other words, "Splendid meal, it's the best grain of the harvested oats" (1991:238). Yet another Irish version ends with the woman saying, "That is good meal," and the fairy replying, "It ought to be good for it is the top grain of Connaught [Connacht]" (NFCS 1100:89). This last one was collected between 1937 and 1939 as part of the Irish Folklore Commission's Schools Collection project, submitted from Lismullyduff, County Donegal, and is close in content to Packy Jim's version, which came to him from his grandmother, Cecily Moss, via his mother. Interestingly, Lismullyduff is very near the border on the north side of Aghyaran and directly opposite Garvagh Blane, County Tyrone, where Packy Jim's grandmother grew up, roughly four miles away.

Segronan Fairies (168–169)

Arguably, this is another variant of migratory legend type 5080 (food from the fairies), but here the dramatic emphasis is on the unseemly curiosity, meddling, and rudeness of the human beneficiary. According to Packy Jim, his outburst, "The De'il stint you to be tired carrying nothing," means "The Devil take you for complaining about such a small burden." In the narrative logic of Irish fairy legends and in the wider belief system that advises reverence and reciprocity when dealing with the fairies, such ingratitude will inevitably be punished (motif Q281). In this legend we also get a glimpse of fairies' physical appearance as about the size of a small boy (motif F239.4.2).

Nick the Nogginweaver (169–170)

Published versions of this fairy legend appear in T. Crofton Croker's *Fairy Legends of the South of Ireland* ([1825] 1862:91–100), an issue of the *Dublin Penny Journal* (Anonymous 1835), and Ó hEochaidh's *Fairy Legends from Donegal* (1977:53–55). Yeats reprints Croker's version, "Master and Man," in his edited collection, *Fairy and Folk Tales of the Irish Peasantry* (1888). The School's Collection of the NFC includes several versions, one remarkably similar in volume 1108, pp. 121–125, from Carrigans, County Donegal. (See http://www.duchas.ie for access to digital scans and crowd-sourced transcripts of the original notebooks from the late 1930s.) Relevant motifs here include F322 (Fairies take or attempt to take bride), F360 (Malevolent or destructive fairies), and F382.3 (Use of God's name nullifies fairies' power). That third motif, involving the fairies being foiled by a protagonist saying, "God bless you," is widespread and emerges in fairy legends of various types and statements of folk belief. See, for example, Hyde (1939:348) or NFC (117:82, 111).

The Water Horse (176–179)

Water-spirit as horse (F420.1.3.3) is a common motif in Irish, Scottish, and Faroese fairy legends, comparable to the Nix of Scandinavian and German folklore. Glassie (1982:803) notes nine published Irish references to the water horse; among the more elaborated narratives are Lady Gregory ([1920] 1970:16–18, 21, 26) and Ó Súilleabháin (1974:113–116). The most common story of the water horse in Ireland involves a farmer taming the supernatural animal to labor at the plow and other tasks, but once he strikes or curses the water horse it turns violent, usually dragging the farmer under water to his death (MLSIT 4086, as suggested by Almqvist 1991a:236–237; 1991b). In a County Sligo version of this story (NFC 172:33), nothing was left of the farmer except his heart, which floated to the surface of the lake, establishing the lake's name as Loch a Chroí (Lake of the Heart). See also NFC 233:4071 and NFC 966:136–137. Likewise, in Scottish stories about the Each Uisge (literally "water horse"), the creature drags a human victim under water to eat every bit of the body except the liver, heart, or lungs, which later emerges (Briggs 1976:115–116; MacDonald 1994–1995:50). Packy Jim's detail about the discovery of Mrs.

McPeake's "lights" being taken as evidence that she was killed by a water horse must be an echo of such narratives. In the Ulster-inflected vernacular of Appalachia, the lights are another term for lungs, or more generally internal organs, rather than specifically the tonsils, as Packy Jim has it. Whether or not there has been a mistake or slippage over time in naming the body part in Packy Jim's version of the story, the widespread core motif seems to feature one organ that the monster does not or will not eat, which subsequently floats to the surface or washes ashore as evidence of the victim's violent demise. Kilfeather (1988) and Almqvist (1991b) include several additional published and NFC manuscript versions. Moreover, they treat the evidence for the age of the legend and the likelihood of Irish versus Scandinavian origin and dissemination.

Saint Patrick (184–186)

A saint overcoming a dragon is an international motif (V229.4; cf. A531 Culture hero kills dragon), lending support to Packy Jim's (and John Cunningham's) suspicion that the story about Saint Patrick killing the serpent of Lough Derg may be something other than or more than a report of literal happenings. In a Fenian tale cited by many, one of Fionn MacCumhaill's warrior band disobeys orders in casting a maggot from a bone into Lough Derg, whereupon it transforms into an enormous rampaging monster termed a worm, *ollphéist* (serpent), or *nathair* (snake). Years of the monster's tyranny pass before Saint Patrick, traveling on his evangelical rounds, arrives at Lough Derg and commences battle. He mortally wounds the monster, which slithers to the depths of the lake. Its blood stains the water and gives the lake its name, "derg" being Irish for red (O'Donovan [1835] 1927:148–149; Lynch 1897:69–71; Evans-Wentz [1911] 1990:443; Cunningham 1984:9–10; P. O'Brien 2006:5). Packy Jim is skeptical, too, about the story of Saint Patrick visiting nearby Magherakeel townland to convert the native chieftains and create a holy well by striking a rock with his staff. He is correct in noting that Moses performed a similar miracle during the desert wanderings of the Jews (Exodus 17:6; Numbers 20:11). Moreover, folklorists testify to the widespread narration of feats attributed here to Saint Patrick with international motifs: A941.5 (Spring breaks forth through power of saint), D1567.6 (Stroke of staff brings water from rock), and V134 (Sacred wells).

The Witch Hare (192–195, 197–198)

Several relevant motifs related to the witch hare include D655.2 (Witch transforms self to hare so as to suck cows), D1385.4 (Silver bullet protects against witches), G211.2.7 (Witch in form of hare), and G275.12 (Witch in the form of an animal is injured as a result of injury to the animal). This constellation of uncommonly specific motifs, when taken in concert and elaborated in narrative, gives rise to a migratory legend type found across Ireland and farther afield. Working with Norwegian materials, Christiansen (1958:48) posits ML 3055 (The witch that was hurt). D. L. Ashliman maintains a webpage that gathers a range of examples from Germanic, Nordic, and Celtic countries, but the familiar pattern of the witch who transforms into a hare and is shot is confined, in his examples, to Ireland, Wales, and Scotland (http://www.pitt.edu/~dash/type 3055.html). Almqvist finds Christiansen's ML 3055 type too broad and applicable to just about any narrative of an injured witch. Therefore he proposes MLSIT 3056 (the old woman as hare) to account for the widespread consistency of the transformation-theft-violence-discovery trajectory of Irish legends (1991a:268–269), which Ní Dhuibhne (1993) neatly summarizes and amply illustrates using NFC materials. Glassie (1982:825–826) offers a thorough annotation of published references to witch hares and butter theft more generally in Ireland. MacDonald (1994–1995) expands the discussion by citing versions from Scotland. Shifting from consistency over space to stability over time, it seems that the core anxiety over having secret enemies endures even after rural agrarian practices and the belief in witchcraft fade. Ní Dhuibhne, again, cites a contemporary legend collected in Dublin in 1980 that preserves the structure and certain thematic aspects of the witch hare legend, now set in a modern urban setting without the earlier supernatural elements. In Ní Dhuibhne's variant— similar to one collected in England by Jacqueline Simpson (1981)—an old woman, who normally attends Mass at a certain hour, feels ill and decides to stay home by the fire instead. She is soon shocked to discover someone attempting to break in by sawing a hole around her lock. When the would-be robber's hand emerges from the hole, she burns it with a poker reddened in the fire. Seeking comfort and assurance at a house of a neighbor, she learns that the neighbor has gone to the hospital to be treated for a burn on his hand (Ní Dhuibhne 1983:57–58; 1993:82). The idea that the familiar neighbor whom you least suspect—the near-hand person from whom you seek support—is in fact plotting against you seems discomfiting enough to account for the evolution of this traditional migratory legend into a contemporary legend, updated to rationalize supernatural elements and to fit a modern, urban world and worldview (Simpson 1981).

The Evil Eye (196–197)

In Packy Jim's account of the trials and tribulations of Black Henry McCutcheon, motif D2071.2.1 (Person kills animals with glance of evil eye) conveys the traditional belief that Dody McGoldrick plays on in order to falsely accuse and further ostracize McCutcheon. Margaret Turner's attempt to thwart Alice the Baffler with her charm-like "hares and witches and dirty butter!" relates to motif D2071.1.5 (Counter magic against evil eye). For a psychoanalytical take on the evil eye belief complex across Europe and the Middle East, see Dundes (1980b). For a collection of case studies from a range of analytical approaches, see Dundes (1981). Jacqueline Borsje (2012) explores the evil eye phenomenon and associated beliefs in medieval Ireland through literary evidence. Robert Maclagan's (1902) exhaustive account of beliefs and associated narratives from largely Gaelic-speaking Scotland—including their association with butter stealing practices—comes even closer to the beliefs and narratives of Packy Jim's time and place.

Notes on the Chapters

Introduction

1. The last two decades have seen several reflexive efforts to illuminate the agendas and assumptions of folklore studies over time. A good place to start is an encyclopedia article by Dorothy Noyes (2004) that offers a concise summation of several conceptions of and motivations for studying folklore. Like Richard Bauman and Charles Briggs in their book-length study *Voices of Modernity* (2003), Noyes identifies the concept of folklore — even before the term was coined in 1846 — as central to the critique of modernity that has gathered momentum since the seventeenth century, then points to the implications of marking certain expressive forms and people as not modern. Diarmúid Ó Giolláin (2000) covers similar intellectual history while relating comparative national case studies to how folklore studies emerged and developed to various ends in Ireland. Most recently, in a succinct volume, Sabra Webber (2015) offers another disciplinary history of ideas that addresses why and how folklore has been studied over time, particularly in Europe and North America.

2. In many ways this project complements *The Individual and Tradition: Folkloristic Perspectives* (2011), which I edited with Tom Mould and Pravina Shukla. Here I am rehearsing briefly some of the arguments I made in my chapter, "At Work in Donegal with Packy Jim McGrath," and in the portion of the introduction I authored.

3. The phrase "performer-centered ethnography" is adapted from Dégh (1995), whose work develops a strand of folklore scholarship, concerned with the relationship between the individual and tradition, which stretches back to the nineteenth century. See references to and discussion of a range of nineteenth- and twentieth-century performer-centered studies in Cashman, Mould, and Shukla (2011:2, 5, 14–15).

4. I am not the first to explore this issue. Notably, Michael Owen Jones (2000) conducted fieldwork with Gary Robertson to explore how an individual may choose from among traditional resources to actively shape his or her "virtual identity," a person's perceived or aspired-to identity. Jones's work rightly emphasizes that individuals need not passively follow tradition; rather, individuals have the agency to choose from among

traditions and handed-down raw materials—alternative behaviors, activities, and objects—in order to construct an identity.

5. The semantic and conceptual differences between the individual, self, and person over time and across space are reviewed thoroughly in Carrithers, Collins, and Lukes (1985) and Morris (1991, 1994). Calling Packy Jim or anyone else an individual is a convenience that comports with commonsense. Packy Jim is himself and no other; where my body ends, that of another human subject may begin. We are all individuals in that uncomplicated way. At the same time there is a debate in the social sciences and humanities about whether the concept of the individual and individualism—a belief in the human subject as a natural autonomous entity and ultimate location of agency and responsibility—are holdovers from the Enlightenment that are becoming less tenable or, more importantly, fair. Sidestepping this debate, I understand that the only Packy Jim I have access to is a self-constructed and other-influenced persona. Persona is derived from the Latin meaning "to sound through," as through a mask in a staged drama. Packy Jim's mask is a social one, a proposed subjectivity designed to associate and inter-relate with other personas, establishing meaning and identity in relation. When I refer to Packy Jim from time to time as an individual, I am simply using a brief convenient label for the kind of human agent who habitually performs, maintains, and revises a persona in social interaction.

6. More typical in contemporary individualistic Western societies, personal experi-ence narratives are not a universally popular or expected genre. H. David Brumble, for example, discusses how traditional Native American conceptions of the self did not give rise to personal narratives of the kind expected by European American editors seeking to publish as-told-to Indian autobiographies in the twentieth century. According to Brumble, the resulting life stories must be read as bicultural documents (1988:11). As we will see, even on the rural Irish border today—contemporary, Western, but not yet entirely individualistic—Packy Jim is atypical in telling more personal narratives, more often than his neighbors.

7. As Linda Dégh points out, Hermann Bausinger was perhaps the first to intro-duce the *Alltagsgeschichte* or personal experience story as a conventional narrative form worth studying as folklore (1994:245). In English-language scholarship, Sandra Stahl (now Dolby) has done the most to bring personal narratives to the attention of folklorists (1977a, 1977b, 1983, 1989). The sociolinguist William Labov has focused productively on generic pattern, structure, and form in personal narrative throughout his career. See William Labov and Joshua Waletzky (1967) and Labov (1972, 1982, 2013).

8. Jason Jackson, personal communication via e-mail, February 10, 2014.

9. Previously referring to the Irish revolutionary period from 1916 to 1922, "The Troubles" has been repurposed as a label more recently to refer to the violent conflict originating in Northern Ireland and spreading at times to the Republic of Ireland and Great Britain from the late 1960s to the late 1990s and sporadically afterward. The recent Troubles began with a civil rights campaign for equal treatment of Catholics being violently suppressed by the Protestant-dominated government and police force. The Protestant establishment viewed civil rights activism as a front for an Irish nationalist agenda and therefore did little to stop the sectarian attacks of loyalist vigilantes and

paramilitary groups. As sectarian violence intensified and rioters clashed with the police, Britain deployed soldiers in 1969, arguably escalating the conflict. In response to events such as Bloody Sunday—when British paratroopers fired into a civil rights demonstration in 1972, killing thirteen and wounding twenty-six—many Catholics turned to armed struggle, joining or supporting republican paramilitary groups, such as the Irish Republican Army, that were committed to fighting the British military, local police, and loyalist paramilitaries in an effort to establish a united Ireland free from British rule.

10. This is not unique to Packy Jim, nor is it an exclusively Irish phenomenon. John McDowell (2011), for example, offers a complementary case study of how personal voice and preoccupations suffuse the public performance of mythic narrative by native people in Colombia and Ecuador.

11. Pursuing worldview as the inspiration for and fundamental objective of ethnography goes back at least to Bronisław Malinowski, who wrote: "What interests me really in the study of the native is his outlook on things, his *Weltanschauung*, the breath of life and reality he breathes and by which he lives. Every human culture gives its members a definite vision of the world, a definite zest of life. In the roamings over human history, and over the surfaces of the earth, it is the possibility of seeing life and the world from the various angles, peculiar to each culture, that has always charmed me most, and inspired me with real desire to penetrate other cultures, to understand other types of life" (1922:517).

12. Compared to Kearney's systematic vision in particular, Dégh further contrasts folkloristic and anthropological approaches to worldview: "Folklorists are more specific in their interpretation of worldview expressed in the confines of folklore utterances than anthropologists, whose description of worldview is more encompassing and inconcrete, sometimes overlapping with culture, ethos, behavior, cognition, magic thinking, etc. Worldview for folklorists is not an organizing factor but rather contextulizing, localizing, concretizing element that turns the global into the local, the empty formula (Honko 1984:273–281) into meaningful reality, and the traditional episode into a familiar occurrence. That is to say, worldview is not an abstraction but part of an active and persuasive elaboration of traditional material, the framing of the folklore text by its ad hoc formulator who fits it into the cultural-conceptual system of its audience. . . . It is also an interpretive vehicle, inseparable from the content of the text and its context" (1994:247).

13. For Tomás Ó Cathasaigh, see Hyde (1939); for Seán Ó Conaill, see Ó Duilearga (1981); for Timothy and Anastasia Buckley, see E. Cross (1942); for Tomás Ó Criomhthain, see Ó Crohan with Robin Flower (1935); for Muiris Ó Súilleabháin, see M. O'Sullivan with Davies and Thomson (1933); for Peig Sayers, see Sayers with MacMahon ([1935] 1974), Sayers with Ennis ([1939] 1962), and Sayers with Almqvist and Ó Héalaí (2009); for Hugh Nolan and Ellen Cutler, see Glassie (1975, 1982, 2006).

Chapter 1. Person and Place, Life and Times

1. At different times, Packy Jim has also identified his birthday as May 31 and his year of birth as 1934. Because he was born at home there are no hospital records to look up. I chose to use May 29, 1933, because when I have asked directly for a birthdate, this

is the one he has offered or confirmed most often. Incidentally, speaking of such choices, "Packie Jim" would be the more common spelling of his nickname, but "Packy Jim" is the spelling he most often uses in letters to me and is the spelling he prefers when directly asked.

2. Townlands are the smallest territorial units recognized in rural Ireland, nested within the larger units of the parish, district, county, province, and country. In this part of Donegal, typical townlands comprise between ten and thirty farms, with individual farms ranging widely from as little as a couple acres to as much as a few hundred acres, with most in the range of twenty to sixty.

3. Also known as the Economic War, the Anglo-Irish Trade War began in 1932 with a new Fianna Fáil government in Ireland under Éamon de Valera refusing to pay the British government agreed upon land annuities—loans offered to tenant farmers wishing to purchase the land they rented, begun before Irish independence. Irish protectionist economic policies, including tariffs for goods imported from Britain, were met with retaliatory British import duties on Irish agricultural goods, which severely crippled the Irish economy already weakened by the Great Depression. Both sides agreed to a settlement in 1938, but the adverse effects in Ireland were long-lasting.

4. At http://www.storyfinders.co.uk you can find, under the Castlederg group, a link to audio of local folklore collector Pat O'Loughlin interviewing Packy Jim (spelled Packie Jim there) about the process of making poitín. More details and an enlightening cultural history of poitín-making can be found in McGuffin (1978).

5. Officially known as An Garda Síochána (Guardians of the Peace), the Gardaí (in Irish) or Guards (in English) are Ireland's police force, organized after independence in 1922.

6. In response to the Land War—a period of agrarian agitation from the 1870s to the 1890s, organized in part by the Irish National Land League—British parliament passed a series of legislation allowing tenants to buy land and structures from landlords, particularly absentee landlords, at reduced and subsidized rates. After 1922 the Irish Free State continued this gradual process by establishing the Irish Land Commission while paying off Britain, with an interruption during the Anglo-Irish Trade War. Whether Britain received its due or not, thousands such as Tommy McGrath steadily sent remits to the Irish Land Commission, every six months, until the original sixty-nine-and-half-year mortgages were fulfilled and the much-hated Anglo-Irish landlord system was quietly and finally laid to rest.

7. Established in 1902, *Ireland's Own* is a family-oriented magazine that publishes puzzles, recipes, fictional short stories, and educational and entertaining articles on Irish history and folklore. The mood is unapologetically nostalgic for simpler times.

8. Knowing that Packy Jim is fond of reading, I have brought or sent him several books over the years—either ones requested or ones that I hoped would either appeal to his interests or that I found complementary to (and might help further explain) the collaborative project in which we were engaged. For the record, to offer a sense of how I may have influenced Packy Jim's thinking about our recorded sessions, let me list here the books I have given him.

The first category includes memoires and ethnographies that revolve around individual tradition-bearers: Tomás Ó Crohan's *The Islandman* (1935), Maurice O'Sullivan's *Twenty Years A-Growing* (1933), Peig Sayer's *An Old Woman's Reflections* ([1939] 1962), Michael MacGowan's *The Hard Road to Klondike* ([1962] 2003), Eric Cross's *The Tailor and Antsy* (1942), Patrick Kavanagh's *Tarry Flynn* (1948) and *The Green Fool* ([1938] 1972), Henry Glassie's *The Stars of Ballymenone* (2006), John Neihardt's *Black Elk Speaks* ([1932] 1988), and Leo Simmons's *Sun Chief* (1942).

A second category includes collections of Irish folklore that I thought would appeal to Packy Jim, and possibly prime the pump for additional narratives from him: Seamas Ó Catháin's *The Bedside Book of Irish Folklore* (1980); Lady Augusta Gregory's *Cuchulain of Muirthemne* (1902), *Gods and Fighting Men* (1904), and *Visions and Beliefs in the West of Ireland* ([1920] 1970); St. John D. Seymour and Harry L. Neligan's *True Irish Ghost Stories* (1926); Michael J. Murphy's *Ulster Folk of Field and Fireside* (1983) and *My Man Jack: Bawdy Tales from Irish Folklore* (1989); Sean O'Sullivan's *Legends from Ireland* (1977); and Henry Glassie's *Irish Folktales* (1985).

Knowing what Packy Jim finds entertaining—adventure stories, mysteries, Westerns, Native Americans, history, and geography—I have given him books in a third category of pleasure reading: Larry McMurtry's *Lonesome Dove* (1985), James Fenimore Cooper's *The Last of the Mohicans* ([1826] 1982), Mark Twain's *The Adventures of Tom Sawyer* ([1876] 1998) and *The Adventures of Huckleberry Finn* ([1885] 1994), Washington Irving's *Rip Van Winkle, and the Legend of Sleepy Hollow* ([1893] 1963), Arthur Conan Doyle's *The Hound of the Baskervilles* ([1902] 1993), Robert Louis Stevenson's *Kidnapped* ([1886] 1982) and *The Master of Ballantrae* ([1889] 1997), Michael O'Hanrahan's *A Swordsman of the Brigade* (1914), Patrick Purcell's *Hanrahan's Daughter* (1944), Maurice Walsh's *The Quiet Man and Other Stories* (2002), Ernst Gombrich's *A Little History of the World* ([1935] 2008), and *Collins World Atlas* (2012). Some of these, such as *A Swordsman of the Brigade*, *Kidnapped*, and *The Hound of the Baskervilles*, were books he did not own but had read in his youth and wanted to read again. I cannot guarantee that he read all of these, but it is a safe bet.

9. Carried out by republican paramilitary groups—the Irish Republican Brotherhood, the Irish Volunteers, the Irish Citizen Army, and Cumann na mBan—the Easter Rising was an armed insurrection, mostly in Dublin, that lasted from April 24 to April 29, 1916, when superior British forces regained control, imprisoned participants, and soon after executed the leaders. Architects of the Rising such as Patrick Pearse did not expect a military victory but rather counted on the symbolic power of a blood sacrifice in the cause of Irish independence, one that would be all the more resonant for coinciding with the celebration of Christ's death and resurrection. In this sense, the Rising was a success, stirring a previously complacent majority to support the establishment of an Irish republic through armed struggle if necessary. The sacrifices of the Rising inspired the 1919–1921 Irish War of Independence, which concluded with independence for twenty-six counties in the south, while six northeastern counties remained part of Britain as Northern Ireland.

10. Packy Jim's proverbial dictum "Love many, trust few, and always paddle your own canoe" recommends self-reliance and minding one's own business. It has been

circulated in print since the early 1800s. For a full explanation and notes on historical usage, see pp. 248–249.

11. Éilís Ní Dhuibne, personal communication via e-mail (June 16, 2014).

12. For community ambivalence over the eccentric artistic personality Peter Flanagan in Ballymenone, see Glassie (1982, 2006). For the same phenomenon in North America, see Ives (1993) and Szwed (1971).

Chapter 2. Authority and Rules

1. Some version of the arduous three-day pilgrimage of fasting, penitence, and vigil in the footsteps of St. Patrick on Station Island in Lough Derg has attracted pilgrims from throughout Ireland and across Europe for at least a millennium (Cunningham 1984). See P. O'Brien (2006) for a survey of how the Lough Derg experience has been evoked in the prose and poetry of William Carleton, Seamus Heaney, Colm Tóibín, and William Butler Yeats, among others. Victor and Edith Turner ([1978] 2011) and Lawrence Taylor (1995) offer anthropological perspectives on the pilgrimage as ritual.

2. This popular story is designated as Irish migratory legend type 6011 in Almqvist (1991a). A representative version from Wexford, as written by the Halls in 1841, appears in Glassie (1985:162–164). Ó Giolláin (1984) offers a comparative study with numerous versions and variants.

3. For more on the form, function, and meaning of local character anecdotes as they are told at wakes and ceilis in Aghyaran, County Tyrone, see Cashman (2008b:6–9, 94–106).

Chapter 3. Power and Politics

1. For more on the symbolic resonances and rhetorical uses of outlaws in Irish legend, song, and popular literature, see Cashman (2000b, 2000d).

2. As a gesture to civil rights activists and nationalists who complained of systemic sectarian prejudice, the B-Specials or B men were disbanded in 1970. Their duties, however, were assumed by another Protestant-dominated security force, the Ulster Defence Regiment (UDR), which was an infantry regiment of the British army consisting mostly of part-time volunteers from the same demographic as the B-Specials. The UDR later joined the Royal Irish Rangers to become the Royal Irish Regiment (RIR) in 1992, but the same complaints about the B-Specials and UDR followed the RIR.

3. The Cumann na mBan (Women's Council [or League]) formed as a republican paramilitary group for women in the prelude to the 1916 Easter Rising. Members served in both support and combat roles during the Rising and the Irish War of Independence.

4. For an overview of the Battle of Pettigo based on documentary sources, see Ó Duibhir (2011:119–130). For accounts informed by documentary sources and local memories, see Cunningham (1984:80–91; 2002:66–68) and Hilley (1999:52).

5. An admirer of Michael Collins more than Éamon de Valera, Tommy voted Fine Gael for the rest of his life with one exception. Packy Jim tells me that when his

father was doting in the hospital, he spoke of his experiences during the 1922 Battle of Pettigo. A nurse called the local Sinn Féin candidate, Joe O'Neill of Bundoran, who perhaps took advantage of Tommy's uncertain mental state in transporting him to the voting station to cast a vote presumably for Sinn Féin.

Chapter 4. Place, History, and Morality

1. The notion of landscape as a vast mnemonic device for narratives treating the past and offering commentary on the present is also born out in the works of, among others, Maurice Halbwachs (1941, 1992), Tim Robinson (1986, 1995), Pierre Nora (1989), Mary Hufford (1992), and Terry Gunnell (2008, 2009). For a case study in this phenomenon from nearby Aghyaran, County Tyrone, see Cashman (2008c). From the local's point of view, the ostensibly unmarked Aghyaran landscape is replete with reminders of local past events that bolster contemporary political viewpoints, in particular an inward-looking nativist republicanism that may long endure due to its deep-rootedness in place.

2. The poem has its fair share of heaving breasts, forced couplets, and purple passages, but to be fair, it did win second prize in the annual *Garda Review* poetry competition.

3. The idea of limited good as an aspect of worldview, especially among economically disadvantaged populations, was first ethnographically elaborated by George M. Foster (1965, 1967). The basic concept involves a finite amount of good in a closed system such that a gain for one person in any realm of human interaction necessarily involves a loss for others.

4. Anthony P. Cohen (1982:11, 17), and after him Maurna Crozier (1989:73), define equalitarianism as a belief in "masking or muting social differentiation," which is different from egalitarianism, "the belief in equality as a moral principle" (cf. Glassie 1982:137–138). See also Cashman (2008b) for evidence of equalitarianism in Aghyaran, County Tyrone.

Chapter 6. Belief and Skepticism

1. Knock in County Mayo was the site of a Marian apparition in 1879 and, like Fatima and Lourdes, it has become a major site of Catholic pilgrimage. Holy water from the shrine is believed by many to be especially efficacious. For a sociologist's take on this apparition and pilgrimage, and what it tells us about Irish cultural history, see Hynes (2008).

2. Compare this with the scriptural evidence Jenny McGlynn marshals to qualify her belief in ghosts (Lysaght 1991). For McGlynn the relevant passage is Matthew 27:52–53, in which holy men emerge from their graves to appear to the living during the Resurrection.

3. Peter Flanagan cites the same passage to the same end using similar wording in Glassie (2006:314).

4. This vernacular theory is not Maggie's alone. It fits well with accounts by Correll (2005) and Ó Giolláin (1990) of the Church's post-Famine efforts to consolidate power and orthodoxy through Tridentine reforms that, among other things, inveighed against the peasantry's fairy faith as backwards and un-Christian.

5. The area around Carrickahony Rock features relatively loose limestone that is suitable for burning in a kiln to make quicklime but is inferior for building. The preferred construction stone is known as white freestone, or just freestone, and comes from farther afield.

6. In addition to Correll's work demonstrating a society-wide range of supernatural belief (2005), Gillian Bennett (1987), Gary Butler (1990), and Barbara Rieti (1991) have documented competing discourses of belief and disbelief in the collected supernatural narratives of populations in urban England and rural French- and English-speaking parts of Newfoundland. Shifting focus from society as a whole to its idiosyncratic members, Linda May Ballard (1980, 1988), Patricia Lysaght (1991), and Bairbre Ní Fhloinn (2012) have observed similar negotiations over belief in the repertoires of individual storytellers across Ireland. It would seem that Packy Jim is in good company with many other individuals who entertain supernatural stories from a critical perspective, believing some stories and story elements but not others, circulating stories in large part to continually interrogate their own beliefs.

7. Folklorists and like-minded historians and oral historians have raised the important point that folk history in its many genres, forms, and media may not always be reliable for conveying the sort of information found in court records, censuses, and annals. But as Américo Paredes (1961) and Brynjulf Alver (1989) argue, folk history gives us a portrait of how events left an impression on people's imaginations and reveals a sense of people's values and preoccupations over time. Moreover, myths and legends in particular are well suited for conveying metaphorical and/or subjective truths. Compare this with Lynwood Montell (1970), Richard Dorson (1971), and Alessandro Portelli (1991). Guy Beiner has applied these propositions to Irish Folklore Commission materials concerning the 1798 Rebellion of the United Irishmen in a much-needed reintegration of the goals and methods shared by folklorists and historians, pointing to something like historical ethnography (2007; see also 2004). Grounded in fieldwork with nonacademic historians such as Hugh Nolan and Michael Boyle, Henry Glassie's *Passing the Time in Ballymenone* contemplates the nature of history-telling and persuasively demonstrates that all history—folk or academic—drives at "a truth larger than that trapped in factual scraps" (1982:651).

8. Remembering a jest from Hughie McGiveney, Michael Boyle played for laughs a story about how Saint Patrick traveled to nearby Inishmore then simply shook his staff in the direction of Ballymenone, acknowledging it without thinking it worth a visit (Glassie 1982:612, 829).

9. These general trends in oral traditions representing the past are elaborated in Jan Vansina's *Oral Tradition as History* (1985). Beiner (2007), again, takes note of several examples in his case study of the folk history surrounding the 1798 Rebellion. For instance, in folk history the leader of the French expeditionary force, General Humbert, becomes

the blank screen onto which storytellers project the more general French disdain for their ill-prepared Irish peasant recruits. Not only does Humbert become the one named figure who serves as a mouthpiece for the views of many, over time he gets replaced in legend and song by his more famous superior, Napoleon Bonaparte. Similar euhemeristic trends and the replacement of original characters by better-known or rhetorically apt characters can be seen in Portelli (1991).

10. Inspired by botanical science, the term "oicotype" (sometimes spelled "oiko-type") was coined by Carl Wilhelm von Sydow to refer to a localized or regionally in-flected variant of a folktale, for example, that is otherwise widespread. Like a plant in a new temperate zone, the oicotype of folklore adapts to a new environment of local tastes and preoccupations though without becoming an entirely new entity. See von Sydow ([1927] 1999; [1932] 1948).

11. The three children—Lúcia dos Santos and her cousins Jacinta and Franciso Marto—reported visitations and instructions first from an angel in the spring through summer of 1917, followed by visitations from the Virgin Mary starting on the Feast of the Assumption, August 15, and culminating with the Virgin's promised "miracle of the sun," witnessed by thousands on October 13. Two secrets from the Virgin revealed by the children included a vision of Hell and guidance for universal conversion and salvation. Packy Jim is correct about the date 1960, when Pope John XXIII announced that the third secret, rumored to be about cataclysmic events, would remain sealed. Given that the Fatima children conveyed the Virgin's prediction of the end of World War I and the beginning of World War II, and this being the Cold War era, much speculation circu-lated about a prophesy of nuclear annihilation. Later Pope John Paul II—who credited Our Lady of Fatima with saving his life during the 1981 attempt on his life on her feast day—allowed text of the third secret to be published. This concerned the deaths of the pope and other clergy, but conspiracy theories that the full secret has not yet been revealed continue to circulate. Published accounts include William Thomas Walsh (1947) and Jeffrey Bennett (2012). Discussion and interpretation of the Virgin's appear-ance and documents relating to the three secrets can be found in "The Message of Fatima" at the Vatican's official website of the Roman Curia (http://www.vatican.va /roman_curia/congregations/cfaith/documents/rc_con_cfaith_doc_20000626_ message-fatima_en.html).

Chapter 8. Worldview

1. A series of articles and chapters complements and extends observations drawn from fieldwork in Aghyaran, County Tyrone, in Cashman (2008b). Initial impressions can be found in Cashman (1999). Customs and storytelling associated with wakes and ceilis are analyzed in Cashman (2006b, 2008a, and 2011). Social and political implications of local mumming are addressed in Cashman (2000a, and 2000c, and 2007b). Cashman (2002, 2007a, and 2008c) investigate sectarian and anti-sectarian expressive culture, practices, material culture, and narrative. Cashman (2006a) explores the implications of nostalgia in local memory and preservationist projects.

2. Although I am in no position to give a thorough synopsis of existentialist or post-modern moral philosophy, a good place to start would be Emmanuel Levinas ([1969] 1994), who bases his ethics on responsibility and obligation to the Other, while taking pains to avoid theological preconceptions and imperatives. Profitably read in conversation with Martin Buber ([1923] 1971) and Jean-Paul Sartre ([1943] 1948; [1983] 1992), Levinas had a profound influence on the postmodern philosopher Jacques Derrida ([1967] 1980; see also Critchley 1992).

Afterword

1. This distinction and these observations about the relative worth of *seanchaí* and *seanchas* versus *scéalaí* and *scéalaíocht* were spelled out by James Delargy ([1945] 1969:6–7) and have been elaborated at greater length throughout Zimmerman (2001).

2. In Stoppard's play, the thing not believed in is England and the conspirators are cartographers.

References

Abrahams, Roger, ed. 1970. *Almeda Riddle: A Singer and Her Songs*. Baton Rouge: Louisiana State University Press.

af Klintberg, Bengt. 1978. *Harens Klagan*. Stockholm: Pan/Nordstedt.

Almqvist, Bo. 1991a. "Crossing the Border: A Sampler of Irish Migratory Legends about the Supernatural." *Béaloideas* 59:210–324.

———. 1991b. "Waterhorse Legends (MLSIT 4086 & 4086B)." *Béaloideas* 59:107–120.

Alver, Brynjulf. 1989. "Historical Legends and Historical Truth." In *Nordic Folklore*, edited by Reimund Kvideland and Henning K. Sehmsdorf, 138–149. Bloomington: Indiana University Press.

Anonymous. 1835. "Old Frank and His Stories: Nick Nowlan, the Noggin Weaver." *Dublin Penny Journal* 4, no. 176: 154–156.

Arensberg, Conrad. 1937. *The Irish Countryman: An Anthropological Study*. New York: Macmillan.

Bakhtin, Mikhail M. 1981. *The Dialogic Imagination*. Translated by Caryl Emerson and Michael Holquist. Austin: University of Texas Press.

Ballard, Linda May. 1980. "Ulster Oral Narratives: The Stress on Authenticity." *Ulster Folklife* 26:35–40.

———. 1988. "Three Local Storytellers: A Perspective on the Question of Cultural Heritage." In *Monsters with Iron Teeth: Perspectives on Contemporary Legend*, vol. 3, edited by Gillian Bennett and Paul Smith, 161–182. Sheffield: Sheffield Academic Press.

Basso, Keith. 1979. *Portraits of the Whiteman: Linguistic Play and Cultural Symbols among the Western Apache*. New York: Cambridge University Press.

———. 1996. *Wisdom Sits in Places: Landscape and Language among the Western Apache*. Albuquerque: University of New Mexico Press.

Bauman, Richard. 1977. *Verbal Art as Performance*. Long Grove, IL: Waveland Press.

———. 1986. *Story, Performance, and Event: Contextual Studies of Oral Narrative*. Cambridge: Cambridge University Press.

———. 1992. "Performance." In *Folklore, Cultural Performances, and Popular Entertainments*, edited by Richard Bauman, 41–49. New York: Oxford University Press.

———. 2004. *A World of Others' Words: Cross-Cultural Perspectives on Intertextuality*. Malden, MA: Blackwell.

Bauman, Richard, and Charles Briggs. 2003. *Voices of Modernity: Language Ideologies and the Politics of Inequality*. Cambridge: Cambridge University Press.

Behan, Brendan. 1957. "Dogmen and Bogmen." *Twentieth Century* 162, no. 969: 419–428.

Beiner, Guy. 2004. "Who Were 'The Men of the West'? Folk Historiographies and the Reconstruction of Democratic Histories." *Folklore* 115:201–221.

———. 2007. *Remembering the Year of the French: Irish Folk History and Social Memory*. Madison: University of Wisconsin Press.

Bennett, Gillian. 1987. *Traditions of Belief: Women, Folklore, and the Supernatural Today*. London: Pelican Books.

———. 1999. "*Alas, poor ghost!*" *Traditions of Belief in Story and Discourse*. Logan: Utah State University Press.

Bennett, Jeffrey. 2012. *When the Sun Danced: Myth, Miracles, and Modernity in Early Twentieth-Century Portugal*. Charlottesville: University of Virginia Press.

Borsje, Jacqueline. 2012. *The Celtic Evil Eye and Related Mythological Motifs in Medieval Ireland*. Leuven: Peeters.

Bourdieu, Pierre. 1977. *Outline of a Theory of Practice*. New York: Cambridge University Press.

Bourke, Angela. 1996. "The Virtual Reality of the Irish Fairy Legend." *Éire-Ireland* 31, nos. 1–2: 7–25.

———. 1999. *The Burning of Bridget Cleary: A True Story*. London: Pimlico.

Briggs, Katharine. 1976. *An Encyclopedia of Fairies: Hobgoblins, Brownies, Bogies, and Other Supernatural Creatures*. New York: Pantheon Books.

———. 1991. *A Dictionary of British Folk-Tales in the English Language*. Part B, *Folk Legends*. London: Routledge.

Brumble, H. David. 1988. *American Indian Autobiography*. Berkeley: University of California Press.

Buber, Martin. (1923) 1971. *I and Thou*. Translated by Walter Kaufmann. New York: Charles Scribner's Sons.

Burke, Kenneth. (1941) 1973. "Literature as Equipment for Living." In *The Philosophy of Literary Form: Studies in Symbolic Action*, 293–304. Berkeley: University of California Press.

Butler, Gary. 1990. *Saying Isn't Believing: Conversational Narrative and the Discourse of Tradition in a French-Newfoundland Community*. St. John's: Institute of Social and Economic Research, Memorial University of Newfoundland.

Carrithers, Michael, Steven Collins, and Steven Lukes, eds. 1985. *The Category of the Person: Anthropology, Philosophy, History*. Cambridge: Cambridge University Press.

Carleton, William. 1855. *Willy Reilly and His Dear Colleen Bawn*. London: Hope.

Cashman, Ray. 1999. "A Letter from Ireland: The News from Ballymongan." *New Hibernia Review* 3, no. 2: 19–35.

———. 2000a. "Christmas Mumming Today in Northern Ireland." *Midwestern Folklore* 26, no. 1: 27–47.

———. 2000b. "The Heroic Outlaw in Irish Folklore and Popular Literature." *Folklore* 111, no. 2: 191–215.

———. 2000c. "Mumming with the Neighbors in West Tyrone." *Journal of Folklore Research* 37, no. 1: 73–84.

———. 2000d. "'Young Ned of the Hill' and the Reemergence of the Irish Rapparee: A Textual and Intertextual Analysis." *Cultural Analysis* 1, no. 1: 51–68.

———. 2002. "Politics and the Sense of Place in Northern Ireland." *Folklore Forum* 33, nos. 1–2: 113–130.

———. 2006a. "Critical Nostalgia and Material Culture in Northern Ireland." *Journal of American Folklore* 119, no. 472: 137–160.

———. 2006b. "Dying the Good Death: Wake and Funeral Customs in County Tyrone." *New Hibernia Review* 10, no. 2: 9–25.

———. 2007a. "Genre and Ideology in Northern Ireland." *Midwestern Folklore* 33, no. 1: 13–28.

———. 2007b. "Mumming on the Northern Irish Border: Social and Political Implications." In *Border-Crossing: Mumming in Cross-Border and Cross-Community Contexts*, edited by Anthony Buckley, Críostóir Mac Cárthaigh, Séamas Mac Mathúna, and Séamas Ó Catháin, 39–56. Dundalk: Dundalgan Press.

———. 2008a. "Storytelling and the Construction of Local Identities on the Irish Border." In *Orality and Modern Irish Culture*, edited by Nessa Cronin, Seán Crosson, Louis de Paor, and John Eastlake, 115–125. Newcastle upon Tyne: Cambridge Scholars.

———. 2008b. *Storytelling on the Northern Irish Border: Characters and Community*. Bloomington: Indiana University Press.

———. 2008c. "Visions of Irish Nationalism." *Journal of Folklore Research* 45, no. 3: 361–381.

———. 2011. "Situational Context and Interaction in a Folklorist's Ethnographic Approach to Storytelling." In *Varieties of Narrative Analysis*, edited by James Holstein and Jaber Gubrium, 181–206. Thousand Oaks, CA: Sage.

Cashman, Ray, Tom Mould, and Pravina Shukla, eds. 2011. *The Individual and Tradition: Folkloristic Perspectives*. Bloomington: Indiana University Press.

Christiansen, Reidar Th. 1958. *The Migratory Legends: A Proposed List with a Systematic Catalouge of the Norwegian Variants*. Folklore Fellows Communications 175. Helsinki: Suomalainen Tiedeakatemia.

———. 1971–1973. "Some Notes on the Fairies and the Fairy Faith." *Béaloideas* 39–41:95–111.

Coffin, Tristram. 1957. "'Mary Hamilton' and the Anglo-American Ballad as an Art Form." *Journal of American Folklore* 70, no. 277: 208–214.

Cohen, Anthony P. 1982. "Belonging: The Experience of Culture." In *Belonging: Identity and Social Organisation in British Rural Cultures*, edited by Anthony P. Cohen, 1–17. Manchester: Manchester University Press.

Collins World Atlas. 2012. London: HarperCollins.

Colum, Padraic. 1907. "An Old Woman of the Roads." In *Wild Earth: A Book of Verse*, 14–15. Dublin: Maunsel.

————, ed. 1922. *Anthology of Irish Verse*. New York: Boni and Liveright.

Cooper, James Fenimore. (1826) 1982. *The Last of the Mohicans*. New York: Bantam Classics.

Correll, Timothy Corrigan. 2005. "Believers, Sceptics, and Charlatans: Evidential Rhetoric, the Fairies, and Fairy Healers in Irish Oral Narrative and Belief." *Folklore* 116, no. 1: 1–18.

Crapanzano, Vincent. 1985. *Tuhami: Portrait of a Moroccan*. Chicago: University of Chicago Press.

Cresswell, Tim. 2004. *Place: A Short Introduction*. Oxford: Wiley-Blackwell.

Critchley, Simon. 1992. *The Ethics of Deconstruction: Derrida and Levinas*. Oxford: Blackwell.

Croker, T. Crofton. (1825) 1862. *Fairy Legends of the South of Ireland*. London: William Tegg.

Cross, Eric. 1942. *The Tailor and Ansty*. New York: Devin-Adair.

Cross, Tom Peete. 1952. *Motif-Index of Early Irish Literature*. Bloomington: Indiana University Press.

Crozier, Maurna. 1989. "'Powerful Wakes': Perfect Hospitality." In *Ireland from Below*, edited by Chris Curtin and Thomas M. Wilson, 70–91. Galway: Galway University Press.

Cunningham, John B. 1984. *Lough Derg: Legendary Pilgrimage*. Monaghan: R. & S. Printers.

————. 2002. *Pettigo and Its People, including a History of the Clan McGrath*. Enniskillen: Erne Heritage Tour Guides.

Dégh, Linda. 1994. "The Approach to Worldview in Folk Narrative Study." *Western Folklore* 53:243–252.

————. 1995. *Narratives in Society: A Performer-Centered Study of Narration*. Folklore Fellows Communications 255. Helsinki: Suomalainen Tiedeakatemia.

————. 2001. *Legend and Belief*. Bloomington: Indiana University Press.

Dégh, Linda, and Andrew Vászonyi. 1976. "Legend and Belief." In *Folklore Genres*, edited by Dan Ben-Amos and Kenneth S. Goldstein, 92–123. Austin: University of Texas Press.

Delargy, James [Séamus Ó Duilearga]. (1945) 1969. *The Gaelic Story-Teller: With Some Notes on Gaelic Folk-Tales*. Reprints of Irish Studies 6. Chicago: University of Chicago Press.

Derrida, Jacques. (1967) 1980. "Violence and Metaphysics." In *Writing and Difference*, translated by Alan Bass, 79–153. Chicago: University of Chicago Press.

Dickens, Charles. (1861) 2002. *Great Expectations*. New York: Penguin Classics.

Donoghue, James. 1935. "The Ballad of Peggy Roe." *Garda Review* (December). Reprinted in Hilley 1999.

Dorson, Richard. 1971. *American Folklore and the Historian*. Chicago: University of Chicago Press.

Doyle, Arthur Conan. (1902) 1993. *The Hound of the Baskervilles: Another Adventure of Sherlock Holmes*. Oxford: Oxford University Press.

Dundes, Alan. (1972) 2000. "Folk Ideas as Units of Worldview." In *Towards New Perspectives in Folklore*, edited by Américo Paredes and Richard Bauman, 120–134. Bloomington: Trickster Press.

————. 1980a. "Thinking Ahead: A Folkloristic Reflection of the Future Orientation in American Worldview." In *Interpreting Folklore*, edited by Alan Dundes, 69–85. Bloomington: Indiana University Press.

————. 1980b. "Wet and Dry, the Evil Eye: An Essay in Indo-European and Semitic Worldview." In *Interpreting Folklore*, edited by Alan Dundes, 93–133. Bloomington: Indiana University Press.

————. 1981. *The Evil Eye: A Casebook*. New York: Garland.

Duranti, Alessandro. 1997. *Linguistic Anthropology*. Cambridge: Cambridge University Press.

Durkheim, Émile. (1893) 1984. *The Division of Labor in Society*. New York: Free Press.

————. (1897) 2006. *On Suicide*. New York: Penguin.

Eliade, Mircea. 1959. *The Sacred and the Profane: The Nature of Religion*. New York: Harcourt Brace.

Ellis, Bill. 2001. *Aliens, Ghosts, and Cults: Legends We Live*. Jackson: University of Mississippi Press.

Evans-Wentz, W. Y. (1911) 1990. *The Fairy Faith in Celtic Countries*. New York: Citadel Press.

Fine, Elizabeth. 1984. *The Folklore Text: From Performance to Print*. Bloomington: Indiana University Press.

Foley, James, et al. 1991. "Harvest Home: Songs and Crack from West Tyrone." Sound recording and notes by James Foley. Belfast: The Arts Council of Northern Ireland.

Foster, George M. 1965. "Peasant Society and the Image of Limited Good." *American Anthropologist* 67:293–315.

————. 1967. *Tzintzuntzan: Mexican Peasants in a Changing World*. Boston: Little, Brown.

Foster, Michael Dylan. 2009. *Pandemonium and Parade: Japanese Monsters and the Culture of Yokai*. Berkeley: University of California Press.

Freud, Sigmund. (1920) 1967. *Beyond the Pleasure Principle*. New York: W. W. Norton.

————. (1927) 1961. *The Future of an Illusion*. New York: W. W. Norton.

Frost, Robert. 2002. *The Robert Frost Reader: Poetry and Prose*. Edited by Edward Coneery Lathem and Lawrance Roger Thompson. New York: Henry Holt.

Gailey, Alan. 1984. *Rural Houses of the North of Ireland*. Edinburgh: John Donald.

Geertz, Clifford. 1957. "Ethos, World-View, and the Analysis of Sacred Symbols." *Antioch Review* 17, no. 4: 421–437.

————. 1973. "Deep Play: Notes on a Balinese Cock Fight." In *The Interpretation of Cultures: Selected Essays*, 412–453. New York: Basic Books.

————. 1973. "Religion as a Cultural System." In *The Interpretation of Cultures: Selected Essays*, 87–125. New York: Basic Books.

Gibbs, Levi. 2013. "Song King: Tradition, Social Change, and the Contemporary Art of a Northern Shaanxi Folksinger." PhD dissertation, the Ohio State University.

Ginzburg, Carlo. (1976) 2013. *The Cheese and the Worms: The Cosmos of a Sixteenth-Century Miller*. Translated by John Tedeschi and Anne C. Tedeschi. Baltimore: Johns Hopkins University Press.

Glassie, Henry. 1975. *All Silver, No Brass: An Irish Christmas Mumming*. Philadelphia: University of Pennsylvania Press.

————. 1982. *Passing the Time in Ballymenone: Culture and History of an Ulster Community*. Philadelphia: University of Pennsylvania Press.

————. 1985. *Irish Folktales*. New York: Pantheon Books.

————. 1997. *Art and Life in Bangladesh*. Bloomington: Indiana University Press.

————. 2003. "Tradition." In *Eight Words for the Study of Expressive Culture*, edited by Burt Feintuch, 176–197. Champaign: University of Illinois Press.

————. 2006. *The Stars of Ballymenone*. Bloomington: Indiana University Press.

————. 2010. *Prince Twins Seven-Seven: His Art, His Life in Nigeria, His Exile in America*. Bloomington: Indiana University Press.

Goffman, Erving. 1959. *The Presentation of Self in Everyday Life*. New York: Anchor Books.

Goldstein, Diane. 2007. "Scientific Rationalism and Supernatural Experience Narratives." In *Haunting Experience: Ghosts in Contemporary Folklore*, edited by Diane Goldstein, Sylvia Grider, and Jeannie Thomas, 60–78. Logan: Utah State University Press.

Goldstein, Diane, Sylvia Grider, and Jeannie Thomas. 2007. *Haunting Experience: Ghosts in Contemporary Folklore*. Logan: Utah State University Press.

Gombrich, Ernst. (1935) 2008. *A Little History of the World*. New Haven, CT: Yale University Press.

Gould, Stephen Jay. 1985. *Ontogeny and Phylogeny*. Cambridge, MA: Harvard University Press.

Green, Richard Firth. Forthcoming. *Elf Queens and Holy Friars: Disciplining Vernacular Belief in the Middle Ages*. Philadelphia: University of Pennsylvania Press.

Gregory, Lady Augusta. 1902. *Cuchulain of Muirthemne: The Story of the Men of the Red Branch of Ulster*. London: John Murray.

————. 1904. *Gods and Fighting Men: The Story of the Tuatha De Danaan and the Fianna of Ireland*. London: John Murray.

————. (1920) 1970. *Visions and Beliefs in the West of Ireland*. Coole Edition. Oxford: Oxford University Press.

Gummere, Francis. 1907. *The Popular Ballad*. New York: Houghton, Mifflin.

Gunnell, Terry. 2008. "Introduction." In *Legends and Landscape: Plenary Papers from the 5th Celtic-Nordic-Baltic Folklore Symposium, Reykjavík 2005*, 13–24. Reykjavik: Iceland University Press.

————. 2009. "Legends and Landscape in the Nordic Countries." *Cultural and Social History* 6, no. 3: 305–322.

Halbwachs, Maurice. 1941. *La topographie légendaire des evangiles en Terre Sainte: Étude de mémoire collective*. Paris: Presses Universitaires de France.

————. 1992. *On Collective Memory*. Edited and translated by Lewis A. Coser. Chicago: University of Chicago Press.

Hartland, Edwin Sidney. (1899) 1968. "Folklore: What Is It and What Is the Good of It?" In *Peasant Customs and Savage Myths*, vol. 1, edited by Richard Dorson, 230–251. Chicago: University of Chicago Press.

Hilley, James, ed. 1999. *Lettercran: An Illustrious Past, an Uncertain Future*. Lettercran, County Donegal: Lettercran Development Association.

Honko, Lauri. 1984. "Empty Texts, Full Meanings: On Transformal Meaning in Folklore." In *Papers I: The Eighth Congress for the International Society for Folk Narrative Research*, edited by Reimund Kvideland and Torunn Selberg, 273–281. Bergen: ISFNR.

———. 1998. *Textualising the Siri Epic*. FF Communications 264. Helsinki: Academia Scientiarum Fennica.

———. 2000. "Text as Process and Practice: The Textualization of Oral Epics." In *Textualization of Oral Epics*, edited by Lauri Honko, 3–56. Berlin: Mouton de Gruyter.

Hufford, David. 1995. "Beings without Bodies: An Experience-Centered Theory of the Belief in Spirits." In *Out of the Ordinary: Folklore and the Supernatural*, edited by Barbara Walker, 11–45. Logan: Utah State University Press.

Hufford, Mary. 1992. *Chaseworld: Foxhunting and Storytelling in New Jersey's Pine Barrens*. Philadelphia: University of Pennsylvania Press.

Hyde, Douglas. 1894. "The Need for De-Anglicising Ireland." In *The Revival of Irish Literature*, by Charles G. Duffy, George Sigerson, and Douglas Hyde, 115–161. London: T. Fisher Unwin.

———. 1939. *Sgéalta Thomáis Uí Chathasaigh: Mayo Stories Told by Thomas Casey*. Irish Texts Society. Dublin: Educational Company of Ireland.

Hymes, Dell. 1975. "Breakthrough into Performance." In *Folklore: Performance and Communication*, edited by Dan Ben-Amos and Kenneth S. Goldstein, 11–74. The Hague: Mouton.

———. 1981. *"In Vain I Tried to Tell You": Essays in Native American Ethnopoetics*. Philadelphia: University of Philadelphia Press.

———. 2003. *Now I Know Only So Far: Essays in Ethnopoetics*. Lincoln: University of Nebraska Press.

Hynes, Eugene. 2008. *Knock: The Virgin's Apparition in Nineteenth-Century Ireland*. Cork: Cork University Press.

Irving, Washington. (1893) 1963. *Rip Van Winkle, and the Legend of Sleepy Hollow*. New York: Macmillan.

Ives, Edward. 1993. *Larry Gorman: The Man Who Made the Songs*. Fredericton: Goose Lane Editions.

Jenkins, Richard. 1991. "Witches and Fairies: Supernatural Aggression and Deviance among the Irish Peasantry." In *The Good People: New Fairylore Essays*, edited by Peter Narváez, 302–335. New York: Garland.

Jones, Michael Owen. 1989. *Craftsman of the Cumberlands: Tradition and Creativity*. Lexington: University Press of Kentucky.

———. 2000. "'Tradition' in Identity Discourses and an Individual's Symbolic Construction of Self." *Western Folklore* 59, no. 2: 115–141.

Joyce, James. (1916) 1993. *A Portrait of the Artist as a Young Man*. New York: Vintage Books.

Kant, Immanuel. (1790) 1987. *Critique of Judgment*. Indianapolis: Hackett.

Kavanagh, Patrick. (1938) 1972. *The Green Fool*. London: Martin Brian and O'Keeffe.

———. 1948. *Tarry Flynn*. London: Pilot Press.

Kearney, Michael. 1975. "World View Theory and Study." *Annual Review of Anthropology* 4:247–270.

———. 1984. *World View*. Novato, CA: Chandler and Sharp.

Kilfeather, Annaba. 1988. "The Water Horse Legends in Ireland." *North Munster Antiqarian Journal* 30:39–45.

Kirshenblatt-Gimblett, Barbara. 1989. "Authoring Lives." *Journal of Folklore Research* 26, no. 2: 123–149.

Kloss, Jürgen. 2011. "Some Notes on the History of 'Brennan on the Moor.'" . . . *Just Another Tune: Songs & Their History* (blog), February. http://www.justanothertune.com /html/brennanonthemoor.html.

Kvideland, Reimund, and Henning K. Sehmsdorf. 1991. *Scandinavian Folk Belief and Legend*. Minneapolis: University of Minnesota Press.

Labov, William. 1972. *Language in the Inner City*. Philadelphia: University of Pennsylvania Press.

———. 1982. "Speech Actions and Reactions in Personal Narrative." In *Analyzing Discourse: Text and Talk*, edited by Deborah Tannen, 219–247. Washington, DC: Georgetown University Press.

———. 2013. *The Language of Life and Death: The Transformation of Experience in Oral Narrative*. Cambridge: Cambridge University Press.

Labov, William, and Joshua Waletzky. 1967. "Narrative Analysis." In *Essays on the Verbal and Visual Arts*, edited by June Helm, 12–44. Seattle: University of Washington Press.

Langness, L. L., and Gelya Frank. 1981. *Lives: An Anthropological Approach to Biography*. Novato, CA: Chandler and Sharp.

Lawless, Emily. 1922. "Fontenoy, 1745." In *Anthology of Irish Verse*, edited by Padraic Colum, 176–177. New York: Boni and Liveright.

Levinas, Emmanuel. (1969) 1994. *Totality and Infinity: An Essay on Exteriority*. Translated by Alphonso Lingis. Pittsburgh: Duquesne University Press.

Lévi-Strauss, Claude. 1966. *The Savage Mind*. Chicago: University of Chicago Press.

Linde, Charlotte. 1993. *Life Stories: The Creation of Coherence*. New York: Oxford University Press.

Livingstone, Peadar. 1969. *The Fermanagh Story*. Enniskillen: Cumann Seanchais Chlochair.

Lynch, P. J. 1897. "Saint Patrick: His Life, Legends, and Miracles." *Donahoe's Magazine* 38:65–73.

Lysaght, Patricia. 1991. "Fairylore from the Midlands." In *The Good People: New Fairylore Essays*, edited by Peter Narváez, 22–46. New York: Garland.

———. 1994. "Bealtaine: Women, Milk and Magic at the Boundary Festival of May." In *Milk and Milk Products from Medieval to Modern Times*, edited by Patricia Lysaght, 208–229. Edinburgh: Canongate Academic.

———. 1996. *The Banshee: The Irish Supernatural Death Messenger*. Dublin: O'Brien Press.

Macafee, Caroline. 1996. *A Concise Ulster Dictionary*. Oxford: Oxford University Press.

MacDonald, Donald Archie. 1994–1995. "Migratory Legends on the Supernatural in Scotland: A General Survey." *Béaloideas* 62–63:29–78.

MacGowan, Michael. (1962) 2003. *The Hard Road to Klondike*. Translated by Valentin Iremonger. Cork: Collins Press.

Maclagan, Robert Craig. 1902. *Evil Eye in the Western Highlands*. London: D. Nutt.

Mac Philib, Séamus. 1988. "*Ius Primae Noctis* and the Sexual Image of Irish Landlords in Folk Tradition and in Contemporary Accounts." *Béaloideas* 56:97–140.

———. 1994–1995. "Legends of Irish Landlords in their International Context." *Béaloideas* 62–63:79–88.

Malinowski, Bronisław. 1922. *Argonauts of the Western Pacific*. London: Routledge and Kegan Paul.

Marshall, John J. 1927. *Irish Tories, Rapparees and Robbers: With Some Account of the Lives and Actions of the Most Notable*. Dungannon: Tyrone.

Marx, Karl. (1844) 1964. *Economic and Philosophic Manuscripts of 1844*. New York: International Publishers.

———. (1867–1883) 2010. *Das Kapital*. Translated by Samuel Moore. Seattle: Pacific Publishing Company.

———. 1994. *Karl Marx: Selected Writings*. Edited by Lawrence H. Simon. Indianapolis: Hackett.

McCabe, Pat. 1992. *The Butcher Boy*. London: Pan Books.

McDowell, John. 2011. "Customizing Myth: The Personal in the Public." In *The Individual and Tradition: Folkloristic Perspectives*, edited by Ray Cashman, Tom Mould, and Pravina Shukla, 323–342. Bloomington: Indiana University Press.

McGlinchey, Charles. 1996. "The Story of Peggy Roe." *Aghyaran* 11:5–7.

McGuffin, John. 1978. *In Praise of Poteen*. Belfast: Appletree Press.

McMurtry, Larry. 1985. *Lonesome Dove*. New York: Simon and Schuster.

Mieder, Wolfgang. 2001. "'Paddle Your Own Canoe': Frederick Douglass's Proverbial Message in his 'Self-Made Men' Speech." *Midwestern Folklore* 27:21–40.

Montell, Lynwood. 1970. *The Saga of Coe Ridge: A Study in Oral History*. Knoxville: University of Tennessee Press.

Morris, Brian. 1991. *Western Conceptions of the Individual*. Oxford: Berg.

———. 1994. *Anthropology of the Self: The Individual in Cultural Perspective*. Ann Arbor, MI: Pluto Press.

Motz, Marilyn. 1998. "The Practice of Belief." *Journal of American Folklore* 111:339–355.

Mullen, Patrick. 1988. *I Heard the Old Fisherman Say: Folklore of the Texas Gulf Coast*. Logan: Utah State University Press.

———. 2000. "Belief and the American Folk." *Journal of American Folklore* 113, no. 448: 119–143.

Murphy, Michael J. 1983. *Ulster Folk of Field and Fireside*. Dundalk: Dundalgan Press.

———. 1989. *My Man Jack: Bawdy Tales from Irish Folklore*. Dublin: O'Brien Press.

Naugle, David. 2002. *Worldview: The History of a Concept*. Grand Rapids, MI: Wm. B. Eerdmans.

Neihardt, John G. (1932) 1988. *Black Elk Speaks: Being the Life Story of a Holy Man of the Oglala Sioux*. Lincoln: University of Nebraska Press.

Ní Dhuibhne, Éilís. 1983. "Dublin Modern Legends: An Intermediate Type-List." *Béaloideas* 51:55–69.

———. 1993. "'The Old Woman as Hare': Structure and Meaning in an Irish Legend." *Folklore* 104, nos. 1–2: 77–85.

Ní Fhloinn, Bairbre. 2012. "'The Cat Was as Big as a Good-Sized Little Calf': A Lacken Storyteller and Some Otherworld Beings." In *Atlantic Currents: Essays on Lore, Literature and Language*, edited by Bo Almqvist, Críostóir Mac Cárthaigh, Liam Mac Mathúna, Séamus Mac Mathúna, and Seosamh Watson, 139–149. Dublin: University College Dublin Press.

Nora, Pierre. 1989. "Between Memory and History: *Les Lieux de Mémoire.*" *Representations* 26:7–25.

Noyes, Dorothy. 2004. "Folklore." In *The Social Science Encyclopedia*, edited by Adam Kuper and Jessica Kuper, 375–378. New York: Routledge.

O'Brien, Flann. (1941) 1974. *The Poor Mouth: A Bad Story about the Hard Life.* Translated by Patrick C. Power. New York: Viking.

O'Brien, Peggy. 2006. *Writing Lough Derg: From William Carleton to Seamus Heaney.* Syracuse: Syracuse University Press.

Ó Catháin, Seamas. 1980. *The Bedside Book of Irish Folklore.* Cork: Mercier Press.

———, ed. and trans. 1985. *Uair an Chloig Cois Teallaigh / An Hour by the Hearth: Stories Told by Pádraig Eoghain Phádraig Mac an Luain.* Dublin: Comhairle Bhéaloideas Éireann.

Ó Crohan, Tomás [Tomás Ó Criomhthain]. 1935. *The Islandman.* Edited and translated by Robin Flower. New York: Charles Scribner's Sons.

O'Donoghue, Thomas A. 1998. "Catholicism and the Curriculum: The Irish Secondary School Experience, 1922–62." *Historical Studies in Education* 10, nos. 1–2: 140–158.

O'Donovan, John. (1835) 1927. "Letters Containing Information Relative to the Antiquities of the County of Donegal, Collected during the Progress of the Ordnance Survey in 1835." Unpublished manuscript in the National Folklore Collection, University College Dublin, reproduced under the direction of Rev. Michael O'Flanagan, Bray, County Dublin.

Ó Duibhir, Liam. 2011. *Donegal and the Civil War: The Untold Story.* Cork: Mercier Press.

Ó Duilearga, Séamus [James Delargy], ed. and trans. 1981. *Seán Ó Conaill's Book: Stories and Traditions from Iveragh.* Dublin: Comhairle Bhéaloideas Éireann.

Offerman, Nick. 2013. *Paddle Your Own Canoe: One Man's Fundamentals for Delicious Living.* New York: Dutton.

Ó Giolláin, Diarmúid. 1984. "The Leipreachán and Fairies, Dwarfs and the Household Familiar: A Comparative Study." *Béaloideas* 52:75–150.

———. 1990. "Perspectives in the Study of Folk-Religion." *Ulster Folklife* 36:66–73.

———. 2000. *Locating Irish Folklore: Tradition, Modernity, Identity.* Cork: Cork University Press.

O'Hanrahan, Michael. 1914. *A Swordsman of the Brigade.* Edinburgh: Sands & Company.

Ó hEochaidh, Seán. 1977. *Síscéalta ó Thír Chonaill / Fairy Legends from Donegal.* Translated by Máire MacNeill. Edited by Séamus Ó Catháin. Dublin: Comhairle Bhéaloideas Éireann.

Ó hÓgáin, Dáithí. 2006. *The Lore of Ireland: An Encyclopedia of Myth, Legend, and Romance.* Woodbridge: Boydell Press.

O'Leary, Daniel. 1946. "Buckley the Brickaloch." *Journal of the Cork Historical and Archaeological Society* 51:182–186.

Oring, Elliott. 1986. "On the Concepts of Folklore." In *Folk Groups and Folklore Genres: An Introduction*, edited by Elliott Oring, 1–22. Logan: Utah State University Press.

———. 2008. "Legendry and the Rhetoric of Truth." *Journal of American Folklore* 121, no. 480: 127–166.

Ó Súilleabháin, Seán [Sean O'Sullivan]. 1942. *A Handbook of Irish Folklore*. Dublin: Educational Company of Ireland.

———. 1967. *Irish Folk Customs and Belief.* Dublin: Three Candles.

———. 1974. *The Folklore of Ireland*. London: B. T. Batsford.

———. 1977. *Legends from Ireland*. London: B. T. Batsford.

———. 2011. *Miraculous Plenty: Irish Religious Folktales and Legends*. Translated by William Caulfield. Dublin: Comhairle Bhéaloideas Éireann.

O'Sullivan, Maurice [Muiris Ó Súilleabháin]. 1933. *Twenty Years A-Growing*. Translated by Moya Llewelyn Davies and George Thomson. New York: Viking.

Paredes, Américo. 1961. "Folklore and History." In *Singers and Storytellers*, edited by Mody Boatright et al., 56–69. Dallas: Southern Methodist University Press.

Pentikäinen, Juha. 1987. *Oral Repertoire and World View: An Anthropological Study of Marina Takalo's Life History*. Folklore Fellows Communications 219. Helsinki: Suomalainen Tiedeakatemia.

Plummer, Ken. 2001. "The Call of Life Stories in Ethnographic Research." In *Handbook of Ethnography*, edited by Paul Atkinson et al., 395–406. Thousand Oaks, CA: Sage.

Plunkett, Joseph Mary. 1916. "I See His Blood upon the Rose." In *The Poems of Joseph Mary Plunkett*, 50. Dublin: Talbot Press.

Portelli, Alessandro. 1991. "The Death of Luigi Trastulli: Memory and the Event." In *The Death of Luigi Trastulli, and Other Stories: Form and Meaning in Oral History*, 1–26. Albany: State University of New York Press.

Porter, James, and Herschel Gower. 1995. *Jeannie Robertson: Emergent Singer, Transformative Voice*. Knoxville: University of Tennessee Press.

Primiano, Leonard. 1995. "Vernacular Religion and the Search for Method in Religious Folklife." *Western Folklore* 54, no. 1: 37–56.

Purcell, Patrick. 1994. *Hanrahan's Daughter*. New York: G. P. Putnam and Sons.

Redfield, Robert. 1952. "The Primitive World View." *Proceedings of the American Philosophical Society* 96:30–36.

———. 1953. *The Primitive World and Its Transformations*. Ithaca, NY: Cornell University Press.

Rieti, Barbara. 1991. *Strange Terrain: The Fairy World in Newfoundland*. St. John's, Newfoundland: ISER Books.

———. 2008. *Making Witches: Newfoundland Traditions of Spells and Counterspells*. Montreal: McGill-Queen's University Press.

Robinson, Tim. 1986. *Stones of Aran: Pilgrimage*. London: Penguin.

———. 1995. *Stones of Aran: Labyrinth*. London: Penguin.

Ryden, Kent C. 1993. *Mapping the Invisible Landscape: Folklore, Writing, and the Sense of Place.* Iowa City: University of Iowa Press.

Sartre, Jean-Paul. (1943) 1948. *Being and Nothingness.* Translated by Hazel E. Barnes. New York: Philosophical Library.

———. (1983) 1992. *Notebook for an Ethics.* Translated by David Pellauer. Chicago: University of Chicago Press.

Sawin, Patricia. 2004. *Listening for a Life: A Dialogic Ethnography of Bessie Eldreth through Her Songs and Stories.* Logan: Utah State University Press.

Sayers, Peig. (1935) 1974. *Peig: The Autobiography of Peig Sayers of the Great Blasket Island.* Translated by Bryan MacMahon. Syracuse: Syracuse University Press.

———. (1939) 1962. *An Old Woman's Reflections.* Translated by Seamus Ennis. Oxford: Oxford University Press.

———. 2009. *Peig Sayers: Labharfad Le Cach—I Will Speak to You All.* Translated and edited by Bo Almqvist and Padraig Ó Héalaí. Dublin: New Island.

Schrempp, Gregory. 1996. "Dimensions of Worldview: Worldview as an Organizing Concept in Ethnographic and Narrative Research." In *Folk Narrative and World View: Vorträfe Des 10. Kongresses der Internationalen Gesellschaft für Volkserzählungsforschung (ISFNR), Innsbruck 1992,* edited by Leander Petzoldt, 21–31. Frankfurt am Main: Peter Lang.

Seal, Graham. 1996. *The Outlaw Legend: A Cultural Tradition in Britain, America, and Australia.* Cambridge: Cambridge University Press.

Seitel, Peter. 1999. *The Powers of Genre: Interpreting Haya Oral Literature.* New York: Oxford University Press.

Seymour, St. John D., and Harry L. Neligan. 1926. *True Irish Ghost Stories.* Dublin: Hodges, Figgis.

Shopes, Linda. 2002. "Making Sense of Oral History." In *History Matters: The U.S. Survey Course on the Web,* February. http://historymatters.gmu.edu/mse/oral/.

Shuman, Amy. 2005. *Other People's Stories: Entitlement Claims and the Critique of Empathy.* Chicago: University of Illinois Press.

Sigerson, George. 1869. "The Mountains of Pomeroy." In *The Harp of Erin: A Book of Ballad-Poetry and of Native Song,* edited by Ralph Varian, 229–230. Dublin: M'Glashan & Gill.

Simmons, Leo, ed. and trans. 1942. *Sun Chief.* New Haven, CT: Yale University Press.

Simpson, Jacqueline. 1981. "Some Rationalised Motifs in Modern Urban Legends." *Folklore* 92:203–207.

Stahl (Dolby), Sandra. 1977a. "The Oral Personal Narrative in Its Generic Context." *Fabula* 18:18–39.

———. 1977b. "The Personal Narrative as Folklore." *Journal of the Folklore Institute* 14:9–30.

———. 1983. "The Personal Experience Story." In *Handbook of American Folklore,* edited by Richard M. Dorson and Inta Gale Carpenter, 268–276. Bloomington: Indiana University Press.

———. 1989. *Literary Folkloristics and the Personal Narrative.* Bloomington: Indiana University Press.

Steiner, Margaret. 1988. "Aesthetics and Social Dynamics in the Folksong Tradition of a Northern Irish Community." PhD dissertation, Indiana University.

Stevenson, Robert Louis. (1886) 1982. *Kidnapped*. New York: Bantam Classics.

———. (1889) 1997. *The Master of Ballantrae*. New York: Penguin Classics.

Stoppard, Tom. 1967. *Rosencrantz and Guildenstern Are Dead*. New York: Grove Press.

Szwed, John. 1971. "Paul E. Hall: A Newfoundland Song-Maker and His Community of Song." In *Folksongs and Their Makers*, edited by Henry Glassie, Edward Ives, and John Szwed, 149–169. Bowling Green: Popular Press.

Taylor, Lawrence. 1995. *Occasions of Faith: An Anthropology of Irish Catholics*. Philadelphia: University of Pennsylvania Press.

Tedlock, Dennis. 1972. "On the Translation of Style in Oral Narrative." In *Toward New Perspectives in Folklore*, edited by Américo Paredes and Richard Bauman, 114–133. Austin: University of Texas Press.

———. 1983. *The Spoken Word and the Work of Interpretation*. Philadelphia: University of Pennsylvania Press.

———. 1992. "Ethnopoetics." In *Folklore, Cultural Performances, and Popular Entertainments*, edited by Richard Bauman, 81–85. New York: Oxford University Press.

Thompson, Stith. 1960. *Motif-Index of Folk-Literature: A Classification of Narrative Elements in Folktales, Ballads, Myths, Fables, Medieval Romances, Exempla, Fabliaux, Jest-Books and Local Legends*. 6 vols. Bloomington: Indiana University Press.

Thoreau, Henry David. (1854 and 1849) 1983. *Walden and Civil Disobedience*. New York: Penguin Classics.

Titon, Jeff Todd. 1980. "The Life Story." *Journal of American Folklore* 93:276–292.

Tuan, Yi-Fu. 1977. *Space and Place: The Perspective of Experience*. Minneapolis: University of Minnesota Press.

Turner, Victor, and Edith Turner. (1978) 2011. *Image and Pilgrimage in Christian Culture*. New York: Columbia University Press.

Twain, Mark. (1876) 1998. *The Adventures of Tom Sawyer*. New York: Dover.

———. (1885) 1994. *The Adventures of Huckleberry Finn*. New York: Dover.

Vansina, Jan. 1985. *Oral Tradition as History*. Madison: University of Wisconsin Press.

von Sydow, Carl Wilhelm. (1927) 1999. "Geography and Folk-Tale Oicotypes." In *International Folkloristics: Classic Contributions by the Founders of Folklore*, edited by Alan Dundes, 137–151. New York: Rowman and Littlefield.

———. (1932) 1948. "On the Spread of Tradition." In *Selected Papers on Folklore*, 11–43. Copenhagen: Rosenkilde and Bagger.

Walsh, Maurice. 2002. *The Quiet Man and Other Stories*. Belfast: Appletree.

Walsh, William Thomas. 1947. *Our Lady of Fatima*. New York: Macmillan.

Weber, Max. (1904–1905) 1976. *The Protestant Ethic and the Spirit of Capitalism*. Translated by Talcott Parsons. New York: Charles Scribner's Sons.

———. (1922) 1964. *The Sociology of Religion*. Translated by Ephraim Fischoff. Boston: Beacon Press.

Webber, Sabra. 2015. *Folklore Unbound: A Concise Introduction*. Long Grove, IL: Waveland.

Wilde, Lady Jane. 1888. *Ancient Legends, Mystic Charms, and Superstitions of Ireland*. London: Ward and Downey.

Wilde, William. (1852) 1972. *Irish Popular Superstitions*. Shannon: Irish University Press.

Wood-Martin, W. G. 1902. *Traces of the Elder Faiths of Ireland: A Folklore Sketch*. Volume 2. London: Longmans, Green.

Yeats, William Butler. 1888. *Fairy and Folk Tales of the Irish Peasantry*. London: Walter Scott.

———. 1902. *The Celtic Twilight*. London: A. H. Bullen.

Zimmerman, Georges Denis. 2001. *The Irish Storyteller*. Dublin: Four Courts Press.

International Motif Index

All motifs cited are drawn from Stith Thompson's *Motif-Index of Folk-Literature* (1960). For additional cross-referencing relevant to Ireland, see Tom Peete Cross's *Motif-Index of Early Irish Literature* (1952). Although one could argue for the inclusion of additional motif numbers, I have identified those that seem most relevant to Packy Jim's stories.

A. Mythological Motifs

A54	Rebellious angels	13–16, 156–158, 246
A106.2	Revolt of evil angels against God	13–16, 156–158, 246
A610.2	Creation of heaven, earth, and hell	14, 157–158, 183
A531	Culture hero kills dragon	184–185, 263
A941.5	Spring breaks forth through power of saint	184–185, 263

D. Magic

D655.2	Witch transforms self to animal (hare) so as to suck cows	192–195, 197–198, 263–264
D1385.4	Silver bullet protects against witches	192, 194, 195
D1567.6	Stroke of staff brings water from rock	186, 210, 263
D2071.1.5	Counter magic against evil eye	197–198, 265
D2071.2.1	Person kills animals with glance of evil eye	196–197, 264–265

E. The Dead

E226	Dead brother's return	153
E265.1.1	Blow received from a spirit at night	152, 182, 208, 260
E272	Road-ghosts	91, 149, 260
E275	Ghost haunts place of great accident or misfortune	91, 148–149, 260

F. Marvels

G. Ogres

J. The Wise and the Foolish

K. Deceptions

M. Ordaining the Future

Q. Rewards and Punishments

T. Sex

V. Religion

W. Traits of Character

X. Humor

Migratory Legend Type Index

Migratory legend types designated with "ML" are from Reidar Th. Christiansen's *The Migratory Legends* (1958). Those designated with "MLSIT" are types suggested by Bo Almqvist (1991a) to adapt Christiansen's system to Irish materials, "SIT" being an abbreviation for "suggested Irish type."

Subject Index

Proper names followed by an asterisk indicate pseudonyms.

Abrahams, Roger, 7

Acheson family, 91, 96, 256, 260

Acheson's Hall, 91–92, 95

Adam and Eve, 183–184, 187

adultery, 54, 60, 61, 258

age, in stories of witchcraft, 202, 217

agency, individual, 4, 5–8, 23, 84, 231, 267n4, 268n5

Aghyaran, Co. Tyrone, 205, 208, 213, 275n1

Alice (Monaghan) the Baffler, 197–198, 201, 202, 214, 265

alienation, 12

allegory, 183–185

Almqvist, Bo, 73, 261, 264

Alver, Brynjulf, 210, 274n7

ambition, 140–142, 200, 211–214, 217, 273ch4n3

analogies, 17, 18

Angel of Pride, 20, 200, 209, 212. *See also* Lucifer

Anglo-Irish Trade War (Economic War), 38, 109–110, 270n3, 270n6

anomie, 12

anxiety: over ambition, 140–142, 200, 212–213, 214, 217, 273ch4n3; over profit and capitalism, 198–202, 213, 214; over secret enemy, 198, 200, 201, 202, 216

Arensberg, Conrad, 3, 181

Armstrong, George, 222

Armstrong, Miss, 92, 95–96

Ashliman, D. L., 264

autobiography, 8, 26–27, 42, 233

autonomy vs. submission, 13, 48, 57–64, 74–83, 122, 246

Bakhtin, Mikhail, 4, 126

"The Ballad of Peggy Roe" (Donoghue), 130–131, 258–259, 273ch4n2

ballads, 88, 130, 133, 258–259

Ballard, Linda May, 274n6

Ballymenone, Co. Fermanagh, 9, 29, 31–34, 96, 124–125, 185, 198, 202, 205–206, 208, 209, 213, 215–217, 220–223, 256

Ballymongan townland, Co. Tyrone, 31

banshee, 145, 159, 163. *See also* fairies

Barr, Bob, ghost of, 179

Barton, Johnny, 112

Basso, Keith, 125, 126

Bauman, Richard, 17, 239, 267n1

Bausinger, Hermann, 268n7

Baxter, Sam, 227

Baxter, Willie, 9, 10

The Bedside Book of Irish Folklore (Ó Catháin), 271n8

297